India's Labouring Poor

Historical Studies, c.1600 – c.2000

Edited by Rana P. Behal and Marcel van der Linden

FOUNDATION BOOKS

Delhi • Bangalore • Mumbai • Kolkata • Chennai • Hyderabad

Published by
Cambridge University Press India Pvt. Ltd.
under the Foundation Books imprint
Cambridge House
4381/4, Ansari Road, Daryaganj
New Delhi 110 002

C-22, C-Block, Brigade M.M., K.R. Road, Jayanagar, **Bangalore** 560 070
Plot No. 80, Service Industries, Shirvane, Sector-1, Nerul, **Navi Mumbai** 400 706
10, Raja Subodh Mullick Square, 2nd Floor, **Kolkata** 700 013
21/1 (New No. 49), 1st Floor, Model School Road, Thousand Lights, **Chennai** 600 006
House No. 3-5-874/6/4, (Near Apollo Hospital), Hyderguda, **Hyderabad** 500 029

First published 2007

ISBN 978-81-7596-496-9

This collection is a revised edition of Rana Behal and Marcel van der Linden (eds), "Coolies, Capital, and Colonialism. Studies in Indian Labour History", International Review of Social History, 51 (2006), Supplement 14.

Published by Manas Saikia for Cambridge University Press India Pvt. Ltd. Printed and bound at Raj Press, R-3 Inderpuri, New Delhi 110 012

CONTENTS

NOTES ON CONTRIBUTORS

Ravi Ahuja, Centre for Modern Oriental Studies, Kirchweg 33, 14129 Berlin, Germany; e-mail: Ravi.Ahuja@urz.uni-heidelberg.de

Sabyasachi Bhattacharya, Centre for Historical Studies, DSA, School of Social Sciences, Jawaharlal Nehru University, New Delhi 110 067, India; e-mail: bappa@bol.net.in

Rana P. Behal, Deshbandu College, University of Delhi, 42 Deshbandhu Society, 15 Patparganj, Delhi 110 092, India; e-mail: rbehal@gmail.com

Michael H. Fisher, Danforth Professor of History, Oberlin College, Oberlin, OH 44074-1095, USA; email: Michael.Fisher@oberlin.edu

Ian J. Kerr, University College, Department of History, University of Manitoba, Winnipeg R3T 2M8, Canada; e-mail: ikerr@cc.umanitoba.ca

Jan Lucassen, Internationaal Instituut voor Sociale Geschiedenis, Cruquiusweg 31, 1019 AT Amsterdam, The Netherlands; e-mail: jlu@iisg.nl

Marcel van der Linden, Internationaal Instituut voor Sociale Geschiedenis, Cruquiusweg 31, 1019 AT Amsterdam, The Netherlands; e-mail: mvl@iisg.nl

Prabhu P. Mohapatra, Department of History, University of Delhi, Delhi 110007, India; e-mail: prabhuayan@gmail.com

Shankar Ramaswami, Department of Anthropology, University of Chicago, 1126 E 59th Street, Chicago, IL 60637, USA; e-mail: shankardelhi@yahoo.com

Willem van Schendel, Internationaal Instituut voor Sociale Geschiedenis and University of Amsterdam, Cruquiusweg 31, 1019 AT Amsterdam, The Netherlands; e-mail: h.w.vanschendel@uva.nl

Rajnarayan Chandavarkar (1953–2006)
Photograph by Perry Hastings. Used with permission

Preface

Rana P. Behal and Marcel van der Linden

At the beginning of the 1990s the discipline of labour history seemed to be in serious crisis. The editorial in Supplement 1 to the *International Review of Social History* in 1993 was seriously concerned that, having peaked during the 1960s and 1970s, interest in labour history had declined very rapidly by the 1990s. The decline of "old labour history" prompted the question whether this was the end of labour history itself. The current phase of globalization, coinciding with the rapid decline of the industrial working class in advanced capitalist countries, the retreat of the state, the emergence of subcontracting, and the demise of the Soviet Union, was the context for nascent doubts about the foundational basis of labour history.

However, recent years have witnessed a growing scholarly interest in historical labour studies, especially in Latin America and South Asia. This revival is different both in its location and in its central concerns. Earlier, the major emphasis of labour history research was on the core countries such as North America, Europe, Australia, and Japan. Now, research on the labour history of the capitalist peripheries is increasingly attracting international scholarship. The concerns of this new labour history are not confined to the traditional working class alone; much attention is also paid to migrants, the self-employed, and indentured labourers.

This new labour history also feels an urgent need to reconstitute the older frameworks, which had revolved around fixed binaries of space, time, and social relations. Increasingly, labour historians have to contend with the existing notions of pre-modern and modern, free and unfree, formal and informal labour relations, and with traditional spatial divisions such as factory and field, urban and rural. With the expansion of the process of informalization and feminization of the workforce, the centrality of the male, unionized factory or transport worker may no longer be tenable. Areas that have gained prominence in recent years include issues of labour mobility, the changing legal construction of labour relations, notions of solidarity, gender relations, multiplicity of labouring identities, and the impact of new technologies on work.

Indian historians have provided an important impulse to these developments. Not only have they published a number of significant studies in recent years – as the select bibliography at the end of this volume emphasizes – they founded, ten years ago, the Association of Indian

Figure 1. Some founders of the Association of Indian Labour Historians, at the founding meeting at Jawaharlal Nehru University in New Delhi, December 1996. Professor Sabyasachi Bhattacharya, the chairperson, is fourth from right.
Collection IISH

Labour Historians, which, partly through its conferences, promotes national and international communication among researchers and fosters young talent.[1] This volume would have been inconceivable without its activities.

That labour history is flourishing in India is not of course a coincidence. The prospect of India as one of the world's major manufacturing hubs and destinations for services outsourcing in the coming decades, along with the phenomenal expansion of the informalization process, has pushed the labour question willy-nilly centre stage. This volume seeks to consolidate and showcase some of the best new research inspired by those developments.

The new research eschews traditional schemes. While recognizing that the category of "labour" was originally connected with the emergence of

1. The Association was founded at a meeting at Jawaharlal Nehru University in New Delhi, in December 1996. The idea arose during a conference on "South Asian Labour: Local and Global Linkages" held in October 1995 at the International Institute of Social History in Amsterdam. In 1998, in collaboration with the V.V. Giri National Labour Institute in Noida, the Association founded the Archives of Indian Labour. See <http://www.indialabourarchives.org>.

modern industrial society, the new labour history feels a need to question the chronological divide that has resulted in a marked emphasis on the colonial period, to the disadvantage of the developments that preceded and followed that period. The temporal divides of the pre-modern/modern/contemporary and the theme of transition across these boundaries have been a major organizing principle of labour history. Labour history has had to contend with the uncomfortable fact of the persistence of pre-modern forms of labour relations and the coexistence of industrialization and deindustrialization. It has become increasingly evident that these lines have been far too sharply drawn. Given the "transitional" nature of social relations under colonialism and the dynamic of caste and convention, some of the contributions to this volume are devoted to the institutional forms and categories of pre-colonial and pre-industrial Indian labour history.

Equally problematic are the classical accounts of labour mobility, which relegated it to the prehistory of class formation. Confronted with the persistence of mobility among workers, these classical accounts interpreted it as incomplete proletarianization and partial labour commitment. The problems with these accounts of mobility are becoming increasingly evident – after a century and a half of industrialization labour mobility remains a dominant issue in South Asian labour history. South Asian labour was mobile in the pre-colonial and colonial periods and remains mobile in the post-colonial era.

This volume opens with a review article by Sabyasachi Bhattacharya, the doyen of the new Indian labour history. Bhattacharya outlines how research has developed in recent decades and makes a forceful appeal for studies comparing South Asia with other areas of the global south. He substantiates his hypothesis that there are important homomorphies between colonial social formations of the past and contemporary under-developed countries.

Michael Fisher's chapter traces the labour history of Indian seamen from the emergence of intercontinental sea trade between India and Europe from the beginning of seventeenth century to the establishment of colonial empires. He locates the changing nature of labour relations, from "free" to "unfree" labour, on board the trans-oceanic ships, in a merchant-capitalist era dominated by Dutch, English, and other northern European joint-stock corporations. In the process of studying the "unevenly changing interactions between indigenous patterns of labour relations and the fundamentally different European models", Fisher's research extends Indian labour history transnationally beyond India's shores and chronologically back to the pre-colonial period.

Ian Kerr's chapter explores the world of pan-Indian circulating and itinerant labour, which worked on wide varieties of construction sites in the pre-colonial, colonial, and post-colonial periods. Underlining the continuity and significance of these groups, he argues that most of the requirements for labour power for construction work in the pre-colonial, colonial, or post-colonial periods were met from within (increasingly better integrated) labour markets involving circulating labour. He further argues that the earlier manifestations of migration in protoindustrial, predominantly agrarian societies with pre-industrial forms of capitalism and different political structures (city-states, the segmentary states of earlier south India, or territorially vast empires for example) have received too little attention. These circulating workers, or people like them, were present early in the history of India and continuously thereafter. Their numbers grew dramatically during the high colonial period due to an explosive increase in the demand for construction labour occasioned by the massive infrastructural building drive by the colonial state.

Jan Lucassen's chapter questions the existing wisdom about labour history, particularly in the orthodox Marxian perception, that collective class-consciousness and action are both linked to the emergence of modern industrialization in western Europe and North America. This perception had a profound influence on the writings of the labour historians of the colonial world of the late nineteenth and twentieth centuries. His research on the history of brickmakers' strikes between 1848 and 1849, at the site of the Ganges Canal builders during the 1840s and 1850s in northern India, offers a critical appraisal of the supposed link between modern industrialization and collective labour action.

Ravi Ahuja extends Michael Fisher's analysis to the late-colonial and post-colonial periods. He looks at the tens of thousands of south Asian seamen who manned European ships in the first half of the twentieth century. Given their profession, these *lascars* were extremely mobile geographically, but very immobile socially. Throughout this period, they were at the bottom of this hierarchically segmented international maritime labour market. Ahuja explains this by pointing out that British and "British-Indian" maritime labour law, the immigration laws of metropolitan countries, and extra-legal structures of exclusion and containment *in combination* were fairly effectual in controlling the mobility of Indian seamen and in reproducing "a segregated pool of poorly paid and legally inferior colonial labour".

Rana Behal shows how, prior to Independence in 1947 and in collaboration with the Indian Tea Association, the Assam Valley tea planters tried systematically to dominate, discipline, and control workers by a combination of two strategies: immobilizing labour within the plantation complex once the workers' had arrived there, and curbing their contact with the outside world. Both strategies aimed to prevent the formation of collective labour organizations. After first showing how the ITA became an extraordinarily effective pressure group within the colonial state, Behal provides a detailed reconstruction of how these strategies were enforced in the day-to-day lives of the coolies.

Prabhu Mohapatra examines the culture and forms of protest among Indian indentured labourers in the West Indies during the last phase of the indentured labour regime (1880–1920). He focuses on four different sets of representations of community identity: the annual Muharram festival, and the public activities of three individuals: two prolific letter writers in the colonial newspapers, and the author of one of the rare literary texts produced by Indians during the period. Mohapatra concludes that no singular identity developed among the Indian diaspora, although all forms of identity bore a relation to the local labour regime.

Shankar Ramaswami takes us to contemporary Delhi. In a pioneering essay, he explores themes of proletarian masculinity and humour among migrant workers in a metalworking factory. Ramaswami's lively narrative describes metalworkers' vocabularies and practices of joking and horseplay, with particular reference to their homoerotic and heteroerotic imageries, as well as to their subtle auto-critiques.

Willem van Schendel concludes the volume with a wide-ranging essay. Focusing on Bengal and north-east India, he examines eight partly overlapping themes that promise to be especially effective in broadening the history of labour in this region. Van Schendel points out, for example, that historians of industrial labour have so far focused disproportionately on the jute factories in colonial Calcutta (Kolkata). He argues that the "dynamic and persistently finely graded labour relations" in agriculture are deserving of greater consideration, as are the amazing variety of gender roles, labour trafficking, the cultures and meanings of labour, and the labour implications of shifting cultivation (*jhum*) and wet-rice cultivation. Van Schendel's essay can be read as a programme for future research.

Originally, it was intended to include an essay by Rajnarayan Chandavarkar in this volume. However, Raj (as he was known to everyone) died unexpectedly on 23 April 2006, while on a visit to the United States. He was fifty-two. As homage to this great scholar, we publish the unpolished draft of his chapter. It is an important contribution to a crucial theme of Indian social history: the decline of the industrial "jobber" (labour recruiter) in the 1940s.

Raj's death is a great loss. Not only was Raj one of the foremost Indian labour historians, he was also an inspiring colleague and a superb teacher. We dedicate this collection of essays to his memory.

Introduction*

SABYASACHI BHATTACHARYA

The discussion of labour history in South Asia was first shaped in the early twentieth century by the hands of the members of a very limited intelligentsia who assumed an adversarial role in relation to capital and colonial state power. Many of them happened to be activists and leaders in the organizations and protest movements of the working classes. Their constituents, sections of the labouring poor, were particularly underprivileged in the general context of economic underdevelopment and low per capita GNP in South Asia.

Their structural location in the colonial socio-economic formation was significant too. During the colonial period, the main characteristic of South Asian countries (I have in mind mainly India, Pakistan, Bangladesh, and Sri Lanka) was that capitalist relations were not sufficiently generalized. There was in this respect a qualitative difference from those metropolitan areas of the world which today are called countries of the North. While in the countries of the North in the late nineteenth and twentieth centuries capitalist relations defined and specified the class structure adequately if not always exhaustively, in colonial South Asia, right up to World War II and perhaps even beyond that, pre-capitalist and capitalist organization of economic life coexisted. The resulting stratification or class structure was inchoate, in the process of being formed – and the working class constituted pre-eminently an example of this incomplete transition.

Even as recently as four decades ago in India one could travel from the industrial city of Jamshedpur into the countryside to the south and virtually travel through time – one could meet industrial wage workers in a capitalist enterprise using advanced technology, and at the other end of the scale people in the hunting and gathering stage of civilization, all while travelling fewer than 300 miles from Jamshedpur to, say, the Bastar forests.

This coexistence of different production regimes which, according to one view, amounted to different stages of evolution to the capitalist mode, imparted a peculiar character to the class structure in colonial South Asia. The intelligentsia, which is to say educated urban professionals, were surrogate leaders and spokesmen of the classes with a low degree of "classness". The low investment in social overheads by the colonial state is well-

* The author wishes to acknowledge his indebtedness to Marcel van der Linden for his suggestions and comments on this essay.

known – and one of its consequences was a low level of literacy, which blocked the articulation of labour demands or the rise of spokesmen from the ranks of the labouring classes. Even a casual observer will notice the marked absence of literate autodidact workers such as the British journeymen and skilled artisans one meets in the pages of E.P. Thompson or Eric Hobsbawm. The result of that low investment was the assumption of this surrogate role by members of the intelligentsia in relation to the working class in factories, mines, and plantations – and the intelligentsia were a numerically insignificant section of the total population, and, further, insufficiently definable in terms of categories of capitalism. "Outsider" leadership, i.e. leadership of labour organizations by persons of non-working-class origin and social status, was a characteristic feature of colonial South Asia.[1] So, the discourse on labour history in South Asia was initially developed by these surrogate spokesmen, representing labour and assuming an adversarial role as advocates in labour's struggle against capital and the colonial state.

The literature on the condition and history of the working classes in the early decades of the twentieth century consisted mainly of writings of that kind. A very popular one for instance, *Coolie: The Story of Labour and Capital in India* by Diwan Chaman Lall, was a mixture of reportage, a participant observer's report on his experiences, and historical reflections.[2] Leaders of the trade-union movement produced similar accounts.[3] The bias in this class of writing was contested by authors who spoke on behalf of the agencies of the state which were concerned with the legislation and regulation of industry.

In 1881 the first Indian Factory Act was passed, applicable to the new factories which existed in Bombay and Calcutta and limited to the objective of preventing the employment of children below the age of nine. From the third decade of the twentieth century, Departments of Industry in the provincial governments were supposed to promote and regulate industry, so there developed a bureaucratic discourse; the spin-off was the publication of works on industrial labour by British civil servants or visiting experts.[4] Among such writings the most influential was one which was not specifically about labour but a general work on the economic

1. S. Bhattacharya, "The Outsiders: A Historical Note", in A. Mitra (ed.), *The Truth Unites: Essays in Tribute to Samar Sen* (Calcutta, 1985), pp. 90–100.
2. Diwan Chaman Lall, *Coolie: The Story of Labour and Capital in India* (Lahore, 1932).
3. These included R.K. Das, *Labour Movement in India* (Berlin, 1923); N.M. Joshi, *The Trade Union Movement in India* (Bombay, 1927); and B. Shiva Rao, *The Industrial Worker in India* (London, 1939).
4. See the following publications: J.C. Kydd, "The First Indian Factories Act (Act XV of 1881)", *The Calcutta Review*, 293 (1918), pp. 279–292; G.M. Broughton, *Labour in Indian Industries* (London, 1924); R.N. Gilchrist, *Indian Labour and the Land* (Calcutta, 1932); A.R. Burnett-Hurst, *Labour and Housing in Bombay* (London, 1925).

development of India by Vera Anstey, who spent some years in India and later became an academic at the London School of Economics; this work was influential in that it was recommended as a textbook in England and India and went through six editions.[5] The emphasis in this class of work was on the problem of getting adequate and regular supply of native labour, supposedly caused by a lack of mobility, failure to respond to wage incentives (an anticipation of what was later to be known in economic theory as the backward bending supply curve of labour), and lack of industrial discipline accounting for low per capita output. As distinct from this construction, Indian labour spokesmen underlined the difficult circumstances under which workers operated in factories, and their generally poor quality of life. In neither of these two streams of discourse did any well-researched historical perspective on Indian labour develop.

The worldwide economic depression in the early half of the 1930s catapulted studies of the condition and history of labour to the public attention. The appointment of a Royal Commission on Labour in India, which published a multi-volume report in 1930–1931, and the focusing of bureaucratic attention on the task of coping with the Depression made an impact on professional social science disciplines and led for the first time to academic research. P.S. Lokanathan's work on labour welfare, A.C. Roy Chowdhury on the standard of living, S.G. Panandikar's *Industrial Labour in India*, and Rhadakamal Mukherjee's *The Indian Working Class* are representative examples of this spurt in academic interest in labour since the Depression.[6] About that time two interesting contributions came from abroad: one from the United States – Buchanan's perspicacious *The Development of Capitalistic Enterprise in India* – and one from England – Margaret Read's work on the conversion of the Indian peasants into factory hands, *The Indian Peasant Uprooted: A Study of the Human Machine*.[7] In both those works the complexities of incomplete transition to capitalism are noted. On the whole the Depression was a wake-up call in labour studies.

The hegemony of European categories of thought often blocked the recognition of the specifics of the South Asian economy and the persistence of pre-capitalist labour forms, especially in Marxist writings. In his celebrated Marxist analysis of historical and contemporary India, Rajani Palme Dutt, for a long time at the top of the Communist Party of

5. V. Anstey, *The Economic Development of India* (London [etc.], 1929).

6. P.S. Lokanathan, *Industrial Welfare in India* (Madras, 1929); A.C. Roy Chowdhury, *Report on an Enquiry into the Standard of Living of Jute Mill Workers in Bengal* (Calcutta, 1930); S.G. Panandikar, *Industrial Labour in India* (Bombay, 1933); R.K. Mukherjee, *The Indian Working Class* (Bombay, 1945).

7. Daniel H. Buchanan, *The Development of Capitalistic Enterprise in India* (New York, 1934), and Margaret Read, *The Indian Peasant Uprooted: A Study of the Human Machine* (London, 1931).

Great Britain and a man of Indian ethnic origin, was content to posit a category of the Indian proletariat on classical Marxian lines, without exploring their specifics. The theory and practice of the Communist International allowed for little else.[8]

However, this tendency in thinking was not limited to communist studies of Indian labour. In the entire corpus of writing on labour history the overwhelming emphasis has always been on the industrial workforce in the organized sector, excluding the vastly greater numbers in the informal or unorganized sector – workers in construction, transport (excluding the railways, which are, of course, very much part of the organized sector), those urban poor irregularly employed in various parts of the service sector such as shops, or small-scale industry, not to mention migrant labourers who for part of the year are present in the margins of the urban labour force and for part of the year are employed as agricultural labourers. Only an exceptional researcher such as Jan Breman addressed problems, historical or contemporary, in this area of study.[9] As late as the 1970s a labour survey of a South Indian city came up against the problem of the complete absence of data on workers in the unorganized sector which constituted, according to this researcher's estimate, about 45 per cent or even more of the labour force.[10] The attention of historians and other social scientists was focused on the organized sector partly because of ready access to data. But what was probably more important – especially to those socialistically inclined – was the stereotypical image of the factory workers, which promoted their role as the advanced section of the labouring classes.

Let me elaborate on that point a little. The larger-than-life image of the industrial proletariat, as compared with the rest of the labouring poor, is due to an attribution of a "historical" role in a vision of things to come, an instrumentalist view of them as vanguards effecting a social transformation through the capture of state power. Whether indeed the industrial worker had such potential in developing colonial countries or whether, as Frantz Fanon believed, they were "in a comparatively privileged position" compared to the rest of the labouring poor and the urban sub-proletariat is a very pertinent question in the light of historical experience.[11] Moreover, the myopic concentration on the industrial wage-worker to

8. R.P. Dutt, *India Today* (London, 1940; repr. Calcutta, 1979). On Dutt see J. Callaghan, *Rajani Palme Dutt: A Study in British Stalinism* (London, 1993), and P. Saha, *Rajani Palme Dutt: A Biography* (Kolkata, 2004).

9. J.C. Breman, *Of Peasants, Migrants and Paupers: Rural Labour Circulation and Capitalist Production in West Bengal* (Oxford, 1985); *idem*, *Labour Migration and Rural Transformation in Colonial Asia* (Amsterdam, 1990).

10. M. Holmstrom, *Industry and Inequality: The Social Anthropology of Indian Labour* (Cambridge, 1984).

11. F. Fanon, *The Wretched of the Earth*, C. Farrington (tr.) (New York, 1965).

the exclusion of the labouring poor in non-wage work or in the informal sector may be based on a wrong reading of Marx. It is true that in his *analytical* scheme the *differentia specifica* underline the sale of labour power for wages in the capitalist mode of production (see for instance *Grundrisse* and parts of *Capital*), but as a *historical* category labour is a more inclusive term in his writings. Thus, when Marx talks of the "reserve army of the unemployed" he talks of the "labourer" generically, compounding wage workers with non-wage workers;[12] he notices labour in "domestic industry" and more importantly in the "sphere of pauperism". Elsewhere he definitely includes not only people who are *sometimes* wage-workers, but even paupers who make up that section of the working class which has forfeited its condition of existence, i.e. sale of labour power.[13]

I would add that in criticizing this narrow focus on the factory proletariat in labour historiography (and in the agenda of some political parties) and in arguing in favour of a more inclusive concept of the "labouring poor" as belonging to non-wage and informal sectors, I am aware that the latter is a fuzzy concept. But possibly a fuzzy concept like the "labouring poor", without sharply defined boundaries, is more appropriate to transitional economies in less developed countries where class boundaries are porous,[14] where gradations shade into each other, where individuals and families are simultaneously located in more than one of the conventional class categories which counterpoise wage labour and non-wage labour. Where the transition to capitalist/wage-labour relationship is incomplete or is not sufficiently generalized, we have what is almost a "permanently transitional" situation, which calls for concepts other than the clear-cut ones of advanced metropolitan economies.[15]

To return to our narrative, the post-Independence period (i.e. after 1947 in India, Pakistan and Bangladesh/East Pakistan, and 1948 in Sri Lanka) saw the burgeoning of higher education and consequently of research. From the 1950s the number of institutions and the size of university faculties increased dramatically; and in the 1960s, area study programmes in North American universities promoted research on South Asia, while the new field of study called "growth economics" and the Five-Year Plans in India during the Nehruvian regime significantly expanded interest in the social sciences. Thus there occurred a rapid growth of professional

12. Karl Marx, *Capital: A Critique of Political Economy*, vol. 1, Ben Fowkes (tr.) (Harmondsworth, 1976), part 7, sections 2 and 4.

13. *Ibid.*, section 5.

14. W. van Schendel, *Three Deltas: Accumulation and Poverty in Rural Burma, Bengal and South India* (Delhi, 1991).

15. S. Bhattacharya, "The Labouring Poor and their Notion of Poverty: Late 19th and early 20th Century Bengal" (Labour and History Series. Working Paper no. 1, V.V. Giri National Labour Institute, Noida, 1998), pp. 1–33; reprinted in *Labour and Development*, 3 (July 1997), pp. 1–23.

academic research in the areas of economics, sociology, and the history of labour in South Asia.

It would be incorrect to talk in terms of a dramatic "end of ideology" in labour historiography, but from the 1950s one saw a certain trend towards de-ideologization. Partly that was the result of the appearance of professional academics, as distinct from the social and political activists whose research had earlier constituted the bulk of the literature on the subject. Frequently, anything problematic began to be framed along the lines of standard neo-classical economics. Thus C.A. Myers contributed to the supply-side explanations of economic underdevelopment in India by arguing that industry was inhibited by both the immobility of labour and its lack of industrial discipline.[16] Morris D. Morris's thesis, on the other hand, was that the lack of any correlation between wage trends and labour supply in the cotton mills of Bombay in the late nineteenth and early twentieth centuries indicates that labour supply was no constraint.[17] K. Mukerji identified long-term trends in the jute textile industry, as did D. Mazumdar in cotton textiles.[18] Amiya Kumar Bagchi addressed the question of labour-supply constraints in his analysis of private investment in India 1900–1939; he rejected that argument, along with other supply-side explanations of colonial underdevelopment.[19]

Historians' contributions in the 1950s and 1960s were in the nature of institutional history, focusing on trade unions. A.S. and J.S. Mathur, V.B. Karnik, G.K. Sharma, S.C. Jha, C. Revri, and Sukomal Sen provided accounts of the growth of the trade-union movement, their chronicles varying in historical depth but uniformly limited to institutional history and rather detached from the roots of its socio-economic context.[20] Most of these trade-union histories merited Hobsbawm's criticism of a similar tradition in British labour historiography: "It tended to identify class and movement, movement and organization or leadership of organization, thus bypassing social realities."[21] Published about this time, the only monograph on Ceylonese labour history, Visakha Kumari Jayawardena's

16. C.A. Myers, *Labor Problems in the Industrialization of India* (Cambridge, MA, 1958).

17. M.D. Morris, *The Emergence of an Industrial Labor Force in India: A Study of the Bombay Cotton Mills, 1854–1947* (Berkeley, CA [etc.], 1965).

18. K. Mukerji, "Trends in Real Wages in the Jute Textile Industry from 1900 to 1951", *Artha Vijnana*, 2 (March 1960); D. Mazumdar, "Labour Supply in Early Industrialization: The Case of the Bombay Textile Industry", *Economic History Review* (2nd series), 26 (1973), pp. 477–496.

19. A.K. Bagchi, *Private Investment in India 1900–1939* (London, 1972).

20 . A.S. and J.S. Mathur, *Trade Union Movement in India* (Allahabad, 1957); V.B. Karnik, *Indian Trade Unions: A Survey* (Bombay, 1960); G.K. Sharma, *Labour Movement in India: Its Past and Present* (Jullundur, 1963); S.C. Jha, *The Indian Trade Union Movement* (Calcutta, 1970); C. Revri, *The Indian Trade Union Movement 1880–1947* (Delhi, 1972); S. Sen, *Working Class of India: History of Emergence and Movement, 1830–1970* (Calcutta, 1977).

21. E.J. Hobsbawm, "Foreword", in J. Foster, *Class Struggle and the Industrial Revolution: Early Industrial Capitalism in Three English Towns* (London, 1974).

The Rise of the Labor Movement in Ceylon, constitutes an exception; although the subject of study is mainly organized trade unionism, it is contextualized within social and economic trends in Sri Lanka between 1880 and 1933.[22]

From the 1970s a movement away from the narrative of the older vintage was manifested in two ways. Empirical research, often of the detailed kind expected in doctoral dissertations, revealed complexities which could not be accommodated in the older paradigm. This is exemplified by C.P. Simmons's work on Bengal coal miners, Chitra Joshi's on Kanpur cotton textile labour, Dick Kooiman's, Rajnarayan Chandavarkar's, and R.K. Newman's on Bombay millhands, and Rana P. Behal's on tea plantations in Assam.[23] After this crop of empirical research in the 1970s came a theoretical critique of the "universalist mode of thinking that constantly produces out of Marxism a master narrative of history".[24] The essence of the critique was that such a master narrative, a construct genealogically traceable to the European Enlightenment, presumptuously tries to explain diverse historical experiences in terms of one unilinear pattern. In the exposition of those diversities emphasis is placed on cultural discourse, a feature that characterizes the "subaltern" approach,[25] and also signals an affiliation claim to the postmodernist linguistic turn or culturalist approach.[26]

Between this approach and that of the proponents of "old history" the battle remains undecided. It has been said in refutation of the culturalist approach that "economic determinism, alleged to be found in Marxist

22. Visakha Kumari Jayawardena, *The Rise of the Labor Movement in Ceylon* (Durham, NC, 1972).

23. C.P. Simmons, "Recruiting and Organizing an Industrial Labour Force in Colonial India: The Case of the Coal Mining Industry, c. 1880–1939", *Indian Economic and Social History Review*, 13 (1976), pp. 455–485; C. Joshi, "Kanpur Textile Labour: Some Structural Features of Formative Years", *Economic and Political Weekly*, 16 (November 1981), pp. 1823–1837; D. Kooiman, "Jobbers and the Emergence of Trade Unions in Bombay City", *International Review of Social History*, 22 (1977), pp. 313–328; R.S. Chandavarkar, "Workers' Politics and the Mill Districts in Bombay Between the Wars", *Modern Asian Studies*, 15 (1981), pp. 603–647; R.K. Newman, *Workers and Unions in Bombay Mills, 1918–1929* (Canberra, 1981); R.P. Behal, "Forms of Labour Protest in Assam Valley Tea Plantations, 1900–1930", *Economic and Political Weekly*, 20 (26 January 1985), pp. 19–26. For some of the later results of this wave of research see S. Patel, *The Making of Industrial Relations: The Ahmedabad Textile Industry, 1918–1939* (Delhi, 1987); D. Kooiman, *Bombay Textile Labour: Managers, Trade Unionists and Officials 1918–1939* (Delhi, 1989); R.S. Chandavarkar, *The Origins of Industrial Capitalism in India: Business Strategies and the Working Classes in Bombay, 1900–1940* (Cambridge, 1994); C. Joshi, *Lost Worlds: Indian Labour and its Forgotten Histories* (Delhi, 2003).

24. D. Chakrabarty, *Rethinking Working-Class History: Bengal 1890–1940* (Delhi, 1989).

25. *Subaltern Studies*, 10 vols (New Delhi, 1982–2000). Vols 1–6 were edited by R. Guha. The later volumes were edited by P. Chatterjee and G. Pandey, D. Arnold and D. Hardiman, S. Amin and D. Chakrabarty, and P. Chatterjee and P. Jeganathan.

26. G. Chakravorty Spivak, "Subaltern Studies: Deconstructing Historiography", in R. Guha (ed.), *Subaltern Studies IV* (Delhi, 1985), pp. 330–363.

theories, is replaced by a sort of cultural determinism".[27] Likewise, Chandavarkar's counter-critique focuses on the homogenizing thrust of a search for a "popular culture" or a "subaltern mind".[28] The explication of the history of labour, or anything else, in terms of popular or "Indian culture" may be no more than a variant of what Edward Said identified as "Orientalism"

It would be an exaggeration to say that the culturalist approach has been widely accepted as a substitute for analysis in terms of class structure and the social conditions of labour. Nor are all historians progressing with equal rapidity towards the post-modernist void. Much of the professional output in recent decades remains anchored in their substantive concern with the "pre-post-modernist" agenda. I feel that an *ante*-postmodernist agenda is not the same as *anti*-postmodernism.

Not only in the writings of the older generation of scholars,[29] but also those of the younger generation,[30] the conceptual framework and the digits of analysis remain unaffected by the culturalist impact. The consequence of that impact has generally been a greater awareness of the cultural dimension. The limited nature of its impact on labour history may be due to several reasons. Methodologically, it is very difficult to establish hypotheses about the culture of the labouring poor in the past; the sources

27. R. Das Gupta, "Indian Working Class: Some Recent Historiographical Issues", in Arjan de Haan and Samita Sen (eds), *A Case for Labour History: The Jute Industry in Eastern India* (Calcutta, 1999), p. 29.

28. R. Chandavarkar, *Imperial Power and Popular Politics: Class, Resistance and the State in India, c.1850–1950* (Cambridge, 1998).

29. For example, R. Das Gupta, "Factory Labour in Eastern India: Sources of Supply, 1855–1946, Some Preliminary Findings", *Indian Economic and Social History Review*, 13 (1976), pp. 277–328; *idem*, "Structure of the Labour Market in Colonial India", *Economic and Political Weekly*, Special Number (November 1981), pp.1781–1806; *idem*, *Poverty and Protest: A Study of Calcutta's Working Class and Labouring Poor 1875–1900* (Calcutta, 1983); *idem*, *Labour and Working Class in Eastern India: Studies in Colonial History* (Calcutta, 1994); R.S. Chandavarkar, *Labour and Society in Bombay* (Cambridge, 1987); *idem*, *The Origins of Industrial Capitalism in India*; G.K. Lieten, *Colonialism, Class and Nation: The Confrontation in Bombay around 1930* (Calcutta, 1984); O. Goswami, *Industry, Trade and Peasant Society: The Jute Economy of Eastern India, 1900–47* (Delhi, 1991); S.K. Sen, *Working Class Movements in India, 1885–1975* (New Delhi, 1994).

30. For example, P. Mohapatra, "Coolies and Colliers: A Study of the Agrarian Context of Labour Migration from Chota Nagpur, 1880–1920", *Studies in History* (New Series), 1 (1985), pp. 13–42; N. Basu, *The Political Parties and the Labour Politics, 1937–1947* (Calcutta, 1992); S. Basu, "Workers Politics in Bengal 1890s–1929: Mill Towns, Strikes and National Agitation" (Ph.D. thesis, University of Cambridge, 1994); A. Das, *Urban Politics in an Industrial Area: Aspects of Municipal and Labour Politics in Howrah, West Bengal, 1850–1928* (Calcutta, 1994); D. Simeon, *The Politics of Labour Under Late Colonialism: Workers, Trade Unions and the State in Chota Nagpur, 1928–1939* (Delhi, 1995); J. Nair, *Miners and Millhands: Work, Culture and Politics in Princely Mysore* (Delhi, 1998); P. Ghosh, *Colonialism, Class, and a History of the Calcutta Jute Hands, 1880–1930* (Hyderabad, 2000); and, for Bangladesh, A.Z.M. Iftikhar-ul-Awwal, *The Industrial Development of Bengal, 1900–1939* (New Delhi, 1982).

used by the cultural historian emanate from literate elite groups and "reading against the grain" of such sources does not always take one very far. Features attributed in this elite discourse are aggregated as "popular" culture, disregarding internal diversities. All this merits historians' attention, but as yet little work founded on historical evidence has emerged in the area.

One area where current research displays its cutting edge is women's and gender studies. There was little substantial research on women workers until recent decades, when a surge in activity took place.[31] Research now ranges from general studies of working women,[32] gradually acquiring a more nuanced approach to the specific local situations of women workers, to a more intensive study of resulting particularities. For instance, Arjan de Haan examines female labour participation in jute mills, and the formation of identities, emphasizing as agents for them the purposeful behaviour of the participants, rather than either culture, be it popular or traditional, or the systemic needs of capitalist/colonial structure.[33] Samita Sen has researched the role of women workers in jute mills, 1890–1940, to explore the interrelationship of gender, class, and communalist/nationalist identities; she underlines the role of gender in wage determination and generally in the development of the working class.[34] There are, of course, many more contributions in this area which address the contemporary situation but lack a historical perspective.[35]

There have been alarm signals from Marcel van der Linden in *International Review of Social History* (1993) and from Ira Katznelson in *International Labor and Working Class History* (1994)[36] warning of a general decline of interest in labour history. I shall not for the present try to answer the question of whether that decline is due to some of the developments in historiography I have touched upon – the "fragmentation" of labour history, the de-ideologization which cut off labour history

31. P. Sengupta, *Women Workers of India* (Bombay, 1960).

32. See for example N. Banerjee, *Women Workers in the Unorganized Sector: The Calcutta Experience* (Hyderabad, 1985); *idem*, "Working Women in Colonial Bengal: Modernization and Marginalization", in K. Sangari and S. Vaid (eds), *Recasting Women: Essays in Colonial History* (New Delhi, 1989), pp. 269–301.

33. A. de Haan, *Unsettled Settlers: Migrant Workers and Industrial Capitalism in Calcutta* (Hilversum, 1994).

34. S. Sen, "Motherhood and Mothercraft: Gender and Nationalism in Bengal", *Gender and History*, 5 (1993), pp. 231–243; *idem*, *Women and Labour in Late Colonial India: The Bengal Jute Industry* (Cambridge [etc.], 1999).

35. A. Basu, *Two Faces of Protest: Contrasting Modes of Women's Activism* (Berkeley, CA [etc.], 1992); L. Fernandes, *Producing Workers: The Politics of Gender, Class and Culture in the Calcutta Jute Mills* (Philadelphia, PA, 1997).

36. Marcel van der Linden, "Editorial", *International Review of Social History*, Supplement 1 (1993), pp. 163–173: Ira Katznelson, "The 'Bourgeois' Dimension: A Provocation About Institutions, Politics, and the Future of Labor History", *International Labor and Working Class History*, 46 (1994), pp. 7–32.

from the mainstream of political discourse about labour in civil society or the state, the exclusion (characteristic of labour history until recently) of large masses of the labouring poor in underdeveloped countries, and the focusing of attention on the minuscule industrial wage worker section. The question to address is: "Where do we go from here?", in the present era of globalization.

First, let us remind ourselves how an interest in labour history developed in many parts of the world in the 1970s. An Indian historian, in a presidential address at the Indian historians' national professional organization in 1982, pointed to the wave of interest in "people's history", "history from below", and the history of the working class in the 1970s.[37] "People's history is a term which might be retrospectively applied", Samuel wrote in 1981, "to those various attempts to write an archive-based 'history from below' which have played such a large part in the recent revival of English social history".[38] Le Roy Ladurie's complaint against economic history, which was "history without people", pointed in the same direction, as did Jean Chesneaux's critique of the "occultation" of the history of the oppressed, caused by the oppressors' and the state's "control over the past".[39] In England alone, according to a bibliography published in 1980, the number of books and articles on the British labour movement published since 1945 exceeded 4,000.[40] That apart, history from below appeared in different guises as new research interests were created – by Hobsbawm in social banditry, by Chevalier in outcasts and dangerous classes, by Laslett in the quotidian family, by E.P. Thompson in the proto-industrial working man, by Rudé in the crowd as an actor on the stage of history, and so on. In the countries of the South one heard similar voices. Rodolfo Stavenhagen in Mexico called for the "de-elitization" of the social sciences.[41] Issa G. Shivji of the "Dar-es-Salaam school of history" in Tanzania called for a new history to replace the historiography which "leaves the large mass of our people out of history".[42] An obscure manifesto issued by the Centre de Estudios de La Realidad Puertoriqueño asked, "What of the history of the historyless, the anonymous people?".[43]

I shall argue that in South Asia and in many countries of the South in general this effort to find the history of the "historyless" had a special

37. S. Bhattacharya, *History from Below: Presidential Address, Modern History Section, Indian History Congress, 1982* (New Delhi, 1982).

38. R. Samuel, "Editorial Preface", in *idem* (ed.), *People's History and Socialist Theory* (London, 1981), pp. xvi, xv–xxxiii *passim*.

39. J. Chesneaux, *Pasts and Futures* (London, 1978); E. Le Roy Ladurie, *The Territory of the Historian* (Chicago, IL, 1979).

40. H. Smith, *The British Labour Movement* (London, 1980).

41. R. Stavenhagen, *Between Underdevelopment and Revolution: A Latin American Perspective* (New Delhi, 1981).

42. I.G. Shivji, *Class Struggle in Tanzania* (New York, 1976).

43. A.Q. Rivera, *Workers' Struggles in Puerto Rico: A Documentary History* (New York, 1976).

significance. In the wake of political decolonization an evaluation began of the construction of the past in the hands of colonial historians on the one hand and nationalist historians on the other. The nationalist paradigm began to be questioned in India. Where was class struggle in the narrative of the Indian people's struggle against British rule? In so far as nationalist historiography was an ideological effort to define and establish national unity in cultural terms, was there a hidden agenda of cultural domination?

And not only in India; consider the debate between Amilcar Cabral, writing of Guinea, and a Tanzanian historian. "What commands history in colonial condition", wrote Cabral, "is not class struggle [...]. In the colonial period it is the state which commands history."[44] Against this it was said that this would reduce all of history into "nothing but the history of the colonial state".[45] In fact, in India this kind of explicit challenge to the nationalist historiography came rather late in the *Subaltern Studies*. Implicitly the challenge had already been posed in the Marxist re-evaluation of the colonial and nationalist tradition in historiography. At any rate, the conjuncture of the interest in history from below in the North and the critique of the older paradigms of history in some countries of the South was the fertile ground on which seeds of labour history produced a crop of new research. What fed this new interest was an urge to recover the people's history. The further labour historians have moved away from that agenda, the more they have lost their audience.

Does the process of globalization since the 1980s present labour historians with a new agenda? At its interface with the South Asian historiography of labour what does "global labour history" connote, if the concept is not merely a label, referring to spatial coverage? Implicitly the question has been touched upon in three ways. First, in the history of India's participation in the international labour market during the nineteenth century in the form of the migration, under the auspices of metropolitan capital, of South Asian labourers to plantations overseas under the indentured labour system; then in the examination of the concept of proletarian internationalism in the Marxian paradigm and its variants from the 1920s in South Asia; and third, in recent decades the question has been noted in a phenomenon brought about by globalization, namely the restructuring of labour both in developed and underdeveloped countries in a new phase of world capitalism. However, in none of these areas has sufficient attention been given to the conceptual basis of re-thinking labour history in global terms.

From the point of view of South Asian labour studies the significant

44. A. Cabral, *Revolution in Guinea* (New York, 1970), p. 56.

45. Shivji, *Class Struggle in Tanzania*, pp. 55–56; for an elaboration of the discussion in the text regarding globalization and labour, see S. Bhattacharya, "International Flows of Unfree Labour", in K.S. Jomo (ed.), *Globalization under Hegemony: the Changing World Economy* (New Delhi, 2006), pp. 195–226.

aspect of a global agenda of research is the possibility of comparative studies straddling national and cultural borders. I suggest that there are certain homomorphies in the colonial social formations in the past and the underdeveloped countries of the South today. On account of these homomorphies, comparison of South Asian socio-economic experiences with those of many countries of the South could be illuminating. I have discussed the special characteristics of the class structure in South Asia consequent on its incomplete transition to capitalism, especially in the colonial period. Marxist Africanists have puzzled over this issue for a long time. Mahmoud Hussein identified an incomplete proletariat in Egypt because they were in an "obstructed transitional stage".[46] Shivji observed that Tanzania had no European or "classical types of class division".[47] Mahmood Mamdani in Uganda noted that "class formation is a process" that had not produced a true class.[48] Richard Sandbrook observed that the proletariat in Kenya had not emerged in a "clearly differentiated" form.[49] Ali A. Mazrui developed a term, "trans-class ambivalence", to cope with the problem of locating migrant labour in an "underdeveloped class structure".[50] Gavin Kitching, researching Kenya, made the drastic suggestion that instead of class concepts only a "concept of exploitation" be employed.[51]

To take another example of similarity: as in South Asia, in African countries it has often been observed that trade-union leadership belonged to "outsiders", non-manual middle-grade employees or clerks; while leaders coming from the rank and file of the working class were rare. Pre-eminent examples are Sekou Touré in Guinea, Tom Mboya in Kenya, and Joshua Nkomo in Southern Rhodesia.[52] Moreover, there are interesting parallels between Indian trade-union history and the history of mutual-aid societies or *mutualidades* transforming themselves into *sociedades de resistencia* and into trade unions in Latin American countries.

Another kind of parallelism to be studied comparatively is in the area of identity politics – the interweaving of communal and class identities. While the Hindu–Muslim issue has been studied in the social and political

46. M. Hussein, *Class Conflict in Egypt, 1945–1970* (New York, 1973), p. 39.
47. Shivji, *Class Struggle in Tanzania*, p. 18.
48. M. Mamdani, *Politics and Class Formation in Uganda* (New York, 1976), pp. 10–11.
49. R. Sandbrook, *Proletarians and African Capitalism: The Kenyan Case, 1960–72* (Cambridge, 1975), p. 191.
50. A.A. Mazrui, "Casualties of an Underdeveloped Class Structure", in W.A. Shack and E.P. Skinner (eds), *Strangers in African Society* (Berkeley, CA, 1979), pp. 261–265.
51. G. Kitching, *Class and Economic Change in Kenya, 1905–1970* (New Haven, CT, 1980), p. 4. See also G. Arrighi and J.S. Saul, *Essays in the Political Economy of Africa* (New York, 1973), which reflects similar concerns and lines of thinking.
52. W.A. Warmington, *A West African Trade Union* (London, 1960), p. 123; B.H. Millen, *The Political Role of Labour in Developing Countries* (Honolulu, HI, 1963), pp. 27–29; E.M. Kassalow, *National Labour Movements in the Post-War World* (New York, 1966), pp. 236 ff.

world of Indian working classes, the eminent anthropologist Max Gluckman looked at a similar problem many years ago in a different terrain, "problems arising from the African industrial revolution": tribal identities among immigrants to the industrial towns were retained/discarded/reinvented, for he said "it is possible for men to dichotomize their actions in separate spheres".[53] These and many other areas of congruence suggest that the patterns of development in labour history in the countries of the South need to be studied in a comparative way as a means of developing a broader perspective.

If, in the coming years, global labour history is to mean something more than aggregation, we have to apply our minds to the necessity of developing a comparative approach towards pattern congruences and diversities, within an agenda of recovering the history of the oppressed who are "historyless"

53. M. Gluckman, "Anthropological Problems Arising out of the African Industrial Revolution", in A. Southall (ed.), *Social Change in Modern Africa* (London, 1961), pp. 67–82.

Working across the Seas: Indian Maritime Labourers in India, Britain, and in Between, 1600–1857*

MICHAEL H. FISHER

INDIAN SEAMEN IN THE EUROPEAN WOODEN WORLD

The advent and expansion of trans-oceanic shipping aboard wooden, wind-powered vessels between India and Europe created uniquely onerous working conditions for the Indian seamen who volunteered to labour aboard – conditions distinct from either coastal or land-based employment in either India or Europe. Indian (and European) seamen on such vessels may have been "free labour" prior to boarding ship, but they were in many respects "unfree labour" while at sea.[1] They were unable to change jobs, to vary the amount of labour extracted from them, to increase the compensation or necessities provided, or to quit – in short, to do much to improve their working conditions generally. They sailed for uncertainly long periods of time, confined to constricted, unhealthy spaces and limited diet, almost constantly facing the various dangers of the open sea under the virtually unavoidable, unrelenting, and unalterable hierarchic authority and often brutal physical discipline of European officers.

For most of this period, wars raged in both Europe and India, so these Indian seamen faced threats from hostile navies as well as piratical and meteorological violence. These seamen engaged in intense and necessarily highly coordinated labour with a relatively small but often mixed group of fellow workers of diverse origins; their solidarities were forged over the arduous voyage, often enduring beyond. Their employment terminated in alien ports, during Europe's "Little Ice Age", with few resources and limited support networks available there except of their own making.

* Research for this article was supported by a generous grant from the American Council of Learned Societies. I would like to thank for their comments participants at the Indian National Labour Institute, Delhi, where I presented an early version of this paper, 4 October 2002. My *Counterflows to Colonialism: Indian Travellers and Settlers in Britain, 1600–1857* (Delhi, 2004) highlights the social and cultural history of lascars and all other Indians living in Britain over this period.

1. For discussion of these concepts, see Tom Brass and Marcel van der Linden (eds), *Free and Unfree Labour: The Debate Continues* (New York, 1997). Intermediary labour recruiters were not unique to the Indian Ocean. In Europe, "crimps" specialized in recruiting seamen (including through coercion or deception); some seamen were slaves. See Amitav Ghosh, *In an Antique Land* (London, 1992), and *idem*, "The Slave of MS. H6", *Subaltern Studies*, 7 (1993), pp. 159–220.

Once ashore, however, they (like seamen generally) were also notoriously free: difficult for port authorities to regulate, discipline, or re-recruit. For centuries, their traditional systems of recruitment and service largely resisted the European-based models of labour relations and regulation which their ship-owning employers sought to impose on them.

The tens of thousands of Indian seamen who served aboard these European, and particularly British, trans-continental ships to Europe during this long transition to "high colonialism" created novel employment patterns aboard and ashore there. Their insistence on recruitment and service under their own headmen and also the economics of their wage and production rates compelled European ship-owners to respond, and often unwillingly defer. Further, when these Indian seamen reached Europe, they interacted through asymmetrical power relationships with the native population and with a range of often conflicting authorities. While some Indian seamen settled there, most participated in transitory communities before returning to India. Many engaged in these maritime labour-gangs as long as they were physically able; others regretted having ventured to Europe even once; a frightfully high percentage did not survive the voyage out, life in Europe, or the passage home. Compiling statistical patterns and drawing upon individual examples, this article considers what it was like to work across the seas between India and Britain during the 250 years from the earliest voyages to the mid-nineteenth century, as much as possible from the perspectives of Indian seamen themselves.

Trade was the lifeblood of the expanding British world-system and Indian maritime labour made British commerce with India possible. Yet, the labour history of these men has only begun to emerge. Much scholarship has described patterns of trade in the Indian Ocean during the pre- and early colonial periods.[2] This article complements this work with consideration of labour relations there. The labour history of European, particularly British, seamen over this period also contrasts with that of Indian seamen.[3] Recent studies have examined Indian seamen working in Britain during later periods when the advent of intercontinental steamships, greater British colonial controls over labour in India

2. See Janet Abu-Lughod, *Before European Hegemony: The World System AD 1250–1350* (New York, 1989); K.N. Chaudhuri, *Trade and Civilisation in the Indian Ocean: An Economic History from the Rise of Islam to 1750* (Cambridge, 1985); Ashin Das Gupta and M.N. Pearson (eds), *India and the Indian Ocean, 1500–1800* (Calcutta, 1987); Holden Furber, *Rival Empires of Trade in the Orient, 1600–1800* (Minneapolis, MN, 1976); Niels Steensgaard, *Carracks, Caravans and Companies: The Structural Crisis in the European–Asian Trade in the Early 17th Century* (Lund, 1973); Sanjay Subrahmanyam, The *Portuguese Empire in Asia, 1500–1700: A Political and Economic History* (London, 1993).

3. See Isaac Land, "Domesticating the Maritime" (Ph.D., University of Michigan, 1999) and "Customs of the Sea: Flogging, Empire and the 'True British Seaman', 1770–1870", *Interventions*, 3 (2001), pp. 169–185; Marcus Rediker, *Between the Devil and the Deep Blue Sea* (Cambridge, 1987).

under "high colonialism", social and economic transformations in colony and metropole, and two world wars profoundly altered the experiences of Indian seamen.[4] During the earlier period analysed here, both the economics of these men's work and the contexts in which they functioned differed markedly from those of the later period. By examining the initial and unevenly changing interactions between indigenous patterns of labour relations and the fundamentally different European models with which they clashed and negotiated, even as power shifted over the centuries, we can begin to extend Indian labour history transnationally beyond India's shores and chronologically back to a relatively early period.[5]

PRE-COLONIAL MODES OF MARITIME LABOUR IN THE INDIAN OCEAN

While there were many pre-colonial patterns of recruitment and service in the Indian Ocean, one that developed most extensively, with disparate advantages for all parties, was the *lascar* maritime labour-gang under a *serang*. A *serang* (a "headman" or labour contractor), recruited each seaman, often customarily termed a *lascar* (from *lashkar*, or *khalasi*, also collectively meaning "a group of armed men, an army", and, more

4. See G. Balachandran, "Conflicts in International Maritime Labour Markets: British and Indian Seamen, Employers and the State, 1890–1939", *Indian Economic and Social History Review*, 39 (2002), pp. 71–100; *idem*, "Circulation through Seafaring: Indian Seamen, 1890–1945", in Claude Markovits, Jacques Pouchepadass, and Sanjay Subrahmanyam (eds), *Society and Circulation: Mobile People and Itinerant Cultures in South Asia, 1750–1950* (New Delhi, 2003), pp. 89–130; N. Benjamin, "The British and Indian Sailors (c.1790–1885)", in P.M. Joshi and M.A. Nayeem (eds), *Studies in the Foreign Relations of India from the Earliest Times to 1947* (Hyderabad, 1975), pp. 485–496; Frank Broeze, "Underdevelopment and Dependency: Maritime India during the Raj", *Modern Asian Studies*, 18 (1984), pp. 429–457; Anne Dunlop, "Lascars and Labourers: Reactions to the Indian Presence in the West of Scotland during the 1920s and 1930s", *Scottish Labour History Society Journal*, 25 (1990), pp. 40–57; Conrad Dixon, "Lascars: The Forgotten Seamen", in Rosemary Ommer and Gerald Panting (eds), *Working Men Who Got Wet: Proceedings of the Fourth Conference of the Atlantic Canada Shipping Project, July 24–July 26, 1980* (Newfoundland, 1980), pp. 265–81; Shompa Lahiri, *Indians in Britain: Anglo-Indian Encounters, Race and Identity, 1880–1930* (London, 2000); R.G.W. Prescott, "Lascar Seamen on the Clyde", in T.C. Smout (ed), *Scotland and the Sea* (Edinburgh, 1992), pp. 199–212; M. Sherwood, "Lascar Struggles Against Discrimination in Britain 1923–45: The Work of N.J. Upadhyaya and Surat Alley", *Mariner's Mirror*, 90 (2004), pp. 438–455; Laura Tabili, "Construction of Racial Difference in Twentieth-Century Britain: The Special Restriction (Coloured Alien Seamen) Order, 1925", *Journal of British Studies*, 33 (1994), pp. 54–98 and *idem*, *"We Ask for British Justice": Workers and Racial Difference in Late Imperial Britain* (Ithaca, NY, 1994).

5. See Norma Myers, "The Black Poor of London: Initiatives of Eastern Seamen in the Eighteenth and Nineteenth Centuries", *Immigrants & Minorities*, 13 (1994), pp. 7–21; M. Sherwood, "Ticket of Leave and Lascar Seamen, Crews for the East India Company", *History Today*, 40 (1990), pp. 6–8; Rozina Visram, *Asians in Britain: 400 Years of History* (London, 2002), and *idem*, *Ayahs, Lascars and Princes: Indians in Britain, 1700–1947* (London, 1984).

specifically, "the crew attached to an artillery piece"). Lascar referred to their condition of employment, so men of very diverse religious communities, regional, linguistic, and caste backgrounds often worked in a single maritime labour-gang. The members of a single gang also might have varying amounts of nautical experience and skills, as well as physical capacities. What they shared was a willingness to engage to serve on a vessel collectively under the immediate command of a serang, who was not the ship-owning employer. Despite their diversity, lascars on a voyage seem generally to have bonded with each other with shared experiences and marine argot and expertise as the glue.

Some serangs, termed *ghat* serangs (literally "dock or landing head man", sometimes termed *seer* or "chief" serang), did not themselves go to sea. Men initially seeking work as lascars went first to a ghat serang, as did experienced but unemployed lascars. Wind-driven shipping depended on the monsoon; between seasons lascars depended for food, housing, and cash advances from ghat serangs, which they more than repaid from future wages. The ghat serang negotiated a corporate contract with each captain for a pre-assembled lascar crew for the voyage (or for loading or unloading a ship in port). Only with the coming of European shipping would these contracts regularly be written rather than verbal.

Other serangs also worked aboard the vessel as petty officers – intermediaries between the ship's captain (sometimes owner-master) and the lascars of their gang. The serang might also serve as ship's navigator (but European ships usually had their own European sailing masters, although the local knowledge of coasts, hazards, currents, and winds which many serangs possessed would be appreciated by any wise ship-master). The serang aboard ship was assisted by one or more subordinate petty officers: *tindals* (*tandail* or *tandel* "the head of a *tanda* or body of men", "a gang boss").[6] Ship serangs and tindals received higher wages from ship-owners and also customary fees from their lascars.

For ship-owners and/or captains, hiring a serang and his maritime labour-gang solved some problems inherent in the industry but also created other tensions. Given the monsoon patterns, wind-powered sailing vessels had to be prepared to leave by particular times or wait until the next annual cycle. A ship idle in port was unproductive. This meant that loading and unloading by longshoremen and assembling the sailing crew prior to departure could be highly time-bound, with all competing ships vying for the same pool of labour for the same short season. Further, captains arriving at an Indian port might not have extensive local connections that

6. See G. Balachandran, "Searching for the Sardar: The State, Pre-Capitalist Institutions, and Human Agency in the Maritime Labour Market, Calcutta, 1880–1935", in Burton Stein and Sanjay Subrahmanyam (eds), *Institutions and Economic Change in South Asia* (Delhi, 1996), pp. 206–236.

would enable recruitment of such labourers on an individual basis. Rather, through customarily arrangements with ghat serangs who possessed effective recruitment networks for labour-gangs, these possible delays might be obviated. Further, communication with – and discipline of – the diverse seamen who composed these labour-gangs would be the ship serang's direct responsibility. This would prove particularly important for European officers, who were culturally and by social class quite different from lascars.

This mode of labour recruitment, however, also had drawbacks for ship captains and owners. They dealt with ghat serangs who controlled the labour supply and therefore wage-rates. The monsoon patterns also provided the ghat serang with leverage at times of peak demand when he could extract the most from desperate captains fearful of missing the sailing season. Serangs also represented to some extent the interests of the lascars collectively, which made them more difficult for officers to divide and subdue. Therefore, the class tensions in any workplace, and particularly in such a total environment as a ship at sea, took on different configurations when a ship was even partially manned by a serang and his lascar maritime labour-gang as opposed to individually recruited seamen. European ships, even when supported by an Indian-based factory run by their East India Company, nonetheless would perforce participate in this indigenous serang system in order to obtain lascars.

When such modes of labour recruitment and service, historically common in the Indian Ocean, interacted with conditions and contexts brought from Europe, even more complications eventuated. European seamen (and non-Indian Asian seamen) had different cultural identities, interests, and expectations from Indian seamen, even if they served on the same ship. European nations had particular laws and customary practices which sometimes conflicted with the serang system concerning fundamental presuppositions about labour relations. Further, capitalist joint-stock corporations – including the English East India Company upon which we will concentrate – functioned differently from other kinds of shipping that plied the Indian Ocean, including by using written contracts and regulations for seamen enforceable by colonial and metropolitian police and judicial courts. Thus, lascar labour-gangs under serangs and European-style shipping comprised two distinct systems that interacted in contested ways that shifted over the centuries.

EUROPEAN SHIPS FIRST SAIL INTO THE INDIAN OCEAN

For increasing numbers of Indian maritime workers, the initial arrival of European ships in the Indian Ocean at the end of the fifteenth century, and then the secular increase in the number of such vessels over the following centuries, created novel opportunities but also significant challenges. We need not rehearse here the larger political and economic changes in the Indian Ocean brought about first by the Portuguese and then by the northern European East India Companies. Rather, we can focus on the labour history of this transition, concentrating on lascars working for the most extensive of the companies, the English.

As the English East India Company entered the ongoing networks of trade in the Indian Ocean from the early seventeenth century onward, virtually all its ships faced the problem of replenishing their onboard labour supply. European seamen died in astounding numbers, in particular from both the harsh conditions aboard ship and tropical diseases on arrival. Many deserted, seeking riches and/or sensual pleasure as soldiers of fortune ashore. The Royal Navy (whose own ships also lost seamen in the Indian Ocean) also conscripted prime European seamen from merchant ships there, at rates occasionally up to one-third of the entire crew.[7] Therefore, almost every arriving ship sought Indian seamen to replace them and enable the ship to return to Europe.

Some East India Company ships, particularly in the early seventeenth century, signed on Indians as individual sailors who contracted personally with ship-owners, as was the practice in Europe. Thus, in 1614, we find three Indian seamen in London negotiating the terms of their employment on the voyage home.[8] Company ships would continue to hire seamen as individuals over the period considered here, but generally this was confined to Europeans or people of mixed ancestry.

Many Company ships perforce or by choice followed the more widespread Indian Ocean pattern of lascar maritime labour-gangs, hired under a serang as a block. While many captains resented their dependence on serangs, the Company soon recognized the right of designated ghat serangs as official labour contractors. For example, in 1699 the Company declared that, in Bengal, "Serang Doud [...] shall be our Serang to furnish our ships with Lascars".[9] The position of ghat serang remained an inheritable proprietary right into the early nineteenth century. Contracts negotiated between the ghat serang and the captain for a passage to Britain often ran for six or more months. The ghat serang received a fee from the captain, prorated for the number and alleged skills of lascars, tindals, and serang whom he supplied. Customarily, half the contracted wages had to be paid in advance by captains, from which the ghat serang deducted debts and fees owed him by lascars before passing the rest on. Each ship's log

7. Benjamin, "The British and Indian Sailors", p. 487.

8. The Company's Directors refused their request to take their three English wives back with them, considering it unfitting "for such women to go among so many unruly sailors" for such a long voyage; Great Britain, Public Record Office, W. Noel Sainsbury *et al.* (eds), *Calendar of State Papers, Colonial Series*, 27 vols, (London, 1860–1926), vol. 2, p. 275.

9. Declaration December 1699, Home Miscellaneous Series 36, fo. 450, British Library [hereinafter BL].

listed lascars by name (with their signature or mark) but in a section customarily separate from the rest of the crew and designated for the lascar labour-gang.[10] On arrival in Britain, the captain was obliged to give his ship's serang the remainder of the contracted wages due the lascars, which the serang then distributed, minus his own fees. The serang also conveyed wages due deceased lascars back to their relatives in India. Even ashore, serangs continued to exercise authority over the lascars in his crew, although there was no legal reason they had to accept it in Britain.

At first, lascars, serangs, and tindals generally had salaries quite comparable with other Indians and Britons of their class. Lascar salaries ranged considerably over time and specific conditions, but in the early seventeenth century were roughly 15 to 22 shillings monthly (equivalent in today's purchasing power of £85 to £125).[11] Indeed, Company officials in India complained from the beginning about what they regarded as excessively high pay. For example, in 1637–1638, an English official at Masulipatnam wrote of the need to hire "these country people at extraordinary great wages to sayle in our ships", due to the shortage of European sailors.[12] Further, captains and Company officials perceived Indian seamen, despite their relatively higher cost, as generally less productive: physically weaker and morally less willing to fight an enemy than Britons.

Due to continued demand for lascars, their wages during the mid-eighteenth century were 23 to 30 shillings monthly (worth approximately £140 to £185 in today's purchasing power).[13] Indian petty officers had appropriately higher wages: 28 to 40 shillings monthly for serangs (in the mid-eighteenth century), slightly less for tindals; serangs and tindals additionally collected fees from their lascars. For comparison, Indian soldiers (*sepoys*) apparently received less than lascars, in the late eighteenth century only 6 to 9 rupees (roughly 12 to 18 shillings) monthly. Army petty officers (*naiks* and *havildars*) received 16 to 20 rupees (some 32 to 40 shillings) monthly.[14] Under the British, however, sepoys usually had

10. The East India Company's records, now in the BL, contain thousands of ship's log and account books.

11. John J. McCusker, "Comparing the Purchasing Power of Money in Great Britain from 1264 to Any Other Year Including the Present", Economic History Services, 2001; URL: http://www.eh.net/hmit/ppowerbp/.

12. William Foster, *English Factories in India*, 13 vols (Oxford, 1906–1927), vol. 1634–1636, pp. 30, 45, 50.

13. Wages are cited in various currencies of fluctuating values. Thus, these are only estimates. See, for example, Court minutes, 14 April 1757 and L/MAR/B/series, *passim*, BL, and Foster, *English Factories*, (1634–1636), pp. 186–187, 280. See also Paul C. van Royen, Jaap Bruijn, and Jan Lucassen (eds), *"Those Emblems of Hell"?: European Sailors and the Maritime Labour Market, 1570–1870, Research in Maritime History*, 13 (1997); McCusker, "Comparing the Purchasing Power of Money in Great Britain".

14. For example, Bengal Secret and Military Consultation, 25 August 1777; Infantry

continuous employment, while lascars worked only seasonally (and, as we will see, generally only on the passage to Britain, not once there or on the return voyage).

The wages paid British sailors on these same trans-oceanic ships rose from 8 to 9 shillings monthly in the early seventeenth century (roughly half that of lascars) to 30 to 45 shillings by the mid-eighteenth century (30 to 50 per cent more than lascars), depending on their experience and level of skill.[15] Thus, there was a marked shift in respective wage levels between lascars and British seamen (British wage increases would widen this disparity significantly by the mid-nineteenth century). In calculating relative costs to ship-owners of lascars versus British sailors, however, owners had to pay the additional expenses of maintenance in Britain and passage home of lascars but not Britons (see below).

Not surprisingly, labour relations between lascars and British officers frequently proved acrimonious. Life on board these relatively tiny and fragile vessels was hellish for all. During the Company's first twenty years, less than half its ships ever returned from Asia; between 1700 and 1818, 160 Company ships sank or were captured.[16] For Indian seamen, linguistic and other cultural differences between them and their British officers often exacerbated the inevitable labour confrontations. Under such conditions, the ship serang served like a shop-steward, representing the lascars against the captain. The time of disembarkation and final "paying off" in Britain, when the contradictory expectations of the crew and owners culminated, often proved a particular time of confrontation. Many serangs and their lascars turned to the East India Company's Court of Directors, British law courts, or other British authorities for redress of grievances inflicted by their British captains; for instance, such petitions have survived from serangs and lascars of fifteen ships between 1667 and 1757.[17] British authorities often supported lascars, given the egregious nature of some of the abuses against them, but also instituted laws highly detrimental to them.

NAVIGATION LAWS SNARE INDIAN SEAMEN IN BRITAIN

For two centuries, the labour market for Indian seamen in Britain was legally suppressed by Parliament. The British mercantilist Navigation Acts, particularly those passed from 1660 on, privileged those ships

Establishment and Bengal Military Consultation, 17 March 1779, National Archives of India, New Delhi.

15. K.N. Chaudhuri, *English East India Company: The Study of an Early Joint-Stock Company, 1600–1640* (London, 1965), p. 105.

16. *Ibid.*, p. 91.

17. Court minutes, 19 November 1679 to 13 October 1742; Dispatches to Bengal, 11 November

defined in law as British.[18] Non-British ships were excluded entirely from certain kinds of trade with Britain and suffered higher tariffs on other designated commodities. For most of this period, the Acts defined as British only those ships with a crew at least three-quarters British – as well as being British-built, British-owned, and British-captained.

Through their constructions of ethnic categories, these Acts profoundly and particularly affected Asian seamen by defining them as "non-British". In contrast, African and Caribbean seamen could be classed as "British". The Royal Navy justified this as necessary to produce a pool of experienced and trustworthy merchant seamen ready for conscription – men the Navy considered worthy fighters. The Navy generally regarded Asian seamen as lacking sufficient physical and moral strength to plunge themselves into battle; in contrast, African-descended sailors reputedly embodied these qualities, as did British seamen, of course. In practice, the Navy impressed and hired substantial numbers of Indians, although this reflected its frequent desperation for manpower rather than its preference. Thus, for example, in 1749 at the end of the War of Austrian Succession, the Navy discharged and consigned to the Company for repatriation fifty-six Indian seamen who had survived its service.[19] Further, British seamen favoured these regulations against Indians – men they increasingly regarded as competitors as British notions of nationality and race developed over these centuries.

The Navigation Acts thus created an unintended surplus of unemployable Indian seamen in Britain. Ships arriving from Asia were excused from the requirement of three-quarters British crew since the government recognized the necessity of hiring Asian seamen there for the voyage home. Yet, on leaving Britain, these Acts precluded ships which wished to be classed as British from employing Asians above one-quarter of the crew.[20] Indeed, the Company's Directors periodically instructed its outgoing ships to have all-British crews, thereby minimizing future dependence on lascars but exacerbating the unemployment of lascars already in Britain.[21]

The Directors and other British authorities struggled henceforth with the consequent perennial problem of growing numbers of stranded and unwanted Indian seamen in their midst. While some owners made provision for the lascars their ships brought to Britain, others did not, simply discharging them into British society. Throughout the period covered in this article, newspaper reports repeatedly blamed the Directors

1757, E/4/616(I), 633, para. 62, BL.

18. The most crucial was Act 12, Car. 2, c. 18 (1660). Parliament periodically modified these acts until largely repealing them in 1849 and 1854.

19. Court minutes, 1–8 November 1749, 6 December 1749; BL.

20. In war, this was relaxed to require only one-quarter of the crew need be British; e.g. Act 13, Geo. 2, c. 3 (1740).

for the presence of so many Indian seamen "daily strowling about [Britain's] Streets, and begging".[22] Thus, the Directors intervened to repatriate lascars by shipping them home, on occasion having to bail them out of British jails first.[23] Generally, in accord with the Navigation Acts, they arranged for lascars to travel back to India free as passengers – but, out of deference to the Company's profits, at the cheapest possible cost, regardless of the detrimental effects of short provisions and unhealthy living conditions this entailed.

Over time, the financial obligations of the Company toward these lascars proved considerable. At the end of the seventeenth century, for example, the Directors allotted 6 pence daily per man while in Britain, plus return passage of £4 to £6 for each lascar and £10 for each serang.[24] Since this was roughly equivalent to the wages already paid them for the voyage in, it doubled the cost of employing a lascar. The Company regularly charged these expenses to the owners of the ships which had brought those particular lascars to Britain, when they could be identified; otherwise, the Company itself had to pay.[25]

In 1689, the Directors tried an innovation to save this passage money. They ordered lascars to work on their voyage home, not for wages since the Navigation Acts largely forbade employment, but simply to cover their costs.[26] Serangs made this impossible by (quite reasonably) objecting to work without pay in violation of the terms of the agreement they had contracted before leaving India. In 1693, for example, Serang Pulsetty on behalf of his five lascars and Mahmood Hussan on behalf of his seven argued successfully against this non-contractual requirement, demanding either payment of wages or free passage as passengers.[27] This 1689 experiment died in the face of the objections by serangs. Nevertheless, in actuality, many captains evidently forced lascars to work – despite officially being passengers with their passages prepaid.[28]

Serangs in Britain also learned how to put political and moral pressure on the Directors. On at least four occasions early in the eighteenth century, serangs sent petitions not only to the Directors, but also to the British royal family.[29] Their faith in the authority of the Crown over the Directors

21. For example, Court Resolution, 8 November 1671; BL.
22. Court minutes, 24 November 1714, 23 December 1713, 17 October 1718; BL.
23. For example, Court minutes, 17 November 1749; BL.
24. The Company allotted £10 each for European privates on the same vessel; e.g. Court minutes, 28 September 1688, 17 February 1693, 23 June 1693; BL.
25. Court minutes, 18 November 1685, 9 November 1687, 21 December 1691, 15 March 1694, 4 April 1700; BL.
26. Court minutes, 24 March 1689; BL.
27. Court minutes, 1 February 1693, 29 March 1693; BL.
28. Act 55 Geo. 3, c. 116 (1814–1815). Parliamentary Papers, Returns (Commons), 1814–1815, vol. 3, paper 471, pp. 217–229.
29. Court minutes, 19 April 1706, 11 December 1706, 21 January 1713, 23 October 1713,

seems indeed to have helped draw attention to their cases, since in each instance officials in the royal establishment wrote the Directors demanding an explanation. On the other hand, so "clamourous" was Ghulam Mahmud, serang of the *St George* who petitioned Queen Anne in 1713, that, although he succeeded in his case in Britain, the Directors blacklisted him and his tindals, ordering Company's officials in India never to employ them again.[30]

During the seventeenth century, the frequent lack of an explicit contract between the serang and the captain often led to strong differences between them over payment of wages and working conditions. After a particularly bitter disagreement between the serang and the captain of the *Montagu* in 1706, the Directors attempted decisively to solve this problem. To avoid in future inciting the "clamorous temper" of the serangs, the Directors ordered each of its port officials in India to require a written labour contract before a ship could leave. The captain and the lascars were all to appear in person and sign an "equitable" agreement, countersigned by the local Company's agent, copies of which were kept by the serang, the captain, and local Company official, with yet another copy sent to Britain.[31]

In reality, few lascars seem to have received their full wages, the total shrinking at the time of payout due to various deductions. These began even before the voyage began. The ghat serang normally took as his share about 20 per cent of the lascar's entire salary, plus any loans or provisions he had advanced. The ghat serang's accountant deducted an additional fee (usually one anna per rupee, 6.25 per cent) for himself. During the voyage, ship serangs appear to have regularly charged lascars under them customary and occasional fees, including fines for alleged violations of discipline and payments for clothing and other supplies. Captains likewise levied fines for sundry alleged infractions and also charged highly for required or optional clothing and supplies from the ship's store. Further, the official British tariffs on all seamen included fees to Greenwich Hospital (for disabled seamen); from the late eighteenth century onward, lascars also had 1 shilling monthly deducted by the Merchant Shipping Office in London and another fee taken by the Navy Agent.[32] In all, of the contracted salary due on disembarkation in Britain, lascars often received less than half. Nevertheless, what they received could be a substantial sum for a working-class man at the time, for example, account books from 1693 show some serangs receiving in London £15 cash each and lascars £4.[33]

Once in Britain, most Indian seamen determined to seek entertainment

4 November 1713, 10–15 February 1721; BL.

30. Court minutes, 2–21 January 1713; BL.

31. Letter Book from Managers, 7 February 1706; E/3/96, BL.

32. *The Times*, 9 December 1814; *Morning Chronicle*, 30 November 1785, 1 December 1785.

33. For example, Court minutes, 29 March 1693, but payments varied widely; see L/MAR/B/

and opportunities. Like many seamen around the world, many lascars quickly spent their pay and fell into destitution. Others, however, found employment, married, and settled in Britain. Marriages in Britain between Indian men and British women would continue as a frequent occurrence and from the seventeenth century onward Indian sailors became a visible feature of British society, particularly, but not exclusively, in the dock areas of east London.[34] Indian seamen who failed in their new country or simply wished to return home relied on the Directors to provide them basic maintenance and free passage back to India. A few saved or earned enough to pay their own passage home, as did eight lascars in 1744.[35] However, many evidently returned to India with little or nothing materially to show for their long labours, although they had learned much about Britain. They thus knew better what to expect when they approached a ghat serang for future voyages bound there.

SERANGS AND EUROPEANS COMPETE IN CALCUTTA

In India, ghat serangs struggled for centuries against European merchants and ship captains, as well as Company officials, over control of the supply of lascars. The expansion of British colonial power, particularly in the three presidency capitals (all major ports), encouraged Company officials and British merchants to exert more control over Indian labour. In 1780, apparently as part of Governor-General Warren Hastings's larger efforts at "reform", the Calcutta government prevented Buddooh Syrang from inheriting the position of ghat serang there. He protested to London that "his late Father had served the Company in providing and training Lascars for the Shipping and Train of Artillery in Bengal", but the Calcutta authorities had appointed someone else to that "office".[36] Buddooh therefore argued that he had been illegally deprived of his property rights, and petitioned the Directors to order restoration of his father's legacy. The Directors recognized the principle that the post was property which should be inherited and ordered an investigation (although it is not clear if they ultimately installed him in the post).

About this time, the Calcutta authorities also supported an appeal by European ship captains and merchants to replace the ghat serangs with a British official as sole supplier and regulator of lascar labour. In 1783, these

series, *passim*, BL.

34. For example, in 1697, some Asian seamen joined the crowds watching the public execution of pirates at Wapping Dock; Harihar Das, "Early Indian Visitors to England", *Calcutta Review*, 3rd series, 13 (1924), pp. 83–114, 84. See also Douglas A. Lorimer, *Colour, Class and the Victorians: English Attitudes to the Negro in the Mid-Nineteenth Century* (Leicester, 1978); Roxann Wheeler, *Complexion of Race: Categories of Difference in Eighteenth-Century British Culture* (Philadelphia, PA, 2000).

35. Court minutes, 20 February 1744; BL.

Table 1. *Pay regulations proposed by Europeans in Calcutta, 1783.*

(In sicca rupees)	During peace	During war
Serang	15	20
1st tindal	12	15
2nd tindal	10	12
1st lascars	6	7
2nd lascars	4	5

Europeans petitioned Governor-General Hastings to appoint a British Registrar of Lascars and also to fix wage rates.[37] Making their argument (but not telling the full story), they wrote of the "great hardships, delays, hindrances, difficulties, and an unnecessary expense in the procuring proper Seafaring Men", due "to a certain Person called a Seer ['chief'] Serang, from whose Impositions both they and the said Seafaring Men are subjected to grievous and heavy losses". The merchants continued that before the ghat serang would supply lascars, he demanded three months wages in advance, much of which he kept himself (they neglected to add that the ghat serang had usually advanced money to lascars awaiting employment). Further, he did not supply all the men until the very last moment before sailing, when desperate captains had to accept whatever low quality and inexperienced men he provided: "the said Seer Serang does frequently instead of able Seamen put on board [...] men kidnapped or forcibly impressed and altogether unused to the sea and unacquainted with the Business of a Seamen." Finally, the merchants set out the monthly wages that they wanted the government to fix by regulation (Table 1).

These proposed wages were approximately the current rate for serangs and tindals, but only about half for lascars.[38] While the merchants thus ostensibly argued for a more bureaucratic and efficient process, they really meant one under British, not Indian, control.

A few months later, the Bengal government indeed passed a regulation that attempted to enforce all that these Europeans requested.[39] This

36. Court minutes, 15 March 1780, see also 18 July 1764; BL.

37. Petition to the Governor-General from the Principal Merchants and Ship-owners of Calcutta, 19 February 1783; Home Miscellaneous Series 190, fos 65–103, BL. Such efforts were not unique to India. See M. Quinlan, "Regulating Labour in a Colonial Context: Maritime Labour Legislation in the Australian Colonies, 1788–1850", *Australian Historical Studies*, 29, 111 (1998), pp. 303–324.

38. Lascars would also receive *batta* (supplement) of 10 rupees monthly, if not provisioned by the owners. See, for example, Court minutes, 14 April 1757 and Marine Department, L/MAR/B/ series; BL.

39. "Rule, Ordinance and Regulation for Ascertaining and fixing the Wages to be Paid to the Native Seafaring Men belonging to the Port of Calcutta", registered with the Supreme Court of Calcutta, 7 July 1783; Home Miscellaneous Series 190, fos 65–103, BL.

established a British "Marine Register Officer" (on the model prevailing in Britain) who would replace the ghat serang. All Indian seamen would pay 1 anna per rupee (6.25 per cent) of their wages plus a 1 rupee fee to be listed in his books. The officer would also find an "abode" for the seamen awaiting assignment. He would hold exclusive authority to supply seamen to all ships, delivering them as requested by captains on twelve days' notice. Soon after this system was imposed, the merchants found to their horror that it failed to deliver the expected results. The ghat serangs held such power – particularly the loyalty of lascars – that they prevented the Marine Register Officer from supplying men. Within a year, the European merchants of Calcutta again petitioned the Company, begging the revocation of this regulation and the return to the old system.

Thus, ghat serangs fended off this and (over the next half-century) further British attempts to take control over lascar labour. In 1790, British applicants for the post of Marine Register Officer promised to deliver all that the European merchants and captains had sought in their earlier petition, to no avail.[40] Then, the Calcutta government ordered its Committee on the State of Marine to investigate and report about the power and alleged abuses of ghat serangs. Yet, in 1793, the British Superintendent of Police in Calcutta reiterated these same accusations about "the rapacity and villainy of Ghaut Serangs", who used their labour monopoly to supply insufficient numbers of inexperienced Indians at exorbitant wages on the eve of sailing, whom European captains perforce accepted rather than miss the season.[41] In 1795, when British employers offered wages that were too low, lascars refused to work.[42] When one British captain resorted in 1798 to kidnapping and sailing off with lascars who had only agreed to load his ship in port, virtually all lascars boycotted work on all British-bound ships, despite Governor-General Wellesley's repeated public assurances that the offending captain would be punished.[43] Further, in 1800, British merchants accused lascars of wholesale arson: taking wage advances and then torching their ships so that they could abscond.[44]

Over the following decades, British authorities increasingly tried to regulate lascar wages and employment conditions. For example, in 1814, the Government of India specified the type and amount of clothing, bedding, and rations (including Indian spices) issued them, as well as the

40. Home Public Consultation, 6 October 1790, nos. 15–17, National Archives of India.

41. Home Public Consultation, 22 November 1793, no. 3, National Archives of India.

42. Home Public Consultation, 29 February 1795, no. 33, and 15 May 1797, no. 18, National Archives of India.

43. Home Public Consultation, 28 June 1799, no. 7; 16 August 1798, no. 22; and 26 November 1798, no. 7; National Archives of India.

44. Home Public Consultation, 4 February 1800, no. 22, National Archives of India, and numerous cases in *Calcutta Monthly Journal* for this period.

volume of space allotted to each seaman for sleeping, and ordered that a surgeon and specified medicines must be aboard.[45] As the Company's own inspectors reported, however, these regulations were often not fulfilled, with lascar death rates of 30 to 40 per cent on some ships inbound and up to 50 per cent on the passage home, when these men were supposed to be unemployed passengers.[46] Similarly, in 1815, Parliament created a "Committee on Lascars and Other Asiatic Seamen" to investigate the entire system of lascar employment which concluded, in part, continued reliance on serangs was "regrettable" but necessary, since no other system could provide and manage the lascars needed.[47] Thereafter, Parliament amended the Navigation Acts to further exclude Asians and required the Governor of each Presidency to certify as truthful a ship-owner's declaration that it was "impossible to procure a crew of British seamen" before that ship could hire a lascar crew in India.[48] Nonetheless, until the mid-nineteenth century, lascars and ghat serangs largely resisted repeated efforts by British merchants and Company officials to take over the system of maritime labour supply, so essential to the anglocentric world-system but also vital to the lives of Indian seamen.

LASCAR EMPLOYMENT TO 1857

Despite such conflicts over recruitment in India, the number of Indian seamen voyaging to Britain from the mid-eighteenth century onward rose significantly, albeit unevenly due to the interactions of socio-economic, cultural, and political forces, most beyond the power of lascars to affect Much of the unevenness reflected fluctuations in overall trade between India and Britain which rose over the late eighteenth and early nineteenth centuries, declined during the post-Napoleonic world depression, and then rose dramatically thereafter.[49]

The advent of intercontinental steam ships and the changing economies and societies of Britain and India also altered the labour history of lascars. Most British captains in India preferred European seamen, so their demand for lascars varied inversely with the supply of British seamen. Many British

45. Marine Department, Papers Relating to the Care of Lascars, 1793–1818; L/MAR/C/902, vols 1–2, pp. 1–13, BL.

46. William Hunter, *Essay on the Diseases Incident to Indian Seamen, or Lascars* (Calcutta, 1804); Lascar Papers, Home Miscellaneous Series 501, vol. 1, fos 1–94, BL.

47. Parliamentary Papers, Returns (Commons), 1814–1815, vol. 3, paper 471, pp. 217–229.

48. Act 55, Geo. 3, c. 116, section 8. For copies of such certificates see Bombay, Political Outward or Order Books for 1818, Maharastra State Archives, Mumbai.

49. For example, British exports to India more than doubled from 108,870 tons (1834–1835) to 252,153 tons (1849–1850) while British imports from India more than tripled from 83,776 to 280,897 tons; Parliament, House of Lords Debate 2 April 1852, Commons debate 19 April 1852, in T.C. Hansard (ed.), *Parliamentary Debates* (London, 1812–) series 3, vol. 120, pp. 546–580, 806–868.

Table 2. *Asian seamen arriving in Britain, 1760–1855.*[50]

Year	Reported arrivals that year
1760	138
1780	167
1803	224
1804	471
1805	603
1806	538
1807	1,278
1808	1,110
1809	965
1810	1,403
1811	929
1812	1,193
1813	1,336
1814–1815*	1,000–1,100
1821–1822	509
1855*	3–3,600

* estimates

sailors were caught up by the Royal Navy during the continuing Anglo-French wars (until 1815) and then discharged wholesale thereafter. Yet, the correlation was not perfect: the mid-1820s, for example, saw a severe shortage of British sailors available for India-bound ships, but the number of lascars hired to go to Britain also declined significantly.[51] Further, Parliament opened new spaces for ever larger numbers of "private" ships as it ended the East India Company's monopoly over trade with India in 1814, suspended for twenty years its right to trade there in 1834, and then took over the Company's authority in 1858. Each of these had powerful implications for lascar employment – and the consistency of records about them. Nonetheless, careful use of available evidence can enable us roughly to delineate the fluctuating patterns of lascar labour going to Britain (Table 2). Many lascars made multiple trips to Britain, and thus appear more than

50. Periodically, the Directors or Parliament ordered compilations of statistics about lascars, but no systematic accounting was maintained. These compilations followed varying principles and categorizations (e.g. occasionally including Chinese and other Asians). Nevertheless, supplemented with informed estimates by British writers of the time, these figures permit an understanding of the scale of lascar presence in Britain. The shipping season covered parts of two calendar years, so some differences between years may not be significant. To 1822, they are based on Lascar Papers, Home Miscellaneous Series 501, vol. 1, fos 1–94, BL; and Parliamentary Papers, Returns (Commons), 1823, vol. 17, paper 491, pp. 149–156. The 1855 estimates come from Colonel Hughes who asserted that 10,000–12,000 lascars served the British merchant fleet, with 5,000–6,000 reaching Britain annually, of whom 3,000–3,600 were Indian. Cited in Visram, *Ayahs, Lascars and Princes*, p. 52.

51. Shipping Committee minutes, 7 January 1825, 20 April 1825, 22 November 1825, 26 July 1826, BL.

once in these figures. Nevertheless, by any reasonable calculation, tens of thousands of lascars reached Britain over this 100-year period.

Lascars continued to serve in substantial labour-gangs, which comprised much of their ship's crew, rather than as scattered individuals. In 1813, for example, only 32 ships arriving from India in Britain reported lascars aboard. Their proportion of lascars ranged from 20 per cent to over 50 per cent of the crew. The average size of a lascar gang was 34 – the largest being 56 and the smallest 16. Overall, of the 3,311 total seamen aboard these 32 ships, about 30 per cent were lascars.[52] In contrast, during the year July 1821–June 1822, only 7 of the 197 ships arriving in London from India reported lascars aboard (in addition, Liverpool, Hull, and Greenock/Glasgow had 22 ships arrive, none with lascars reported). This was only 22 per cent of the number of ships arriving with lascars in 1813. On these 7 ships, however, lascars still comprised large labour-gangs: 110, 107, 86, 72, 66, 38, and 30 lascars respectively (there were only 91 British and 21 "other foreign" sailors on these 7 ships).[53] That equalled 509 lascars, less than 5 per cent of the total seamen arriving, compared to 10,000 Britons and 1,000 "foreigners" (some of whom may have been Indian sailors serving as individuals, rather than in lascar labour-gangs). This was a much smaller proportion of the total manpower and less than half the absolute number of lascars of 1813. Yet, ships on this intercontinental trade had grown larger; the average size of a lascar crew was 73 men, over double that of 1813. Thus, relatively fewer ships carried virtually all of the incoming lascars in larger crews than earlier.

Many British officers treated lascars brutally. Such brutality stands clearly revealed, for instance, in the memoirs of Captain Robert Eastwick, who spent his career (1792–1825) mostly on ships in Asia. He considered lascars as virtual animals, easily panicked, useless in a crisis, and not worth saving in a wreck. On one voyage from England to India in 1810, his ship, the *Elizabeth*, carried 320 lascars (mostly passengers being returned home).[54] When this ship sank off Dunkirk, Eastwick remorselessly used an oar to beat off as many lascars as he could, so that the lifeboat in which he saved himself would not swamp (as he himself shamelessly and unregretfully reported). Of the lascars aboard, 310 died in the wintry waters (along with many Europeans and 8 Indian female servants). To some Britons, including men like Eastwick, lascars appeared not as individuals but as a collective mass.

Lascars were, however, not cheap labour. In terms of the actual voyage to Britain alone, the Company calculated that it neither gained nor lost

52. Lascar Papers, Home Miscellaneous Series 501, vol. 1, fo. 124, BL.

53. Parliamentary Papers, Returns (Commons), 1823, vol. 17, paper 491, pp. 149–156.

54. Robert Eastwick, *Master Mariner: Being the Life and Adventures of Captain Robert William Eastwick*, Herbert Compton (ed.) (London, 1891), pp. 262–282; *The Times*, 1 January 1811.

money by using lascars instead of British sailors. The Directors believed that due to differences in physical and moral strength (especially in cold weather), three lascars were equivalent in manpower to two Europeans, so lascar wages were comparably only two-thirds as much.[55] Lascars also received less expensive provisions and less sleeping space. Similarly, prize money for capturing enemy ships also followed the two-thirds formula.[56] Thus, on a given passage to Britain, the Company expended no more for the larger number of lascars it felt necessary than for better-paid British sailors. Each lascar, however, received one-third less than each Briton.

Further, after lascars reached Britain, they entailed substantial financial and political costs for the Company. Until 1834 (when Parliament suspended its right to trade in Asia), the Company contracted with private lodging-keepers, suppliers, and surgeons in London to shelter, feed, clothe, cure, and manage these men at fixed rates per capita and also with ship-owners to carry them back as pre-paid passengers. During the 1804–1813 period, the Company's average expenditure for maintaining each lascar in Britain and returning him to India was £37, totalling for all lascars £363,600 for that decade (equivalent to over £19 million today).[57] This per capita expenditure was much more than the entire wage paid the lascar for the voyage (roughly a shilling per day on the passage in; most lascars were unpaid returning home). Employing British sailors carried no such expense following the end of their contract.

Additionally, the British public and Parliament held the Company morally and legally responsible for all Indians in Britain, especially allegedly indigent or anti-social ones. Yet, the Directors lamented in vain to Parliament in 1815, their lack of police powers over lascars: "the impossibility in this free country of confining those persons within the prescribed limits, and of thereby preventing their intercourse with the dregs of society, which gives the Lascars of vicious dispositions facility in selling their bedding and clothing, and of contracting loathsome disorders".[58] Thus, even at times of peak demand, the Directors only reluctantly recognized the necessity of hiring lascars. To keep down the number arriving in Britain, the Company wanted as large a pool of British seamen on its outgoing ships as possible, to compensate for their expected losses. Thus, for example in 1808, the Directors reiterated that all their outbound ships must have entirely British crews – even though they were

55. Shipping Committee minutes, 22 February 1804, 18 June 1828; Draft of Charter-Party, L/MAR/1/17, fo. 43, BL; Parliament, House of Commons debate 25 November 1801, William Cobbett, *Parliamentary History of England*, 36 vols (London, 1806–1820), vol. 36, pp. 288–302.
56. For example, Shipping Committee minutes, 24 September 1813; Court minutes, 13 August 1823, BL.
57. Lascar Papers, Home Miscellaneous Series 501, vol. 1, fo. 120, BL; McCusker, "Comparing the Purchasing Power of Money in Great Britain".
58. Lascar Papers, Home Miscellaneous Series 501, vol. 1, fos 69–75, BL.

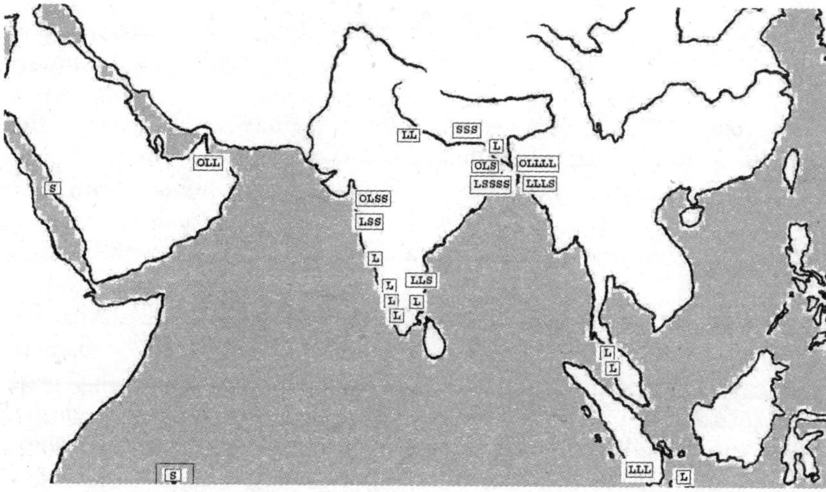

Figure 1. Self-reported origins of the serang/tindals (O), lascars (L), and ship's servants and sepoys (S) of the *Hercules*, sailing from Calcutta to England, 1818.

allowed one-quarter non-British crews under the Navigation Acts.[59] Parliament also periodically discouraged lascar employment in the Atlantic.[60]

Only rarely can we discover the origins of the lascars in a crew. Many served under Europeanized or culturally ambiguous names, although it is clear from ship-logs and account books that people from many ethnic and religious communities might serve together in a single lascar labour-gang, often generically labeled "Indian". A rare example where the crew's self-reported origins were recorded was the ship *Hercules* (sailing from Calcutta to Britain in 1818). Figure 1 demonstrates that this nominally "Indian" crew of fifty included: six lascars from southeast Asia; a tindal, two lascars, and a servant from the Arabian Peninsula (plus a servant from Mauritius); in addition to thirty-nine men from India.[61] While most of those from India came from Bengal Presidency, fifteen (including Serang Baxo [Bakhsh]) had origins along India's southern or western coasts.

59. Lascar Papers, Home Miscellaneous Series 501, vol. 1, fo. 24, BL. In later years, with increasing shortages of British seamen, the Directors allowed up to a quarter of the crew on outgoing vessels to be Indians, which still made them legally British ships.

60. For example Act 42 Geo. 3 (1802), c. 61 which officially prohibited lascars from serving on ships west of the Cape of Good Hope, and Act 55, Geo. 3 (1815), c. 116 which amended the Navigation Acts to exclude Asians from the category "British".

61. Note: one servant gave Cheran Chupah [*sic*] as his birthplace, which cannot be identified. Further, Mauritius is located further south than indicated. In addition, the six seaconnies (helmsmen) came from Penang, Malinga, and Malacca, and three from Manila, while the captain, two officers, gunner, and carpenter were all Europeans; Home Miscellaneous, volume 253, fos

The geographic diversity of the serang and tindals, and between them and the other crew members, highlights how the ghat serang assembled them ad hoc in Calcutta. Unlike Indian labour-gangs in factories or indentured labourers, whom a headman (*sardar* or *kangani*) often recruited from his own home village or region, these maritime workers came together through their employment, and forged bonds during their passage. Their subsequent solidarity in Britain as mutually supportive shipmates suggests how powerful that experience was.

LASCAR SOLIDARITIES IN BRITAIN

Once ashore in Britain, lascars in a labour-gang often continued their ship-born camaraderie, under their serang. He negotiated for them corporately against their employers and other British authorities. He also assisted British authorities by exerting discipline over his lascars. Nonetheless, other identities, including homeland and individual lascar interests, cross-cut these solidarities and created others.

The period following the lascars' arrival was often one of confrontation with their employers and other groups in Britain. Some lascars stayed aboard temporarily and unloaded their ships, receiving extra pay for this.[62] Such work, however, placed them in conflict with British – particularly Irish – stevedores, with whom they occasionally fought.[63] Frequently, lascars disembarked and appealed under the leadership of their serang directly to British authorities for redress of grievances.[64] One serang, Doud Gouber Gash, (speaking through a translator) in 1823 described his role as "an officer looked up to as the father and protector of his men, and appointed by them as the receiver and distributor of their wages, and guardian of their privileges".[65] This serang, who had made several previous voyages to Britain, led his lascar crew to complain to London's Lord Mayor: he "handed a long epistle to his Lordship, in which the petitioners

135–138, National Archives of India. Confirming these patterns, similarly diverse lascar crews are found for other ships in Home Miscellaneous, volume 253, fos 203–206; volume 425, fos 6–8, National Archives of India. See also Balachandran, "Circulation through Seafaring".

62. The autobiography of Joseph Emin (1726–1809) is a rare recounting of the life of a man who worked his way from Calcutta to London as a seaman in 1751, unloading his ship, and then living there periodically for a decade. See his *Life and Adventures of Joseph Emin, An Armenian, Written in English by Himself* (London, 1792) and Michael H. Fisher, "Asians in Britain: Negotiation of Identity through Self-Representation", in Kathleen Wilson (ed.), *A New Imperial History: Culture, Identity and Modernity in Britain and the Empire, 1660–1840* (Cambridge, 2004), pp. 91–112.

63. For example, Irish stevedores fought Asians in two such riots in 1813. Shipping Committee minutes, 14 July 1813, 31 August 1813, BL.

64. For example, Court minutes, 3 January 1798; Shipping Committee minutes, 28–30 June 1815, 12–19 July 1815, 2 August 1815, 1 September 1815, 6–15 December 1815, 19–26 June 1816, 27 May 1818, 8 July 1818, 13–27 January 1819, 2 February 1819, BL.

65. *The Times*, 4 July 1823.

described themselves as in a state of starvation, and treated with great cruelty in this free country". They refused to leave until they had been paid. The British captain admitted that he owed them wages, but asserted they would only run away and squander it; he promised to pay them when they boarded.

British authorities sometimes regarded such acts or protest as desertion and riot, arresting the serang "ringleader" to suppress the rest.[66] Other times, depending on the particular circumstances and how effectively serangs represented their cases, British authorities – including the Directors, Naval Agent, municipal officials, and law courts – might consider and act on lascar complaints.[67] For example, in 1813–1814, the Naval Agent in London reportedly collected £262 10 shillings in fees deducted from lascars' pay (at 1 shilling per month each), but collected for lascars £1,571 in disputed wages from ship-owners.[68] To some extent, therefore, lascars had agency in gaining compensation for provable breaches of contract or regulations by ship-owners.

In the lodgings that the Company provided (until 1834), the barracks was divided into rooms, each with a heating stove. Self-organized groups of seven to twenty-five lascars from the same ship generally lived and cooked in the same room under the direction of their serang, apparently reflecting solidarities formed aboard the harsh voyage as well as ethnic and religious identities. However, while on board and then in the lodgings ashore, members of a crew apparently cooked and ate separately, divided by religious identity.[69] Lascars also clashed with both native Britons and other seamen.

There were repeatedly large-scale riots which pitted Indians against British service workers and seamen in London's streets. For example, in 1803, three lascars armed with cutlasses broke into the City of Carlisle public house in Whitechapel, seeking to recover the substantial sum of £150 they claimed that local sex-workers there had stolen from them. The landlord had them arrested. The Directors bailed them out, paid the damages, and put them aboard an outgoing ship, not to protect the British community from them, but rather the reverse: "for their better protection from the women of the town".[70] Elite British fears about the predations of the British poor, especially the female British poor, on Asian seamen would recur. Just two years later, in October 1805, lascars took over the

66. For example, *The Times*, 23 September 1796.

67. Court minutes, 26 May 1802, 21July 1802, 16 July 1806; Home Miscellaneous Series 501, fos 1–93, BL.

68. *The Statesman* [Calcutta], 21 July 1813; *The Times*, 9 December 1814, 3d; Shipping Committee minutes, 22 July 1813, BL.

69. Emin describes initially eating separately from Europeans, and never mentions dining with the lascars onboard; Emin, *Life*, pp. 44ff.

70. *The Times*, 6 October 1803.

streets of Shadwell, east London, in a large-scale tumult in which fifteen people were hospitalized and nineteen arrested.[71] Only a month after that, lascars seized the streets east of the Tower of London one Friday night, claiming a sex-worker there had robbed one of their number.[72] In 1808, a quarrel between a drunken but armed British sailor and a single lascar brought 400 lascars out into the streets in his support. A passing squad of British militia drove them back with bayonets.[73]

Larger identities like Indian, Chinese, Arab, or Malay also apparently remained potent onboard ship and in Britain. For example, the same ship might have both lascars and Chinese seamen, although they evidently customarily served in separate labour-gangs; tensions between them occasionally flared in London. Indeed, in 1785 groups of Indians fought Chinese.[74] Similarly, in 1806, 150 Indians fought 300 Chinese who were supported by some Arab seamen.[75] The alleged causes were an escalating conflict initially generated on the ship *Skelton Castle*, which had sailed to London with 150 lascars and 20 Chinese seamen aboard, and jealousy over some local British women. In London, other Chinese (and Arabs) apparently supported these 20 Chinese seamen against the lascars who had sailed with them. Since most lascars and Arabs were Muslim, and most Chinese seamen were not, this was evidently not a religious conflict.

On a smaller scale, in 1808, three Muslim Malay seamen killed a Muslim Indian lascar, Imambacchus. An Englishwoman, Sarah Williams, testified that she had been living with the victim in a room nearby on Cable Street, east London, for the previous month. One night, she took 7 shillings from one of the Malay seamen, Glosse, to get drunk and then left the Blue Gate public house (on nearby Ratcliffe Highway) with him for sex. The victim arrived just then and caught them. The Malay seaman was joined by a Malay shipmate and a third Malay from another ship. Together, they mortally wounded the lascar. Testifying on behalf of the victim were a Muslim serang and two lascars from the accused's own ship. The jury convicted the Malays of manslaughter. Though clearly based in sexual rivalry, the sides in the affray were formed around solidarities based on origin that cut across shipmate lines.[76]

After 1834, when Parliament suspended the Company's right to trade in Asia and therefore its legal responsibility to lodge and feed lascars, private entrepreneurs, including some Indians, established lodging houses of their own, particularly in east London's docklands – Poplar and Limehouse.

71. *The Times*, 15 October 1805.
72. *The Times*, 26 November 1805.
73. *Annual Register* (1808), 50, Chronicle, p. 13.
74. *Annual Register* (1785), 27, Chronicle, pp. 242–243.
75. *Annual Register* (1806), 48, Chronicle, pp. 450–451; *The Times*, 7 October 1806, 3a–b.
76. Proceedings of the Old Bailey, 1 June 1808, pp. 280–288, case 395.

This soon became known as the "Oriental Quarter". Given the exclusively male population of arriving seamen, and the common cultural expectation that women were necessary to provide particular services, a distinctive pattern developed. The Indian male rooming-house operator often had a British woman partner.

One of these proprietors, Abdool Rahman of Surat, came to England as a lascar in the 1840s but decided to settle. He first established himself as a crossing-sweeper (clearing passage for ladies and gentlemen across the dung-laden street in exchange for gratuities) at St Paul's Churchyard, and learned much about British society. When Nepali Ambassador, Jung Bahadur, visited London in 1850, Abdul Rahman joined his suite as a translator for his servants.[77] He then used the money he received to establish himself as operator of two lodging-houses designed for lascars in Blue Gate Fields, Limehouse. Allegedly, he also provided opium. After some twenty years there, Abdul Rahman finally sold his houses and shipped back to India as a serang.[78]

In 1842, the Church Missionary Society surveyed and reported the dire "state of the Lascars in London". Subsequently, evangelicals proposed a charity house, and gathered £15,000 (including Indian donations totalling £5,000).[79] In 1856, "The Strangers' Home for Asiatics, Africans, and South Sea Islanders" opened in Commercial Road, Limehouse, under the leadership of its Secretary and Manager, Lieutenant-Colonel R. Marsh Hughes, late of the Company's army.[80] This linking of various ethnicities of the working classes collectively as "Strangers" reflected current British attitudes. Since Parliament had reimposed legal responsibility for lascars on the Company in 1854, its Directors contributed hundreds of pounds of the Company's money to this Home annually until 1858.[81] The Home assumed many of the paternalistic functions earlier exercised by the Company, including identifying, maintaining, and managing lascars (and other indigent Indians), working with their serangs in prosecuting police and legal charges against defaulting ship-owners, and arranging for lascar employment or passage home.

77. *Indian News*, 16–17 June 1850, cited in John Whelpton, *Jang Bahadur in Europe: The First Nepalese Mission to the West* (Kathmandu, 1983), pp. 232–233.

78. Joseph Salter, *Asiatic in England: Sketches of Sixteen Years' Work among Orientals* (London, 1873), pp. 30–31, 275–278.

79. Foreign Political Consultation, 1 May 1857, National Archives of India; Hughes Letter 24 January 1879, Political Department Home Correspondence, L/P&J/2/59, BL; *Illustrated London News*, 56 (1870), pp. 253–254; Salter, *Asiatic in England*, pp. 6–7.

80. Court minutes, 14–28 November 1855, 16 April 1856, 22–30 December 1857, 12–26 January 1858, 3–10 February 1858, 3–10 March 1858; Political and Military Committee Memoranda, 22 December 1857, BL; Salter, *Asiatic in England*, pp. 66ff; *The Times*, 20 November 1855.

81. Court minutes, 1856–1858, *passim*, BL. The Home continued until 1927.

CONCLUSION

After the mid-nineteenth century, there were many changes in the lives and employment patterns of lascars. Steamships required fewer skilled seamen, so many Indians ended up instead as poorly paid manual or service labourers – shovelling coal into boilers or attending on passengers.[82] Tensions also increased between British seamen and Indian lascars, particularly as the former unionized and exerted political pressure to legally advantage themselves and disadvantage Indians. According to a 1848 House of Commons Report, lascar wages were only 10 rupees (5 shillings) per month, tindals 12 rupees, and serangs 20 rupees, while British able seamen received 90 rupees (45 shillings).[83] These factors, and the abundant supply of lascars, drove down wages to only a fraction of their actual seventeenth- and early eighteenth-century levels (to about the rates proposed by Calcutta merchants in 1783). The 1850s also saw many stories in the British press about lascars as arsonists of British ships.[84]

In India, British authorities continued to pressure ghat serangs in order to seize control over lascar labour. Among the markers of this shift was the 1850 Merchant Seamen Act passed by the Governor-General in Council (and revised in 1859) which required brokers to procure seamen to be licenced by a government-appointed Registrar, with all seamen agreeing to contract on a prescribed form with fixed monthly wages, and a definitive list of seamen delivered by each captain to the Registrar.[85]

In Britain, racial attitudes also shifted over the late nineteenth century, to the detriment of Indians. These had many causes including the bloody conflicts in India (1857) and Jamaica (1865), as well as pseudo-scientific ideas derived from Darwinism and British imperialism generally. Scholars including Dixon, Dunlop, Prescott, Sherwood, and Tabili draw different interpretations from evidence about attitudes toward Britons, especially British seamen, toward Indian lascars serving or living among them.[86]

Over the 250 years considered in this article, lascars entered and altered the maritime labour market on sailing ships between India and Europe. Their efforts, and those of serangs, to work on European ships but outside

82. See Daniel Thorner, *Investment in Empire: British Railway and Steam Shipping Enterprise in India, 1825–1849* (Philadelphia, PA, 1950); R.O. Roberts, "Comparative Shipping and Shipbuilding Costs", *Economica*, New Series, 14, 56 (1947), pp. 296–309.

83. D.C. Alyin's Evidence in Second Report of the Select Committee of the House of Lords Appointed to Inquire into the Policy and Operation of the Navigation Laws, House of Commons paper no. 431 of 1848, cited by N. Benjamin, "The British and Indian Sailors".

84. For example, *Annual Register* (1851) Chronicle, 4 March 1851, pp. 20–21; *The Times*, 8 October 1853, 18 October 1853, 20 October 1853. See also Benjamin, "The British and Indian Sailors", p. 492.

85. *Ibid.*, pp. 489–490.

86. Dixon, "Lascars: The Forgotten Seamen"; Dunlop, "Lascars and Labourers"; Prescott, "Lascar Seamen on the Clyde"; Sherwood, "Lascar Struggles"; Tabili, "Construction of Racial Difference", *idem*, *"We Ask for British Justice"*

European recruitment and employment patterns, remained remarkably strong over this period. Thus, as Balachandran argues for a later period, their labour history is the "site of interactions of many working class histories [...] where categories of race, class, and nation collide and contaminate one another [...] where we can derive insights into historical negotiations of rival, overlapping, and complementary solidarities".[87]

87. Balachandran, "Conflicts in International Maritime Labour Markets", pp. 71–100.

The Brickmakers' Strikes on the Ganges Canal in 1848–1849*

JAN LUCASSEN

INTRODUCTION

For a long time it seemed indisputable that collective actions of wage labourers in general and strikes in particular were a typically European and American phenomenon, closely linked to the Industrial Revolution and its consequences. Modern imperialism and the concomitant spread of industrialization and modernization brought these phenomena to the rest of the world. Some decades ago, however, an awareness arose that even before that famous watershed in history people knew how to organize a strike.[1] Although this critical reappraisal of the supposed link between the Industrial Revolution and labour tactics led, albeit slowly, to a renewal of interest in the early labour history of Europe, its implications for the labour history of other continents have not yet received the attention they deserve. If we want to take that next step, the question could be formulated as follows: "If strikes could take place in pre-industrial Europe, why not also in other pre-industrial parts of the world?"

At first sight such a question does not seem very useful for India if we follow the line of argument put forward most eloquently by Dipesh Chakrabarty. Since his influential studies from the 1980s on the Calcutta jute-mill workers, the historiography of Indian labour can be characterized – in the words of Deep Kanta Lahiri Choudhury – as follows: "Studies began from the 1880s and characterized the period 1880–1919 as the 'prehistory' of labour mobilization in India and as the period of the emergence of 'community consciousness' within Indian labour."[2]

* I would like to thank Sabyasachi Bhattacharya, Ian Kerr, and Marcel van der Linden for their useful remarks on earlier versions of this article.

1. C.R. Dobson, *Masters and Journeymen: A Prehistory of Industrial Relations 1717–1800* (London, 1980); Catharina Lis, Jan Lucassen, and Hugo Soly (eds), *Before the Unions: Wage Earners and Collective Action in Europe, 1300–1850*, Supplement 2 to the *International Review of Social History* (1994).

2. Deep Kanta Lahiri Choudhury, "India's First Virtual Community and the Telegraph General Strike of 1908", Supplement 11 to the *International Review of Social History* (2003), pp. 45–71, 45–46; cf. Ian J. Kerr, "Working Class Protest in 19th Century India: Example of Railway Workers", *Economic and Political Weekly*, 20 (26 January 1985), PE 34–40, PE 34; Dipesh Chakrabarty, "Communal Riots and Labour: Bengal's Jute Mill Hands in the 1890s", *Past and Present*, 91 (1981), pp. 140–169; *idem*, *Rethinking Working-Class History: Bengal, 1890–1940*

In fact, the idea that the prehistory of Indian labour begins only in the 1880s has a long pedigree which goes from the 1970s and 1980s via Sukomal Sen all the way back to Daniel Houston Buchanan in the 1930s and to Rajani Kanta Das in the first decades of the twentieth century;[3] detailed studies by scholars such as Morris David Morris seem to confirm it.[4] Das started his studies of the Indian workers in 1912, took a degree from the University of Wisconsin in 1916, and for some time was a lecturer in economics at New York University. In his publications, most of which came out in Germany, he traces the first strike in India back to 1882 and the first trade union to 1890.[5] Both Buchanan and Sen essentially agreed with Morris's opinion, although Sen adds the first labourers' petition in 1884 and some earlier strikes, especially the 1862 strike at Howrah Railway Station.[6]

Recent critics of Chakrabarty, especially Rajnarayan Chandarvarkar, have questioned the accepted wisdom that links industrialization, class-consciousness, and labour organization.

> [Such] interpretations of the working classes in general have been severely limiting, but in the case of India, in particular, they proved especially damaging. Economic backwardness, in this reasoning, made the very notion of a working class unthinkable, just as the peculiar institutions of India seemed to place it in a special category of its own. [...] Most crucially, this teleology imposed upon the

(Princeton, NJ, 1989); and for a critique, Subho Basu, "Strikes and 'Communal' Riots in Calcutta in the 1890s: Industrial Workers, Bhadralok Nationalist Leadership and the Colonial State", *Modern Asian Studies*, 32 (1998), pp. 949–983.

3. Rajani Kanta Das, *The Labor Movement in India* (Berlin [etc.], 1923); *idem*, *Factory Labor in India* (Berlin [etc.], 1923); *idem*, *Plantation Labour in India* (Calcutta, 1931); Daniel Houston Buchanan, *The Development of Capitalistic Enterprise in India* (New York, 1934); Sukomal Sen, *Working Class of India: History of Emergence and Movement 1830–1970* (Calcutta [etc.], 1977); *idem*, *May Day and Eight Hours' Struggle in India: A Political History* (Calcutta [etc.], 1988).

4. Morris David Morris, *The Emergence of an Industrial Labor Force in India: A Study of the Bombay Cotton Mills, 1854–1947* (Berkeley, CA [etc.], 1965), p. 110 (the earliest date of a collective action Morris gives is 1875, all others started in the 1880s); *idem*, "The Growth of Large-Scale Industry to 1947", in Dharma Kumar (ed.), *The Cambridge Economic History of India*, vol. 2: *c 1757– c.1970* (Cambridge, 1983), pp. 553–676.

5. Das, *Factory Labor in India*, p. 187 ("the first labor union"; cf. Das, *Labor Movement in India*, p. 14); *ibid.*, p. 190 ("the earliest strikes"); *idem*, *Plantation Labour in India*, p. 95 (first strikes on plantations in 1884).

6. Sen, *Working Class of India*, pp. 75, 78–79. He adds that prior to 1862 "there were also cessations of work in Calcutta by the palanquin-bearers in 1823 and by the river-transport porters in 1853. Subsequently in September 1862, the coachmen of bullock-carts in Calcutta stopped work. Similarly, the meat-sellers under Bombay Municipal Corporation stopped work in 1866. At Ahmedabad also the tailors and brick-field labourers ceased work in 1873. But all these cessations of work by the toilers in different professions should not be confused with the strike of the modern industrial workers like the railway workers' strike in 1862." Without any further reference, Dharma Kumar, ("Regional Economy (1757–1857): South India", in Kumar, *Cambridge Economic History*, pp. 352–375), states that in southern India c.1800 "weavers' strikes were frequent" (p. 368).

> working classes an arbitrary and misleadingly narrow definition as an industrial labour force. In this sense, the industrial labour force was abstracted from its connections with other categories of labour who were proletarianized in nineteenth- and twentieth-century India by similar social processes [...].[7]

Consequently, there is less and less reason to neglect what we might call pre-industrial labour history in the case of India. Nevertheless, this is still an almost completely underdeveloped field.

Not as an explicit attempt to take sides in this discussion, but rather on empirical grounds, Ian Kerr in his *Building the Railways of the Raj* questioned the absence of collective labour resistance in India before 1880[8] and the nature of that protest. Even before 1880, Kerr found a variety of forms of collective resistance by the men and women who built the railways. In his taxonomy, rather loosely formulated, they range from indirect to direct actions and from passive to highly active resistance. All the forms he mentions can be summarized as follows: indirect and passive resistance; disagreement over piece-rates, leading to a withdrawal of labour before an agreement had been reached; absconding with the advances received before the actual work had started; petitioning; stopping work over various issues, of which the most important were payments lower than agreed or than expected, delays in payment, constrainment to use working gear which workers consider awkward or harmful in daily practice (in particular in the case of piece-work); violence against property, such as machines; and violence against persons, including overseers and bosses.

Nearly twenty actions that can be characterized more or less as strikes are mentioned by Kerr for the half century in which the railways were built in India; this represents on average about one strike every two years (see Table 1 overleaf).

It would be wrong to think that Kerr's book is very much focused on these collective actions, however impressive the list that can be derived from it. In fact he stresses that his book "is not a history of worker agency; it is a story of how the British got the railway built. That the workers had agency I accept, but, except tangentially, this book does not seek to explore that agency."[9] Nevertheless he is fairly sure that all the collective actions he has identified have nothing to do with a conscious criticism of nor resistance to large questions such as proletarianization or capitalism, but instead must be interpreted simply as very definite clashes of interests between employers and employed.

If Kerr is right, the question then arises where the tactics and strategies

7. Rajnarayan Chandarvarkar, *Imperial Power and Popular Politics: Class, Resistance and the State in India, c.1850–1950* (Cambridge, 1998), pp. 6–7.

8. Kerr, "Working Class Protest", PE–34, is much more explicit than Ian J. Kerr, *Building the Railways of the Raj: 1850–1900* (Delhi [etc.], 1995).

9. Kerr, *Building the Railways of the Raj*, p. 14. For Kerr's ideas on a proletarian consciousness see *ibid.*, pp. 169, 182, 192.

Table 1. *Strikes and similar collective action by construction workers on public building sites in India (1858/1859–1903)*

Date	Place	Type of workers	Type of action
1858–1859	Bombay, Baroda and Central India Railway (BB&CIR)	Brickmakers	Resistance to the introduction of new brass moulds; later a strike because of a lack of such moulds
1858–1859	Bombay, Baroda and Central India Railway (BB&CIR)	Brickmakers	Resistance to the introduction of new brass moulds; later a strike because of a lack of such moulds
June 1859	Sind Railway	Navvies (Jaisalmeris) Kutch masons	Strike because of arrears in wage payments Strike because of non-acceptance of overseers
1859 (late)	Tanjore	Navvies	Refusal to work for too low wages
1859–1860	Trichinopoly district of Madras	Navvies	Pre-emptive strike in order to raise piece-rates for earthwork
1860	Tapti viaduct of the BB&CIR	Navvies	Strike in order to raise piece-rates
March 1863	Bhore and Thal Ghat	N/A	Disorder and worker unrest
1872	Jhelum Bridge	Divers	Strike for higher wages
March 1878	Vellore Bridge (Madras)	Navvies (coolies of the pariah caste)	Violence against European supervisor

August 1880	Sohan Bridge	Riveters	Strike
1883	Harro Bridge	Divers	Strike for higher wages
1884 rainy season	Narayanganj–Dacca–Mymensingh State Railways	Brickmakers	Strike for higher piece-rates
1886	N/A	N/A	Strike for higher wages
c.1888	Ganges Canal at Mayapur	Stonemasons	Slowdown in order to alter the shift from piece to time work
1889	Sind–Peshin Line	Skilled workers	Strike for higher wages
May 1890	North Arcot district	Navvies	Petition for prompt and full payment of wages
1897–1898	Godavari Bridge at Rajahmundry	Punjabis engaged in well-sinking	Combination to slow down the work speed and thus to prolong the job
1899	N/A	N/A	Strike
1903	Damodar Bridge	Riveters	Strike

Sources: Ian J. Kerr, *Building the Railways of the Raj: 1850–1900* (Delhi [etc.], 1995), pp. 104, 122–123, 144–145, 173, 176–181, 184; *idem*, "Labour Control and Labour Legislation in Colonial India: A Tale of Two Mid-Nineteenth Century Acts", *South Asia*, 27 (2004), pp. 7–25. The following cases only in *idem*, "Working Class Protest in 19th Century India: Example of Railway Workers", *Economic and Political Weekly*, 20 (26 January 1985), PE34– PE40: 1859 Tanjore (PE–36), Bhore and Thal Ghat 1863 (PE–36 and PE–39, n. 27), the 1899 strike (PE–35 and PE–39, n. 14, after Lajpat Jagga's unpublished M.Phil. thesis of 1978; the case in c.1888 in L.R. Nicolls, "Agricultural Engineering in India (VIII)", *Engineering*, 46 (1888), pp. 175–177, 176. Not included are disturbances related to the Santhal uprising and mutiny; Kerr, *Building the Railways of the Raj*, pp. 35–37, 125, 184; G. Huddleston, *History of the East Indian Railway* (Calcutta, 1906), pp. 23–25, 36, 280–281, nor collective actions by enginemen, clerks, signallers, and other railway personnel, as recorded from 1862 onwards by Kerr.

of such collective labour actions had been learnt and how they were improved. In other words, was there – at least from a certain point in time – a tradition, and, if so, how did it develop? Following Kerr's rather scanty suggestions on this point one can envisage three possibilities: this type of collective action was new and started with and because of the railway building in India; or it represents a translation of a general repertoire of resistance from other parts of society, such as peasant unrest; or it represents a tradition vested in professionally migrating skilled workers who offered themselves at public works.[10]

In this essay a series of collective actions will be presented, including several strikes that broke out in the dry season of 1848–1849 among the brickmakers engaged in building the Ganges Canal. The fact, moreover, that these events are reasonably well documented offers some scope to follow up Kerr's carefully and very modestly presented but at the same time truly seminal ideas. The very existence of this rather extensive strike at least suggests there might have been a tradition of collective resistance in India among workers engaged on large public works. As in Europe, it seems that such a tradition existed before the building of the railways, in particular among those who built canals and dykes; this would push the history of collective action much further back in time, as far back indeed as the late Middle Ages in western Europe.[11] If that is an easy conclusion at first sight, only a careful description of such actions can lead us to tackle the much more difficult questions about the mentality and consciousness of those involved, as well as the development over time of their activity. Therefore, the task now is first of all to describe what happened during that 1848–1849 strike. In a few concluding remarks I shall discuss the extent to which these events link up with Kerr's work.

BRICKMAKERS ON THE GANGES CANAL

The Ganges Canal, in Uttar Pradesh, to the north-east of New Delhi, is one of the largest canals in the word. It is all the more remarkable for the

10. Nor should it be forgotten that the employers too developed traditions in dealing with labour unrest, as Kerr shows. The same goes for the government, as is shown by the passing of the Workmen (Dispute) Act (X) of 1860; cf. Kerr, *Building the Railways of the Raj*, p. 184, and *idem*, "Labour Control and Labour Legislation in Colonial India: A Tale of Two Mid-Nineteenth Century Acts".

11. Jan Lucassen, "The Other Proletarians: Seasonal Labourers, Mercenaries and Miners", in Lis *et al.*, *Before the Unions*, pp. 171–194, 179–183; Piet Lourens and Jan Lucassen, *Arbeitswanderung und berufliche Spezialisierung: Die lippischen Ziegler im 18. und 19. Jahrhundert* (Osnabrück, 1999), pp. 23–24; cf. Terry Coleman, *The Railway Navvies: A History of the Men Who Made the Railways* (Harmondsworth, 1968); James E. Handley, *The Navvy in Scotland* (Cork, 1970); Anthony Burton, *The Canal Builders* (London, 1972); and Peter Way, *Common Labour: Workers and the Digging of North American Canals 1780–1860* (Cambridge, 1993).

Figure 1. The Ganges Canal at Roorkee: watercolour (1863) by William Simpson (1823–1899). *British Library, Picture Library, Record no. C6562–04, WD 1012. Used with permission*

fact that it was constructed around the middle of the nineteenth century. The main canal, running from Haridwar to Kanpur, measures 349 miles (562 kilometres) (excluding branch canals) and in 1850 the total cost was estimated at more than 14 million rupees. No wonder it took sixteen years (1839–1854) to finish, although most of the work was done between 1848 and 1854 under Major Proby T. Cautley, who had succeeded Major W.E. Baker as Director in January 1848.

For the construction of the Ganges Canal, its total length had been divided into six sections. The First or Northern Division measured only twenty-four miles but was the most difficult to build because of the high fall, the complicated canal head in Haridwar and the majestic aqueduct over the Solani River. With its twenty-four miles, this First Division covered less than 8 per cent of the total length, but it absorbed 45 per cent of the total estimated cost of the whole canal. Besides, all the experience had to be gained on that First Division.[12] Because, as far as we know, the

12. Proby T. Cautley, *Report on the Ganges Canal Works: From Their Commencement until the Opening of the Canal in 1854*, 3 vols and one atlas (London, 1860), vol. 3, pp. 292–295 (Appendix Q); *idem*, *Ganges Canal* [text in English, Hindi, and Urdu] (n.p., 1854), pp. 8, 12, 20; *idem*, *Estimate of the Probable Expense to be Incurred in Constructing the Ganges Canal Works [...]* (Umballa, 1850), pp. ii–iv. Cf. Robert B. Buckley, *The Irrigation Works of India, and Their Financial Results* (London, 1880), pp. 1–10, 88–112.

labour unrest during the building of the canal took place only in that First Division, I shall restrict this discussion to a brief description of the organization of the work on that Division, and in particular to the brickmaking activities.

This Division starts at Haridwar, where the canal receives its water from the river Ganges, which follows its parallel course to the east of the canal. From Haridwar the canal first runs westwards via Jawalpur and then turns south to Roorkee, where the builders established their headquarters and where, in 1847, an engineering college was set up, to become the basis of a modern university.[13] From Roorkee the canal continues south to Asafnagar Falls and finally to Manglaur, which actually forms part of the Second Division. Roorkee was the scene of the strike of 1848.

From a plan drawn up on 17 June 1848 by Cautley, who wanted to reorganize the central space, we can gain an idea of what Roorkee looked like at the time of the strike. At the centre, not far from the canal that could be crossed by a bridge, were bungalows for the European staff and the workshops, first the old quadrangle with the smithy and iron department and to the west of it the model room quadrangle which was extended to the south for the carpenters. Cautley wanted to place a small portable steam engine in this carpenters shop for lathes and other machinery so that "this Department should in some measure become a school not only for a native workman but for the students in the college". Also in the middle of Roorkee was the college under Headmaster Conductor, H. Bingham; and there was a hospital. On 22 February 1849 Cautley reported that a brick manufactory had been established near the workshop and the model room as there was so much earth from the cutting left over from levelling operations.[14] Around these central brick buildings at the time were "numerous thatched buildings which are in perpetual danger of the fires, which occur in the quarter of the bildars", especially because of the very large collection of wood needed for the carpentry work.[15]

The daily supervision of this First or Northern Division was entrusted to two executive engineers, under the Director. Lieutenant Henry Yule of the Bengal Engineers was responsible for the "Works Department" until 15 April 1848, when he left for Calcutta. His successor was Lieutenant A.G. Goodwyn, who shortly before had had to face the death of his child, fell ill himself, and afterwards joined the Army of the Punjab. Being unable himself to work for quite some time, from 17 October 1848 to 22 March

13. See http://rurkiu.tripod.com.

14. National Archives of India, New Delhi, Military Board [hereafter, NAI, MB], Proceedings, 25 May 1849, 1263–1264; cf. *ibid.*, 18 August 1848, 7481–7483; *ibid.*, 17 September 1849, 10792–10794; *ibid.*, 04 January 1850, 324–326; [Proby T. Cautley,] *Report on the Ganges Canal from Hurdwar to Cawnpore and Allahabad* (Calcutta, 1845), pp. 76–80.

15. NAI, MB, Proceedings, 11 July 1848, 4684–4687; a prophetic observation, as will be shown later.

1849 Goodwyn left the actual running of things to his assistant Thomas Login.[16]

The care of the new "Materials Department" was in the hands of James Finn of the Artillery Regiment, who arrived on 24 September 1847. That is not to say that only the "Works Department" had dealings with the labourers, since Finn in his "Materials Department" had to produce on the spot things like bricks and lime. One could say that the first executive engineer was generally responsible for the earthworks, masonry, and the Roorkee workshops (for sawing, carpentry, and ironwork), while the second saw to production of the bricks and lime needed by his colleague.

The two executive engineers of the First Division were assisted by six assistant executive officers, each at a salary of 250–400 rupees a month plus a marching allowance of 100 rupees at 4 annas per mile (which means 400 miles of monthly marching, on horseback of course, but still a considerable distance). Because each of them was responsible for financial expenditure of 50,000 to 100,000 rupees a month, they all had to provide security of 5,000 rupees each before being entitled to receive any salary.[17] Thomas Login was in charge of the workshops in Roorkee, while Lieutenant A. Allen was the engineer overseeing the timber yard and T.S. Murdoch the iron yard. Two others were attached to the nearby Solani Aqueduct. Second Lieutenant G. Price of the 1st European Regiment Fusiliers oversaw the navvies and James Parker looked after the masonry, while one William Kay was responsible for the works at Ranipur Rao. Because each maintained a bungalow in Roorkee, except for William Kay who lived in Jawalpur, they were at an advantage over most of the canal officers of the other Divisions, who passed most of their time under canvas, as Cautley remarked.[18]

Further, in their Division various assistant executive officers commanded an overseer at 65 rupees a month. All these men were still young during the eventful season 1848–1849, being between twenty-four and thirty-two years old. Overseer Sgt Russell Kelly was attached to the Roorkee workshops, Sgt William Johnstone to the Solani Aqueduct, and Sgt Thomas Martin to the works at Ranipur Rao. James Finn commanded four overseers, the sergeants G.N. Dodd (in Roorkee), Edward Durrant (especially for the brick fabrication in Roorkee), George Barrett (in Mahewar), and George S. Murray (in Salempur).[19] Three Englishmen and

16. NAI, MB, Proceedings, 1 August 1848, 6605; *ibid.*, 3 April 1849, 18181–18182; *ibid.*, 10 April 1849, 18313; *ibid.*, 21 August 1849, 6060–6064; *ibid.*, 8 January 1850, 13700.

17. NAI, MB, Proceedings, 8 May 1849, 1293–1298; *ibid.*, 2 November 1849, 10085–10108; *ibid.*, 23 November 1849, 11314.

18. Cautley, *Report on the Ganges Canal from Hurdwar*, p. 68; NAI, MB, Proceedings, 2 November 1849, 10089–10093.

19. NAI, MB, Proceedings, 5 October 1847, 6621; *ibid.*, 1 May 1849, 90–94; *ibid.*, 21 August 1849, 6060–6064; *ibid.*, 2 November 1849, 10104–10105; *ibid.*, 18 December 1849, 12468–12469;

four Indians were employed in the English offices of the Works and the Materials Departments. The best-paid Englishman there earned 100 rupees a month, the worst was paid 35 rupees, while the salaries of the Indians varied between 25 and 45 rupees a month. If we consider the entire establishment just mentioned, there were (excluding Cautley at 1,000 rupees monthly with a small staff) eighteen Englishmen and three Indians in the higher ranks in the First Division. In the lower ranks another seventy-six Indians belonged to the establishment, with monthly salaries ranging between 4 and 30 rupees. Apart from a master carpenter, a master smith, a master bricklayer and his assistant, a native doctor, and a few *moonshees* (writers), most of them were *chuprassis* (messengers), and *barkandazis* (police constables). The *barkandazis* under their *jemadars* not only secured the personal safety of the establishment, but just as importantly were in charge of guarding the treasury in which the money for wages was kept.

This handful of Englishmen with their Indian staff[20] had to manage the construction with the help of dozens of Indian contractors, who themselves directly or indirectly had hired thousands of Indian workers. The importance of the cooperation among the Europeans as well as between Europeans and Indians is illustrated by the straightforward judgement by Baker about one of the assistant executive engineers:[21]

> I do not consider Mr Kay to be deficient in professional knowledge, but he is wanting in judgement and temper and appears incapable of managing natives or making a proper use of the native agency without which executive works cannot be carried on in this country. As Executive Officer Mr Kay must have the control of assistants (who would be commissioned officers) and overseers, but he has not had the education nor has he the manners and habits which would command the respect or ensure the cordial cooperation of his European subordinates. I would therefore propose that Mr Kay should continue under the orders of Lieutenant

Cautley, *Report on the Ganges Canal from Hurdwar*, pp. 65–66. For Johnstone see also "Building Materials", *Papers Prepared for the Use of the Thomason Civil Engineering College, Roorkee*, no. 1 (Roorkee, 1862, 3rd edn), p. 38; for Allen see NAI, MB, Proceedings, 9 March 1849, 16788–16789. Sometimes other Europeans and a single Indian official too are mentioned in the period under review. They included J.H. Butler, Asst Surgeon from 25 April 1849 (*ibid.*, 11 May 1849, 490), and Luthfoollah Khan, promoted to native doctor on 30 April 1849 (*ibid.*, 29 June 1849, 3456).

20. Apart from the four Indian clerks in the First Division, the canal works employed in all only two Indians in the higher ranks – as Cautley's overview for January 1849 shows: the sub-assistant civil engineers Petamber Sing (superintending the preparation of bricks over fifteen miles at the head of the Fourth Division) and Madho Ram (taking cross sections for the Cawnpore branch canal in the Sixth Division and in May 1849 superintending a brick kiln). See NAI, MB, Proceedings, 1 May 1849, 90–94; *ibid.*, 3 July 1849, 3669. For Indian salaries see *ibid.*, 21 August 1849, 6063.

21. NAI, MB, Proceedings, 5 October 1847, 6618–6619, W.E. Baker on 15 September 1847 about William Kay.

Yule and that he should be employed during the ensuing cold season in the construction of the dam across the Ranipur Rao.

Concern over the capability of Europeans to oversee Indians also arises from the case of Sergeant Thomas D. Hawthorne.[22] A clerk from Newport in Hampshire, he arrived in India in October 1836 to join the army while not yet twenty-one. Ten years later, Hawthorne was in the Second Company, 4th Battalion Artillery, and taking the opportunity of joining the College of Civil Engineers at Roorkee, he became an assistant overseer on the Third Division of the Ganges Canal in January 1849. He found himself answerable to a German, Philip Volk, very skilled in canal building, but not very proficient in English.

To the indignation of Cautley, who considered "that in receiving men from the Civil Engineers' College, we ought at least to expect a guarantee against drunkenness", Sergeant Hawthorne turned out to be, in the words of his character testimonial, "indolent and indifferent regarding works". He even "took to drinking spirits in latter time, so as to become intoxicated". His misbehaviour was considered to be so grave that a court session was held under Volk's presidency. Its proceedings were witnessed by Beni Purshad, the native doctor attached to the Third Division, Sundul Lal, the *moonshee* attached to Hawthorne's establishment, Muburdust Khan, the *duffadar* of the guard in charge of the treasury, Imambux and Hyder Khan, both *barkandazis* of the same guard, and Godzarr, the sergeant's *chaprassi*. Not only do we receive in passing a fair idea of the immediate circles in which an assistant overseer on the Ganges Canal lived, we also hear why drunkenness was considered to be "a vice, which, beyond all others, unfits a man for the Department of Public Works". First, the money in the treasury, indispensable for the payment of wages, was no longer safe, which of itself implied a lack of confidence in the *duffadar* and the *barkandazis* of the guard; second, after a time the subcontractors did not know how to continue their work; finally, such conduct as Hawthorne's obviously undermined the always precarious position of the all too small contingent of Englishmen commanding the Indian workforce.

Who were the Indian workers? First there were the earthworkers or *bildars* (occasionally between 400 and 500 are mentioned at 4 rupees per month; and additionally 10 *tindals* at 6 to 7 rupees);[23] then there were masons and other skilled workers; and finally the men who made the

22. NAI, MB, Proceedings, 24 July 1849, 4629–4636; for Volk see *ibid.*, 9 November 1849, 10480.

23. NAI, MB, Proceedings, 5 January 1849, 14616. In the sources *bildar* seems to be used as an occupational term, meaning an unskilled worker or assistant. As far as I can see, there are no indications that one specific caste, in particular that of the *beldars*, is meant; Kerr, *Building the Railways of the Raj*, pp. 110–112.

materials, workmen in the central smiths' and carpenters' shops, and brickmakers. As they were the main strikers, let us see what we know about their work and their backgrounds.

Between 1842 and 1854, during a dozen of the dry seasons which was the only time bricks could be made, in the First Division alone 211 million bricks were made for the building of bridges, aqueducts, locks, and other constructions. An almost incredible number, as Cautley himself realizes, adding to his report "a popular idea of its vastness may be given by stating that if the above number of bricks were laid endwise they would form a line upwards of 40,000 miles in length".[24] How many people were involved in this fabrication? We do not have direct information to enable us to answer the question, so we must work towards it stepwise; this entails perhaps a somewhat lengthy exercise, but it is essential because we cannot proceed to understand and appreciate the strike without detailed knowledge of the actual labour force.

A production of 211 million bricks in 12 years means on average 17.6 million bricks per season. If made by hand – taking on average 190 working days per season and a daily production per moulder of 800 bricks – that would require about 120 moulders working simultaneously.[25] In fact, the numbers would have been different since not all seasons were equally busy, and from 1848 onwards moulding machines were used. Enough data are available for a few years to reconstruct the total number of workers engaged in brickmaking, and to allow a more detailed breakdown of the composition of this workforce (see Table 2).

As this table clearly shows, the variation between the different seasons depends primarily on the number of *bildars* needed for digging the clay and carrying it from the pits to be mixed with water and moulded. The distance between the two places in fact determined the number of *bildars* engaged in the preparatory phases of the brickmaking process.

Unfortunately, in Table 2 a rough estimate is available only for the season 1846/1847 to indicate the ratio between all workers of the First Division engaged in making green bricks and those engaged in the firing process. However, for a limited number of kilns on the Ganges Canal in about the same years enough data are available not only to corroborate these results, but to supply more details about the different tasks involved: loading, firing, and unloading of the kiln, and possibly also the transport from the kiln, or "clamp", to the construction site (see Table 3, p. 60).

24. Cautley, *Report on the Ganges Canal Works*, vol. 3, Appendix A, p. 19.

25. The number of days is taken from *ibid.*, vol. 1, p. 65; daily production per moulder of 800 can be found in NAI, MB, Proceedings, 25 May 1849, 1286 (an estimate by Finn which seems to be more realistic than the 1,000 which one also can find). Cf. Major Baker who, in 1847, planned for brickmaking for the Solani Aqueduct, 149 brick moulders per day plus 3,309 labourers; *ibid.*, p. 66.

Table 2. *Reconstruction of the composition of the labour force engaged in brickmaking at the First Division of the Ganges Canal during the seasons 1846/1847 to 1849/1850*

	1846/1847	1847/1848	1848/1849	1849/1850
Number of *bildars* per moulder:				
– for excavating		incl. below	incl. below	incl. below
– for carrying clay to *pukka* terraces (called *tughars*)		3	3	1
– for breaking clods and rough tempering of the clay		1	incl. above	incl. above
– for mixing and carrying the prepared clay (called *garrah*) to the moulder		3	2.5	2.5
– for carrying ashes and water		1/6	1/6	1/6
Moulder	1	1	1	1
Total number of workers or *bildars* in a moulder's gang	N/A	8 1/6	6 2/3	4 2/3
Total number of moulders	149	150	N/A	200
Total number of workers making green or *kutcha* bricks (also called "bucks")	[1,250]	1,225	[1,000–1,200]	933
Total number of workers loading ("packing"), firing, and unloading kilns and clamps	[2,200]			
Grand total per day	3,458			
Percentage of workers making green bricks	36			

Sources: 1846/1847: Proby T. Cautley, *Report on the Ganges Canal Works: From Their Commencement until the Opening of the Canal in 1854*, 3 vols and one atlas (London, 1860), vol. 1, p. 66; 1847/1848: *ibid.*, vol. 3, pp. 8–9, and National Archives of India, New Delhi, Military Board [hereafter, NAI, MB], Proceedings, 12 September 1849, 9091 (Roorkee); 1848/1849: Cautley, *Report on the Ganges Canal Works*, vol. 3, p. 15, and NAI, MB, Proceedings, 25 May 1849, 1285–1286 (Roorkee and Mahewar, August–October 1848); 1849/1850: Cautley, *Report on the Ganges Canal Works*, vol. 3, p. 16, and NAI, MB, Proceedings, 13 June 1850, 2262 (Roorkee, Mahewar, Dhunowree, and Salempur in May 1850). See also F.D.M. Brown, "Brick-making near Roorkee", in J.G. Medley (ed.), *Professional Papers on Indian Engineering*, First Series, 4 (1867), pp. 158–165, 160, and 165 (four men and two boys per moulder).

Table 3. *Percentage breakdown of costs of moulding 100,000 bricks and firing them in puzawahs, or clamps, Ganges Canal, 1848–1851*

%	1st Division 1848	3rd Division 1850	3rd Division 1851
Pukka bricks at kiln	19	9.2	12.7
Fuel	43	59.1	59.9
Loading or piling	22	19.2	17.1
Firing or burning	4	N/A	N/A
Unloading	11	N/A	N/A
Miscellaneous	N/A	0.9	0.6
Establishment	1	11.6	9.7
Total	100	100	100
Total cost in rupees per 100,000 bricks	772	501	450

Sources: 1st Division (old kiln Roorkee 25 June 1848 – 120,000 bricks): NAI, MB, Proceedings, 12 September 1848, 9089; 3rd Division 1850 (based on data for 32 kilns, costing on average 501 rupees) and 1851 (based on data for 31 kilns, costing on average 450 rupees): "Building Materials", *Papers Prepared for the Use of the Thomason Civil Engineering College, Roorkee*, no. 1 (3rd edn, Roorkee, 1862), pp. 47–48.

Combining the two tables we may suppose that twice as many labourers were involved in the firing process – either in fixed kilns or in clamps (*puzawahs*) – as in moulding.[26] All these data and considerations would lead to the conclusion that for one moulder the following additional labourers are needed: between four and seven for excavating, preparing, and drying the clay, and fifteen for the firing process, which might have included a number especially engaged for all sorts of transport, mainly carting of fuel to the kiln and of bricks from the kilns to the sites where they were needed for masonry and other purposes.[27] The great number of people involved in preparing the *puzawah* (piling, firing, and sorting of the ready bricks according to quality) should not surprise us, for to load such a stack of 100,000 bricks two to three months were needed. A total sum of 80–100 rupees spent would amount to 40 rupees per month, or indeed ten individuals at 4 rupees a month each, which corresponds to the wages found so far.[28]

26. This is confirmed by the data concerning Mynpooree District ("Building Materials", p. 38). For unknown reasons, other dispersed data show much higher costs for green bricks and much lower (up to impossibly low) costs for loading, firing, and unloading (see data for Dinapore in NAI, MB, Proceedings, 12 Septemeber 1848, 9084, and for the Fifth Division of the Ganges Canal in "Building Materials", p. 49).

27. "Building Materials", p. 38 (according to Finn at the Western Jumna Canals, an extra 150 rupees was needed to carry the ready bricks from the kilns to the works, both for larger bricks that cost 450 rupees at the kiln and for smaller ones of 350 rupees).

28. *Ibid.*, p. 46.

Figure 2. Clamps along the Hooghly river, near Calcutta, ready to be dismantled (right and left), with, in the foreground, stacks of green bricks drying, on which two workers are standing. Hand-coloured photographic print by Frederick Fiebig (c.1851–1852).
British Library, Picture Library, copy neg. B 23209, Photo 247/1(21). Used with permission

Although there are still many uncertainties, that seems to be the best result we can achieve at present. Such an exercise might seem futile, but we shall see that a breakdown of the labour force is important to understand the labour protest properly, as it is always necessary to pinpoint precisely which labourers are involved, in what type of collective action, and which are not. The total workforce on the brick elds of the First Division, an estimated 3,000 men during the season 1848/1849, might be broken down as follows: 150 moulders with 1,000 assistants, and 1,850 in charge of ring the bricks. Among the groups of moulders it is highly likely that women were present as well as men, but there is no positive evidence here to prove it.[29] What was the social background of these brickmakers, and where did they come from?

Kerr draws a distinction between wandering specialists and local labour,

29. Women are not mentioned in any of the sources I have seen so far about Roorkee before the 1860s. From then on they seem to have been quite common, as J.G. Medley writes: "Generally the moulder has one woman to take away the bricks as he makes them"; J.G. Medley, *Roorkee Treatise on Civil Engineering in India,* 2 vols (Roorkee, 1866, 1st edn; 1869, 2nd edn), vol. 1, p. 30 (in second edn p. 33). For female brickmakers earlier on – but in far-away Bengal – see n. 31 of the present article.

Figure 3. *Puzawah*, or large Indian clamp.
Proby T. Cautley, Report on the Ganges Canal Works: From Their Commencement until the Opening of the Canal in 1854, *3 vols and one atlas (London, 1860), vol. 2, p. 197.*

who could be sent to construction sites "temporarily and involuntarily because village power-holders made them do so" in exchange for only one meal a day; or they could go there at their own initiative to earn some supplementary income. These semi-proletarians after all remained involved in the economy of their villages and the wage rates offered by constructors were not always high enough to induce them to come. Of course, dire need and especially famine might leave them with little option, but many cases are documented where such local semi-proletarians preferred not to apply to public works for employment.[30]

Unfortunately, up to now we have only very scant information on the origin of the brickmakers on the First Division of the Ganges Canal. Although it is known that under certain circumstances specialized potters of the Kumhar caste made bricks on government production sites, in this case that does not seem to have been very likely, at least not local Kumhars. There simply would not have been enough in the small area concerned, and reports of travelling bands of Kumhars are not known.[31] Cautley's report

30. Kerr, *Building the Railways of the Raj*, pp. 170–173; cf. Cautley, *Report on the Ganges Canal Works*, vol. 2, pp. 544–547, 550, 557, 562–563, on the nomadic professional navvies called *oades*.

31. NAI, MB, Proceedings, 3 October 1848, 10835–10856 (report by J.S. Irwin, executive engineer Ramgur Division, Hazareebaugh, 12 July 1848: "It will be seen that the moulding and kilning were to be done by contract by coomars as I believe is usual in department Public Works." In this case the moulding was done by women assisted by men; it was also mostly women who brought bricks to the kilns.).

of 28 February 1849 speaks vaguely of "both Hill men and Labourers from the plains" in the Sixth Division north of Kanpur.[32] In another report (written about the same time on the basis of a report by James Finn of 2 February 1849) about the First Division, he compares contractors at small manufactories in the villages "twenty miles west and ten miles east of Roorkee" and the big contractors in Roorkee proper. The former must be seen as family enterprises with one or two moulders and their assistants, because their seasonal production fluctuated between one and four lakh. They were able to produce bricks at between 42 and 72 rupees per 100,000, because they could select places for production where good clay and plenty of water were available, and decide when to make bricks and when to attend to their household affairs. The brick fields in Roorkee were fixed, and clay and water had to be transported to them. Furthermore, migratory workers always need to be able to work continuously in order to take home enough money for after the season. Therefore they and the contractors who hired them had to be paid much more.

Where did the contractors and their men come from? As we shall see, in September 1848 Finn tried to find moulder contractors in Meerut, Ambala, Karnal, and Dehra Dun, all from 50 to 100 kilometres from Roorkee and apparently places from where they had come in previous seasons. When with the cold weather of 1851/1852 all attempts at firing, or even making, bricks failed and the brick fields were totally cleared out, the parties of masons had to be broken up, and that caused a delay to the works because, Roorkee being remote, the men came from far away, from "Oude, Rajpootana and the country north of the Sutlej". It is not impossible that these were also regions brickmakers came from. Specialists in firing bricks came from the region north of Benares.[33]

Some individual workers assume for us an identity of a sort, because accidents which might befall workers and any compensation the canal works were obliged to pay are discussed in correspondence between the engineers. That is why we know of "Newoz" (also spelt differently), the son of Bhojrey, and thirty-six years and six months old. This "dark black coloured" man was five feet and two inches tall, had "one mark of smallpox on the upper part of the right side of the spine and on the anterior part of either thigh". He was a married Chamar from the village of Gowrah, in the pargana of Mohomdabad (most likely Mahmudabad is

32. NAI, MB, Proceedings 1 May 1849, 101.

33. Cautley, *Report on the Ganges Canal Works*, vol. 1, p. 92 (the northern Punjab is situated north of the Sutlej). For Oude see *ibid.*, vol. 3, pp. 4 and 6, where Cautley writes that one of the methods for building brick kilns "was taught us by men obtained from Benares"; and NAI, MB, Proceedings, 12 September 1848, 9095: "Major Baker not three years ago [...] did not think it possible to burn bricks with wood in the upper parts of the Doab, indeed that the practice was unknown north of Benares. I rather think brickmakers were afterwards sent for from that Province".

meant) in the province of Lucknow. A hardworking *bildar*, Newoz had already been engaged for half a year before he was severely injured on 30 June 1848 while digging under the canal embankment. About 11.30 am on that day he was brought to Muhes Chenader Dey (also spelt Mohes Chunder Dey), the assistant surgeon in the hospital in Roorkee. Newoz was found to have broken his right thigh bone in two places as well as his seventh rib, his loins were severely lacerated, and his bladder was totally paralysed. Dey attended him for eight months but then had to declare that the poor man's injuries were so complicated that it "has totally incapacitated him for any business whatsoever". Ten months later J.H. Butler, the Civil Surgeon of the Ganges Canal, could establish no improvement, whereupon Finn was permitted by the military board to grant Newoz a life pension of 2 rupees a month to enable him to return to his home in the Lucknow territory and to support himself there.[34]

A second labourer we know by name is the *bildar* "Nunkoo" (or Nankoo), who died on 25 October 1848 as the result of severe head injuries caused by a fall into the well excavated for a foundation block of the Solani Aqueduct. Nunkoo had been employed for two years at 4 rupees per month. It was decided to grant 50 rupees to Jugmuttra, the thirty-year-old widow he left at home. They were Hindus of the Lodha caste, residing in Ramnuggur village, in the pargana of Rudauli, in the Oude District. The *tindal* Lokey and the *bildar* Matudeer stood as witnesses in support of the claim for a pension for this man's widow, which was to be drawn in Lucknow.[35]

That is all we know about the origins of those workers. On the basis of such scant evidence we may perhaps conclude that the workers in the First Division, including the 600 to 900 brick moulders, the 1,200 to 1,400 brick firers, and the hundreds involved in transport on the brick fields, were drawn from a vast area stretching up to 500 kilometres to the west and north, but especially to the east and southeast of Roorkee.

Brickmakers, like navvies, were recruited through intermediaries, contractors. Although the engineers complained that, unlike in Europe, there were not enough large contractors in India, it is clear that contractors did play a crucial role. James Finn, in charge of the supply of material, remarked:

> I have been very fortunate in my extensive dealings with the contractors for *Puzawah* made bricks, lime and carriage of firewood. Of brick contractors I had

34. NAI, MB, Proceedings, 30 March 1849, 17878–17882; *ibid.*, 18 May 1849, 855–856; *ibid.*, 18 September 1849, 7971–7972. The distance that Newoz had to travel was roughly 275 kilometres as the crow flies if Gowrah is situated in the pargana of Mahmudabad and 450 kilometres if it is part of the pargana of Muhammadabad.

35. NAI, MB, Proceedings, 19 June 1849, 2684–2688. Rudauli is c.350 kilometres from Roorkee as the crow flies. A third incident, involving a *bildar* called Jurowar, is reported (but without further details) in NAI, MB, Proceedings, 9 May 1850, 375–377.

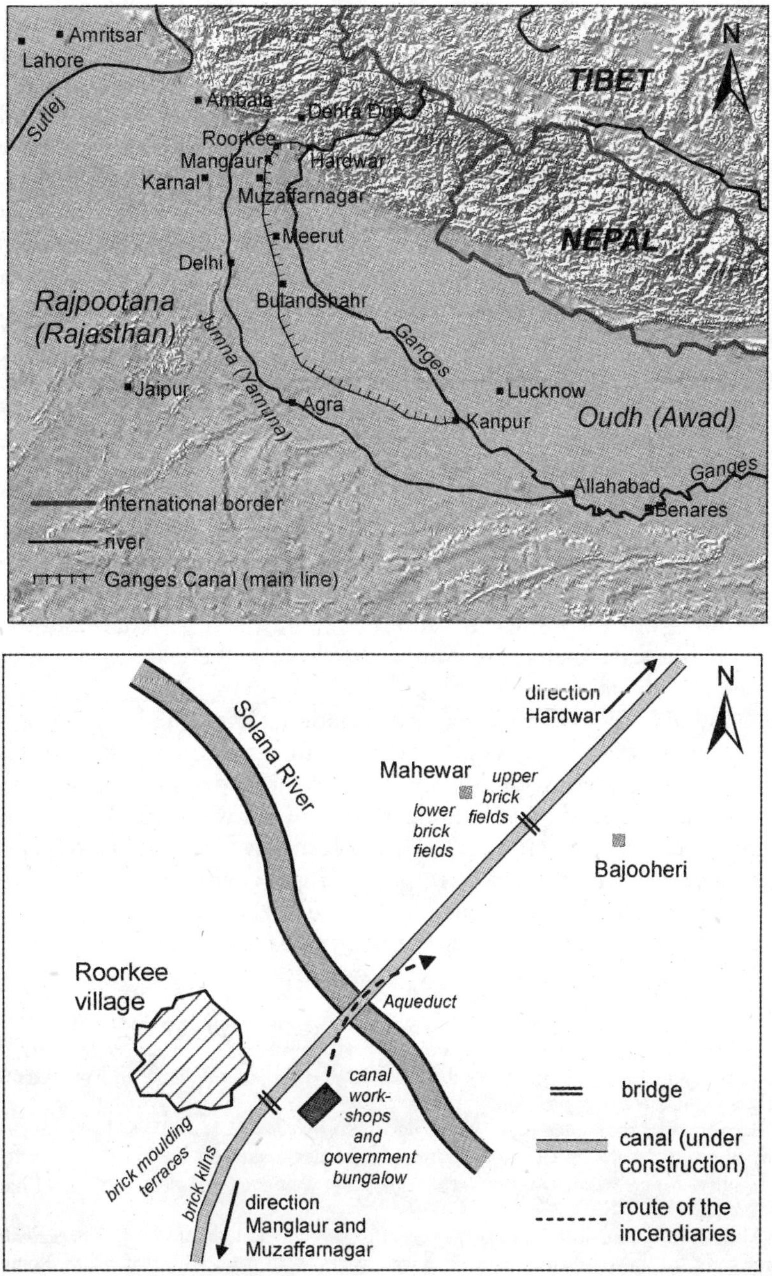

Figure 4. Maps of the Ganges Canal's main line (upper map) and part of the First Division of the canal under construction in 1848–1849 near the village of Roorkee (lower map).
Mapwork by Jelle van Lottum

> from 40 to 50 in constant employ, about the same number of lime contractors and sometimes as many as 400 contractors with 2,000 carts bringing firewood from the forest.[36]

Finn might have been fortunate with his kiln and clamp contractors, but with moulders – who operated completely separately from the firers – he experienced many difficulties. During 1842–1846 his predecessors had made a loss of 25,225:5:7[37] rupees compared with advances of 79,666:13:1 rupees, and these losses proved to be irrecoverable:

> With one exception, the contractors against whom balances existed, were men of straw; every effort was made to get them to fulfil their engagements, or to refund, but all failed: and it was determined by Major Baker, the director at that time, that legal proceedings instituted against them, could lead to no other result than the addition of a large amount for law expenses to the heavy losses which had already been sustained.[38]

The insignificant losses to Finn of 150 rupees paid to two lime contractors who died before their contracts were completed were also irrecoverable, according to him because "they were in such poor circumstances that they left nothing but their starving families behind them".[39] That last remark seems to indicate that these contractors have to be envisaged rather as cooperative subcontractors than as large entrepreneurs.

Although we have no direct information about the social relations within groups of workers who contracted for moulding during the season 1848/1849, our reconstruction shows that they consisted on average of seven persons headed by the moulder himself, but we do not know if these groups received a collective task wage or just time wages with a 50 per cent premium for the moulder, who received 6 rupees per month against a wage of 4 rupees for his assistants, called *bildars*.[40] There is no further information on this crucial point until twelve years later:

36. Cautley, *Report on the Ganges Canal Works,* vol. 3, p. 21; cf. NAI, MB, Proceedings, 15 August 1848, 7446–7447. As 2,200 workers were engaged in the firing phase (cf. Table 2), this means that on average one brick contractor may have represented fifty workers; however, if the carters have to be included in the total figure, the average is more likely to have been forty workers per kiln (or clamp gang).

37. Prior to 1957, the Indian rupee was divided into sixteen annas, one anna being four pices. Conventionally, a colon is used to separate rupees, annas, and pices.

38. Cautley, *Report on the Ganges Canal Works,* vol. 3, pp. 2–3.

39. *Ibid.*, p. 21.

40. Although the sources for 1848–1849 seem to be equivocal about the dominance of time wages, it is still possible that in reality piece wages were paid, which in their reports the engineers, for convenience' sake, converted to time wages as given here. Cf. "Building Materials", p. 45: contract rates for regular moulding with an output of 1,200 to 1,500 bricks per day in the Third Division varied from 55 to 70 rupees per lakh, depending on the difficulty of procuring water. These piece-rates are consistent with the time-rates normally mentioned in the sources.

> At Roorkee a moulder made generally from 800 to 1000 bricks per diem [...]. The number of attendants on each moulder, to supply clay, water, &c. will depend on the distance of the moulding ground from where the clay is dug, and of both of these from the water [...]. On account of the assistance that can be given to the brick-moulder by his family working at intervals, brick-moulding may be advantageously done as piecework, i.e. a certain sum given per thousand bricks moulded and stacked.[41]

However tentatively, some conclusions can be proposed. First, that in Roorkee moulders and firers were organized separately whereas in the villages the small family-based teams of brickmakers seem to have controlled the whole process. Second, that a moulding gang in Roorkee was headed by one moulder, acting probably as *primus inter pares*. Finally, it is not impossible that the firing gangs showed a similar social structure.

THE 1848–1849 STRIKES AND THEIR AFTERMATH

A straightforward account of the strikes of the 1848/1849 season must start with a caution. Even more than in the previous section we have to bear in mind Kerr's caveat: "Although we can only know of these resistances as they come to us, refracted through British eyes and minds, from English-language sources, their presence is clear."[42] Nevertheless, that is all we have. All we can do is try to use these sources as critically as possible.

In order to understand the events of 1848 and 1849 we should go back in time a little, to January 1842 when brickmaking started in Roorkee. Roorkee was then still a small town near the jungle, where suddenly British engineers established their headquarters, turning upside down the local labour market. It was a development not anticipated because, still in 1845, in the words of Cautley, "the price of labour is so cheap and therefore the value of machinery [...] is much less than it is in Europe"; that was soon to change.[43] As Cautley later remarked:

> [...] when works were first established at Roorkhee, and in the forest tracks north of it, the executive Officers were forced to pay high, to get men to come to the works at all: there was an uncertainty about the works being continued, labourers did not understand on what terms they were to work, uncertainty of

41. "Building Materials", p. 25.
42. Kerr, *Building the Railways of the Raj*, p. 169; see also p. 14.
43. Cautley, *Report on the Ganges Canal from Hurdwar*, p. 31, and Cautley, *Report on the Ganges Canal Works*, vol. 3, p. 2. Cf. NAI, MB, Proceedings, 29 June 1849, 3456, where the Military Board comments: "There is no question that when they began, that part of the country was very thinly populated, as the canal progresses, its entire neighbourhood will soon be densely populated, and things will then from competition be very cheap. These are all the good effects of roads and canals."

getting hire and ignorance of our system of regular payment made it a very difficult matter to get either men or carriage.[44]

However, on assuming the directorship from Major Baker on 11 January 1848, Major Cautley, pressed by the members of the Military Board in Calcutta, thought that it was time to change this situation, which was in his eyes abnormal and no longer warranted. He wanted to turn to wages which he had always paid to similar workers elsewhere ("and that at a time when the Sunday holiday was not allowed by the Government"), wages which were usual on the Eastern Jumna Canals. That meant 3:8 rupees per month for *bildars* instead of the 4 rupees which was usual in Roorkee, a wage reduction of half a rupee, or 12.5 per cent. To put those wages in perspective: poverty in that period was defined as net urban household income of less than 3 rupees per month.[45]

Cautley's argument ran as follows: "The labourer is certain of getting employment and regular pay, and the owner of a cart is certain of getting his cart employed, there is now therefore every reason why we should endeavour to reduce our rates to the proper standard of the country."[46] Besides, Cautley wanted to introduce as many labour-saving devices as possible, for example a new type of kiln (the small Scinde model by Captain Weller of the Engineers) in order to replace the *puzawahs*; or the establishment of a brick manufactory in the centre of Roorkee, and moulding tables instead of the Indian way of moulders squatting to perform their work.[47] On 1 July he could not wait to start the new season along these new lines: "I look sanguinely to the result of next season's operation being much more satisfactory."[48]

But the advantages of all these changes were not as evident to the labourers as they were to the new director. The collective protest that arose went through four phases. First, the refusal and absconding of some contractors and their workmates in September and October; second, two or three work strikes in October; third, several acts of machine breakage between October and March; and fourth, incendiary fires at the end of March, finally followed by conflict with the lime contractors. As soon as

44. Cautley, *Report on the Ganges Canal from Hurdwar*, p. 31; and *idem*, *Report on the Ganges Canal Works*, vol. 3, p. 2.
45. Christopher A. Bayly, *Rulers, Townsmen and Bazaars: North Indian Society in the Age of British Expansion, 1770–1870* (Cambridge, 1983), p. 306.
46. NAI, MB, Proceedings, 25 May 1849, 1266–1267; cf. *ibid.*, 12 September 1849, 9081–9098.
47. These moulders worked on specially prepared terraces, constructed before the start of the campaign in the dry season; bricks were partially "table-made", and Scinde kilns were introduced; see NAI, MB, Proceedings, 12 September 1848, 9095, and *ibid.*, 16 January 1849, 14993–15006. For working while standing instead of squatting, see Kerr, *Building the Railways of the Raj*, p. 174. More details about the working of these new kilns can be found in Cautley, *Report on the Ganges Canal Works*, vol. 3, pp. 9–10.
48. NAI, MB, Proceedings, 12 September 1848, 9087.

Cautley announced the wage reduction – it was on the occasion of Lieutenant Goodwyn's departure from the First Division at the beginning of the brick season 1848/1849 – trouble started. James Finn wrote on 2 February 1849 that it had been very difficult to find moulding contractors:

> [...] in September last Lieutenant Goodwyn had some contractors brought for me from Meerut, and others came from Umballa and Kurnal on my own requisition, but none of them would take a contract for kutcha bricks such as we make here, and exclusive of carriage of earth to the jughars, for less than 100 Rs per lac. I prevailed on one man who came from Deyra Doon [now Dehra Dun], and on another, who resides in the village of Roorkee, to take contracts on trial, at the rate of 75 Rupees per lac, and being anxious to introduce the system of kutcha brickmaking by contract, I assisted these people, by lending them the requisite tools for their work. The bricks made by these parties were invariably counted by one of the European overseers, and the men were paid by me. Yet, after working for about one month and a half, the former party went off without settling accounts, and the latter implored to be allowed to give up their contract, as they declared they could not make anything by it. Whether the Roorkee people did gain by their contract, or not, I do not know, but that the contractor from Deyra Doon did not I am certain, for his party was composed of strangers who seeing our people unemployed on Sundays, would not work for him on those days, and during the remainder of the week, they performed less work for him, than our people did for us.[49]

The reaction of the brick contractors need not astonish us. These men were very well able to manipulate the labour market and were fully a match for the British engineers, as the following example shows from the Third Division under Volk at the beginning of 1849.[50] Cautley reports on a section near Bulandshahr, where the abovementioned Sergeant Hawthorne was stationed:

> At the village of Muhmudpoor or between that and Berkhera, excavation has been commenced on a small scale, but – as usual on the commencement of work – the contractors are holding off in the hopes of higher rates, and on my visit I only saw one small party engaged in digging. [...] Contractors always keep in the background at first, in the hopes of obtaining higher rates, small bodies of this class are put forward as feelers, to report on the state of things in the Division, and the probabilities of their being well or ill used, under or overpaid. We are forced moreover to establish a connection between the Divisions so that rates may be regulated agreeably to circumstances, as it is clear that if one Executive Officer gives a higher rate than another, the one giving the lower rate will find himself deserted.

49. James Finn's report of 2 February 1849 to Cautley is to be found in NAI, MB, Proceedings, 25 May 1849, 1281–1286; earlier on, brick contractors with *puzawahs* were the rule (NAI, MB, Proceedings, 23 June 1848, 3635–3636).

50. NAI, MB, Proceedings, 18 May 1849, 890–892.

In this case E. Garstin, an engineer and a member of the Military Board, commented on the rates that according to him were very high: "We must continue to draw this to Major Cautley's ears, in the hope that by degrees it will be lowered as people flock to the work. We must not forget that in this part of the country there are few or no workpeople."

Finn's only alternative for engaging contractors was to employ all moulders directly and to pay them "task wages", which meant, as far as I can see, time wages at Cautley's new rate but with the obligation of a minimal and explicitly defined performance as to the quantity and quality of bricks moulded: "their work is checked every day by the overseers; when it happens that the workmen do not turn out the given number of bricks, they are invariably fined, in proportion to the shortness of their work". At about the same time new machinery was introduced at the brick fields in Roorkee. First one and then more of Hall's horse- and later bullock-drawn brickmaking machines were imported in October 1848. The machines had to be fed with clay and water, whereupon the properly mixed clay was extruded directly into moulds. Each machine required nineteen men to work it. As the new machines could produce 11,000 bricks in a day, the labour productivity of the moulding gangs could be raised to five times what it had been. Overall growth in productivity was naturally less than that because of the cost of the machinery itself, especially of the four bullocks needed to pull the beam of the pug mill.[51] As it happened, only one machine was operative in the season 1848/1849, which meant that some 7 per cent of total production was mechanical and the rest manual.

Against the expectations of the Military Board and Cautley, direct employment as well as the introduction of the machinery caused brick production to be more rather than less costly. In the words of Finn about the commencement of the working season October 1848 to June 1849, written down a year and a half later:

> [...] the brick moulders were the most intractable and troublesome class of men on our works. We had then about 150 moulders employed daily at Roorkee and at Mahewar, and their combined and frequent efforts to evade the doing of a fair day's work, or to extort from us a higher rate of pay, caused much anxiety to all concerned in the manufacture of bricks. If an attempt was made to coerce a moulder, or even if fault was found with the quality or quantity of work performed by one or more of them, the whole would quit working collectively, take their moulds in their hands, and walk to their huts, in spite of all remonstrance. I can well remember, that they served us in this manner twice in one week at Roorkee.[52]

51. Cautley, *Report on the Ganges Canal Works*, vol. 3, p. 10. According to "Building Materials", p. 27, productivity increased only 40 per cent.

52. NAI, MB, Proceedings, 13 June 1850, 2261–2262; cf. Cautley, *Report on the Ganges Canal Works*, vol. 1, p. 91, and vol. 3, pp. 10–12.

These strikes – phase 2 – seem to have been caused by the direct interference of the European overseers, which was much resented by the skilled moulders, accustomed to producing green bricks with their own gang without any interference, except for counting and quality control of the dried bricks by the engineers afterwards. Under the new system of direct employment with task wages, their attempts to maintain a certain degree of independence were not appreciated by Finn or Cautley.

But that was not all, for besides strikes there was obstruction of the machinery by the moulders – phase 3 . Cautley summarized it as follows in his book: "For the first three months, owing probably to the awkwardness of the men employed, it was constantly getting out of order, and considerable interruption to progress was the consequence."[53] He could easily have omitted his "probably" because, in his own words written ten years before, "One great object in the introduction of machines for the purpose of making bricks was to beat down the monopoly of the brick moulders, in whose hands we were placed most completely."[54] And we need have no doubt that at the arrival of Hall's patent pug mill in Roorkee, Cautley, Finn, and assistant Durrant would have crowed about it to any moulder who might have wanted to complain at its presence. They would have spoken too soon.

On Friday 25 October 1848, the third day after the machine had become operational, the beam of the pug mill broke. On Wednesday 30 October work recommenced, but on Saturday 2 November the cistern of the pug mill failed. In January 1849 the same machine was twice out of order and on 8 February the machine gave up altogether and could not be used again before 21 March.[55] January was a bad month anyhow for all concerned, because of heavy rains. About 6 lakhs of *kutcha* bricks were lost, which is one week's work of all the moulders and their mates. Finn reported on 22 February: "The brick making machine turns out a maximum 8,000 bricks a day, but it is perpetually giving trouble by getting out of order, at this moment it is under repair." It seems that the engineers were convinced that none of these problems occurred by accident, but at the same time the culprits were never caught. One of the consequences was that the engineers needed to have recourse to the surrounding villages again to have their bricks moulded and fired.[56]

53. *Ibid.*, vol. 3, pp. 10–14.

54. NAI, MB, Proceedings, 13 June 1850, 2261.

55. NAI, MB, Proceedings, 25 May 1849, 1265. However, Finn was to write in his quarterly report for November 1848 to January 1849: "Hall's Brick making machine has been, for the last quarter nearly steadily at work, without accidents the daily turn out being about 10,500 bricks. Two of Ainslie's Brick making machines have reached Roorkee, from England."(Proceedings, 23 October 1849, 9435.) Ainslie's machines turned out to be worthless and – even more importantly – some years later Hall's machine was no longer in use in Roorkee and all bricks were made by hand again ("Building Materials", p. 26).

56. NAI, MB, Proceedings, 29 June 1849, 3453.

After all this trouble Cautley commented on 22 February 1849: "Mr Finn has much to fight against, contractors to make kutcha [green] bricks won't stay at Roorkhee", allegedly – according to the contractors – because they "cannot get their labourers to work on a Sunday, when the whole of the monthly paid people, and in fact the whole of the Canal Establishment have a holiday at that day".[57] As the following events will show, that seems to be at best a poor explanation for the refusal of the workers to continue under the new conditions, as are Cautley's statements later in his book about "the most intractable and troublesome class of people that were on the works".[58]

That Cautley was well aware of the difficulties involved in wage reductions is clear too from the following phrase in the same letter of 22 February: "The same reduction [of wage rates] ought to be made in carpenters and masons, but it requires some tact to reduce the pay of these people without interrupting progress." All in all, Cautley was still confident because, according to him, from 21 March obstructive behaviour stopped, as "they saw that we could turn out from the machine 11,000 bricks per day, independently of themselves", and the moulders "became the most docile of our people, and after a while, they were glad to receive 6 rupees per month for a full day's work".[59] That rate is remarkable because it was both before that time and afterwards the normal rate for moulders. Is it possible that, after all, Cautley had had to give in on the point of wages not only to the moulders but to the *bildars* too, and that in the end the wage reductions had to be rescinded?[60]

Whatever the case, in a way the worst was still to come – phase 4. When Lieutenant Goodwyn returned from the Punjab at the end of March, as officiating executive engineer in the Northern Division he was met immediately by the moulders. They complained about the wage reduction and reiterated their complaints on 27 March, not only to Goodwyn, but in the evening to Lieutenant Yule as well, but without success because Goodwyn stuck to the rate of the director. On that same evening of 27 March 1849, a fire broke out. Next day, Goodwyn wrote a detailed report

57. NAI, MB, Proceedings, 25 May 1849, 1265.

58. Cautley, *Report on the Ganges Canal Works*, vol. 1, p. 91, and vol. 3, pp. 10–12.

59. NAI, MB, Proceedings, 25 May 1849, 1267; cf. "Brick-making in India", in J.G. Medley (ed.), *Professional Papers on Indian Engineering*, first series, 2 (1865), pp. 137–144, 138: "As is the case with every innovation on the customs of Orientals, a person would find a good deal of friction at first starting, but the people employed should in six weeks' time give no trouble." Against this racial argument see Sabyasachi Bhattacharya, "Cultural and Social Constraints on Technological Innovation and Economic Development: Some Case Studies", *Indian Economic and Social History Review*, 1 (1965), pp. 240–267.

60. F.D.M. Brown, "Brick-making near Roorkee", in J.G. Medley (ed.), *Professional Papers on Indian Engineering*, first series, 4 (1867), pp. 158–165, 160, also gives 6 rupees per month for moulders at the pug mill and 4–5 rupees for the other labourers, as well as 2–3 rupees for the boys.

to the director, from which it is interesting to quote extensively because of its details:[61]

> I regret much to have to report the occurrence of several fires among the thatched sheds of the public works at Roorkee last night. These fires were evidently incendiary and have caused considerable destruction of Government property. Ajuba Chowdry of Mr. Finn's hackeries states that about 9 or 9.30 on the night of the 27th inst. he ran outside Mr. Finn's bullock shed on an alarm of fire being given by a driver, and saw that the North Western shed for the accommodation of carpenters etc. was burning, the thatched roof being in a blaze. That he immediately busied himself and set drivers to work getting the bullocks out of their shed, and whilst so employed discovered that the range of huts occupied by himself and others as dwellings had been fired. He hastened to the spot and was in time to extinguish the flame. Whilst running he saw a man making off in the gloom, but did not pursue him being anxious to put out the fire in his hut. About an half hour after this Mr. Finn's soorkhie sheds was discovered to be in flames and was consumed almost instantaneously. About half past 10 or 11 o'clock the shed used by the sawyers, situated between the Roorkhi Bridge and Government Bungalow was discovered to be in a blaze, and burned with such rapidity, that little could be done beyond drawing away some timbers, which, lying at a moderate distance from the fire, permitted the approach of bildars for that purpose. About 11.30 o'clock the stacks of thatching grass at the South West end of the aqueduct were in a blaze and the incendiary or incendiaries appeared to have crossed the river to have attempted to burn the line of lime sheds along the aqueduct on the Mahewar side. They succeeded in thrusting fire into the thatched roofs of 4 or 5 sheds but as Mr. Parker had stationed men on the look out to frustrate any attempts of this kind, the fires were seen and extinguished before they could spread or do any material damage. About 12 o'clock an attempt was made to burn the shed near the weighing machine within the coffer-dam and so bold were the incendiaries that this was done within 200 yards of the spot where I was in person directing the efforts which were being made to check the conflagration of thatching grass. The fire having been discovered before it burst out in any strength was extinguished without much difficulty. The fire engine had been brought to bear on the burning ruins of the sawyers shed and when the flames were reduced so that no apprehension was entertained for the safety of the Government and private buildings in the vicinity, the engine was taken down the aqueduct to the grass stacks and played on them during the remainder of the night, neatly checking further ravages of the fire. But failing to extinguish it, about daylight it became practicable to commence unstacking the bundles of grass.

For Goodwyn, there was no doubting the cause of these incendiaries, which cost 1088:14:8 rupees plus 385 rupees for Finn's *soorkie* pounding

61. NAI, MB, Proceedings, 6 July 1849, 3757–3766: Goodwyn's report of 28 March and Cautley's comments of 10 April 1849. I do not know what position Yule (Goodwyn's predecessor) had at the First Division at that time.

sheds and one range of outhouses for artisans (the equivalent of the wage reductions for at least 120 *bildars* for one whole season). He wrote:

> I am inclined to think that the cause which has led to this wanton destruction of property has been discontent of the bildars at the rate of wages which they at present receive. On my first appearance on the works after rejoining my appointment and also yesterday I was saluted with sundry complaints on this point as also was Lieut. Yule in the evening. As of course the complainants could not be listened to and as perhaps they had supposed that the higher rate of pay Cos. Rs. 4 – per mensem instead of Cos. Rs. 3:8 – might be reverted to on my return, it is probable that the nearly general dissatisfaction found vent among the leaders of the malcontents by active participation in this outrage, which the remainder either approved of or would take no active steps to prevent. That such was the case is I believe the opinion of all the officers present. The greatest difficulty was in getting the bildars out to work, and unless the incendiaries had been pretty confident of the sympathie [sic] of perhaps the majority of the bildars, I do not think they would have acted as they did after the alarm was given and everyone was on the alert. I am using every exertion to discover the delinquents and have offered a reward of Co. Rs. 200 to anyone who will give information leading to the conviction of one of them.

The only solution Goodwyn had to offer to the director was to

> [...] post one bildar at each thatched shed on the works during the night for the next month. [...] I propose simply excusing them from day work, the bildars acting as chowkeydars and changing the men constantly so that at the expiration of a month, on the discontinuance of the practice of guarding these sheds, no one can fancy himself aggrieved.

On top of these measures Cautley ordered the removal of every grass hut in the neighbourhood of the workshops.

Cautley, as before, tried to minimize the seriousness of the incident and to disassociate it from his wage-rate reductions. He even omitted the entire episode from his book, which does not fail to mention the strikes and the machine-breaking. In his letter to the Military Board of 10 April 1849 he wrote that, according to a semi-official letter of Goodwyn, "the opinion of Mr Finn and others is that the incendiary was a villager, and that the bildars had nothing to say to it, but that it is useless speculating as to how the fires originated". Cautley himself doubled Goodwyn's premium of 200 rupees. In the light of all the events since the beginning of the 1848/1849 brickmaking season we may, without any hesitation, attach much more credence to Goodwyn's than to Cautley's interpretation of the incendiaries of 27 March 1849.

How all those engaged in the labour conflicts of that steamy season came to terms with what had happened is not clear, but it might possibly be significant that Major Proby Cautley fell seriously ill and had to leave for the hills north of Dehra to recover. As early as December 1848 he was afflicted with a fever while making his tour of inspection in the neighbourhood of Meerut on his way to continue his duties on 18 January 1849; a further attack felled him in July, this time for several months.[62] Furthermore, on 1 November 1848 he recommended to the Military Board that they raise the salaries of most specialists on the canal, not only the English ones, but most especially the Indians, such as the head artificers. Without such increases for such men as the treasurer, the head masons, carpenters, and smiths, he deemed it impossible to attract the best people to the service.[63] The *bildars* employed at the machine might have found some blessed oblivion at the Haridwar Fair (10–11 April 1849), when they were allowed two days off, of which one was paid.[64]

At the end of the 1848/1849 season James Finn concentrated on a new adversary, the lime contractors. Whereas during the greater part of that season slaked lime had been delivered by the contractors at 30 rupees per 100 maunds, Finn proved able to reduce the rate to 22:12 rupees in the quarter May–July, which amounted to a saving of 7:4 rupees, or nearly one-quarter of the original rate. In his own words:

> This was effected by my having laid in a large stock of the material from which circumstance I was for the time independent of the old contractors. By inviting new people to take contracts, I created an opposition, and thereby though with an indefinite deal of trouble I broke up the old monopoly which had existed since the time I took charge.

Unfortunately we do not know very much about this trouble, but later on Finn lifted a corner of the veil:

> As our work progressed and competition was engendered, I thought an opportunity offered for getting [the lime] at a reduced rate, and to a certain extent I succeeded in the second season of our operations. In the following year, however, I proceeded too far; I paid no more than 23 rs. 12 a. per 100 maunds; the consequence was, that the supply fell off; contractors would not come forward, and I was reduced to the necessity of advancing the rate by 1 rs. 8 a. per 100 maunds. [...] ever since November 1850 the price of lime has remained fixed at 25 rs. 4 a. per 100 maunds, and I believe this to be a fair rate both for contractors and Government.[65]

62. NAI, MB, Proceedings, 28 August 1849, 6496–6500; *ibid.*, 9 November 1849, 10481, and 18 December 1849, 12575.

63. NAI, MB, Proceedings, 2 November 1849, 10093–10101; cf. also *ibid.*, 18 August 1848, 7500–7501.

64. Cautley, *Report on the Ganges Canal Works*, vol. 3, p. 13. Cf. Basu, "Strikes and 'Communal' Riots", pp. 957–958, for the significance of such festivals for workers and for labour relations; and Bayly, *Rulers, Townsmen and Bazaars*, pp. 127, 159, 184, 280 for the Haridwar Fair.

65. NAI, MB, Proceedings, 5 March 1850, 16488; Cautley, *Report on the Ganges Canal Works*, vol. 3, p. 21.

A price reduction of 25 per cent turned out to be impossible for the lime contractors in the long run, but one of 15 per cent was, apparently, feasible.

In sum, at great cost the engineers seem to have won their position against the moulders for the time being. However, was it worth it? Certainly so at first sight, and that is of course stressed by Finn to Cautley and by Cautley to the members of the Military Board who regarded the high material costs "the disease of the Canal Department". The manufacturing costs of the bricks had indeed been greatly reduced in Roorkee, from 1194:9:2 rupees per lakh on 30 April 1848 to 705:2:7 rupees by 31 July 1849, but Finn himself adds: "It is but fair however to attribute this reduction partly to the introduction of a new system of burning in flame kilns and the present regular order of our brick fields."[66]

None of that had anything to do with moulders' wages and labour relations, and more caveats are warranted before we exult prematurely. To begin with, the real quarterly cost of brick manufacturing in the Northern Division had never been under 900 rupees (including carriage), and during the months under scrutiny were in fact 920 rupees per lakh, as Finn later stated.[67] Further, it is questionable to what extent all relevant costs were charged on the materials account, as Table 4 (p. 77) shows.

Finally, even if we could arrive at more realistic overall costs for the moulding process – which undoubtedly were higher than officially reported by Cautley to his superiors – we must put moulding costs in perspective. As Table 2 (p. 59) shows and as Table 5 (p. 78) reveals in more detail, the impact of the cost of the moulding process on the end result of the manufacturing process was much less important than suggested by all the efforts of the engineers to introduce new labour relations.

Taking all this into consideration, it seems reasonable to conclude that first, production costs of green bricks were rather low in comparison with the cost of fuel and the firing process; second, that labour costs dominated the cost of the moulding process, although we should never forget the cost of damage caused by the labour conflicts; third, that the reduction of moulding costs was achieved mainly by reducing the distance between the digging and tempering sites of the clay and the moulding point rather than by reducing wage rates; finally, that the labour conflict was more about principles than about real costs.

The principles involved touched on the question of the greatest autonomy possible for the workers in organizing their tasks among themselves, when set against the power of the engineers to overrule them. Major Cautley best summarized his self-designated task in the commemorative booklet published to mark the completion of the canal in 1854:

66. NAI, MB, Proceedings, 5 March 1850, 16489–16490.

67. Cautley, *Report on the Ganges Canal Works*, vol. 3, p. 23.

Table 4. *Price of bricks as charged by the Materials Department of the Northern Division to the Works Department of the same Division (including carriage and stacking), 1848–1850*

Period	Rs per lakh	Remarks about items probably excluded
Working season 1847/1848:		
February–April 1848	1,210	Rebuilding of nearly all kilns probably excluded
May–July 1848	1,300	Rebuilding of nearly all kilns probably excluded
Working season 1848/1849:		
August–October 1848	1,150	Purchase and transport of Hall's brickmaking machine almost certainly excluded
November 1848 – January 1849	1,070	Repairs to that same machine probably excluded
February–April 1849	970	Construction of Scinde and flame kilns at Mahewar probably excluded
May–July 1849	920	Purchase and transport of two of Ainslie's machines (2,500 rupees for one machine) certainly excluded; damage by incendiaries (a minimum 1,500 rupees) and posting of night watches certainly excluded
Working season 1849/1850:		
August–October 1849	920	
November 1849 – January 1850	900	Repairs to Ainslie's machines probably excluded
February–April 1850	900	

Sources: Cautley, *Report on the Ganges Canal Works*, vol. 3, Appendix A, esp. p. 23; British Library, London, OIOC, India and Bengal letters received 2 February 1849, Narrative of the Proceedings of the Government of the North Western Provinces, Judicial and Revenue Department, Revenue 30 December 1848 for the 3rd quarter of 1848, p. 71 (price of Ainslie's brickmaking machine).

> [T]hose who execute works of Civil Engineering in countries overflowing with every resource that mechanical skill and individual enterprise can supply [should not] overlook those peculiar difficulties which beset the Engineer's path in India *where his resources are chiefly in himself*, and where he must not only be the designer of works but the head mason, the head carpenter, *the head brick and lime burner*, in fact the man of all detail work, or of all general design.[68]

It is perhaps symbolic of this imposed ideal of British rule that in 1850 a clock tower was erected in the centre of Roorkee, "this item being

68. *Idem*, *Ganges Canal*, p. 21 (italics mine).

Table 5. *Costs of making kutcha or green bricks at the Materials Department of the Northern Division of the Ganges Canal (in rupees).*

Working season	Monthly wages		Cost of green bricks				
	Hand moulders	Assistants	Wages of hand moulders and their assistants	Bullocks, establishment and sundries	Total	Total	
			Per 27,000 green bricks			Per 100,000 green bricks	As % of fired bricks
1847/1848	7	4	35:10:8 (91%)	3:4:0 (9%)	38:14:8 (100%)	143:15:9	11.5
1848/1849	6	4/3:8	28:10:8 (89%)	3:8:0 (11%)	32:2:8 (100%)	119	12.2
1849/1850	6	4	20:10:8 (87%)	3:2:6 (13%)	23:13:2 (100%)	88:4:3	11.3
1850/1851	(6)	N/A	N/A	N/A	N/A	96:9:9	12.4
1851/1852	(6)	N/A	N/A	N/A	N/A	93:13:4	11.6
1852/1853	(6)	N/A	N/A	N/A	N/A	90:7:9	9.9

Source: Cautley, *Report on the Ganges Canal Works*, vol. 3, pp. 8–9, 15–18, 23 (partially reconstructed).

Figure 5. The clock tower erected in the centre of Roorkee in 1850, view from inside the canal workshops. The agstaff on the top has been omitted by the artist.
Proby T. Cautley, Report on the Ganges Canal Works: From Their Commencement until the Opening of the Canal in 1854, *3 vols and one atlas (London, 1860), vol. 2, p. 381.*

indispensable for securing regularity of attendance. A ag staff on the top of this tower, regulates by the rise and fall of its appended ag, the periods for collecting and dismissing the parties on the works between Roorkee and Mahewar."[69]

After all, in later reports, as we have seen, moulders still earned 6 rupees monthly, sometimes even 7, and *bildars*4 rupees, or even 5.[70] Moreover, the perpetrators of violence seem never to have been caught, apparently due to the silent approval of the other workers, such as the rers (who were never reported as taking part in the protests), and the carpenters and other craftsmen, who all had wage reductions to fear – as they must have

69. *Idem,Estimate of the Probable Expense,* p. 71; cf. *idem,Ganges Canal* p. 13 ("clock and tower and sonorous bell").
70. *Idem, Report on the Ganges Canal Works,* vol. 3, p. 121 (data for 1857); "Building Materials", pp. 26–27.

realized all too well. All these facts together make it doubtful whether Cautley really had won his battle.

CONCLUSIONS

All the various collective actions by the brick moulders in Roorkee between September 1848 and March 1849, that is to say during the entire brickmaking season from start to end, must be seen as manifestations of a consistent protest against the reduction of wage rates and the intensification of inspection by the Military Board and its representatives. This long and sustained chain of protests by over a thousand workers does not display the supposedly primitive characteristics of labour protest in India before 1880, which, according to Buchanan and later Sukomal Sen and others, mostly involved short-term work stoppages by none too many labourers, badly organized, and reflecting no class-consciousness.[71]

Of course the material presented here does not allow us to conclude in a straightforward way that the brick moulders in Roorkee had something approaching class-consciousness. On the other hand it certainly does allow us to surmise that they were perfectly aware of what was at stake. As far as the sources permit us to say anything about the consciousness of these men, their dedicated and systematic attempts to change the minds of the engineers to make them reverse the wage reductions do not suggest that they should be relegated to something like "the infantile, blundering and frustrated" peasant rebels in the way characterized by Ranajit Guha.[72] Their consciousness reminds us rather of the men and women engaged in the urban tax, famine, and other revolts of the early nineteenth century, described by Chris Bayly in terms of "guild-type organisations of the artisans and labourers", such as the Muslim weavers of Benares who, in 1813, combined their efforts and used court action in the face of deteriorating economic conditions.[73]

What is the significance of the stories told about the brickmakers' strikes of 1848–1849? Do they represent just a new item to be added to the list of collective labour actions that has been reconstructed from Ian Kerr's

71. Buchanan, *Development of Capitalistic Enterprise,* p. 426; Sen, *Working Class of India,* pp. 70–88.

72. Ranajit Guha, *Elementary Aspects of Peasant Insurgency in Colonial India* (Delhi, 1983), p. 76: "The peasant rebel of colonial India, the infantile, blundering and alas, invariably frustrated, precursor of a democratic revolution in the subcontinent had set out to learn his very first lesson in power, but in this earlier period prior to the emergence of a modern bourgeoisie, an industrial proletariat and advanced ideas of democracy he could do so by translating it backwards into the semi-feudal language of politics to which he was born."

73. Bayly, *Rulers, Townsmen and Bazaars,* p. 313 (quotation); cf. also pp. 295–296, 313–333.

74. Cf. Sjaak van der Velden, "Strikes in Global Labor History: The Dutch Case", *Review,* 26 (2003), pp. 381–405; an early example of Indian strike statistics is to be found in Buchanan, *Development of Capitalistic Enterprise,* p. 428.

work? What if they represent perhaps the first recorded and fully documented strike in Indian labour history? It may be that, in the end, it is indeed only a single building block in a vast collection of strikes that can be analysed statistically, as has been done in other parts of the world.[74] But perhaps it is more. For the moment, the events of 1848–1849 at least meet the requirements which make them important for the development of Indian labour history in the way proposed a few years ago by Dipesh Chakrabarty, when he said:

> [...] one has to look at labour not as labour but as a series of activities embedded in particular histories, in particular practices of embodiment. To my mind it is only when we begin to do these things that Indian labour history will break out of the enduring hold, partly productive and partly unproductive, of European sociological thought on our thinking.[75]

Let us try in the same vein to draw a few more conclusions about the character of this series of labour conflicts.

First, it must be emphasized that the reports on which this narrative is based show a remarkable absence of astonishment, indignation, panic, or disappointment among the British engineers. Their reports are detailed and factual, as the lengthy quotations show. The engineers do not ask for military or other assistance; rather they seem to be confident that they can deal with the matter. That is remarkable because officially, since 1819, labour contracts could be enforced by penal law.[76] However, on the Ganges Canal Works such legal actions seem never to have been seriously considered. Of course Cautley and his executive engineers regretted that losses had to be written off, but neither they, nor their superiors in Calcutta, made much ado about the thousands of rupees lost.[77] On the side of the engineers there was a tradition in dealing with labour unrest which was certainly apparent by 1848, but which was probably much older. If that were the case, would this conclusion hold good too for the labourers at public works in general and for brickmakers there in particular?

Second, if so early a tradition of collective labour protest and action among Indian labourers can feasibly be claimed, how would it have to be characterized? The events of 1848–1849 in Roorkee, if seen as a logical sequence of manifestations of the same labour conflict, cannot be ascribed

75. Dipesh Chakrabarty, *Culture in Working Class History: A Discussion* (Noida, 1998), p. 21.
76. Cautley, *Report on the Ganges Canal Works*, vol. 3, p. 128.
77. Cf. Kerr, *Building the Railways of the Raj*, pp. 180–181, 183, confirms this attitude for 1859 and later. A decade after the strike, Cautley wrote emotionally about the nature of the striking labourers; Cautley, *Report on the Ganges Canal Works*, vol. 3, p. 10.
78. Chandarvarkar, *Imperial Power and Popular Politics*, esp. pp. 147–150. I side with Chandarvarkar in his disagreement here with David Arnold, "Industrial Violence in Colonial India", *Comparative Studies in Society and History*, 22 (1980), pp. 234–255, especially where Arnold asks "How were these rural traditions [of violence] transmitted to modern industry?" (p. 239).

simply to the proneness of Indian workers to spontaneous and violent action. In this regard I completely agree with Chandarvarkar's critique, especially his linking it to discussions about workers' violence in early modern Europe.[78] Kerr's interpretation of the labour unrest at railway building sites as a protest against proletarianization is not convincing – if only because he shows at the same time that large groups of navvies and other labourers at public works had been proletarianized before then.[79] It is the latter group which seems to have been most active in the collective resistance of 1848–1849 at the First Division of the Ganges Canal. Unfortunately, it is much easier to say what is wrong about the interpretation of the collective identity or consciousness of the 1848 strikers than to offer any alternative. However, it seems to me that even those seasonal and therefore possibly part-time labourers understood very well the consequences of changes to their labour conditions and labour relations, understood that collective action was the only appropriate answer, and knew how to apply a whole repertoire of activities in order to defend themselves – to a great extent successfully.

Third, and finally, we come to consider the question of when such workers' collective consciousness first emerged and developed in India, when it increased, slowed down or diminished – at least for these groups of earthworkers, brickmakers, and the like. But it is a question which cannot be answered in the analysis of one strike, although the fact that, first, a detailed study of railway building and, now, an early glimpse at canal building have delivered so many examples of collective labour resistance might imply that more research in this and earlier periods will bring us ever more evidence of workers' consciousness and identity, long before the advent of large factories, and before the building of the railways of the Raj or for that matter canal building; and perhaps even before modern imperialism and colonialism.[80]

That was also realized by J.A.P. Macgregor, one of the members of the Military Board, who wrote in 1830:

> It may not, perhaps, be irrelevant to enquire, under what system were the various public and private works constructed, which are to be found throughout

79. Kerr, *Building the Railways of the Raj*, pp. 90, 171–172. For the professional excavators who for centuries had been engaged in circular labour migration (including "the beldars of Bihar and western Bengal") see Ian J. Kerr, "Free or Unfree? Railway Construction Labour in Nineteenth-Century India", in Tom Brass and Marcel van der Linden (eds), *Free and Unfree Labour: The Debate Continues* (Berne, 1997), pp. 405–426, 414–415.

80. For indications of earlier proletarianization see Bayly, *Rulers, Townsmen and Bazaars*, p. 281; and Shireen Moosvi, "Skilled Labour Migration in Pre-Colonial India, 16th–18th Centuries" (Paper presented to the 19th International Congress of Historical Sciences, Oslo, 6–13 August 2000); cf. also Jan Lucassen, "A Multinational and its Labor Force: the Dutch East India Company, 1595–1795", *International Labour and Working Class History*, 66 (2004), pp. 12–39.

> Hindostan, such as Canals, Roads, Bridges, Tanks, Aqueducts, Temples, Palaces, Mosques, Tombs etc. etc. etc. whether undertaken at the expense of native governments, or of individuals, before the introduction of European skill and capital to India. The answer to this query in all probability would be, that they had been chiefly executed by contractors, under the supervision of Government officials, especially nominated for that purpose. And one need only inspect the masonry of the works above numerated to perceive, that the best description of materials must have been furnished by the contractors of the olden time, since their workmanship may be deemed superior to that of modern builders.[81]

Such an enquiry, especially as to the workers behind these contractors and constructions, is now more welcome than ever before.

81. NAI, MB, Proceedings, 11 May 1830, 327.

On the Move: Circulating Labor in Pre-Colonial, Colonial, and Post-Colonial India*

IAN J. KERR

In 1770 a British official in Madras observed groups composed of men, women, and children who formed "a kind of travelling community of their own under a species of Government peculiar to themselves, with laws and customs which they follow and observe wherever they go".[1] These itinerant, coveted groups of earth and stone workers – "even courted by Princes" – circulated from worksite to worksite where they dug tanks (small reservoirs), ditches, and wells, and built roads and fortifications. They lived close to their worksites in "temporary hutts which they throw up for the occasion, and always chuse a spot distinct from any village, wandering from one place to another as is most convenient".[2]

Circulating labor (a phrase that captures frequent movement better than migrant labor), with a particular but not singular emphasis on construction labor, provides the subject matter of this paper.[3] The paper seeks, spatially, to identify the substantial, pan-Indian presence of circulating workers; temporally, to establish the presence of many such workers in the pre-colonial, early colonial (e.g. 1770 Madras), high colonial (later nineteenth/early twentieth century) and post-colonial periods; and conceptually, to explore how we might situate these workers within the history of India.

* A draft of this paper was presented at the International Workshop, "Towards Global Labour History: New Comparisons", at the V.V. Giri National Labour Institute, New Delhi, November 2005. I am grateful to those whose efforts made the conference a success and my attendance possible. I benefited from helpful critics at the Delhi conference, and from an editor of this collection, Rana Behal. Prasannan Parthasarathi, Niels Brimnes, Adapa Satyanarayana, and Ian Petrie kindly identified useful sources. Katy Hunt provided invaluable assistance. A Social Science and Humanities Research Council (Canada) Standard Research Grant supported my research.

1. British Library, Oriental and India Office Collections [hereafter OIOC], George Paterson, MS Eur.E379/2, "The Paterson Diaries," entry dated 23 November 1770. The diaries cover the years 1769–1775. Paterson, a keen observer, was the secretary to successive East India Company naval commanders-in-chief.

2. OIOC, Paterson Diaries, 23 November 1770.

3. Because migrant labor and itinerant labor are commonly used, I deploy both as rough synonyms for circulating labor. However, I do suggest that migrant labor is not the best label for many of the groups discussed in this paper.

CONCEPTUAL CONSIDERATIONS

A pioneering study of migrant labor in Europe, 1600–1900, stated that "little serious attention" had been paid to migrant workers despite their importance to European labor markets.[4] Various obstacles, the author noted, had hampered the study of migratory labor: one was the fragmentation of migration history into a number of sub-specialties – of which labor migration is one – that weakened the search for more inclusive, integrated understandings of human mobility; another was the limited integration of the recent findings of migration history into more general expressions of historical understanding. Migration history must emerge fully from its specialized ghetto if it is to enrich the more general social, cultural, and economic narratives.[5] The movement across space in the search for employment is the normal condition under which large numbers of people lead their lives. And, on the other side of the coin, many demands for labor power could not have been met without the presence of migrant labor – a situation as true in the twenty-first century as in the preceding centuries.

A distinct sub-grouping within migratory labor is particularly ignored in the European literature. These are the itinerant workers who – like those in Madras in 1770 – practiced ambulatory occupations (including trade and transportation), and who traveled in family groups.[6] Research on this "striking case of migrants [...] has been marginal at best".[7] The same groups, moreover, were marginalized, even criminalized, by the authorities and local inhabitants in the areas through which they moved. They became the quintessential social outsiders, the feared, despised or degraded "others" despite their importance to local economies. Those labeled gypsies were the most severely affected. The historiography has reflected societies' treatment of these groups: their imputed criminality, marginality, and poverty – their "stigmatization" – has preoccupied scholars to the detriment of understanding their important economic functions.[8]

4. Jan Lucassen, *Migrant Labour in Europe 1600–1900: The Drift to the North Sea*, Donald A. Bloch (tr.) (London, 1987), p. 1.

5. My brief summary of the European literature is derived from Jan Lucassen and Leo Lucassen, "Migration, Migration History, History: Old Paradigms and New Perspectives", in Jan Lucassen and Leo Lucassen (eds), *Migration, Migration History, History: Old Paradigms and New Perspectives* (Berne, 1997), pp. 9–38. "State-centrism", "modernization-centrism", and "Euro- or Atlantocentrism" are terms used by the Lucassens.

6. Leo Lucassen, "A Blind Spot: Migratory and Travelling Groups in Western European Historiography", *International Review of Social History*, 38, (1993), pp. 209–235, 210. This article is reprinted in Leo Lucassen, Wim Willems, and Annemarie Cottaar, *Gypsies and Other Itinerant Groups: A Socio-Historical Approach* (Basingstoke, 1998), pp. 135–152.

7. Leo Lucassen, "Eternal Vagrants? State Formation, Migration, and Travelling Groups in Western-Europe, 1350–1914", in Lucassen and Lucassen, *Migration, Migration History, History*, pp. 225–251, 225.

8. *Ibid.*, pp. 225–227.

Thirdly, a set of classificatory concepts – expressed in different historiographical streams and therefore contributory to disciplinary fragmentation – has had a negative impact on the history of migratory labor. These include distinctions between free and unfree migrations, labor migrants versus refugees, the movements of peoples versus the processes whereby migrants become settled in new locations (with the latter often focussing on issues of assimilation, integration, racism and ethnicity), and finally a powerful set of political, temporal and geographical predispositions that limit the quest for more broadly-based, integrated understandings.

The latter include, firstly, "state-centrism" in which migration is seen to be that which occurs across state borders triggered largely by state action and/or constrained or encouraged by state policies. This shunts to the sidelines "voluntary" labor migration, be it within or across state borders. A second predisposition, "modernization-centrism", leads to a focus on migratory labor in industrializing or post-industrial Europe; in short on the period during which the processes of modernization (defined in a certain way) took hold. Since this was also a period of intensified state building, "state-centrism" is intensified, and the connection of migration with more recent and disruptive (much of the migration literature stresses uprooting) socio-economic changes is reinforced. Thus, earlier manifestations of migration in proto-industrial, predominantly agrarian societies with pre-industrial forms of capitalism and different political structures (e.g. city-states, the segmentary states of earlier south India, or territorially vast empires) receive less attention.

Thirdly, there is "Euro-" or "Atlantocentrism", leading to an emphasis on studies of migration in western Europe or across the Atlantic, with the latter encompassing the "voluntary" migrations to North America and parts of Latin America (e.g. Italians to Argentina), and the African slave trade to North America, the West Indies, and Brazil. This third predisposition has lost much of its restraining power in recent years but more spatially encompassing approaches to migration continue to be influenced by state-centric and modernization-centric analyses.[9]

Readers familiar with the literature on migration and migratory labor in the Indian context will recognize the presence of many of the characteristics glossed above. However, this is not a bibliographical essay and space does not permit extensive reference to the good studies that are available. Suffice it to say that fragmentation and inadequate integration into general histories is present. To take but one example: much writing about migration can be found in the diaspora literature which often focuses on

9. The ambitious synthesis by Lydia Potts, *The World Labour Market: A History of Migration*, Terry Bond (tr.) (orig. publ. 1988; London, 1990) testifies to the weakening of "Euro- or Atlantocentrism" and the continued force of "state-centrism".

cultural factors; the same migratory streams studied from economic perspectives often display little familiarity with the diaspora literature, and vice versa. State-centrism, too, is a pronounced predisposition as is modernization-centrism.

The overall result has been a good but skewed understanding of certain categories of circulating labor in colonial and post-colonial India; little understanding of circulating labor in pre-colonial India; virtually no study of the long-term presence of forms of itinerant labor established in the pre-colonial period and continuously present throughout the colonial and post-colonial eras; and, therefore, the near absence from the literature of the large bodies of workers, including construction workers, who populated those ignored worlds of labor. Indeed, if we did not have the distinguished writings of Jan Bremen – writings anchored in post-colonial contexts – joined recently by those of Ravi Ahuja on the early colonial period, circulating labor would be virtually ignored in academic writing.[10]

The focus on rural migration to the industrializing cities – modernization-centrism – emphasizes novelty and discontinuity. The increased presence of migrant labor is attributed to unpleasant changes, uprooting, unleashed in the colonial period that forced people out of their hitherto harmonious, stable, economically supportive, agrarian existences located in the sedentary worlds of thousands of peasant villages. This belief and its imputation of subsequent change (for the better or for the worse depending on one's political stance) to the policies of the colonial administration and the interests of metropolitan and indigenous capitalists dies hard. A central question is not whether colonialism and industrial capitalism affected village India – they did – but what pre-existing conditions they affected.

Indeed, a pervasive myth tied to a powerful ideology works to deny the change and mobility of peoples that characterized pre-colonial India. Modernization-centrism and state-centrism reinforce that myth although few scholars intend such a result. Moreover, the contrary finding of recent research notwithstanding, the myth persists. Ravi Ahuja noted that "recent writings on India's colonial period thus often tend to disconnect its pre-colonial from its colonial past, in order to construct incompatible exogenous and indigenous 'principles' of social organization".[11] The ideal of a harmonious, stable, communitarian Hindu India living in a state of contentment until disrupted by Moslem invasions and British colonialism

10. Jan Bremen, *Of Peasants, Migrants and Paupers: Rural Labour Circulation and Capitalist Production in West India* (Delhi, 1985); *idem*, *Footloose Labour: Working in India's Informal Economy* (Cambridge, 1996); Ravi Ahuja, "Labour Unsettled: Mobility and Protest in the Madras Region, 1750–1800", *Indian Economic and Social History Review* [hereafter *IESHR*], 35 (1998), pp. 381–404; *idem*, "Labour Relations in an Early Colonial Context: Madras, c.1750–1800", *Modern Asian Studies*, 36 (2002), pp. 793–826.

11. Ahuja, "Labour Relations in an Early Colonial Context", p. 793.

is a component of Hindutva ideology. David Ludden writes: "Closure and sedentarism are characteristics of civilization in South Asia that have been formed as knowledge by intellectual and political elites in their competitive pursuit of cultural power."[12]

The pre-colonial, colonial, and post-colonial reality was very different from the sedentary myth. Indians (and other South Asians) were and are mobile. Ludden suggests that "half of the population of India in the eighteenth century" would have been made up of a great variety of mobile people ranging from seasonal migrants to "hunters, herders and transporters" living out their lives in "a terrain of perpetual movement".[13] Even the many inhabitants of the tens of thousands of peasant villages who did (and do) form the majority of the population were not immobilized in their little worlds. Marriage arrangements – and hence kin networks – normally extended beyond the borders of a single village; pilgrimages and periodical fairs (secular, religious and both) drew people out of their villages; itinerant traders and artisans came to villages to sell goods and services; poor peasants and landless laborers found seasonal employment outside their residential village or migrated permanently to nearby or distant places.

Others moved from urban place to urban place. When, for example, the Mughal court moved – as it often did – thousands of hangers-on (servants, artisans, merchants etc.) dependent on imperial patronage, or the support of those the Mughals patronized – moved with them. And what of the extended labor markets for soldiers, and the subsequent mobile life of the soldier, so well described by Dirk Kolff and others?[14] Circulation, not immobility, needs to be "a fairly general framework within which to look at Indian society and the transformations it underwent in the modern period, that is at least from the eighteenth century, if not from an even earlier period".[15]

Circulating labor moves to varied temporal rhythms and across different expanses of space. Even when one excludes the many who travel to work daily and return daily to their residences – they are better conceptualized as commuters ("daily migrants" stretches the meanings of migrant and

12. David Ludden, "History Outside Civilisation and the Mobility of South Asia", *South Asia*, ns 17 (1994), pp. 1–23, 3. Research by an anthropologist like P.K. Misra also gets "ghetto-ized". See P.K. Misra, "The Study of Nomads", in Surajit Chandra Sinha (ed.), *Research Programmes on Cultural Anthropology and Allied Disciplines* (Calcutta, 1970), pp. 151–197.

13. David Ludden, "Caste Society and Units of Production in Early-Modern South India", in Burton Stein and Sanjay Subrahmanyam (eds), *Institutions and Economic Change in South Asia* (Delhi, 1996), pp. 105–133, 109.

14. Dirk H.A. Kolff, *Naukar, Rajput & Sepoy: The Ethnohistory of the Military Labour Market in Hindustan, 1450–1850* (Cambridge, 1990).

15. Claude Markovits, Jacques Pouchepadass, and Sanjay Subrahmanyam, "Introduction: Circulation and Society under Colonial Rule", in *idem* (eds), *Society and Circulation: Mobile People and Itinerant Cultures in South Asia 1750–1950* (Delhi, 2003), pp. 1–22, 3.

migration) – one is left with large numbers whose search for employment requires longer-term circulation. Another important variable is who migrates? A male head of household only? An unmarried male? A female only (as in some labor markets for domestics or sex workers – although sex workers are not necessarily female)? An entire family or even larger units joined by ties of residential propinquity, kinship, friendship, or all three? Moreover, migrations are sometimes staggered: first, the male head of household, then his family, and later other kinfolk. The causative push-pull factors and the legal and regulatory frameworks within which migration takes place are equally complicated.

Some of the differences have been touched upon in the paragraphs above. The differences are many and their different combinations make for a complicated matrix of possibilities. The possibilities include, for example, at the end points of many continuums the (a) permanent departure of a single male from a previously fixed abode in India to a specific, permanent place in a distant part of the globe, to (b) frequent movement from worksite to worksite within an Indian region of a family comprised of father, mother, and children embedded in a larger circulating group of similar workers belonging to the same caste or tribe.

More published research may make it possible to construct a useful taxonomy of the types of South Asian migrant labor and the causes and conditions of its movements. However, exercises in overly detailed classification can lead to formal, sterile analyses, so the good sense to know when such efforts reduce rather than enhance understanding of complex, dynamic situations will be needed. Regardless, we are a considerable distance from any such effort: too much is still unknown about many forms of migrant labor in India during the past 500 years – and since 1500 is not particularly consequential in this matter, why not the past 1,000 years. Until we know a good deal more we cannot write with authority about the ways in which migrant labor and laboring has – or has not – changed in India from pre-colonial to post-colonial times.

For now, it suffices to distinguish between those who commute to work, those who migrate to find work, and those who are itinerant and circulate for much of their lives. Even within these simple divisions, however, boundaries are blurred. Itinerants usually travel in family groups (often as part of larger collectivities of families) since, to be truly itinerant, there can be no place called home where other family members remain. However, others among the migrant workers may also travel in family units to a place of employment where they will remain for many months or longer. Thanks to the monsoon-induced rainy season, there is a pronounced seasonality to much outdoor construction work in India.

The remainder of this paper focuses on some of the inadequately studied, often numerous, economically important bodies of workers whose existences as itinerant laborers can be traced from pre-colonial to colonial to post-colonial times. Construction workers made up a sizeable fraction of circulating labor (although not all construction workers circulated – many were commuters) but they were by no means the only participants.[16]

CIRCULATING LABOR: THE BANJARAS

One of the most eye-catching of the circulating groups was the Banjaras.[17] Their main occupation was to transport bulk commodities – they were the common carrier of pre- and early colonial times although they did engage in other occupations including cattle dealing. Huge herds of Banjara bullocks moved salt, sugar, corn, and rice across the sub-continent. A Banjara *qafila* (caravan) often contained 10,000 or more bullocks, each bullock laden with 250–350lb of goods. Journeys up to 2,000 miles were undertaken. Most Banjaras had no fixed home. The life of the men, women and children of the *qafilas* was that of travel from one daily encampment to the next as the bullocks progressed at roughly 10 miles per day. Most Banjaras, except for the young and the infirm, walked alongside the animals.

Banjaras were present in India from early times.[18] They flourished in the Sultanate and Mughal period – from the north-west deep into the Deccan – because, in those centuries of widespread military campaigning, they came to transport crucial supplies to armies in the field. Instead of maintaining a costly, standing commissariat the sultans and Mughal emperors hired Banjaras. Once hired – and they were astute bargainers – the hundreds of *tandas* (camps – the macro unit headed by a chief, a *naik*, into which Banjaras were divided; the *naik* bargained for the *tanda* and enforced tribal laws; individual Banjara families owned the bullocks; some *tandas* were Hindu, others Moslem) were faithful to their contracts and, because of their indispensable services, usually permitted unimpeded passage across India.[19] However, in the event a *qafila* was attacked the well-armed Banjaras defended themselves vigorously.

Tightened, more widespread British control over India in the early decades of the nineteenth century marked the beginning of the end of six

16. Weavers also moved in the search for better economic opportunities. See Douglas E. Haynes and Tirthankar Roy, "Conceiving Mobility: Weavers' Migrations in Pre-Colonial and Colonial India", *IESHR*, 36 (January–March 1999), pp. 35–67.

17. My account is based on Robert G. Varady, "North Indian Banjaras: Their Evolution as Transporters", *South Asia: Journal of South Asian Studies*, ns 2 (1979), pp. 1–18; and Laxman D. Satya, "Colonial Sedentarisation and Subjugation: The Case of the Banjaras of Berar 1850–1900", *Journal of Peasant Studies*, 24 (1997), pp. 314–336.

18. Romila Thapar, *Early India From the Origins to AD 1300* (Berkeley, CA, 2002), p. 459.

19. *Banjaras* were migrant workers providing transportation services. However, they were not wage-laborers but rather groups of cooperating families with shared cultural traits, most of whom owned their means of production.

centuries of Banjara success as transporters. Colonial authorities increasingly sought to control and to settle the wide-ranging, armed, independent Banjaras and similarly peripatetic groups.[20] The colonial authorities, in fact, wanted a sedentary, peasant India. The next 150 years saw the Banjaras struggle to survive and adapt. Railways, the great technology handmaiden of industrial capitalism and the instrument of a strengthened colonial state, opened in India from 1853 onwards and reached a tentacular 23,627 route miles in 1900, largely ended the Banjaras' role as long-distance, bulk commodity transporters.

Ironically, in western India, Banjaras (regionally *Vanjaris*) in and around Bombay came to have a major presence among those who worked as railway station porters.[21] Driven out of their role as transporters and into marginal farming, the men then migrated to Bombay in the search of work (albeit, like many other such groups, retaining links to the land and often leaving their families in the villages).

Some Banjaras turned to criminal activity thus intensifying the tendency of colonial authorities to brand them, collectively, a criminal tribe. Others focussed more on what had always been a subsidiary Banjara enterprise, the cattle trade, by driving their herds to local *melas* (fairs) where they bought and sold livestock. Some settled down at fixed locations where they engaged in cattle grazing and agricultural pursuits, perhaps mixed with some cattle dealing.

A later development (1950s) in the area of motorized road transport gave some Banjaras new opportunities in the business of cattle dealing. The advent in India of the long platform lorry (previous lorries were too small to be useful to the Banjaras) enabled enterprising Banjaras to transport twenty or so bullocks or twenty-five to thirty calves a couple of hundred miles in one day. Quick, flexible, direct fair to fair transport of cattle had become possible and profitable so, with bullock power still essential to the agrarian economy and *melas* the main loci of cattle dealing, some Banjaras successfully continue in the cattle business. However, now the men ride the lorries. They complain about the amount of time they spend away from their families and remember nostalgically the days when they accompanied their herds on foot.[22] If we developed a complex categorization of circulating work, the lorry-riding Banjara would have to be located at a different spot on the matrix from either his cattle-dealing early twentieth-century ancestors or his eighteenth-century ancestors who

20. Satya, "Colonial Sedentarisation", pp. 314–336, stresses this theme. Also see the wider-ranging, more-nuanced contribution by Radhika Singha, "Settle, Mobilize, Verify: Identification Practices in Colonial India", *Studies in History*, ns 16 (2000), pp. 151–198.

21. Dennis Weitering, "Carrying the Load Together: Mumbai Railway Coolies and their Quest for Labour, Income and Social Security", (M.A., University of Nijmegen, 2003), pp. 48–52.

22. Varady, "North Indian Banjaras", p. 11.

manned the great *qafilas*. The forms and content of such work change over time

The Banjaras were kept amused during their long journeys by accompanying conjurors, astrologers, jugglers, musicians, and entertainers with dancing bears and trained monkeys.[23] This reminds us just how diverse the occupations of migrant labor were in India. Some people provided goods and services essential to the economies of which they were a part; others, no less mobile, provided entertainment and other activities that formed an integral part of the rich tapestry of daily life and popular cultures.

Neeladri Bhattacharya provides a fine description of the "vast network of peddling trade" in colonial Punjab extending across the North-West Frontier.[24] Although dominated by Labanas, Khojas, and Banjaras, this network included others who forged the multiple links along which flowed the goods and services that connected villages, towns, and cities over extended distances. Different communities were associated with particular activities but "the boundaries were permeable, the identities multiple and intertwined". "Tramping entertainers and specialists were an intimate part of village life, supplying villagers with their ritual and cultural needs, with entertainment, news and rumours."[25]

Acrobats, blacksmiths, genealogists, goldsmiths, Khaswalas (sellers of brushes and ropes made of grass), musicians, and Qalandars with their trained monkeys, plus many others, were parts of the vibrant, mobile mix. As Servan-Schreiber reminds us:

> Across a wide swathe of roads in northern India, wandering castes of Bhojpuri singers earn their living even today [early twenty-first century] by performing and singing a variety of tales and songs. Gorakhpanthi ascetics dressed in the ochre garb, Nat dancers with long hair and wearing skirts like women, Noniya singers formerly attached to saltpetre manufactures, Madari Sufis holding the green banner of Islam to receive their alms, and Teli singers accompanying caravans towards the Nepal Terai, all continue to travel either alone or in small groups, instruments in hand.[26]

CONSTRUCTION: PRE-COLONIAL AND COLONIAL

However, numerous among the migrant workers from deep into the pre-colonial period to the twenty-first century were those engaged in

23. *Ibid.*, p. 4 and n. 35.
24. Neeladri Bhattacharya, "Predicaments of Mobility: Peddlers and Itinerants in Nineteenth-Century Northwestern India", in Markovits, Pouchepadass, and Subrahmanyam, *Society and Circulation*, pp. 163–214, 168.
25. *Ibid.*, p. 168.
26. Catherine Servan-Schreiber, "Tellers of Tales, Sellers of Tales: Bhojpuri Peddlers in Northern India", in Markovits, Pouchepadass, and Subrahmanyam, *Society and Circulation*, pp. 275–305, 275–276.

construction work. Quite likely, in fact, they were the most numerous, given the ubiquity of construction work. They migrated within rural India, from rural to urban areas and vice versa, as well as from urban area to urban area. An important feature of construction-type work is that it occurs everywhere and continually, albeit time-limited where any specific project is concerned. Lifetime work at a specific construction site rarely occurs although a worker, occasionally, might find a lifetime of work within commuting distance of his or her residence.

This large body of workers was not a homogenous group – no more so than the multiple kinds of things they built (compare, at the extremes, the construction of a small reservoir with the building of the Taj Mahal; or a road in rural Punjab with the city of Chandigarh). Many occupations and many castes or tribes (or possessors of other cultural signifiers) engaged in construction work and they migrated to worksites over different distances, according to different temporal rhythms, individually or in differently sized and differently composed social units. Indeed, many who worked in construction did so as commuters.

In Mughal times, as in later times, the workers and artisans collected at a construction site (construction of Akbar's Fort at Agra required 3,000 to 4,000 artisans, laborers, and functionaries daily) were "both local and those brought from different regions of the country".[27] Highly skilled artisans were part of the construction workforce as were women and children who carried earth in little baskets on their heads from borrow pit to tip. Mughal paintings "help us to identify skilled and non-skilled labour: the latter, often scantily clothed, run about doing sundry jobs".[28] Women laborers appear in Mughal paintings but not children, although we know children were present at construction sites in the nineteenth century.

An important grouping among those engaged in construction was the workers in earth and stone like those described in Madras in 1770. Similar groups existed throughout India but they were not identical, despite sharing a similar niche in the labor market and a mobile life style. The different socio-cultural groups of earth-workers tended to be broadly regional in their ambulatory patterns: for example Odhs in the Punjab, Nuniyas in the central Gangetic valley, Oddar in southern and western India. The latter, with names specific to the regional languages of the south and west (e.g. Vaddar in Kannada) were known generically to the British as Wudders. Likely originating in Telegu speaking parts of the Deccan south, they were most probably the workers seen by Paterson in 1770.

We know, too, that some communities in the grouping (quite likely most) had a history that extended deep into India's past. One finds

27. Ahsan Jan Qaisar, *Building Construction in Mughal India: The Evidence From Painting* (Delhi, 1988), p. 11.
28. *Ibid.*, p. 12.

speculation in the Eliot manuscripts that Vaddars – referred to as a "numerous and widely spread Caste" may have been Buddhists in the eleventh century.[29] And, dating from the same century, we have a specific story about a foundation victim (the need to have a human sacrifice to ensure the permanence of a building or the embankment of a reservoir) that states that Raja Jayasinha Siddharaja, (who ruled the Caulukya kingdom located in Gujerat/southern Rajasthan, also know as the Solankis of Anahilapataka, i.e. Patan, from 1094–1143) abducted "a woman of the Od or navvy caste, but she cursed him that his lake at Patan should never hold water, and it never did until Mayo, a Dheda scavenger, was sacrificed".[30] Tradition places the arrival of itinerant earth-working communities in south India, in and around Madurai, to the Nayaka kingdoms established in the late sixteenth century after the break-up of the great Vijayanagara dynasty.[31]

Paterson, we know, testified to the considerable presence of nomadic earth-workers in Madras in the 1770s. He labeled them a "particular cast [*sic*] of people called Tank diggers" thus indicating one of their main activities in south India where, especially in the dryer Deccan interior, water storage was a major concern. He mentions groups as large as 2000 men, women and children whose

> [...] sole business is to dig Tanks, Ditches, Wells, carry Earth, work in Gardens, on Fortifications etc. Their only instruments are a Mamotty (a broad kind of hoe with a short handle) and a basket. And as they excell in this kind of work, one doing more than three or four Coolies, they are much sought after and even courted by Princes to remain in their Country.[32]

When John Sullivan wrote to the East India Company Court of Directors on 3 February 1779 about a canal to permit water to flow from the Krishna and Godaveri Rivers into the Cauvery River he argued it would not – as some feared – draw laboring people too much from cultivation because of a "peculiar institution" among the Hindus whereby a group "of great numbers" and "peculiar robustness" separate "from all other orders of the Society" dug canals.[33] Sullivan said these people were known by the "name expressive of their occupation (Tank Diggers) [...]" and that they had no fixed residence but wandered about with their

29. OIOC, MS Eur. D317, Eliot Manuscript, pp. 211–213.
30. William Crooke, *Religion & Folklore of Northern India*, prepared for the press by R.E. Enthoven (new edn, New Delhi, 1926), p. 110.
31. J.H. Nelson, *The Madura Country: A Manual Compiled by Order of the Madras Government* (Madras, 1868), Pt 2: "Ethnology, Fauna and Flora", p. 88.
32. OIOC, Paterson Diaries, 23 November 1770, p. 98.
33. OIOC, Mackenzie Collection: General, vol. 59: Water Works in the Carnatic, "Appendix to the Memoir on Watering the Circars", by Alexander Dalrymple (London, 1793) in which a long extract from Sullivan's letter is found plus Dalrymple's comments.

families in search of work. Alexander Dalrymple reproduced and commented on Sullivan's letter in 1793. Dalrymple recounted his experience on the works of Fort St George (at Madras) in 1756 where "multitudes" were employed to argue Sullivan was "mistaken in supposing all other are by caste excluded from the labour of removing earth".

It was an important correction. The nomadically inclined groups like the Wudders were never the only earth-workers; indeed, they were rarely the majority at the many big construction projects undertaken from the 1840s onwards. Dalrymple stated that an argument for the proposed canal was the vast numbers it would employ – numbers, he implied, that would include general laborers from the immediate locality in addition to the nomadic groups. One suspects that throughout the eighteenth, nineteenth, and part of the twentieth centuries the circulating groups acted as pacesetters whose effectiveness as earth-movers set the standards by which employers established payment rates for earth-work. To re-emphasize an important point: construction work usually employed many whose sole or main occupation was not construction. Construction work was a fluid category ill-suited to the subsequent enumerative practices of colonial or post-colonial census takers who consistently understated the numbers involved.

Subsequent descriptions of earth-working groups are similar to those provided in the late eighteenth century. Substantial numbers, nomadism, a preference for contracted piece-work negotiated by a headman on behalf of the group, community cohesion and the internal enforcement of community norms and values including, according to Paterson, decapitation by the mamotty for serious crimes, collective work by men, women, and children using the simplest of tools, and the fact that these groups moved earth much more effectively than ordinary laborers find repeated description.

In the first decade of the nineteenth century, the keen observer Francis Buchanan encountered similar groups during his travels across Mysore, Kanara, and Malabar. He called them "Woddas, or Woddaru [...] a tribe of Telinga origin" who retained the Telegu language despite their presence throughout Tamil- and Kannada-speaking areas.[34] Buchanan's description deserves extended reproduction because it raises issues important to the discussion pursued in this paper. It is, moreover, the most fulsome of the early ethnographies and, since it was read by later observers, an influence on their perceptions of the Wudders and similar groups.[35]

34. Francis Buchanan, *A Journey From Madras Through the Countries of Mysore, Canara, and Malabar*, 3 vols (London, 1807), vol. 1, p. 310. Most writers hold that the Wudders originated in Telegu-speaking areas although some suggest they moved to what is now Andhra from places in what is now Orissa.

35. *Ibid.*, pp. 310–311.

> They dig canals, wells and tanks; build dams and reservoirs; make roads; and trade in salt, and grain. Some of them are farmers, but they never hire themselves out as *Batiguru*, or servants employed in agriculture. Some of them build mud-houses; but this is not a proper occupation for persons of their cast [*sic*]. The old and infirm live in huts near villages; and dig and repair tanks, or wells, or perform other such labour; while the vigorous youth of both sexes travel about in caravans with oxen and asses, in pursuit of trade. In these caravans they carry with them all their infants, and their huts, which latter consist of a few sticks and mats. They follow armies to supply them with grain, and in time of peace take to the lower *Carnatic* grain, *Jagory*, and tamarinds, and bring up salt. In *Hyder's* government they were very numerous; but, having been forced by *Tippoo* to work at his forts without adequate pay, a great number of them retired to other countries. As they are a very useful set of people, they are now encouraged, and are fast returning. There are no distinctions among them that prevent intermarriages, or eating in common.

Buchanan continues with a description of the customary practices of the Wudders, including simple marriage ceremonies, the presence of a modest bride-price, eating all meat except carrion, drinking spirituous liquors, burial rather than cremation of the dead, a claim to being pure *Sudras*, and a Vaishnava faith – a description similar in general outline, if not always in specific detail, to many subsequent accounts of the Wudders.

The subsequent accounts did not represent the construction of an "ideal" discourse about an unchanging, stereotypical earth-working group divorced from actual observation. Later writers (many of whom had read Buchanan) in the gazetteers, the census reports, and the distillation of much from those into the multi-volume, early twentieth-century handbooks of castes and tribes often engaged in their own direct observation and enumeration (the writers often had field experience as administrators or other colonial postings). Nonetheless, some distillation and essentializing took place. Used suggestively and not proscriptively, the essentialized fierceness of lions, cleverly used by Edward Said to illustrate the construction of powerful discourses, can be used to understand how, with each iteration, the distinctive characteristics of the Wudders as nomadic "others" got reinforced.[36]

The foundational account by Buchanan, however, is striking for its portrayal of occupational and generational fluidity among the Wudders. The old and infirm were not itinerant; the Wudders were earth-workers and traders – indeed, in parts of Buchanan's description, they seem more like Banjaras; and the Wudders as a whole showed little internal differentiation and no barriers to intermarriage. Bhattacharya's assessment quoted above deserves repeating: different communities were associated

36. Edward Said, *Orientalism* (New York, 1979), pp. 93–94.

with particular activities but "the boundaries were permeable, the identities multiple and intertwined" [37]

STIGMATIZATION

Later accounts became more judgmental and more inclined to place Wudders – and similar groups – into less permeable but more internally differentiated categories. Nelson, writing in 1868, refers to them as strong and hard-working but also "drunken, gluttonous and vicious".[38] He said Wudders could not be trusted, since they sometimes took advances from half a dozen employers in one week and worked for none of them if they could. The 1885 *Poona District Gazetteer* refers to itinerant Vadars (significantly classified under the sub-heading "unsettled tribes"), likely of Telegu extraction, who entered the area in the 1850s and who were divided into three divisions: Gadi-vadars or cartmen, Jate-vadars or grindstone men, and Mati-vadars or quarrymen. Members of the three divisions could eat together but did not intermarry.[39] By the time Edgar Thurston published (1909) his monumental compendium *Castes and Tribes of Southern India*, the Odde, the Tamil name Thurston uses for his Wudder entry – with other regional names used within the entry – the Kallu Vaddas (stone-workers and builders) considered themselves superior to Mannu Vaddas (earth-workers) with whom they would neither intermarry nor eat – at least in Mysore.[40] The colonial gaze with its instrumental need for classification and enumeration went on to divide the Vaddas into twenty-three exogamous septs.[41]

Thurston's material also includes the presence among the Wudders of groups that had taken to "crime as a profession" and who had become "skillful burglars and inveterate robbers".[42] Stone Wudders were chiefly represented because, as builders and stone-cutters, they went about "under the pretence of mending grindstones" during which they "obtain much

37. Bhattacharya, "Predicaments of Mobility", p. 168. Satya, "Colonial Sedentarisation", pp. 314–336 makes similar observations about the pre- and early colonial *Banjaras.*

38. Nelson, *The Madura Country*, p. 88.

39. *Gazetteer of the Bombay Presidency*, 17, Pt 1: Poona (Bombay, 1885), pp. 426–428. They were called "excellent workers, almost always working by the piece", but also "poor" and not inclined to take to "new pursuits".

40. Edgar Thurston, assisted by K. Rangachari, *Castes and Tribes of Southern India*, 6 vols (Madras, 1909), vol. 5, pp. 422–436. The Wudders have been studied by Chandrashekhar Bhat, *Ethnicity and Mobility: Emerging Ethnic Identity and Social Mobility among the Waddars of South India* (New Delhi, 1984). His book draws upon some of the sources I use. It also provides a case study of a Waddar settlement in Karnataka (started in the mid 1940s) and the processes of Wudder sedentarization and upward social mobility.

41. Bernard S. Cohn, *Colonialism and its Forms of Knowledge: The British in India* (Delhi, 1997) explores the processes of classification and enumeration.

42. Thurston, *Castes and Tribes*, p. 434.

useful information as to the houses to be looted or parties of travellers to be attacked".[43] By the early twentieth century Wudders also had begun to appear in manuals describing what the authorities labeled – as a legal category subject to special rules – criminal castes and tribes.[44] The socially distinctive tribes of India had, since early times, an ambivalent relationship with Hindu caste-societies (which, to repeat, were not homogenous, monolithic, and static). They were distinct but they were also in continual interaction with settled caste societies: indeed, as itinerant groups, they moved in the interstices between those settled groups to whom they provided crucial goods and services. "As the 'Other' they also defined the 'Self' and were categorically considered culturally inferior, though not always oppressed."[45]

T.N. Atre captured well the important yet marginalized and stigmatized roles nomadic groups played in the lives of Maharastrian villagers in the late nineteenth and early twentieth century. His *Gaav Gada*, published in 1912 in Marathi and translated into English (2000), includes a chapter on "The Nomads".[46] Atre identified regular visitors to a village, usually at harvest time, whom he labels *vatandars*. They usually had a fixed schedule and maintained "themselves either by selling their wares, doing odd jobs, or by begging". *Vatandars* were contrasted to "wanderers who do not necessarily stick to any traditional schedule" whom he labels "*uplani* or outsiders". He then goes on to describe in considerable detail the many groups that fit within his two categories. He states that many know "some art or form of entertainment" but "if one pulls the veil aside a little, one would be convinced that their main object is begging and thereafter cheating, deceit, theft and in some cases clandestine sexual relations".

Earth-working Wudders (*uplani*) traveling in groups of five to fifteen families were among those Atre described. They settled on the village outskirts in grass-covered tents along with their donkeys, sheep, and goats. They took contracts from the engineers but the women and children also begged in the villages. They also sold the same stone articles as the *beldars* – an example of the permeable categories mentioned earlier. Atre calls some sub-castes of Wudders criminals and describes their illegal activities and methods of operation. Indeed, much of his chapter on "The Nomads" is devoted to stigmatization, to the discussion of the criminal behavior of

43. *Ibid.*

44. The Criminal Tribes of India Series, No. 1: Rai Bahadur M. Pauparao Naidu, *The History of Railway Thieves With Illustrations & Hints on Detection* (4th edn, Madras, 1915), pp. 119–144.

45. Aloka Parasher-Sen, "Introduction", in *idem* (ed.), *Subordinate and Marginal Groups in Early India* (New Delhi, 2004), p. 5. Parasher-Sen includes tribes and foreigners among the "outsiders"; Satya, "Colonial Sedentarisation", provides a more harmonious picture of villager/nomad relationships, at least where Berar and the Banjaras was concerned.

46. T.N. Atre, *The Village Cart*; a translation of T.N. Atre's *Gaav Gada* by Ram Deshmukh (Mumbai, 2000). Nomads are covered in ch. 6, pp. 118–138. All quotations are from this chapter.

the migrant groups. He concludes by advocating the active use of colonial laws and police powers to control the nomads. Atre, it should be noted, served in the colonial administration as a low-level revenue officer and then as a sub-judge.

The colonial authorities did seek to marginalize, compartmentalize, and criminalize itinerant groups like the Banjaras and the Wudders. Surveillance of their activities was increased and regulatory and legal mechanisms instituted to control them. If many itinerant groups had an ambivalent but accepted role in pre-colonial India, the state-centrism and anxieties (after all, the alien few ruled the indigenous many) of the colonial authorities fostered a less accommodative view. Itinerant groups came to be seen as threats, actual or potential, to social stability and regime security. Traditional patterns of circulation came to be seen as a "radical contestation of colonial rule".[47] Sedentary subjects were more easily controlled: the myth of sedentary, immobile India was partially created out of the emergent realities and ideologies of the high colonial period. The itinerant "Others" were marginalized, stereotyped, and then stigmatized in ways that paralleled the repressive treatment of vagrant groups in Europe detailed by Leo Lucassen.[48] Those considered particularly threatening were collectively designated criminal tribes and castes and brought under the draconian provisions of the Criminal Tribes Act (Act XVII of 1871).[49]

The authorities placed some Wudder sub-groups on the list of criminal tribes. Some of these, in turn, entered the ethnographic literature as Donga Wuddiwars "or [literally] thieving Wudders, from their fact of their having taken to crime as a profession".[50] Police at the Kolar Gold Field reported in 1913–1914, and again in 1915–1916, that close watch had been kept on the movements of criminal gangs with "thieving proclivities" such as the Wudders and the Korachars.[51] Later classificatory schemes such as those of scheduled castes and tribes initiated in 1935 found the Wuddurs in Mysore State listed among the scheduled castes, while in other jurisdictions they were considered criminal tribes. The classificatory confusion continued in post-colonial India where, in some areas, Wuddurs were

47. Arnaud Sauli, "Circulation and Authority: Police, Public Space and Territorial Control in Punjab, 1861–1920", in Markovits, Pouchepadass, and Subrahmanyam, *Society and Circulation*, pp. 215–239, 216.

48. Lucassen, "Eternal Vagrants", esp. pp. 225–227, 240–248.

49. See, as one example from a growing literature, Sanjay Nigam, "Disciplining and Policing the 'Criminals by Birth'", Pt 1: "The Making of a Colonial Stereotype – The Criminal Tribes and Castes of North India"; Pt 2: "The Development of a Disciplinary System, 1871–1900", *IESHR*, 27 (1990), pp. 131–164, 257–287.

50. Thurston, *Castes and Tribes*, p. 434.

51. Mysore Geological Department, *Report of the Chief Inspector of Mines for the Year 1915–16* with statistics for the calendar year 1915 (Bangalore, 1918), p. 24.

designated a criminal and wandering tribe, in other areas a backward and depressed class, and in yet other areas an untouchable and depressed caste.[52] A section of the earth-working Oudhia (Odh) caste in North India also found themselves listed among the so-called criminal tribes.[53] Neither the fondness for classification nor the notion of collective criminality disappeared in 1947.

However, to return to Thurston and to the issues of migrant labor and occupational niches: his sources attest to the variety of occupations in which early twentieth-century Wudders were involved. Those included felling trees in the forested hills of the Kurnool district from which their bullocks dragged the timber. Significantly, some Wudders were reported to have settled permanently on the outskirts of large towns where men and women found jobs as sweepers in sanitation and conservancy activities. Others had found work in the Mysore manganese mines. Nonetheless, varieties of construction work continued to be most favored. Finally, Thurston quotes with approval a comment about British navvies. They were, he wrote, largely unknowns who risked their lives to construct the facilities upon which "modern civilized life largely depend" and whose "claim on our sympathies is universal". These remarks, he states, "apply with equal force to the Oddes, who numbered 498,388 in the Madras Presidency at the census, 1901".[54] He did not add that in the case of the Wudders, "civilized life" was equally indebted to the labor of women and children.

THE HIGH COLONIAL PERIOD

The high colonial period witnessed an explosive increase in the demand for construction labor of all kinds. Across India, the 1891 Census enumerated 110,142 involved in the production of building materials but considered that number to be an understatement because, among other reasons, many engaged in brick-burning returned themselves as potters, their traditional caste occupation. 1,027,597 were returned as "artificers in building". Those involved in "earth-work &c" numbered 1,647,710. These numbers total 2,785,449: a considerable number but too small, since some among the 23,820,277 returned as "general labour" (primarily unskilled agricultural laborers according to the Census), found their way into construction work – if only temporarily on projects near to their places of residence.[55]

Earth-workers were required in huge numbers for large-scale canal and

52. Bhat, *Ethnicity and Mobility*, pp. 36–38.

53. Stephen Fuchs, *At the Bottom of Indian Society: The Harijan and Other Low Castes* (New Delhi, 1981), p. 57.

54. Thurston, *Castes and Tribes*, pp. 435–436.

55. *General Report on the Census of India, 1891* (London, 1893), esp. pp. 103–112.

reservoir building – the massive Ganges canal was begun in the 1840s – and the subsequent century witnessed a series of large hydraulic projects in many parts of India ranging from the canals and canal colonies of the Punjab to the Krishnarajasagar dam in Mysore. Similarly, the lengthy construction of New Delhi (c.1912–c.1935) as the capital of the British Indian Empire required large numbers of earth-workers and more skilled construction workers (notably masons but also electricians, plumbers, and other skilled trades).

22,000 laborers were employed on the new capital in April of 1914 and 1915, and 30,000 in 1929.[56] Some 13,300 artisans and workmen were enumerated in New Delhi and 60,000 in old Delhi at the 1931 Census.[57] How many counted in old Delhi were employed in New Delhi is unknown, but some clearly were.[58] 9,000 men, women and children (all but the younger children worked) were housed in the coolie camp at Safdar Jang and the rest were in camps scattered throughout the area.[59] The mud, thatched-roof huts in the camps were described as "unfit for human habitation".[60] Pay and working conditions could be deplorable. One member of the RLC found an emaciated, naked 11-year-old boy working for 2 annas a day.[61]

The substantial but fluctuating supply and demand for construction workers for New Delhi was met primarily by people who migrated from Bikanir and Rajasthan. Skilled workers, however, came from across North India.[62] Initially, much of the migration of the unskilled workers was seasonal with many returning to their villages as the agricultural cycle dictated. However, increasing numbers made Delhi their permanent home and seasonal or other forms of circulation gave way to residence in or near Delhi. This, however, created a problem in the late 1920s and early 1930s when the major public works required for the new capital were completed and the demand for construction workers slackened. Unemployment grew and wages, never generous, were lowered.[63]

Figures 1a and 1b opposite provide a fascinating glimpse of the latter stages of the construction of monumental New Delhi. The photographs show the laying of the topmost stone on the crown finial of the North Block of the Secretariat on 30 September 1927. Masons, overseers, an

56. Royal Commission on Labour in India. *Evidence*, 2, Pt 2: Punjab, *Delhi and Ajmer-Merwara: Oral Evidence* [hereafter RLC, *Oral Evidence*] (London, 1931), pp. 138, 195.
57. *Census of India, 1931: Delhi, Report and Tables* (Lahore, 1933), p. 43.
58. Royal Commission on Labour in India Evidence, 2, Pt 1: *Punjab, Delhi and Ajmer-Merwara. Written Evidence* [hereafter RLC, *Written Evidence*], (London, 1931), p. 154.
59. *Census of India, 1931: Delhi, Report and Tables*, p. 43.
60. RLC, *Written Evidence*, p. 155.
61. RLC, *Oral Evidence*, p. 211.
62. RLC, *Written Evidence*, p. 154.
63. *Ibid.*

(a)

(b)

Figure 1a and 1b. Laying the topmost stone (one of two) of New Delhi, the crown finial on the North Block of the Secretariat, 30 September 1927. The close-up in the upper panel includes, standing left to right, H.W. Pippet, (junior) foreman mason; Rai Bahadur Sardar Baisakha Singh, contractor; Khan Bahadur Muhammad Sulaiman, executive engineer, CPWD; Lala Shadi Ram and Lala Chela Ram, sub-divisional officers, CPWD, and H.A.N. Medd, resident architect. The sitting participants are overseers and masons.

The two photographs from which this composite image was created are found in the photographic collection of the Centre of South Asian Studies, University of Cambridge, Box A91, Medd, H.A.N., Album #4: "New Delhi: Building the Government Offices", pp. 12 and 13. The images are reproduced with the kind permission of the Centre of South Asian Studies.

executive engineer, a major contractor Baisakha Singh, and the resident architect are posed triumphantly far above the ground in a silent, telling tribute to the labor of tens of thousands of men, women and children that built imperial New Delhi.

The example of New Delhi illustrates a number of the features of circulating construction labor suggested in this paper: (1) the concentration of large numbers of workers drawn from widespread areas at the sites of major construction projects; (2) the presence of many people whose main occupation remained agriculture (albeit often as landless laborers), and who circulated back into agricultural employment at certain times in the year; (3) the difficult conditions under which the construction people worked and lived. An additional pattern present among the New Delhi construction workers – the decision of a substantial number to make the Delhi region their permanent home – was a variation present in situations where, as in large urban projects, employment prospects and other inducements made permanent residence seem appealing. The construction at Jamshedpur earlier in the twentieth century and at Chandigarh in the mid-twentieth century may have offered similar scenarios. Dam and ever-moving railway construction rarely led to the permanent sedentarization of hitherto circulating labor.

A full appreciation of the emergent – and then increasingly integrated construction labor markets – will require an extended study of contractors. They were the crucial intermediaries. They are one of the most neglected groups in the history of Indian labor – or, for that matter, in the history of the growth and development of the Indian bourgeoisie.[64] Contractors came in all shapes and sizes. Some were little more than *mukaddams* (roughly headmen) who could assemble and command a small gang of laborers. Some like Baisakha Singh, a trained engineer who gave evidence to the Royal Commission on Labour and who won construction contracts at New Delhi in the 1920s, employed over 2,000 workers at far-flung locations (500 at New Delhi). He provided labor, materials, and project supervision.[65] Larger contractors used smaller labor contractors – layers of intermediaries existed – and advances often glued those who provided labor power to those who employed labor.

Ten million or so workers were needed to build India's railways between 1850 and 1900 and large numbers continued to be needed into the 1970s. Railway construction at any given spot often required migrant laborers, among whom many were Wudders and similar groups.[66] The Wudders were prized by railway engineers and contractors for their

64. See Burton Stein, "Towards an Indian Petty Bourgeoisie: Outline of an Approach", *Economic and Political Weekly*, 26 (26 January 1991), pp. PE9––PE20.

65. RLC, *Oral Evidence*, pp. 134–135.

66. Ian J. Kerr, *Building the Railways of the Raj 1850–1900* (Delhi, 1995), pp. 196–226.

Figure 2. Kistna Bridge, Construction of the Western River-Training Embankment, c.1892. *From an album "Kistna Bridge, Bezwada 12 spans of 30 Feet", F.J.E. Spring, L.C.E, M.I.C.E., engineer-in-chief. Held in the Library of the Institution of Civil Engineers, London and reproduced with the kind permission of the Institution.*

formidable earth- and stone-working capacities. Wudders were among those present at the construction of the East Coast State Railway's Kistna Bridge at Bezwada in the early 1890s.[67] Part of that massive project is shown in Figure 2 above. The photograph captures well the large numbers of workers that would crowd upon a major construction site.

I have detailed elsewhere the processes by which labor for railway construction up to 1900 was mobilized and utilized.[68] Here I wish to emphasize that railway building as a labor-intensive activity continued until 1947 and well beyond. If India had 23,627 route miles of railways in 1900, it had 40,524 in 1947 and, after the division of lines between India and Pakistan, India alone climbed back to roughly 40,000 route miles in 2001, indicating the construction of roughly 6,500 new miles of track. Moreover, the closing decades of the twentieth century saw Indian Railways convert many miles of meter-gauge line to the more prevalent

67. *Ibid.*, p. 108.
68. *Ibid.*, esp. ch. 4.

broad gauge (5 feet 6 inches) – this required a good deal of construction-type labor. These projects frequently used itinerant labor.

Railways, hydraulic projects, highways, and other great construction activities (e.g., the Bhakra Nangal hydro and irrigation dam, underground railways in Calcutta and Delhi) ensured the continued demand for construction workers in post-colonial India. Indeed, India's great urban areas have been and continue to be the sites of massive construction efforts. The Delhi capital region is a major case in point. The construction of monumental New Delhi discussed above has been followed by massive waves of expansion and construction since 1947: a development spurred by the 1947–1948 influxes of refugees and the subsequent massive population growth of India's capital region. The numbers are likely underestimates but one study indicates that in nine of the years between 1955 and 1970 the building industry in Delhi each year employed over 50,000 workers with the lowest year (1963) being 23,500 and the highest (1967) 71,200.[69]

THE POST-COLONIAL PERIOD AND SOME CONCLUDING OBSERVATIONS

Thus, most construction work in the pre-colonial, colonial or post-colonial periods must be examined as a related activity whose requirements for labor power were met from within (increasingly better integrated) labor markets involving circulating labor. A study conducted in the 1970s noted that migrant labor had integrated the construction labor market.[70] Migrant labor stabilized (depressed might be a better word) wage rates and flattened labor supply curves. Contractors on big projects imported migrant labor when the cost of local labor rose. The migrants, more desperate for work, were cheaper although they had to be imported. "Thanks to the availability and mobility of migrant laborers, construction employers can, given sufficient time, avoid a general labor shortage or a highly inelastic labor supply, even if local labor supply becomes increasingly inelastic."[71]

However, change has occurred recently in some instances of large-scale construction. A railroad engineer writing in the late 1990s stated that twenty to thirty years earlier:[72]

69. C.K. Johri and S.M. Pandey, *Employment Relationship in the Building Industry: A Study in Delhi* (New Delhi, 1972), p. 2.

70. International Bank for Reconstruction and Development [World Bank], Bank Staff Working Paper no. 223, "Some Aspects of Unskilled Labor Markets for Civil Construction in India: Observations Based on Field Investigation", prepared by Swadesh R. Bose, November 1975, pp. 34–35.

71. *Ibid.*, p. 35.

72. *A Treatise on Konkan Railway* (Navi Mumbai, c.1999), p. 147.

> Contractors and agents used to bring gangs from Orissa, after paying an advance to the workers' families and the village headmen. Able-bodied people from entire villages were brought in, to work almost sixteen hours daily, breaking up only for meals, which used to be cooked centrally. They were by far the most efficient gangs. They were gangs from other places as well, during the working season. Camels and donkeys used to be used for leading and massive works would be completed in this way.

This description could easily have been that of nineteenth-century construction. The work of the Odhs in later nineteenth-century Punjab was described thus: "the men dig, the women carry the earth to the donkeys, which they always have with them, and the children drive the donkeys to the spoil bank".[73] However, the railroad engineer was comparing construction in the 1960s and 1970s with what occurred when the 760-km West Coast Konkan line between Roha and Mangalore was built in the 1990s. He went on to say that "now, with modern methods available and the fact few people are willing to do such a hard job, work is done through mechanical means".[74] Insofar as large-scale projects like the Konkan line were concerned – projects where capital-intensive practices made economic sense – the 125-year use of great agglomerations of laborers, many of them migrants, had ended.

The pivotal groups of construction workers discussed in this paper were those who practiced an itinerant life-style and who moved in family groups to a succession of construction sites. We know them best by a series of regional caste/tribe names multiplied into variant forms by the vagaries of British transliterations of Indian names into English. Among the most important groups were the Odhs of the Punjab, Rajasthan, and Western Uttar Pradesh, the Nuniyas of the Gangetic valley, the Beldars of Bihar and western Bengal, and, best documented, the groups the British called "Wudders" who were found in western, central, and southern India.[75] These groups, or people like them, were present early in the history of India and continuously thereafter. They flourished in the high colonial period when an explosive increase in the demand for construction labor occasioned by massive railway and hydraulic projects made their earth and stone-working abilities highly valued. They were rarely the only migrant workers at construction sites but they were the pace-setters. Engineers consistently referred to them as the "professional navvies" of India who worked more rapidly than any other group.

73. W. Crooke, *The Tribes and Castes of the North-Western Provinces and Oudh*, 4 vols (Calcutta, 1896), vol. 4, p. 95.

74. *A Treatise on Konkan Railway*, p. 148.

75. There was persistent speculation in the folklore/ethnological periodicals that these groups shared a common origin. For examples see *Panjab Notes and Queries, A Monthly Periodical Devoted to the Systematic Collection of Authentic Notes and Scraps of Information regarding the Country and the People*, R.C. Temple (ed.), 2 vols (1884).

Mobile and accustomed to waged work (albeit filtered through the collectivity via piece-work payments) the itinerant construction workers initially adapted easily to the changing conditions of the colonial period. They became enmeshed in the relationships of capitalism – certainly railway construction was a project of colonialism and capitalism (intertwined but not identical processes and structures) – via processes Marx labeled the formal subsumption of labor under capitalism.[76] However, and despite the appreciation many engineers and contractors had for their capacity to work hard, they also came under the suspicious eye of colonial authorities. Some among them became the objects of police surveillance and legal restrictions. The rich and fascinating ethnographic descriptions became a basis for the disapproval of itinerant lifestyles and the attributions of collective criminality.

Ecological, social, legal and economic pressures in the twentieth century increasingly led to the sedentarization of itinerant construction workers – and other itinerant groups like the Banjaras. Employment as migrant construction workers was not necessarily abandoned but the distinctive, centuries-old lifestyles of the Wudders and others had to give way to more settled lives. Moreover, in an ever more populated India nomadic peoples ran out of space. As P.K. Misra observed in 1970, social, economic, and political changes had led nomadic peoples everywhere to settle down – a process "marked in India too and this process has been further accentuated on account of the rapid planned development".[77] If Odhs in the mid-nineteenth century building canals in the Upper Doab were reluctant to take work further south because the more developed state of agriculture in the Lower Doab provided limited space in which they could graze their large herds of cattle and donkeys, then their successors in the mid-twentieth century found themselves more hemmed in.[78] The economic development the itinerant navvies of India helped to bring about – the infrastructures of modern civilized life praised by Thurston – contributed to their sedentarization.

In addition to the importance of circulating labor within construction labor markets these groups offer a jagged terrain that throws into sharp relief the history of South Asian labor within the transitions of capitalism and the emergence, maintenance and demise of formal colonialism. It is a history within which the nomadic proclivities of the itinerant groups have been steadily circumscribed. In the early twenty-first century, fewer itinerant workers exist than they did a century ago although the general category of migrant workers has shown no such diminution. The more

76. My use of Marx 's concept is discussed in Kerr, *Building the Railways of the Raj*, pp. 7–9.
77. Misra, "Study of Nomads", p. 151.
78. Ian Stone, *Canal Irrigation in British India: Perspectives on Technological Change in a Peasant Economy* (Cambridge, 1984), p. 58.

pronounced fluidity captured in the term circulating labor has given way to patterns of mobility perhaps better understood as varieties of migrant labor wherein longer-term residence becomes interspersed with periods of movement.

Mobility and Containment: The Voyages of South Asian Seamen, c.1900–1960*

RAVI AHUJA

LASCARS IN A SEGMENTED LABOUR MARKET

In the political and economic context of imperialism, the enormous nineteenth-century expansion of shipping within and beyond the Indian Ocean facilitated the development of a new and increasingly transcontinental regime of labour circulation. The Indian subcontinent, it is well known, emerged as a seemingly inexhaustible source for plantation, railway, and port labour in British colonies across the globe. Moreover, the new and predominantly seaborne "circulatory regime"[1] itself relied to a considerable extent on the labour power of South Asian workers, on the *lascar*, as the maritime counterpart of the "coolie" labourer was called.

The number of Indian workers on the decks and in the engine rooms and saloons of merchant vessels grew considerably along with the rise of long-distance steam shipping in the last quarter of the nineteenth century. During the interwar years, on average about 50,000 South Asian seamen were employed on British merchant vessels alone and many thousands more by German and other European shipping companies. In this period, lascars made up roughly a quarter of all ratings on British merchant ships – a proportion that remained fairly stable well into the 1960s, despite the end of the colonial regime.[2]

* Research for this article was undertaken during a fellowship at the Centre for Modern Oriental Studies (Berlin) and funded by the German Research Council. I have greatly profited from the lively discussions of the Centre's Indian Ocean History Group (K. Bromber, J.-G. Deutsch, M. Frenz, F. Hartwig, P. Krajewski, and B. Reinwald). Earlier versions were presented at the 4th International Conference of the Association of Indian Labour Historians (Noida, March 2004), at the biennial conference of the German African Studies Association (VAD, Hanover, June 2004), and at the 18th European Conference on Modern South Asian Studies (Lund, July 2004). I am grateful for the critical comments and valuable suggestions received from many colleagues, especially from Gopalan Balachandran, Sabyasachi Bhattacharya, and Marcel van der Linden, though I do not wish to implicate any of them in my conclusions. The location of archival material is indicated by the following abbreviations: ILO (Archives of the International Labour Organization, Geneva); NAI (National Archives of India, New Delhi); NMML (Nehru Memorial Museum and Library, New Delhi); OIOC (Oriental and India Office Collections of the British Library, London); PRO (Public Record Office, London).

1. See Claude Markovits, Jacques Pouchepadass, and Sanjay Subrahmanyam (eds), *Society and Circulation: Mobile People and Itinerant Cultures in South Asia 1750–1950* (Delhi, 2003), p. 3.
2. Laura Tabili, *"We Ask for British Justice": Workers and Racial Difference in Late Imperial*

A sailor's work implies extraordinary mobility across territorial frontiers and cultural spheres. It is, therefore, tempting to conjure up images of a transcultural, uncontainable, and freely roaming proletariat of the seven seas. However, the social history of South Asian steamship workers sits rather uneasily with apologetic "globalization" narratives that celebrate unending beach parties of happy "hybridity" or revel in "the Dance of the Flows and the Fragments".[3] Nor does it corroborate Linebaugh and Rediker's hypothesis of an inclusive and revolutionary maritime work culture in the Atlantic of an earlier period.[4] Instead, as Sherwood, Tabili, and others have shown, the maritime labour market of the nineteenth and twentieth centuries was structured into a rigidly racist hierarchy with South Asians at its bottom.[5]

This segmentation was no mere teething trouble of an emerging global labour market. Rather, in the course of its development, ethnic segmentation intensified and consolidated into a defining and permanent structural property of the maritime labour market. While wage differentials between European and South Asian seamen had apparently been volatile, moderate, and not always to the disadvantage of the latter in the seventeenth and eighteenth centuries, they became more marked and consistently defined in terms of a racist taxonomy in the early 1800s.[6] By the mid-nineteenth century, lascars received as little as between one-fifth and one-third of the pay of European "able-bodied seamen" – a ratio that remained unchanged up to the 1980s.[7]

Britain (Ithaca, NY [etc.], 1994), p. 47; *Labour Gazette*, X.2 (Bombay, October 1930), p. 159; S.G. Sturmey, *British Shipping and World Competition* (London, 1962), p. 296; Gopalan Balachandran, "Circulation through Seafaring: Indian Seamen, 1890–1945", in Markovits *et al.*, *Society and Circulation*, pp. 89–130, 98.

3. The expression is from Fred Cooper's incisive critique of such trends: "What is the Concept of Globalization Good for? An African Historian's Perspective", *African Affairs*, 100 (2001), pp. 189–213, 193. Such narratives unfortunately overshadow the newly invigorated field of Indian Ocean studies. This could, for instance, be witnessed at the largest recent international conference in this field, on "Cultural Exchange and Transformation in the Indian Ocean World" (UCLA, April 2002, conference volume forthcoming).
4. Peter Linebaugh and Marcus Rediker, *The Many-Headed Hydra: The Hidden History of the Revolutionary Atlantic* (London, 2002).
5. Marika Sherwood, "Race, Nationality and Employment among Lascar Seamen, 1660 to 1945", *New Community*, 17 (1991), pp. 229–244; Tabili, *"We Ask for British Justice"*, pp. 41–57.
6. Michael H. Fisher, *Counterflows to Colonialism: Indian Travellers and Settlers in Britain 1600–1857* (Delhi, 2004), pp. 34f., 144.
7. OIOC, Bombay Marine Proceedings [hereafter, BoMP], IOR/P/6705, A223–224 (August 1903); Reports from the Departmental Committee on Manning of Merchant Ships with Addenda and Statistical Tables (London, 1896), p. 15; Dinkar Desai, *Maritime Labour in India* (Bombay, 1940), pp. 93–96; Lascar Diet Scale, OIOC, Economic & Overseas Dept, Seamen, IOR/L/E/9/973 (1934–46); J.L. Mowat, *Seafarers' Conditions in India and Pakistan* (Geneva, 1949), p. 57; Conrad Dixon, "Lascars: The Forgotten Seamen", in Rosemary Ommer and Gerald Panting (eds), *Working Men Who Got Wet* (Newfoundland, 1980), pp. 265–281, 278; Frank Broeze, "The Muscles of Empire – Indian Seamen and the Raj, 1919–1939", *Indian Economic and Social*

The segmentation of the maritime labour market thus displayed a remarkable stability. With regard to our present discussion, this implies that the seamen's extraordinary spatial mobility did not effect an equalization of their wages or other terms of contract. Hence the lascars' trans-territorial itinerancy did not, even in the long run, undermine the "barrier" that separated this ethnically defined segment of an occupational group from their better-paid European colleagues, and effectively prevented them from moving on to labour markets offering much higher wages in the various metropolitan cities they called at during their voyages. Statements of ship-owners, merchant navy officers, and colonial officials confirm these observations by pointing out time and again that an extremely low rate of desertion was among the principal advantages of replacing "white" and even Chinese seamen with lascars.[8] Even in 1929, when an unusually large number of lascars jumped ship in British ports, the India Office registered no more than eighty desertions. In 1931, the British government's efforts to introduce a more efficient scheme of preventing illegal immigration of Indian seamen met with a lukewarm response from the shipping companies, most of which stated that the problem was "trifling in extent".[9]

As various studies have shown, the first traces of lascar settlement in Britain date back to the eighteenth century. In the mid-nineteenth century, South Asian seafarers contributed to the development of an "Oriental Quarter" in London and by the early twentieth century small communities of former Indian seamen, many of whom had jumped ship, sprang up in several British port cities.[10] There is no point in questioning the *qualitative* importance of these early communities, as several of them were to turn into anchor points for chain migration – most famously in East London where a small group of lascars from Sylhet (today a district of Bangladesh bordering on the Indian state of Assam) grew over time into a large

History Review, 18 (1981), pp. 43–67, 44; R. Hope, *A New History of British Shipping* (London, 1990), pp. 441, 455; Tabili, *"We Ask for British Justice"*, p. 45; G. Balachandran, "Recruitment and Control of Indian Seamen, Calcutta, 1880–1935", *International Journal of Maritime History*, 9 (1997), pp. 1–18

8. Dodwell-Castle Line (James Chambers & Co., Liverpool) to Mercantile Marine Dept, Board of Trade, 28 August 1930, OIOC, Commercial & Revenue Dept, IOR/L/E/7/1125, file 2139; Graham's Trading Co. (Agents of Brocklebank's Cunard Service) to Secretary to Govt of Bengal, Maritime Dept, 11 February 1925, *ibid.*

9. High Commissioner for India [hereafter, HCI], General Dept, to Secretary to Government of India [hereafter, GoI], Commerce Dept, 26 November 1931, NAI, Dept of Commerce, Merchant Marine II, August 1932, file 67, M. II/32, s.nos. 6–8, part B, folios 3, 11.

10. Rozina Visram, *Ayahs, Lascars and Princes: The Story of Indians in Britain 1700–1947* (London, 1986), pp. 34–59; *idem*, *Asians in Britain: 400 Years of History* (London, 2002), pp. 57–69; Fisher, *Counterflows to Colonialism*, pp. 65–71, 137–179, 381–392; Norma Myers, "The Black Poor of London: Initiatives of Eastern Seamen in the Eighteenth and Nineteenth Centuries", *Immigrants & Minorities*, 13 (2–3) (1994), pp. 7–21.

immigrant community. The same happened in other cases, such as that of firemen from the Mirpur area of Kashmir (today in Pakistan) who opened up avenues of immigration for many of their neighbours to northern England and the Midlands.[11] However, whenever officials searched for the immigrant lascar before the 1950s the figures they arrived at were hardly significant, despite the fact that tens of thousands of South Asian seamen had called at British ports every year since the last quarter of the previous century.[12]

Moreover, the rise of the steamer, by rendering shipping more independent of the seasons, abbreviated the period during which lascars had to wait in British ports to embark on the return voyage to India, which apparently reduced their presence in Britain despite rapidly growing employment figures.[13] In the twentieth century, Indian seamen found themselves stranded in Britain in large numbers only at certain junctures, especially during the two World Wars. The more fortunate were readily employed by British factory owners, while others experienced the Empire's benevolence towards its colonial subjects in squalid detention camps.[14] Nevertheless immigration into metropolitan capitalist countries by way of seafaring remained negligible in *quantitative* terms. No more than 8,000 Indians, it has been estimated, lived in Britain before the 1950s.[15] Even if lascars made up a considerable share, this figure confirms the reports mentioned above that the rate of "desertion" of Indians from British merchant vessels was surprisingly moderate under the prevailing conditions of steep wage differentials.

Furthermore, though Indian seamen outnumbered all other non-British segments of the UK merchant marine's labour force, they appear to have been less likely to settle in British port cities. The Deputy Chief Constable of the Cardiff police thus estimated in 1929 that 200 Indian seafarers lived in this town as opposed to "some 6,000 Arabs, West Indians, Malays,

11. Katy Gardner, *Global Migrants, Local Lives: Travel and Transformation in Rural Bangladesh* (Oxford, 1995), pp. 34–65; Caroline Adams (ed.), *Across Seven Seas and Thirteen Rivers: Life Stories of Pioneer Sylhetti Settlers in Britain* (London, 1994), pp. 39–66; Yousuf Choudhury, *The Roots and Tales of the Bangladeshi Settlers* (Birmingham, 1993), pp. 69f.; Roger Ballard, "The Context and Consequences of Migration: Jullunder and Mirpur Compared", *New Community*, 11 (1–2) (1983), pp. 117–136.

12. A committee set up in 1910 to investigate the problem of Indian and other colonial "destitutes" in Britain (and lascars settling in Britain were in official circles automatically assumed to be "destitutes") could, for instance, trace no more than 250 Indians for the period 1888 to 1910; Visram, *Asians in Britain*, p. 69.

13. For earlier problems of lascar accommodation during the winter season see Fisher, *Counterflows to Colonialism*, pp. 148–178.

14. *Report of the Bombay Chamber of Commerce* [hereafter, RBCC] *1916* (Bombay, 1917), pp. 55–56, 329–335; Dinkar Desai, *Among Indian Seamen in Great Britain* (Bombay, 1946); Adams, *Across Seven Seas*, pp. 46f.; Ballard, "The Context and Consequences of Migration", p. 125.

15. Visram, *Asians in Britain*, pp. 254–269.

Maltese and other seamen".[16] If few lascars became immigrants, that was not because they had no one to turn to after jumping ship in a British port – several of the life accounts collected by Caroline Adams bring out clearly that the necessary links were firmly established before World War II and intending immigrants were well informed about where to find fellow countrymen (like the Sylheti Ayub Ali Master who ran a coffee shop in London's Commercial Road) who would help them to get a footing ashore.[17] Yet, on the whole, South Asian maritime labour networks were not transformed into networks of large-scale migration before the 1950s.

How do we explain the fact that only a small minority of Indian seamen climbed the barriers of wage discrimination? Why was the shipping industry never forced to level out maritime labour market disparities despite the lascars' high potential for mobility and increasing trade-union pressure? This article argues that the remarkable stability of these discrepancies was due to changing and interlocking sets of formal and informal institutional devices that may be called "scenarios of regulation". These "scenarios" are understood as the labour market's inherent structure, as its form of realization, and not in neoclassical terms of external intervention in this market. Various devices of these scenarios were aimed at restricting the lascars' freedom of movement. They were created in at least three overlapping spheres of regulation: British and "British Indian" maritime labour law, the immigration laws of metropolitan countries, and extra-legal structures of exclusion and containment. While each of these spheres of regulation by itself would have been unequal to the task, the combination of devices from all of them, it is argued, was fairly effective in controlling the mobility of Indian seamen and facilitated the reproduction of a segregated pool of poorly paid and legally inferior colonial labour in the international maritime labour market over more than a century. This article's concluding section briefly discusses the transformation of these scenarios of regulation after 1947 and sketches wider implications of these findings for research on ethnically segmented labour markets.

MARITIME LABOUR LAW

In the early years of the twentieth century, the British Board of Trade appointed a Mercantile Marine Committee to enquire into the causes and potential dangers of the dramatic increase in the employment of foreign, and especially lascar, seamen. The powerful British shipping industry

16. E.W. Huddleston, Shipping Advisor of High Commissioner, 25 February 1929, NAI, Dept of Commerce, Merchant Marine I, June 1929, file 451, M. I(8)/29, s.nos. 1–5, part B, fo. 9.

17. Adams, *Across Seven Seas*, pp. 39–45; Nawab Ali's account, *ibid*., pp. 73, 77; Haji Shirajul Islam's account, *ibid*., p. 98; Haji Kona Miah's account, *ibid*., p. 133.

defended, successfully as it turned out, their preference for Indian seamen against the criticism of the jingoistic Navy League and Havelock Wilson's seamen's union. The ship-owners' arguments were elaborated in a rambling pamphlet by one Captain W.H. Hood. He claimed that South Asian seamen rescued British merchant shipping from the "blight of insubordination" brought about by the employment of the English "Jack Tar", and in order to substantiate his assertion he quoted the following account by a shipmaster:

> In a South African port three British steamers lay in dock side by side, one a transport with the usual British crew, the others manned respectively by lascars and Chinese. From the latter vessels not a man during their stay in port had been absent from his duties, while fully two-thirds of the transport's crew were being kept "unspotted from the world in the local gaol, serving sentences for continual drunkenness and absence without leave".[18]

Several statements of this sort could be cited.[19] All of them fuse, of course, two constructs of the dominant social ideology of the time: first the image of the child-like "docile coolie",[20] and secondly the idea of the morally immature "white proletarian". Yet even if shipmasters expressed their thoughts in terms of a well-established idiom of authoritarian paternalism, these thoughts are likely to have been informed by their experiences of quotidian social praxis. As for the "docility" of lascars on the shores of South Africa, consider, for instance, that until later than World War II employers could legally insert a clause into the special employment contracts of Indian seafarers, the so-called "lascar agreements", which in African and North American ports expressly denied them the customary right to shore leave.[21] This permissible clause or "stipulation" had received the legal sanction of the colonial administration under pressure from the immigration policies of the USA and other states, something which will be discussed more fully in the next section. Consider also that the combined efforts of shipping industry and colonial administration prevented any formal regulation of the working hours of South Asian seamen throughout the same period.[22] That meant not merely longer working hours, but practically unlimited control

18. W.H. Hood, *Blight of Insubordination: The Lascar Question and Rights and Wrongs of the British Shipmaster* (London, 1903), p. 63.

19. Relevant evidence has been presented at length in Ravi Ahuja, "Die 'Lenksamkeit' des 'Lascars'. Regulierungsszenarien eines transterritorialen Arbeitsmarktes in der ersten Hälfte des 20. Jahrhunderts", *Geschichte und Gesellschaft*, 31 (2005), pp. 323–353.

20. See Kaushik Ghosh, "A Market for Aboriginality: Primitivism and Race Qualification in the Indentured Labour Market of Colonial India", in G. Bhadra, G. Prakash, and S. Tharu (eds), *Subaltern Studies X. Writings on South Asian History and Society* (New Delhi, 1999), pp. 8–48.

21. OIOC, Economic & Overseas Dept Collections, Seamen, IOR/L/E/9/974; *ibid.*, IOR/L/E/9/977, fol. 242.

22. For the employers' arguments see *RBCC 1921*, vol. 1 (Bombay, 1922), pp. 146–147, and Fakirjee Cowasjee, Report on the 13th International Labour (Maritime) Conference, Geneva,

over the *person* of the lascar, who risked being charged with breach of contract if he refused to be at the disposal of the shipmaster at any time, either when the ship was at sea or when it lay in port.[23] It is therefore less useful to reduce the construct of the "docile lascar" to another element of a coherent "discourse" than to approach it as a peculiarly coloured and refracted reflection of practices of political and economic domination – practices that need to be understood in their own right.

What needs to be emphasized here is that the word "lascar", which up to the early nineteenth century had been a general designation for seafarers from the whole Indian Ocean region,[24] was slowly transformed into a legal category to distinguish lascars from "seamen" – the legal status of the former being different and markedly lower.[25] In the early decades of the twentieth century, the question of who was a lascar time and again occupied government legal experts in England and India: lascars, most agreed, were seafarers resident in "British India". Since Aden was an important recruitment port and under the Government of Bombay, there was some consensus that Adenese seafarers too should be included. Yet many of them in fact came from Somalia, while one-third of all seamen

10–26 October 1929, NMML, M.A. Master Papers, IV, Printed Material, file 39. Hence, working hours were not regulated by law nor collective agreement but by custom, while overtime was not paid for. See Replies to Questions Relating to Hours of Work [...] [for International Labour Conference 1929], NMML, M.A. Master Papers, 1. Subject Files, E. National Committees and Commissions, file 780; Replies furnished by the Indian Merchants' Chamber, Bombay to Questions Relating to Hours of Work and Organisation of Work on Board Ship, NAI, Dept of Commerce, Merchant Marine II, August 1929, file 465–M. I/29, s.nos. 1–27, part A, p. 97; Memorandum on Regulation of Hours of Work of Indian Seamen (undated, probably 1944), NMML, M.A. Master Papers, I. Subject Files, F. International Committees and Commissions, file 896. According to an official statement in 1927, actual average weekly working hours were 61 hours for "deck lascars", 84 hours for *sukhanis* (helmsmen), 56 hours for "engine room lascars" and 63 to 70 hours for "saloon staff"; Shipping Master, Calcutta, to Government of Bengal [hereafter, GoBe], Marine Dept, 14 June 1927, *ibid.*, pp. 35–36.

23. Desai, *Maritime Labour in India*, pp. 65–72; A. Marr, Secretary to GoBe, to GoI, Commerce Dept, 23 June 1921, OIOC, GoI Commerce Proc., IOR/P/11247, A7–10; see also *RBCC 1921*, vol. 2 (Bombay, 1922), pp. 867–869; B.A. Malik, Memo on Regulation of Hours of Indian Seamen, 1 August 1945, NMML, M.A. Master Papers, subject file 896; GoI, Dept of Commerce, Memorandum on Wages, Hours of Work, Manning, 8 June 1946, *ibid.*, subject file 903, p. 4; R.K. Das, *History of Indian Labour Legislation* (Calcutta, 1941), pp. 129f. See also references to the imprisonment of Indian seamen for refusing overtime work in Erich Kirchenknopf, "Bericht über die auf Veranlassung des Deutschen Verkehrsbundes angestellten Untersuchungen: 1. Indische Seeleute an Bord deutscher Schiffe; 2. Indische Seeleute an Land", Ms. (1929), Bundesarchiv, Stiftung Archiv der Parteien und Massenorganisationen der DDR (SAPMO), ZPA I 4/6/23, pp. 55f.

24. Janet Ewald, "Crossers of the Sea: Slaves, Freedmen, and Other Migrants in the Northwestern Indian Ocean, c. 1750–1914", *American Historical Review*, 105 (2000), pp. 69–91, 75.

25. Leo Barnes, *Evolution and Scope of Mercantile Marine Laws Relating to Seamen in India* (Bombay, 1983), pp. 36–39; Sherwood, "Race, Nationality and Employment among Lascar Seamen", pp. 231–233 and *passim*.

recruited in Bombay were Indian Christians from the Portuguese colony of Goa. Moreover, could "Eurasians"[26] be employed as lascars, and what kind of agreement applied to subjects of Indian princely states? Even more controversially, what was to be done about the sizeable community of Chinese seafarers resident in Calcutta at a time when a "yellow-peril" campaign in Britain targeted East Asian seamen?[27]

The reason for such debates was that the freedom of movement of seafarers under "lascar agreements" was much more restricted than that of "white" seamen and subject to different regulations from those of other so-called "coloured seamen". Most importantly, lascar seamen could not be engaged for single journeys (from Bombay to London for instance), for "lascar agreements" were concluded either for a round-trip voyage or for a period of twenty-four months, and later twelve months. In any case, shipmasters could discharge lascars only in Indian ports, and South Asian seamen could in no circumstances terminate their contracts in any port outside "British India".[28] That regulation ostensibly protected the lascar from being abandoned in a European port where, it was assumed, he would invariably become destitute and a burden to the respective municipality or British consulate. Shipping companies were accordingly held responsible for the repatriation of all lascars any master of one of their vessels might have left behind in any port outside India.[29]

Yet there are indications that Indian seamen did not necessarily appreciate that kind of "protection". Harsh conditions on a particular vessel, or the simple desire to sign on under "European articles" for much higher pay, were good reasons for claiming discharge on reaching a Western port. What was declared as the lascars' "privilege" was mainly in the interest of ship-owners who were, according to England's Merchant Shipping Act of 1894 and subsequent legislation, entitled to transfer even unwilling lascars to any vessel of their or any other company as long as it

26. "Eurasian", in colonial phraseology, was the designation for children of Indian mothers and European fathers.

27. For a summary of the relevant debates and legislation between 1888 and 1920, see GoI, Dept of Commerce, to Government of Bombay [hereafter, GoBo], Marine Dept, 15 September 1920, OIOC, BoMP, IOR/P/10793, A345f. See also *RBCC 1904* (Bombay, 1905), pp. 105–106, 498–520; OIOC, Bengal Marine Proceedings [hereafter, BeMP], IOR/P/10315 (1918), A33–34 (February 1918), A3 (September 1918); *ibid.*, IOR/P11178, A36 (March 1922); OIOC, BoMP, IOR/P/7750, A355–360 (July 1907); *ibid.*, IOR/P/7750, A503 (October 1907); *ibid.*, IOR/P/9596, A17 (January 1915); *ibid.*, IOR/P/10546, B42 (March 1919); *ibid.*, IOR/P/10793, A347f (November 1920); *ibid.*, IOR/P/11008, A181–185 (1921); *ibid.*, IOR/P/11188, A79–83 (1922); Engagement of Natives of India under Lascar Articles, OIOC, Dept Papers, Commercial & Revenue Dept (1904–41), IOR/L/E/7/481.

28. OIOC, Commercial & Revenue Papers, IOR/L/E/7/853, file 7563; Desai, *Maritime Labour in India*, pp. 204–207; Tabili, *"We Ask for British Justice"*, p. 185.

29. Barnes, *Evolution and Scope of Mercantile Marine Laws*, pp. 168–178. See also Sherwood, "Race, Nationality and Employment among Lascar Seamen", pp. 230–232, 235.

was bound for India.[30] Hence an Indian seaman's only chance to terminate a contract outside South Asia was to break it, thereby committing the criminal offence of "desertion" and forfeiting all payments due from his employer.

That denial of the right to claim discharge restricted the room for manoeuvre available to Indian seamen in two ways. First of all, it reinforced the segmentation of the international maritime labour market by raising the barrier lascars had to surmount when they attempted to leave the low-pay and inferior-rights sector of the market, which was no doubt an ingenious method of reducing the freedom of movement of a potentially highly mobile occupational group. Second, any individual vessel was insulated from the wider world of maritime labour even when lying in port, which reinforced steep hierarchies on board ship – hierarchies that could be contested less easily than on vessels with non-Indian crews. The lascar's (formal) freedom of contract was thereby reduced and so was his bargaining position, both in the labour market ashore and towards his superiors at sea. Maritime despotism (including the frequent application of physical violence) was even more attractive as a mode of managing the labour process when there was little risk that the crew would sign off at the next port and large demurrage fees build up before replacements could be found.

That might explain why representatives of conflicting interests held similar views regarding the nature of the lascars' labour relations. While W.H. Hood, the ship-owners' mouthpiece, rejoiced in 1903 that Indian seamen were "more completely the servants of the shipowner [...] than any other group of men doing similar work",[31] the liberal trade unionist Dinkar Desai denounced the lascars' legal status in 1941 as a "form of servitude".[32] Desai made his remark a full decade after a new stipulation had been inserted into the "lascar agreements" by the Legislative Assembly, which gave an Indian seaman the right to claim discharge if he proved he could obtain employment in a higher grade, if he provided a substitute, created no additional costs for the owner, and on condition that the shipmaster gave his consent.[33] Even this microscopic change had been opposed by the employers, for instance by the Bombay Chamber of Commerce, which had warned that a relaxation of the stipulations

30. See the various papers on "lascar agreements" in OIOC, Economic & Overseas Dept Collections, Seamen, IOR/L/E/7/977. See also Reports from the Departmental Committee on Manning, p. 15.

31. Hood, *Blight of Insubordination*, p. 48.

32. Desai, *Maritime Labour in India*, pp. 204–208; see also R.N. Saksena, *Seamen in India* (Dehra Dun, 1951), pp. 102–104.

33. International Labour Organization, Monthly Report of the Indian Branch [hereafter, ILOrep] June 1931, ILO C1903/31, pp. 62–63 (excerpt from *Gazette of India*, 23 May 1931, part 1, p. 412).

regulating the termination of agreements would "enable a seaman to break his contract [*sic*] on a very flimsy pretext and [...] cause intolerable inconvenience to the shipowner".[34] Constraints on the lascars' freedom of movement by way of maritime labour law were thus defended tooth and nail.

IMMIGRATION POLICIES

When the SS *City of Norwich* arrived at New York in April 1921 the situation on board ship was extremely tense.[35] The shipmaster had entered in his logbook a physical assault on a British engineer by a group of Indian stokers that included a foreman (*tindal*). Immediately after entering the port of Brooklyn two lascars jumped ship. Soon after, thirty-three Punjabi firemen, led by the engine-room *serang*, Fazel Ahammed, went ashore to lodge a protest against the behaviour of the shipmaster with the British Vice Consul and then with the agent of the Ellerman shipping line, the proprietors of the vessel. The master, they claimed, had broken the contractual obligation of providing warm clothing on the North Atlantic route. Moreover, they complained that the food rations were not in keeping with the agreement and that members of the crew had been maltreated. The incident gained some publicity when it was taken up by a New York lawyer of Indian origin named Henderson and one Alfred W. McCann, a journalist described by the British Consul General as "pronouncedly anti-British and strongly Sinn Fein".[36]

The thirty-three seamen went to court, but there are contradictory statements as to whether they tried to return on board ship and were denied access by the master, or themselves refused to take up their stations again. In any case, the shipmaster logged them as "deserters", hired a new crew, and put to sea. After almost a year, the US Circuit Court of Appeals reversed an earlier decision. The judges did not pronounce with regard to the seamen's allegations, although they opined that they seemed unfounded. Instead they focused on the question of whether the seamen had been wrongfully discharged by the shipmaster. They concluded that the lascars had had "no justification" for withdrawing from the ship; had therefore committed the crime of "desertion", and were to be punished under the provisions of England's Merchant Shipping Act of 1894 by forfeiture of wages and by imprisonment.[37] We should recall here that

34. *RBCC 1930*, vol. 1 (Bombay, 1931), pp. 188f.
35. This incident is documented in considerable detail in NAI, Dept of Commerce, Lascar Seamen, May 1922, s.nos. 94–95, filed.
36. Gloster Armstrong, British Consulate General, New York, to Principal Secretary for Foreign Affairs, 17 March 1922, *ibid.*
37. Fazel Ahammed *et al.* against SS *City of Norwich*, Opinion of United States Circuit Court of Appeals, for the Second Circuit, *ibid.*

incarceration as a punishment for "desertion" or "absence without leave" was abolished for "white" seamen in the twentieth century but perpetuated for lascars by the Indian Merchant Shipping Act of 1923 well into the post-colonial period.[38]

The colonial records are silent as to what became of the thirty-three Punjabi firemen, but they include a clipping of one of McCann's articles. He reported that the lascars were "panic stricken" when the marshal suggested during the court's opening session that they should be brought to Ellis Island, which after World War I had been turned into an internment camp for unwanted immigrants: "Through an interpreter they said they knew all about this terrible place, and would not go there." All of them left the court building soon afterwards and we have no information about whether they managed to escape confinement and deportation.[39] What the records clearly indicate is a considerable uneasiness among colonial administrators in India about the "*Norwich* incident". A Board of Trade official remarked: "This is a most unsatisfactory case. The charges may be vague & the facts obscure, but we know perfectly well that properly treated lascars would never desert at New York, with the threat of Ellis Island hanging on them."[40] Another bureaucrat agreed that they "were not likely to desert in New York without very good cause".[41] The immigration policy of the United States was, in other words, a strong barrier under normal circumstances against a breakdown of ship's discipline and the absconding of a large part of the crew.

The case of the SS *City of Norwich* demonstrates how labour law and immigration policy combined in restricting the mobility of Indian seamen: the lascars committed not one but two offences when they left their ship. First, under British and "British Indian" maritime labour law, Indian (as opposed to "white") seamen had a legal claim neither to terminate their contract outside their home country nor take shore leave during their engagement. Leaving the ship without the shipmaster's consent, therefore, always amounted to "desertion" even when the crew took legal action against the master for breach of contract. Secondly, the immigration laws of the United States and of other countries[42] further impinged upon the seamen's customary right to shore leave and made them liable to prosecution for the offence of "illegal entry" if they insisted on it.

38. Desai, *Maritime Labour in India*, pp. 204–208; Barnes, *Evolution and Scope of Mercantile Marine Laws*, pp. 175–176.

39. Alfred W. McCann, "Starved at Sea, Hindoos Assert", *New York Globe*, 16 May 1921.

40. Note by H.M. Lindsay, Commerce Dept, GoI, 14 January 1922, NAI, Dept of Commerce, Lascar Seamen, May 1922, s.nos. 94–95, filed.

41. Note by ? [illegible], Commerce Dept, GoI, 16 January 1922, *ibid.*

42. Lascars were, for instance, permitted to land in French ports only if they possessed "a certificate attesting that they would be engaged in a British port" (which was, as we have seen, contrary to British and "British Indian" maritime labour law); Desai, *Maritime Labour in India*, p. 61.

Figure 1. Lascars on board the SS *Viceroy of India* (1929). This specimen of "official ship photography" shows Indian seamen on board ship, not in their usual working clothes, but in an orientalized dress uniform. The differentiation in the dress code of maritime workers according to their origin may be understood as a visualization of the legal as well as informal distinctions between the labour relations of lascars and (white) seamen.
National Maritime Museum Picture Library. Used with permission.

Figure 2. Seamen outside Dunbar House, West India Dock Road (1920s). The men on this photograph are apparently on land leave and outside the reach of ship discipline. Their choice of attire contrasts starkly with the supposedly oriental ship uniforms provided by the shipping companies (cf. Figure 1).
Tower Hamlets Local History Library and Archives, Bancroft Library. Used with permission.

The first technique of regulation supplemented the economic subordination of labour by imposing an inferior legal status on the lascars and so created labour relations akin to those conceptualized in the English "master and servant law".[43] The second technique made it considerably more difficult to sidestep the barriers raised by the first and effectively protected shipmasters and shipping companies against indictments for breach of contract. As one colonial official remarked on the occasion of the *Norwich* case, "[so] far as the Indian Merchant Shipping Laws are concerned there does not seem to be any provision under these laws under which Govt. could bring an action against a master of a vessel guilty of an infringement on the terms of the agreement".[44]

In a period when the centre of the world economy shifted to North

43. See *ibid.*, pp. 204–208. For a thorough discussion of the genealogy of "master and servant law" in the British Empire see Douglas Hay and Paul Craven (eds), *Masters, Servants, and Magistrates in Britain and the Empire, 1562–1955* (Chapel Hill, NC [etc.], 2004).
44. Note by Under-Secretary to the Commerce Department, GoI, 12 January 1922, NAI, Dept

America and a growing share of merchant shipping was attracted to its ports, the immigration policies of the United States acquired an ever growing importance for South Asian maritime employment, despite the legal restrictions we shall turn to in the next section. More than 7,000 lascars entered North Atlantic ports of the USA during the summer months of 1937 on European vessels, 6,000 of them on British merchant ships.[45] If Indian seaman were frequently denied land leave, that was due also to a US regulation introduced in the early 1920s under which ship-owners had to pay a security of $500 for each lascar on board their ships, a sum that was withheld in case the lascar "deserted".[46] This fine was raised to $1,000 in the 1930s, when a bill was introduced into the US Senate "authorising officials to board ships entering the United States' ports and remove or deport seamen of races ineligible for United States citizenship". British officials and employer representatives as well as the Indian nationalist press agreed that the purpose of these measures was not only to prevent Indian immigration but to protect the US domestic shipping industry against British competitors, which enjoyed a considerable advantage through their privileged access to cheap colonial labour from the Indian subcontinent.[47]

However, British settler colonies pursued similar policies. In 1902–1903, for instance, the Australian Federal Ministry persisted, against the criticism of the British Colonial Secretary, in giving a mail contract to the P&O Company only on condition that lascars were not to be employed on mail steamers for Australia. The two reasons given for the policy were apparently to preserve the "purity of their race and to encourage the recruitment of British seamen".[48]

With regard to British immigration policy towards Indian seamen we can be very brief since the field has been explored thoroughly by several

of Commerce, Lascar Seamen, May 1922, s.nos. 94–95, filed. It is probably against this background that "facilities for making complaints" against the shipmaster were included in the Indian Merchant Shipping Act of 1923, though their efficacy is rather doubtful. See P.G. Kanekar, *Seamen in Bombay: Report of an Enquiry into the Conditions of Their Life and Work* (Bombay, 1928), p. 35.

45. ILOrep August 1939, ILO C1903/129, p. 42 (excerpt from *The Bombay Chronicle*, 27 August 1939).

46. *Report of the Committee of the Bengal Chamber of Commerce 1922*, vol. 2 (Calcutta, 1923), p. 332.

47. OIOC, Economic & Overseas Dept Collections, Seamen, IOR/L/E/9/974; ILOrep January 1932, ILO C1903/38, p. 59 (excerpt from *The Leader*, 27 January 1932); Jam-e-Jamshed, 26 January 1932, quoted in Government of Bombay, *Native Newspaper Report* [hereafter, BNNP] *for the week ending 30 January 1932*, p. 198.

48. Jam-e-Jamshed, 31 July 1903, quoted in *BNNP*, 1 August 1903, p. 14. See also Praja Bandhu 19 January 1902, quoted in *ibid.*, 25 January 1902, pp. 12–13; Rast Goftar, 17 May 1903, quoted in *ibid.*, 23 May 1903, p. 9; Gujarati, 21 June, quoted in *ibid.*, 27 June 1903, p. 12; Voice of India, 11 July, quoted in *ibid.*, 11 July 1903, p. 10; Gujarati, 2 August 1903, and Mahratta, 2 August 1903, quoted in *ibid.*, 8 August 1903, p. 15.

historians, especially Marika Sherwood, Laura Tabili, Rozina Visram, and most recently by Gopalan Balachandran. While xenophobic campaigns against "coloured seamen" date back to the late nineteenth century, the economic downturn after World War I exacerbated hostility to immigrant workers. The number of non-European seamen who had found employment ashore had increased during the war and there were many more who competed with unemployed British sailors for engagements after peace had been concluded.

In 1919 the Aliens Restriction (Amendment) Act required ship-owners to give preference to British seamen, while "destitute coloured seamen" were to be deported. The latter part of that regulation could not legally be applied to seamen from "British India" who were not "aliens" but "Imperial citizens" and had, therefore, the right to stay in Britain. In practice, however, Indian seamen were treated as "undesirable residents" and found it difficult to obtain work in British ports.[49] Eventually the India Office decided to commission vessels at their own expense to transport lascars to ports in the Indian Empire if they agreed to repatriation on the promise of being paid a gratuity.

The official records do not convey the impression that those lascars who accepted the offer felt they had narrowly escaped "destitution" only thanks to an "act of grace" by the India Office – an image propagated by the contemporary British press.[50] Thus, when the *Kurmark* passed the Suez Canal in 1921 with 150 "Adenese" and 63 Punjabi "destitute seamen" the situation on board was extremely tense. The Indian seamen insisted on land leave in Aden, on *halal* meat, and on the immediate payment by the India Office of the debts they had incurred with their creditors who were also on board. They were infuriated as they felt they had been cajoled into returning to India with false promises. The shipmaster pointed out that the port captain had told him he was "very sorry to oblige me to sail with such a crowd of Bolshevicks [*sic*] aboard".[51]

The regulation of 1919 was consolidated by the infamous Coloured Alien Seamen Order of 1925 that forced "coloured" seamen to register themselves with the police when residing in Britain, and provided that they could be deported if they were deemed "destitute". Of the South Asian seamen, Goan Christians and subjects of princely states were immediately

49. Visram, *Asians in Britain*, pp. 196–224. See also Sherwood, "Race, Nationality and Employment among Lascar Seamen", pp. 234f.; Tabili, *"We Ask for British Justice"*, pp. 33–36; Gopalan Balachandran, "Conflicts in the International Maritime Labour Market: British and Indian Seamen, Employers, and the State, 1890–1939", *Indian Economic and Social History Review*, 39 (2002), pp. 71–100, 83f.; *idem*, "Circulation through Seafaring", pp. 113f.

50. "Coloured Seamen Repatriated", *The Western Mail* (Cardiff), 12 September 1921; see also Visram, *Asians in Britain*, pp. 201–205.

51. Shipmaster SS *Kurmark* to Director, India Office Shipping, 7 October 1921, OIOC, Commercial & Revenue Papers, IOR/L/E/7/1103, fos 49–51; Resident, Aden to Secretary of State for India, 1 October 1921 (telegram), *ibid.*, fos 74–75.

affected by this regulation as they were not residents of "British India". However, more than a few lascars from areas of the subcontinent under direct British rule were deported under this Order since most could give no documentary proof of their origin. Many were, after all, ship-jumpers whose only proof of identity, the "Continuous Discharge Certificate", had stayed behind on the vessel where it was always kept in the shipmaster's cabin for as long as the agreement lasted. When they were issued with seamen's passports after registration, they were often categorized as "British protected persons", and not as Imperial subjects, which left them vulnerable to deportation. This government order was not revoked until 1943, when war had once again increased the demand for seamen.[52]

However, the efficiency of racist immigration and labour laws should not be overstated since there were many ways to subvert them.[53] India Office officials pointed out, for instance, that "in some cases lascars who are deserters are smuggled in by boarding-house masters among Arab stoke-hold crews" in order to obtain engagements under European articles.[54] Exceptionally well documented is the story of a steward named A.G. Straker who played on the vagueness of ethnic and national identification with considerable virtuosity to enlarge his room to manoeuvre on the maritime labour market. Hence, he sometimes claimed to be a resident of Britain and sometimes to be a "Eurasian" from India. In 1923, an infuriated India Office bureaucrat noted that Straker "makes a business of travelling between India and the UK being constantly repatriated from one Country to the other". A number of officials made it a point to hunt him down and eventually identified him as a native of Jamaica. Imperial law could constrain the mobility of seamen but never control it totally.[55] Yet immigration policy set limits on the ingenious appropriation by "coloured" seamen of the opportunities offered them in an increasingly global maritime labour market. Their situation might have been similar to that of Hašek's good soldier Švejk, who could subvert the authority of his superiors but could not end the war.

COMPETING LABOUR NETWORKS

Extra-legal mechanisms were no less important than labour and immigration laws in the regulation of maritime labour relations in general and of

52. Tabili, "*We Ask for British Justice*", pp. 113–134; Tony Lane, "The Political Imperatives of Bureaucracy and Empire: The Case of the Coloured Alien Seamen Order, 1925", *Immigrants & Minorities*, 13 (2–3) (1994), pp. 104–129. See also Balachandran, "Conflicts in the International Maritime Labour Market", pp. 83f.
53. See Tabili, "*We Ask for British Justice*", pp. 128f.
54. Summary of letter from High Commissioner for India, 26 November 1931, NAI, Dept of Commerce, Merchant Marine II, August 1932, file 67, M. II/32, s.nos. 1–11, part B.
55. OIOC, Commercial & Revenue Papers, IOR/L/E/7/1165, file 3594.

the seamen's mobility in particular. Elsewhere I have discussed at length the "networks of subordination" involving various middlemen and institutions through which shipping agents recruited and shipmasters controlled the lascars – networks that were simultaneously appropriated as "networks of the subordinated" for purposes at variance with employer interests.[56]

With regard to mobility, this latter aspect of "subaltern" appropriation has been brought out clearly by scholars who have looked at the origins of lascar settlement in Britain. Immigrant Indians, often former seamen or boatswains themselves, founded boarding houses in British port towns that attracted ship-jumpers and provided them not only with accommodation but often also with jobs – by the 1930s not infrequently in one of the mushrooming Indian restaurants.[57] South Asian maritime labour networks also expanded into the British mainland in the form of pedlar rings which sold artificial silk shawls and cheap household goods from door to door,[58] and we have already mentioned that maritime labour networks were transformed into networks of large-scale migration in the 1950s and 1960s. However, in combination with various legal regulations, the same networks that were able to integrate, connect, and facilitate mobility also had the capacity to exclude, insulate, and constrain the freedom of movement of seamen. It is to these legal regulations that we shall now turn.

Various regulations sanctioned by the Government of India since 1887 limited the geographical space in which Indian seamen could legally be employed. From 1893 onwards, lascars could be engaged only for voyages between the latitudes 60° N and 50° S during the winter months between October and March. Moreover, the engagement of Indian seamen on voyages in this season to all American North Atlantic ports beyond 38° N, namely Boston and New York, and to the Baltic, was ruled out too. Such a piece of protective legislative racism was based on the assumption that "Asiatics" could not stand cold weather as well as the hardy Jack Tar. The "lascar line" was another type of legal constraint on Indian seamen's mobility excluding them, in effect, from some of the most important routes of world shipping. This regulation remained a binding clause in the

56. Ravi Ahuja, "Networks of Subordination – Networks of the Subordinated: The Case of South Asian Maritime Labour under British Imperialism (c.1890–1947)", in Harald Fischer-Tiné and Ashwini Tambe (eds), *Spaces of Disorder: The Limits of British Colonial Control in South Asia and the Indian Ocean* (forthcoming).

57. Adams, *Across Seven Seas*, pp. 39–52; Choudhury, *The Roots and Tales*, pp. 71–75. See also Tabili, *"We Ask for British Justice"*, p. 143.

58. Letter from Geo. Smith & Sons, Agents for Ellerman's City Line, 17 September 1925, NAI, Dept of Commerce, Shipping, September 1926, file 606–S, s.nos. 1–18, part A, p. 22; Summary of letter from High Commissioner for India, 26 November 1931, NAI, Dept of Commerce, Merchant Marine II, August 1932, file 67, M. II/32, s.nos. 1–11, part B. See also Balachandran, "Conflicts in the International Maritime Labour Market", pp. 85–87; *idem*, "Circulation through Seafaring", pp. 117–120.

prescribed forms of "lascar agreements" for decades, and was only briefly relaxed during World War I when the demand for merchant seamen reached unknown heights.[59]

Between the World Wars, the British shipping industry (and later the emerging Indian seamen's trade unions) persistently demanded the abolition of this clause, arguing that lascars had shown their ability during the war to bear the harsh climatic conditions of a North Atlantic passage and that improved conditions on steamships had made such voyages less demanding.[60] In August 1938 the Government of India suspended the regulation experimentally for a period of three years.[61] When the experiment was reviewed a year later, it was reported that the returned seamen's state of health was "satisfactory". Moreover, it was emphasized that no European seaman had lost his job because of the clause's suspension: "Inquiries made at the Government Shipping Office, Bombay, reveal that the only persons hit by the decision are Malayan and Chinese deck hands [...]."[62] That was apparently not considered a problem and had, in fact, been one of the explicit objectives British shipping companies had been pursuing with their demand to abolish the clause. "[O]n account of extensive smuggling of opium, and desertions of Chinese, we are considering the advisability of changing to Lascars", wrote executives of the Dodwell-Castle Line,[63] while the agents of Brocklebank's Cunard Line observed that

> [...] it has been found that both the Chinese and Malay crews are very liable to desert on arriving in the USA, thus causing a considerable loss to the owners of the line. It has also been our experience that Malay and Chinese crews are not as efficient as lascars on steamers trading from Calcutta to America in addition to which the former invariably give more trouble to the masters of our vessels.[64]

59. GoI, Dept of Commerce and Industry, to GoBo, Marine Dept, 12 February 1920, OIOC, BoMP, IOR/P/10793, A 73–75.
60. NAI, Dept of Commerce, Merchant Marine II, September 1938, F. No. 11, M. II (2)/37, s.nos. 1–9, part A. See also ILOrep January 1933, ILO, C1903/50, p. 67 (report about a meeting of the members of the Deck Department of the National Seamen's Union of India, Bombay, 20 December 1932); *Labour Gazette* (Bombay), XVI.10 (June 1937), p. 764 (report on All-India Seamen's Conference). For a view in favour of continued spatial exclusion of lascars, see *Labour Gazette* (Bombay), XIV.4 (December 1934), p. 285 (statement of Imperial Merchant Service Guild). See also Balachandran, "Conflicts in the International Maritime Labour Market", pp. 96–98.
61. ILOrep August 1938, ILO, C1903/117, pp. 41–42 (excerpt from *Hindustan Times*, 25 August 1938).
62. ILOrep June 1939, ILO, C1903/127, p. 42 (excerpt from *The Times of India*, 1 June 1939).
63. Dodwell-Castle Line (James Chambers & Co., Liverpool) to Mercantile Marine Dept, Board of Trade, 28 August 1930, OIOC, Commercial & Revenue Department Papers, IOR/L/E/7/1125, File 2139: Lascars, employment outside winter limits, main file (1920–1931). See also Andrew Weir & Co., London and Glasgow, to Captain Darvell, Shipping Master, Calcutta, 10 February 1925, *ibid.*
64. Graham's Trading Co. (Agents of Brocklebank's Cunard Service) to GoBe, Maritime Dept,

The suspension of geographical prohibitions on lascar employment thus enabled employers to shift from Asian maritime labour networks they found less amenable, to those of the lascars. From another perspective, the abolition of legal restrictions did not entail a "de-regulation" enabling all maritime workers, as so many atomistic individuals, access to the labour market irrespective of socio-economic bonds. Access was regulated mainly by complex, predominantly extra-legal and non-public maritime labour networks which connected shipping agents, like the famous Mackinnon Mackenzie Company, and colonial port officials in Bombay and Calcutta with "licensed shipping brokers" and other recruitment agents (*ghat serangs*), and with trade unions and village clubs, with boarding-house keepers and moneylenders, village elders, and so-called *serangs*, who were the equivalents of British boatswains. In this case, the National Seamen's Union of India (which may be conceived of as a publicly operating and institutionalized element of the Bombay network and whose traces can be located more easily) urged the colonial government "to move shipping companies to engage Indian, rather than Malay and Chinese, seamen" on ships bound for North America.[65] In this case, an Indian labour network responded to labour market competition by attempting to reduce the trans-territorial movements of Malay and Chinese colleagues. In other words, not only did it manage to link itself to the North Atlantic maritime labour market, it contributed to the exclusion of competing Asian networks.

That was no isolated case – the networks of Indian seamen, like other labour networks under capitalism,[66] were not mechanisms solely of incorporation. While they opened up avenues of trans-territorial mobility for some, they contributed to blocking them for others. Competition in the international maritime labour market was discernible not only between British and Indian seamen, but also between various maritime networks of the Indian Ocean region and even within South Asia. Hence, not all traditionally seafaring communities of coastal India gained access to the market for steamship labour – the south-eastern shores of India were heavily under-represented, while interior regions with little reputation for seamanship like Northern Punjab acquired some prominence. In the late nineteenth century, Punjabis and Pashtuns appear to have more or less driven out the Zanzibari "Sidis" from the engine rooms of British steamships, where the latter had so far been favoured as stokers.[67] By

11 February 1925, *ibid*; see also Graham & Co. to GoBe, Maritime Dept, 15 March 1915, OIOC, BoMP, IOR/P/10793, A 75–76.

65. ILOrep January 1933, ILO, C1903/50, p. 67 (report about a meeting of the members of the Deck Department of the National Seamen's Union of India, Bombay, 20 December 1932).

66. See Eric Wolf, "Incorporation and Identity in the Making of the Modern World", in *idem*, *Pathways of Power: Building an Anthropology of the Modern World* (Berkeley, CA [etc.], 2001), pp. 353–369, 366–368.

67. Hood, *Blight of Insubordination*, p. 11; see also Hope, *A New History of British Shipping*, p. 324; Ewald, "Crossers of the Sea", pp. 83f.

this time, thousands of Indian lascars were shipped as passengers to various ports of the Indian Ocean region, where they were engaged on steamships in preference to local labour.[68] Abdul Majid, however, a *ghat serang* from Sylhet, met with little success in the 1920s and 1930s when he tried to convince the colonial authorities in Singapore that Chinese seamen should be replaced by "loyal British subjects" from Bengal and Malaya.[69] During World War II, the Indian Seamen's Union (Calcutta) endorsed the replacement of 2,000 striking Chinese seamen by lascars, in 1942.[70]

There was also stiff competition between the labour networks of the two main recruitment ports for steamship labour in India, Calcutta and Bombay. Shipping companies had established permanent links with labour networks rooted in specific localities: P&O preferred Muslim stokers from particular areas of northern Punjab, deck-hands from certain coastal villages in Gujarat or Ratnagiri, and Catholic stewards from the *velhas conquistas*, the "old conquest" areas of coastal Goa; the Clan, British India, and other steam navigation companies favoured firemen from the "seamen's zone" of central Sylhet; others hired Maldivians as deckhands whenever possible.[71]

Yet there was a permanent wage differential – Calcutta lascars received lower wages, and even the food rations their agreements entitled them to were smaller and less expensive – a discrepancy legitimized with bizarre anthropological arguments.[72] In 1929, the Bombay-based Indian Seamen's Union demanded prohibition of the practice among shipping companies of

68. R.H.H. Hopkins, Shipping Master Bombay, to Bombay Marine Department, 2 December 1913, OIOC, BoMP, IOR/P/9596, A309. See also Report by the Shipping Master Calcutta, 17 August 1918, *ibid.*, IOR/P/11008, A 207.
69. Indian Employment Bureau, M.A. Majid, Singapore, to J. Foley, Under-Secretary to Board of Trade, Mercantile Marine, 2 September 1938, PRO, CO273/639/9, fol. 11–15.
70. Indian Seamen's Union, Resolution on the Pending Grievances of the Indian Seamen, 31 August 1943, NMML, M.A. Master Papers, I. Subject Files, A. Scindia Steam Navigation Company, file 150.
71. OIOC, BoMP IOR/P/9083 (September 1912), A347; W.A. Cosgrave, Off. Deputy Commissioner Sylhet, to Commissioner Surma Valley and Hill Districts, 21 August 1913, OIOC, Commercial & Revenue Papers IOR/L/E/7/696, file 405; Shipping Master Bombay to GoBo, 15 January 1918, OIOC, BoMP IOR/P/10326, B19; Shipping Master Bombay to Bombay Marine Dept, 10 March 1920, OIOC, BoMP IOR/P/10793, A160; Reply to the Report of the Seamen's Recruitment Committee (Clow Committee), August 1923, OIOC, BeMP IOR/P/11312, A41, p. 58, 65; Kanekar, *Seamen in Bombay*, pp. 5–18; GoBo, Conditions of Industrial Labour in the Bombay Presidency, Royal Commission on Labour in India: *Evidence* (London, 1931) [hereafter, RCLI Evidence], vol. 1, part 1 (Bombay, Written Evidence), p. 149; written statement by Bombay Seamen's Union, *ibid.*, pp. 293f; written statement by Mackinnon, Mackenzie & Co., *ibid.*, pp. 544f; Olga Esther Baptista, "The 'Coor' System – A Study of Goan Club Life" (M.A., University of Bombay, 1958), pp. 89, 175; Choudhury, *The Roots and Tales*, pp. 58f.
72. Desai, *Maritime Labour in India*, pp. 47f.; Saksena, *Seamen in India*, pp. 66f.; OIOC, BoMP IOR/P/6705, A299 (October 1903); OIOC, Economic & Overseas Department Collections, Seamen (1925–1941), IOR/L/E/9/973.

"importing" crews from Calcutta, which had triggered violent clashes between seamen of the two ports.[73] Conversely, in the early 1930s, a breakaway union of Bengali Muslim stewards, led by the conservative Muslim League politician and future Pakistani prime minister H.S. Suhrawardy, tried to exclude Goan saloon crews from the Calcutta labour market.[74] The demand to remove wage differentials was voiced somewhat more insistently only after non-particularistic trade-union policies gained some influence and trade-union links between the two ports intensified in the 1930s.[75]

Yet as late as 1948, the president of the National Seamen's Union, the largest of Bombay's seafarers' organizations at the time, "maintained that there should be separate unions for the ports of Bombay and Calcutta because conditions in the two ports were so dissimilar", giving weight to his opinion by drawing attention to divergent ethnic and religious affiliations: "while the saloon staff in Bombay are almost entirely Goan Christians, in Calcutta the saloon staff are predominantly Muslims".[76] The union represented by this spokesman was by no means "communalistic" or exclusivist along ethnic lines; several of its key leaders, including the president himself, were, for instance, Muslims, though large parts of its membership were not. Their attitude rather reflected the competition between maritime labour networks based in distinct *social* spaces – a particularism of locality that was sometimes given plausibility by appealing to the ethnicized common sense of the time.

Of all maritime labour networks, that of the Goan stewards was surely the best organized – the power of outside recruitment agents, money-lenders, and commercial boarding-house keepers had been limited by cooperative village clubs, the *kur*, of which about 300 existed in Bombay in the 1920s and several in Calcutta and Karachi. The kurs had been created since the mid-nineteenth century by *communidades* of certain agrarian villages for the exclusive use of Catholic and "respectable" migrants from

73. Written statement by Indian Seamen's Union (Bombay), RCLI Evidence, vol. 1, part 1 (Bombay, Written Evidence), pp. 290–293; written statement by Mulchand M. Kripalani, Hon. General Secretary, Indian Seamen's Union (Karachi), *ibid.*, p. 232; verbal testimony by Tarachand J. Lalwani and Mulchand M. Kripalani, Indian Seamen's Union (Karachi), *ibid.*, vol. 1, part 2 (Bombay, Oral Evidence), pp. 41f; verbal testimony by Mohammed Ibrahim Serang and P.G. Kanekar, Indian Seamen's Union (Bombay), *ibid.*, p. 224. See also oral testimony by R. Liddle, Marine Superintendent, British Indian Steam Navigation Company, Calcutta, RCLI Evidence, vol. 5, part 2 (Bengal, Oral Evidence), p. 304.

74. Principal Officer, Mercantile Marine Dept, Calcutta District, to Secretary to the GoI, Dept of Commerce, 21 July 1931, NAI, Dept of Commerce, Mercantile Marine II, January 1932, F. No. 32, M. II./31, s.nos. 1–3, part B. See also ILOrep July 1931, ILO C1903/32, p. 80 (excerpt from *The Pioneer*, 2 July 1931).

75. ILOrep C1903/119, pp. 34–35 (excerpt from *The Labour Times*, Madras, October 1938). See also Broeze, "The Muscles of Empire", pp. 66 and *passim*.

76. Mowat, *Seafarers' Conditions in India and Pakistan*, p. 79.

that village.[77] However, since the turn of the century they had also provided the organizational basis for a very early development of trade unions. The constitution of the Bombay Seamen's Union, at the time one of the strongest maritime unions in the port, prescribed as late as 1926 that members of its Committee had to be managers of "village clubs" and that only Goan Christians were acceptable as members. Before the major seamen's unions in Bombay opened up to all sections of ship workers in the late 1920s,[78] resolutions were often concerned with preserving as a Goan domain all employment in the saloon departments of P&O and other shipping lines.[79] When the British parliament decided in 1935 that tramp-shipping subsidies should be granted only for vessels employing "British subjects", even the Portuguese Embassy in London turned to the British Foreign Office in protest.[80] Eventually, the Goan labour networks proved to be too well entrenched to be marginalized by such legislative measures. Even in the late 1950s almost all stewards and cooks recruited in Bombay were Goan Christians.[81]

SERANGS AND SURVEILLANCE

If maritime labour networks contributed to structuring the access of the various communities of seafarers to the international maritime labour market, they were as much involved with regulating the individual mobility of seamen during their voyages. Detailed information regarding the labour process of lascars on British steamships is hard to come by, since many of the daily routines of surveillance and command, being delegated to Indian serangs, were conducted in languages British officers and engineers could not follow and consequently left few traces in their written documents. Further research is required in this field, but the evidence presently available suggests that the "informal" social relations between

77. The only systematic and unfortunately unpublished study of these "village clubs" is Baptista, "The 'Coor' System".
78. Verbal testimony by J.P. Lobo and Patrick DeSa, Bombay Seamen's Union, RCLI Evidence, vol. 1, part 2 (Bombay, Oral Evidence), pp. 227–232; A. Colaco (ed.), *A History of the Seamen's Union Bombay* (Bombay, 1955), pp. 15–20, 70f. See also Ahuja, "Networks of Subordination"; Broeze, "The Muscles of Empire", p. 56.
79. See for example "The humble petition of the members of the Goa Portuguese Seamen's Club, the Portuguese Seafarers' Union and the Asiatic Seamen's (Saloon Crew) Union" to Sir G.A. Lloyd, Governor of Bombay, 23 July 1920, OIOC, BoMP, IOR/P/10793, A273–274.
80. OIOC, Economic & Overseas Department Collections, Seamen (1925–1941), IOR/L/E/9/955. See also Balachandran, "Conflicts in the International Maritime Labour Market", pp. 89f.
81. Seamen's Employment Office, Bombay, No. of Seamen on Articles as on 15th May 1956, NMML, M.A. Master Papers, I. Subject Files, E. National Committees and Commissions, file 867; C.P. Shrivastava, National Board of Seafarers, to ?, dated 14 July 1956 [*sic*, probably 1957], *ibid.*, B. Shipping, file 482.

serangs and lascars augmented the various legal techniques of limiting the incidence of "desertion" we have so far looked at.

The serang was no doubt an ambiguous social type, combining the features of crimp and patron, of foreman and subcontractor. He was his employer's agent, and spokesman for the crew, a moneylender, and organizer of the village clubs and trade unions.[82] The ambiguous social position of these middlemen was also revealed in their role in regulating the lascars' spatial mobility. As has already been mentioned, serangs could be involved in extending their networks into the hinterlands of Britain and other metropolitan countries.[83] Yet any serang who wished to stay in merchant shipping and hold continuous engagements strove to develop permanent links to a certain shipping company, to a particular shipmaster or chief engineer. That was possible since employers, from the 1920s, apparently undertook greater efforts to regularize the labour relations of a skilled core of their crews and to foster a cadre of serangs who were well acquainted with the peculiarities of the labour process on their ships and had a reputation for being able to control their men, make them work, and prevent them from absconding in metropolitan ports.[84]

However, if colonial officials and spokesmen for the shipping industry asserted that crews "fell to pieces in a few days" and turned into "unwieldy indisciplined mobs" without the leadership of a powerful serang, some caution is in order. Balachandran has argued with some reason that these circles systematically overstated the community bonds of lascar crews and the power of the serang, which until the 1940s enabled them successfully to legitimize a pseudo-traditional recruitment method, based on a complex system of mostly informal payments (or "bribes"), that offered considerable cost advantages to employers but

82. See G. Balachandran, "Searching for the *Sardar*: the State, Precapitalist Institutions, and Human Agency in the Maritime Labour Market", in Burton Stein and Sanjay Subrahmanyam (eds), *Institutions and Economic Change in South Asia* (Delhi, 1996), pp. 216–220; Ahuja, "Networks of Subordination".

83. See above, in the section "Competing Labour Networks".

84. The British India Steam Navigation Co., by far the largest recruiter in Calcutta, manned 127 ships in this port in 1929/30, for which purpose they kept a register of 226 deck serangs, 200 firemen serangs, 782 *sukhanis* (helmsmen) and 200 butlers (foremen in the saloon department) who were given preference in engagement. As every ship required one foreman of each category and four helmsmen, the ratio between the registered and the employed was less than 2:1. Moreover, it was stated that no serangs had been added to the register for six or seven years, except when the necessity of immediate replacement occurred. The preference for fairly regular employment patterns with regard to these categories of seamen was also expressed in the payment of a pension or gratuity to serangs who had been in the company's service for twenty-five years. Oral testimony by R. Liddle, Marine Superintendent, British Indian Steam Navigation Company, Calcutta, RCLI Evidence, vol. 5, part 2 (Bengal, Oral Evidence), pp. 297–303. For further evidence of the tendency towards (partial) regularization of the maritime workforce see my "Die 'Lenksamkeit' des 'Lascars'".

was increasingly unpopular and contested by the seamen and even the serangs.[85]

Before the 1950s, however, bonds of kinship and locality *did* usually connect at least the core of a crew to their respective serangs, whose recommendations on recruitment were usually accepted by the ship-master. Crews were likely to become more heterogeneous in periods of great demand for maritime labour power, especially during the two World Wars. Community bonds might have been somewhat less pervasive in Calcutta than in Bombay, though the available evidence suggests – *pace* Balachandran – that the networks of Sylheti firemen, who worked the engine rooms of most steamers manned in Calcutta, were rather closely meshed.[86] Even when the boatswain was not a family or village elder, most seamen needed credit to be able to discharge the various extra-legal fees that had to be paid to various middlemen before they received their agreement, and for this many of them had to turn to a serang too, or to a *bariwallah*, as boarding-house owners were called in Calcutta. These creditors frequently, though not always, came from the same or a neighbouring locality and lascars seem to have been unable in many cases to discharge their full debts even after receiving an advance on signing their articles.[87]

85. Written Statement by R. Liddle, Marine Superintendent, British Indian Steam Navigation Company, Calcutta, RCLI Evidence, vol. 5, part 1 (Bengal, Written Evidence), pp. 363; Oral testimony by H.F. Darvell, Shipping Master Calcutta, *ibid.*, vol. 5, part 2 (Bengal, Oral Evidence), pp. 277, 298; Report of the Sub-Committee Appointed by the Owners to Consider Government of India Memoranda Relating to Conditions of Employment of Indian Seamen (not dated, c.1946); NMML, M.A. Master Papers, I. subject Files, E. National Committees and Commissions, file 786; see also [L.W. Balcombe,] Calcutta Liners Conference (Crews) to E.S. Krishnamoorthy, GoI, Dept of Commerce, 19 February 1946 (confidential letter), *ibid.* See also Balachandran, "Recruitment and Control of Indian Seamen".

86. See Report of the Seamen's Recruitment Committee (Clow Committee), OIOC, BeMP, IOR/P/11178, A1 (December 1922), folio 3. The Clow Committee here opined (possibly under trade-union influence) that community bonds were of minor importance in Calcutta ("no close attachment between the *serang* and his crew"). For a concurrent opinion of a trade unionist and social reformer see also Kanekar, *Seamen in Bombay*, p. 29. Balachandran seems to accept this view to a certain extent ("Recruitment and Control of Indian Seamen", pp. 12f., 18; "Circulation through Seafaring", pp. 108–111, and personal communication with the author). However, life accounts collected by Adams (*Across Seven Seas*: Nawab Ali, p. 72, Haji Shirajul Islam, pp. 95f.; Abdul Malik, p. 111; Haji Kona Miah, pp. 128–130, Shah Abdul Majid Qureishi, pp. 146, 148; Abdul Wahab, p. 209), memories of former Sylheti seamen as presented by Choudhury (*The Roots and Tales*, pp. 35–43, 53–56, and *passim*) and Gardner's fieldwork in Sylhet (*Global Migrants, Local Lives*, pp. 41, 79f.) suggest a qualification of this assessment, which was also refuted by other officials and most eloquently by the Calcutta Shipping Master: H.F. Darvell to GoBe, Maritime Dept, 17 March 1925, NAI, Dept of Commerce, Shipping, October 1927, file 104–S.(4), s.nos. 1–6, part A (confidential), pp. 5f. See also Maritime Labour Advisory Committee, Memorandum on Recruitment of Indian Seamen, 9 April 1947, p. 3, NMML, M.A. Master Papers, I. subject files, F. International Committees and Commissions, file 916.

87. Oral Testimony by H.F. Darvell, Shipping Master Calcutta, RCLI Evidence, vol. 5, part 2 (Bengal, Oral Evidence), p. 270; Desai, *Maritime Labour in India*, pp. 44–48.

Hence, bonds of community were backed up (in Calcutta even more than in Bombay)[88] by bonds of debt, and this combination, together with the legal provisions of the "lascar agreements", created considerable disciplinary power for the serang on board ship. This power did not remain unchallenged and there were probably numerous instances when lascars clashed with serangs, who often acted in concert with ships' officers over the payment of informal commissions. Such conflicts usually remained unrecorded as most of them were resolved or suppressed informally on board ship.[89] Some, however, came to such a head that they were noticed by state authorities. One such incident occurred in Salford in January 1920, when the greater part of the stokers of the SS *Shanghai* refused to make payments the serang had tried to enforce and insisted on being discharged. The owners saw no other way to solve the conflict than to transfer "the Serang and four of his relatives" to a different ship from the rest of the firemen.[90]

The refusal or inability of a lascar to pay the share of his wages the serang expected from him could thus lead to extremely tense relations on board ship. Under the dual necessity of fulfilling his own financial obligations and of maintaining his authority, the serang could not afford to permit non-payment. For the same compelling reason, he could not allow defaulting debtors to desert the ship, even laying aside the necessity of his maintaining his reputation with the employers as an efficient supervisor. Lascars, therefore, faced not just the formal power of the law, but also the informal might of the serang when they asserted their freedom of movement. If they came from the same village as their foreman, they had to consider, moreover, that he would hold their families responsible for their debts.

Interviews with veteran lascars, conducted by Caroline Adams in the East End of London in the early 1980s, permit rare glimpses into the

88. Report of the Seamen's Recruitment Committee (Clow Committee), Appendix B: Report on the Preliminary Inquiry in Calcutta, NAI, Dept of Commerce, Lascar Seamen, August 1922, s.nos. 1–7, part A, pp. 37–38.

89. However, the Calcutta Shipping Master put on record that in the year after the creation of his office, 1925, at least ten complaints had been received by his office from seamen every week, most of which had been directed against serangs, but that complaints had been much less in the following years. Oral testimony by H.F. Darvell, Shipping Master Calcutta, RCLI Evidence, vol. 5, part 2 (Bengal, Oral Evidence), pp. 267f. See also oral testimony by R. Liddle, Marine Superintendent, British Indian Steam Navigation Company, Calcutta, RCLI Evidence, vol. 5, part 2 (Bengal, Oral Evidence), p. 279.

90. NAI, Dept of Commerce, Lascar Seamen, May 1921, s.nos. 156–157, Filed. For lascar-serang conflicts over payments see also F.S. Purnett, Chief Collector of Customs in Sind and Shipping Master Karachi, to Commissioner of Sind, 21 February 1913, OIOC, BoMP, IOR/P/9342, A212; R.H.H. Hopkins, Shipping Master Bombay, to Secretary to GoBo, Marine Dept, 29 March 1913, *ibid.*, A213–214; Indian Seamen's Union, Resolution on the Pending Grievances of the Indian Seamen, 31 August 1943, NMML, M.A. Master Papers, I. Subject Files, A. Scindia Steam Navigation Company, file 150.

ensuing informal restraints on the mobility of South Asian seamen. They recalled serangs and watchmen sharply watching and preventing them from jumping ship, and remembered warnings that the serang would do "afraiding things" to deserters who were caught. One former seaman reported that his serang had been reluctant to hire the son of a "respectable" family, considering these prone to desertion, and had, therefore, taken a "vow" from his uncle to ensure he did not jump ship.[91] Once again, the serang's power to prevent desertion was by no means absolute: desertion was rare in western ports, but in Calcutta almost 1,000 or about 2 per cent of all engaged Indian seamen "deserted and failed to join their vessels" during some years.[92] Yet that rate was apparently perceived by shipping interests as an indication of a high level of discipline.

The life accounts collected by Adams also disclose a strong feeling of empowerment among many of the former lascars. Seafaring had opened up the world to them; they were proud of the greater mobility they had achieved in comparison with their co-villagers and were unwilling to give that up.[93] Yet mobility and containment simultaneously shaped the everyday lives of lascars on their voyages around the world and both the silences and the explicit statements of their accounts reflect this contradiction. Very strikingly, the narrators hardly ever refer to everyday life on board ship and confine themselves to recounting at length their onshore experiences in South Asia, Britain, and elsewhere. Statements like "I didn't like the ship because it was like a prison" give an inkling as to why this was so.[94]

In colonial records there is a remarkable recurrence of the theme of lascar suicides, especially among firemen; that may be interpreted, too, as a hint at the strong sense of confinement that could emerge on board spatially, as well as socially, insulated steel vessels. Hence, the British Consul in Port Said stated in 1904 that fifteen suicides of lascars had been reported to him within the last two years, and he suspected that conflicts with serangs about the payment of "fees" were at the bottom of them. "In theory", Cameron reasoned, the lascar,

> [...] can go on shore at the next port and complain to the Shipping Master; but, if practically he is a prisoner on board, it is possible that the man reviewing the hopelessness of his position may find the only solution in jumping overboard,

91. Haji Shirajul Islam's account, in Adams, *Across the Seven Seas*, p. 96; Shah Abdul Majid Kureishi's account, *ibid.*, p. 148.

92. Annual Report of the Calcutta Shipping Office for 1912–1913, OIOC, BeMP, IOR/P/9151, A24; Annual Report of the Calcutta Shipping Office for 1913–1914, OIOC, BeMP, IOR/P/9385, A41. But see also the considerably lower figure (383 or 0.9 per cent) in Annual Report of the Calcutta Shipping Office for 1921–22, OIOC, BeMP, IOR/P/11178, A6.

93. Adams, *Across Seven Seas*, p. 14; Nawab Ali's account, *ibid.*, p. 69; Shah Abdul Majid Kureishi's account, *ibid.*, pp. 145f.

94. Nawab Ali's account, *ibid.*, p. 79.

whether to commit suicide on the high seas or to take his chance of reaching the shore of the Suez Canal.[95]

In the early 1930s, the frequency of unnatural deaths among lascars during sea voyages became the object of (largely fruitless) investigations on the part of the Government of India.[96] And even German shipping authorities noticed an unusual frequency of suicides of "coloured" trimmers and stokers in the early years of the twentieth century.[97]

POSTSCRIPT AND CONCLUSIONS

The first decade of Indian independence saw major changes in the scenario of maritime labour regulation, though the British shipping industry remained the most important employer of South Asian seamen by far. In fact, the old "informal" recruitment system that had shown its first cracks in the 1920s, and had been further undermined under the pressure of increasing labour demand during World War II, was now more systematically replaced by corporatist modes of controlling the supply and reproduction of labour – a process I have discussed elsewhere.[98]

As for the regulation of maritime labour mobility, the partition of India and economic developments in Britain affected many of the patterns that had emerged in the era of steam shipping. Areas like the North-West Frontier Province, West Punjab, Sylhet, Chittagong, or Noakhali, which so far had provided a large number of seamen, were all of a sudden separated from Calcutta and Bombay, the two major ports of recruitment, by a contested international border. Yet the effects of partition on maritime labour migration were not identical for the western and eastern

95. W.H. Howell, Board of Trade, Marine Dept, to Under-Secretary of State for India, 12 December 1904, OIOC, BoMP, IOR/P/7191, A228; D.A. Cameron, British Consul in Port Said, to Board of Trade, Marine Dept, 3 November 1904, *ibid.*, A229. However, not only serangs, but also engineers and other "white" officers could make a seaman's life so difficult as to induce him to put an end to it. See for example A. Challis, London City Mission, to Board of Trade, 13 January 1913, OIOC, BoMP, IOR/P/9083, A469.

96. See for instance NAI, Dept of Commerce, Merchant Marine II, January 1932, F. No. 54–M. II/31, S. Nos. 1–42, part B. Various other files regarding "death on board ship" can be found in the 1932 and 1933 indices of this series of records, though several were apparently "not transferred" to the NAI. See also oral testimony by H.F. Darvell, Shipping Master Calcutta, RCLI Evidence, vol. 5, part 2 (Bengal, Oral Evidence), p. 279.

97. The shipping authority of Bremen, home base of the Hansa DFG (the largest German employer of Indian seamen), noted that 61 per cent of the 106 trimmers and stokers who committed suicide between 1901 and 1912 were "coloured". See Hartmut Rübner, "Lebens-, Arbeits- und gewerkschaftliche Organisationsbedingungen chinesischer Seeleute in der deutschen Handelsflotte. Der maritime Aspekt der Ausländersbeschäftigung vom Kaiserreich bis in den NS-Staat", *Internationale wissenschaftliche Korrespondenz zur Geschichte der deutschen Arbeiterbewegung*, 4 (1997), pp. 1–41, 19.

98. Ahuja, "Die 'Lenksamkeit' des 'Lascars'".

regions of the subcontinent. In Bombay, Punjabis and Pashtuns had apparently all but disappeared from the lists of the newly founded Seamen's Employment Office by the second half of the 1950s, while the presence of seamen from the shores of South India became more noticeable.[99] In Calcutta, the shift brought about by partition was more gradual: of the 19,000 seamen who signed on in 1955, more than 10,000 were East Pakistanis; even today Bangladeshis have a certain presence among the crews of Indian merchant ships.[100]

However, younger seamen tended to be Indian citizens and there were organized efforts by a paramilitary group called the West Bengal National Volunteer Corps to give each month fifty Indian youths, most of them without any maritime background, a very basic training as firemen after they had been drilled in military discipline and patriotism for several weeks.[101] For reasons deserving further exploration (including the introduction of a passport and visa system in 1952), cross-border migration of maritime workers appears to have lost by and by much of its attraction or practicability (though it did not disappear completely), while hopes to create job alternatives by enticing shipping away from Calcutta to the East Pakistani ports of Chalna and Chittagong did not materialize.[102]

Of the older networks, only those linking Goan Catholics and the Konkani Muslims to Bombay appear to have survived as *maritime* labour networks.[103] That does not mean the other informal infrastructures of incorporation simply disintegrated. Contrary to current conceptualizations ascribing an inherent impermanency to "informal" networks as opposed to an assumed greater durability of "formal", state-based institutional structures, several South Asian maritime labour networks showed a remarkable capacity for endurance and resilience. Several of them bypassed the new restrictions imposed on them by the Indo-Pakistan

99. C.P. Shrivastava, National Board of Seafarers, to ??, dated 14 July 1956 [*sic*, probably 1957], NMML, M.A. Master Papers, I. Subject Files, B. Shipping, file 482.

100. National Welfare Board for Seafarers, Special Subcommittee for Welfare in Ports, Proceedings, Examination of K.C. Ray, 8 August 1956, NMML, M.A. Master Papers, I. Subject Files, E. National Committees and Commissions, file 863; interview with Abdulgani Y. Serang, General Secretary, National Union of Seafarers of India, 10 March 2003.

101. National Welfare Board for Seafarers, Special Subcommittee for Welfare in Ports, Proceedings, Visit to TS *Bhadra* and Examination of Captain Mody, 8 August 1956, *ibid.*

102. Adams, *Across Seven Seas*, p. 61; Choudhury, *The Roots and Tales*, pp. 86–90; see also Mowat, *Seafarers' Conditions in India and Pakistan*, pp. 81–83.

103. Seamen's Employment Office, Bombay, No. of Seamen on Articles as on 15 May 1956, NMML, M.A. Master Papers, I. Subject Files, E. National Committees and Commissions, file 867; interview with Abdulgani Y. Serang, General Secretary, National Union of Seafarers of India, 10 March 2003 (who stressed the continuity of employment from Goa, while that from the Konkan had somewhat declined); interview with Joseph Mascarenhas, former Chief steward and third-generation seaman from Concolim (Goa), 13 March 2003 (who mentioned for example that the seamen's villages of Assolna, Velim, and Concolim still maintained an association of clubs in Mumbai with more than 10,000 members).

border by turning into networks of large-scale international labour migration. In this process, "informal" infrastructures were once more intertwined with "formal" political and legal arrangements.

One of the most important leaders of the pre-Independence seamen's unions, Aftab Ali, a Sylheti who had been a lascar himself, became a prominent politician in East Pakistan. In the 1950s and 1960s, he used his influence to arrange for the legal immigration of thousands of former seamen (as well as other Sylhetis) to the United Kingdom, where industry had a demand for large numbers of immigrant workers. Consequently, London's Sylheti immigrants, a small group of a few hundred at the end of World War II, emerged in the course of the 1960s as a major migrant community comprising about 35,000 people.[104] The "voucher system", which permitted the immigration of a certain quota between 1962 and 1966, was also appropriated by another former maritime labour network, that of the Mirpuris, to transform itself into an infrastructure of migration.[105]

The objective of this essay was, however, not merely to reconstruct the pattern of spatial mobility or immobility of South Asian seamen, but also to test the validity of a set of more general hypotheses in this specific case. It started from the understanding that the notion of a "labour market" is merely an abstraction "summarizing complex human arrangements",[106] which need to be reconstructed historically. Moreover, it was assumed that such complex arrangements cannot be reduced to "purely economic" relations, as they necessarily involve political and social forms of regulation. Ethnic segmentation of a labour market is thus not merely a simple derivative of pre-existing differentials in the price of labour power between metropolitan and colonial regions,[107] but also the result of ongoing formal, public, and state-based as well as informal, private, and network-based regulatory activities.[108]

Thus, in the case under review, wage differentials between European "seamen" and Indian "lascars" were apparently less pronounced before the emergence of a large-scale global market for steamship labour; ethnic segmentation was the concomitant of this process of spatial integration rather than the residue of earlier differentials between weakly linked

104. Adams, *Across Seven Seas*, pp. 58, 61–66; Gardner, *Global Migrants, Local Lives*, pp. 43–47, 56f.

105. Ballard, "The Context and Consequences of Migration", p. 125.

106. Wolf, "Incorporation and Identity", p. 366.

107. For this view see Edna Bonacich, "The Past, Present, and Future of Split Labour Market Theory", *Research in Race and Ethnic Relations*, 1 (1979), pp. 17–64, 19 and *passim*.

108. However, the distinction between "informal" and "formal" regulation is understood as an auxiliary tool for analytical purposes, while in reality both types would often merge into each other (as for instance in the case of trade unions, which were, as we have shown, often based on informal networks but aspired to legal recognition).

regions. Moreover, neither the exclusion of one of the racially defined groups nor an ethnic division of labour ensued from the wage differential between "seamen" and "lascars":[109] Europeans and South Asians continued to do the same work on deck, in engine rooms and saloons, though not side by side on the same ships.

Such permanency of ethnic segmentation in the market for steamship labour is the more striking if we consider the seamen's inordinately high level of spatial mobility, which suggests a tendency towards an equalization of labour relations. The phenomenon of permanent segmentation can be explained, however, by taking into account the interacting levels of political domination and social power that reduced the actual ability of the lascars to appropriate to their own purposes the movements of their workplaces between low-pay and high-pay regions.[110] Such an explanation would have four constituents.

First, the very uneven access to resources of state power in both Britain and India available to the highly monopolistic British shipping industry on the one hand, and to British as well as Asian and African maritime workers on the other, which was reflected in the consistent racial differentiation of maritime labour law. Secondly, the equally uneven access to resources of state power available to metropolitan working classes on the one hand and to colonial labourers on the other, in combination with concerns about political stability on the part of the metropolitan ruling bloc, which was reflected in restrictive immigration policies. Thirdly, the spatial unevenness of processes of labour market integration under capitalism, which was reflected in the emergence of closely meshed and mainly informal maritime networks in *some* regions – networks that were ethnic in form but social in content and had the ability to control access to this labour market and exclude competitors from other regions lacking networks of equal strength. And fourthly, the uneven distribution of resources of informal power between the social interests constituting these maritime labour networks, which was reflected in the fact that they functioned *predominantly* (though not consistently) as informal devices for further limiting the access of Indian seamen to higher-pay and superior-rights segments of the labour market.

109. These are the alternative "resolutions" of the problem of "split labour markets" suggested by Edna Bonacich, *ibid.*, p. 18.

110. For a study that stresses the importance of access to state power in conflicts between social groups involved with "split labour markets" see Yoav Peled and Gershon Shafir, "Split Labor Market and the State: The Effect of Modernization on Jewish Industrial Workers in Tsarist Russia", *American Journal of Sociology*, 92 (1987), pp. 1435–1466. For the contribution of (predominantly informal) social networks to the ethnification of labour market segmentations see Wolf, "Incorporation and Identity", pp. 366f. By introducing the concept of "scenarios of regulation", I try to come to grips with the interconnectedness of these seemingly separate practices of political and social power.

This scenario of regulation was subject to historical change. The end of colonial rule and the emergence of an Indian shipping industry, the rise and demise of post-colonial corporatism, the coming of container shipping and passenger aviation, the shift of major metropolitan shipping lines to other Asian labour networks: all were major developments transforming the position of South Asian seamen in the international maritime labour market. However, the regulation of the Indian seaman's freedom of movement continues to be an issue of conflict. When in March 2003 this author talked to Abdulgani Serang, the General Secretary of the National Union of Seafarers of India, he maintained that the employment situation had deteriorated considerably since 11 September 2001, when Indian seamen were barred from US ports. Even in the era of so-called "globalization", incorporation and mobility share a cabin with exclusion and containment.

Power Structure, Discipline, and Labour in Assam Tea Plantations under Colonial Rule

RANA P. BEHAL

The tea industry, from the 1840s onwards the earliest commercial enterprise established by private British capital in the Assam Valley, had been the major employer of wage labour there during colonial rule. It grew spectacularly during the last quarter of the nineteenth century, when tea production increased from 6,000,000 lb in 1872 to 75,000,000 lb in 1900 and the area under tea cultivation expanded from 27,000 acres to 204,000 acres.[1] Employment of labour in the Assam Valley tea plantations increased from 107,847 in 1885 to 247,760 in 1900,[2] and the industry continued to grow during the first half of the twentieth century. At the end of colonial rule the Assam Valley tea plantations employed nearly half a million labourers out of a labour population of more than three-quarters of a million, and more than 300,000 acres were under tea cultivation out of a total area of a million acres controlled by the tea companies.[3]

This impressive expansion and the growth of the Assam Valley tea industry took place within the monopolistic control of British capital in Assam. An analysis of the list of companies shows that in 1942 84 per cent of tea estates with 89 per cent of the acreage in the Assam Valley were controlled by the European managing agency houses.[4] Throughout India, thirteen leading agency houses of Calcutta controlled over 75 per cent of total tea production in 1939.[5] Elsewhere I have shown that the tea companies reaped profits over a long time despite fluctuating international prices and slumps.[6]

One of the most notable features of the Assam Valley tea plantations was that, unlike in the cases of most of the other major industries such as jute, textiles, and mining in British India, it never suffered from a complete

1. Rana Partap Behal, "Some Aspects of the Growth of the Tea Plantation Labour Force and Labour Movements in Assam Valley Districts (Lakhimpur, Sibsagar and Darrang) 1900–1947" (Ph.D., Centre for Historical Studies, School of Social Sciences, Jawaharlal Nehru University, 1983), p. 34.
2. *Report of the Assam Labour Enquiry Committee, 1906* [hereafter, *RALEC*] (Calcutta, 1906), p. 12.
3. Behal, "Some Aspects", ch. 2.
4. *Assam Directory and Tea Areas Handbook, 1942* (Calcutta, 1942).
5. *Report of the Plantation Inquiry Commission 1956: Part 1: Tea* (Delhi, 1956), p. 23.
6. Behal, "Some Aspects", pp. 84–85.

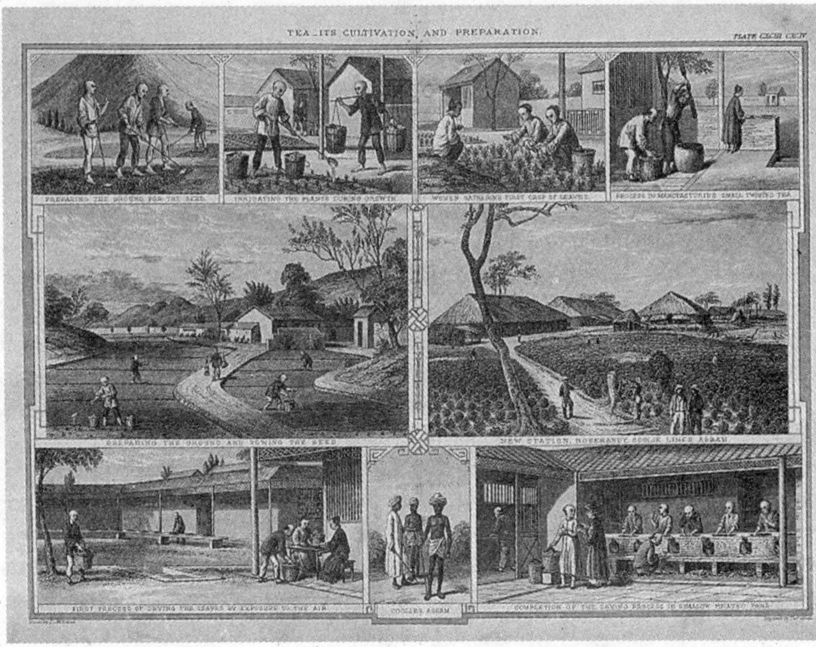

Figure 1. Engraving showing the different stages in the process of making tea, around 1850. Tea production is pictured here idealistically as a well-organized process in an idyllic, pastoral environment, with the coolie lines as comfortable housings.
Joseph Lionel Williams after Thomas Brown, 1850, Wellcome Library, London, V0019221, at http://www.plantcultures.org/pccms/action/showItem?id=389#description

stoppage of production during its long history. That is remarkable considering the fact that it employed arguably the largest labour force at the lowest level of wages of any private capitalist enterprise in the history of colonial India. It had one of the worst records of labour relations and constantly complained of "labour troubles", nor was it trouble-free in other areas of its production, most of which was export-oriented. Fluctuation of tea prices in an increasingly competitive world market was a constant source of anxiety to the management of tea companies, but production and expansion occurred without interruption. I venture to suggest that the explanation of this success story lies in the very nature of the tea industry's power structure and the hierarchies constructed and evolved during its long history.

This power structure evolved and operated at two levels. At the upper level the tea companies, with their headquarters in the United Kingdom and managing agents in Calcutta, instituted a centralized authority in the form of an apex body, the Indian Tea Association, manned by senior executives of tea companies and retired officials of the Indian Civil

Services. It functioned both as a lobby for the industry in the corridors of power and as a planner and implementer of its strategies of production, organization, and labour policies in the tea plantations. This power structure was bolstered by the industry's social and political connections with the colonial authority to influence policy on labour matters, particularly to prevent legal impediments to the use of extra-legal and coercive forms of labour control on the plantations.

At the lower level, on the ground, these strategies and policies were enforced through a hierarchical power structure centred on the managerial authority of European planters and their assistants. The key emphasis throughout was on immobilizing labour within the plantation complex after its arrival there, and at the same time curbing its contact with the outside world. Both strategies aimed at preventing the formation of collective labour organizations. The planters developed strategies to dominate, discipline, and control labour, both in work and living spaces, through legal and extra-legal methods. Most remarkably, the planters adapted to the exigencies of changing legislative and political situations in the region and were able to manipulate them to their advantage. At both levels the authorities operated in tandem and implemented remarkably successful strategies and policies prepared by the apex body. In the following pages we shall try to trace the story of how this power structure evolved and functioned in the Assam Valley tea plantations. We shall begin at the top.

THE INDIAN TEA ASSOCIATION

The early years of experimentation and slow growth suddenly gave way, during the 1860s, to frantic expansion of tea plantations, which generated a highly speculative boom,[7] one which was itself triggered by Lord Canning's "fee-simple rules" of land grants to planters at throwaway prices.[8] The developments in the tea industry taking place after 1865 laid the foundation of a power structure that actually continued to operate for more than two decades after Independence.

The first such development was that managing agency houses took control of the management of tea gardens, which led to the amalgamation of smaller gardens into large-scale enterprises. By the end of the century

7. Sir Percival Griffiths, *The History of the Indian Tea Industry* (London, 1967), pp. 61–99; Radhey Shyam Rungta, *The Rise of Business Corporations in India 1851–1900* (London, 1970), pp. 97, 103, 279–280.

8. The wasteland settlement policy, adopted by the government during the 1850s and 1860s, was to facilitate the grant of large acreages for tea cultivation to European planters. The terms were further liberalized in 1861 under Lord Canning's "fee-simple rules" under which land was sold for 2.8 to 5 rupees per acre without any clearance conditions attached. Instead of giving a lease the land was put up for sale at auction. This encouraged large-scale land grabbing. See Behal, "Some Aspects", pp. 17–19.

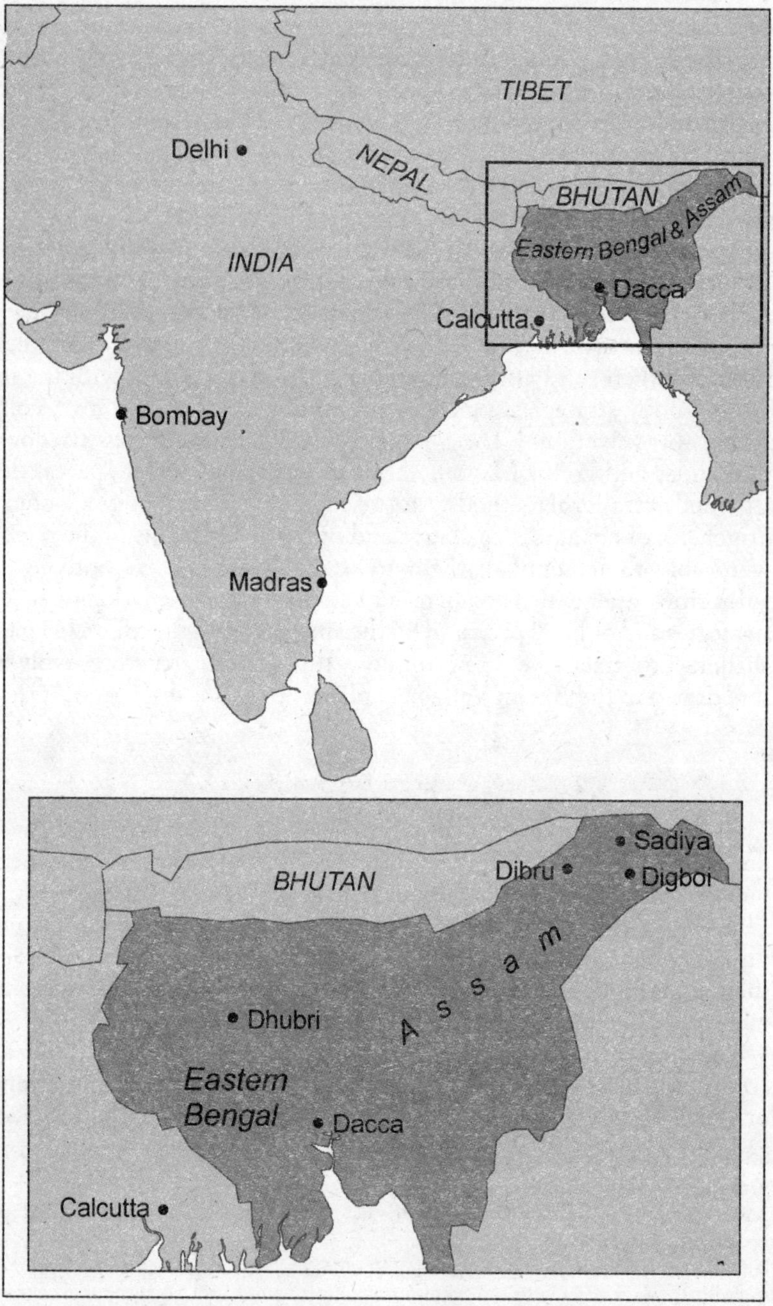

Figure 2. Map of Assam and eastern Bengal at the beginning of the twentieth century. *Artwork by Jelle van Lottum*

seven top managing agency houses controlled nearly 61 per cent of all tea gardens.[9] The overall business strategies of manufacture, transport, and marketing of tea began to be implemented through a hierarchy of managers, superintendents of tea gardens in Assam, managing agents in Calcutta, and the companies' headquarters in Britain. The industry acquired cohesion and became a well-organized business lobby with the formation of its apex body, the Indian Tea Association (ITA) in 1881. By the beginning of the twentieth century the ITA and its branches had become an important European pressure group which successfully influenced government policy affecting the industry in particular and the province of Assam in general.

European planters were the chief body of non-officials who were asked by the government to participate in the local committees set up for the purpose of developing local communications and other infrastructure. Similarly, until 1915, most of the local boards were heavily loaded with ex-officio and elected European planter members.[10] In 1906 a Legislative Council was established as a result of the 1905 settlement which formed East Bengal and Assam into a Governor's province. The new Council was dominated by Europeans, who made up practically two-thirds of its membership.[11] When the question of its enlargement came up with the Morley-Minto Reforms of 1909, the ITA, backed by the Bengal Chamber of Commerce, succeeded in pressuring the government to allocate two seats to the tea interests in the Council.[12] In 1912, when the Assam Legislative Council was constituted, the tea industry alone was allocated three out of the eleven elected seats.[13] However, no representation was given to labour in the three councils.

The Assam Legislative Assembly constituted under the Act of 1935 had 7 European and 2 Indian planting members representing only 1,319 voters. On the other hand tea garden labour representing 34,279 voters was given only 4 seats.[14] The European group continued to be influential with the provincial government even after a "popular" ministry was formed in 1937. The official historian of the tea industry acknowledged rather uncomfortably that in Shillong the European group counted for a great

9. These managing agency houses also controlled most of the other industrial, financial, banking, and shipping enterprises in eastern India and enjoyed tremendous political influence with the British government and its bureaucracy, both in India as well as in the UK; A.K. Bagchi, *Private Investment in India* (Cambridge, 1972), pp. 161–162; D.H. Buchanan, *The Development of Capitalistic Enterprise in India* (New Delhi, 1966).

10. A. Guha, *Planter Raj to Swaraj: Freedom Struggle and Electoral Politics in Assam 1826–1947* (New Delhi, 1977), pp. 30–31.

11. *Ibid.*, p. 75.

12. *The Report of the General Committee of the Indian Tea Association, 1909* [hereafter, *ITA Report*] (Calcutta, 1909), pp. 144–146.

13. Guha, *Planter Raj to Swaraj*, p. 82; *ITA Report, 1912* (Calcutta, 1912), p. 6.

14. Guha, *Planter Raj to Swaraj*, p. 220.

deal and, indeed, found itself called on to play an embarrassingly prominent part in the making and unmaking of provincial governments.[15]

The ITA's views, expressed through deputations, memorials, and representations, as well as through behind-the-scenes contacts with officials, received the most privileged consideration by the colonial state. In 1901 the Chief Commissioner of Assam, Henry Cotton, recommended an increase in the monthly wage paid to labourers on plantations and took some corrective administrative actions on the basis of inspection reports from the district officials. The ITA's campaigning through the Anglo-Indian press and lobbying of senior government officials in Calcutta led to trouble for Cotton from his superiors, and marred his future prospects in the Indian Civil Services.[16] However, there were exceptions: the rejection of the Anti-Enticement Bill in 1914 by the Secretary of State for India, which was cleared by both provincial and central governments after some hard lobbying by the ITA, and the withdrawal in 1926 of Act XIII of 1859.[17]

But that did not mean that the ITA was becoming unimportant. For example, when the planters were confronted with new realities when labour protests were assuming collective forms, like strikes and the exodus during 1921–1922, the ITA successfully lobbied the Assam government to use its propaganda and law-enforcement machinery to suppress labour militancy. Assam's government responded immediately and appointed a special officer to supervise propaganda work,[18] at the same time complying with the planters' request for a number of platoons of the Assam Rifles to be deployed in troubled districts to assist the civil police in suppressing a strike on the Dibru-Sadiya Railway, and dealing with an outbreak of rioting among tea garden labourers in the Assam Valley.[19] Further, most of the revolts were ruthlessly handled by local police, and by court prosecutions and convictions to varying terms of rigorous imprisonment.[20] That the ITA's influence was not at all diminished was

15. Griffiths, *History of the Indian Tea Industry*, pp. 527–528.

16. Behal, "Some Aspects", p. 166; National Archives of India, New Delhi [hereafter, NAI], Government of India, Department of Revenue and Agriculture, Emigration, A Proceedings, nos 6–8, file no. 90 of 1901, pp. 122–136.

17. After the withdrawal of penal clauses from the Immigration Labour Act in 1908 the ITA submitted a memorial to the government asking for new legislation to counter the "enticement" of labour in the tea gardens in Assam. The Secretary of State for India rejected the bill on the grounds that it involved "principles" which could not be accepted. It was a reference to the strong anti-slavery sentiments prevailing in Britain. For details see Behal, "Some Aspects", pp. 158, 166; for more details of Act XIII see below.

18. *ITA Report, 1921* (Calcutta, 1921), p. 5.

19. Assam State Archives, Guwahati [hereafter, ASA], Government of Assam, Financial Department, Immigration Branch B, nos 20–112, March 1922, pp. 105–107.

20. *Annual Report on Labour Immigration into Assam* [hereafter, *Assam Labour Report*], *1920–21* (Shillong, 1921), p. 2. In Sonaguli and Kacharigaon tea estates thirteen and twenty-six

made clear when the Government of India, before passing the Tea Districts Emigrant Labour Act XXII of 1932, sent copies of the draft of the bill to the ITA for their views on its provisions. That action was followed by several interviews and meetings between the planters' representatives and government officials. Consequent upon their discussions, the amendments recommended were accepted in the final draft of the bill.[21]

In the latter part of the 1930s the political climate in Assam, as in other parts of India, began to change, with increasing political activity and the formation of elected provincial governments under the Government of India Act 1935. The arithmetic of electoral politics in Assam prevented the formation of a stable single-party government and ushered in an era of short-term multi-party coalition governments. The European group acquired a balancing position between the Congress and the non-Congress groups.[22] The ITA's main concern at this juncture was to prevent any of the coalition groups in power from taking legislative action that it considered inimical to tea interests. With Sir Percival Griffiths, a retired civil servant and later the historian of the Indian tea industry, as its political adviser the ITA prepared strategies to manipulate and support those political groups in forming governments which it considered amenable and easy to influence. Their basic approach was summed up in the following excerpt from communications sent by the Chairman of the Calcutta ITA:

> It seems to me to be of vital importance for the industry to realise the dangers which lie ahead, and to do everything possible to consolidate its position. If with a friendly Government we can do anything, which will prevent hostile Legislation, either being introduced if Congress returned to power, or if

labourers respectively were convicted and sentenced to various terms of rigorous imprisonment. In Dhandai, Bamgaon, and Khairabri tea estates, sixty-five, six, and twelve labourers respectively were arrested, out of whom forty-nine were sentenced to rigorous imprisonment. In Barkathani tea estate two labourers were convicted – one ran away and the other was sentenced to two years' rigorous imprisonment on the charge of assaulting a manager. The ringleaders in the Amguri and Borsilla tea estates were prosecuted and directed to execute bonds of 50 rupees each, with two sureties to keep the peace for six months, in default of which they were to undergo six months' simple imprisonment. In Suffry tea estate, the Sub-Divisional Officer came with the Assam Rifles and forced the workers to disperse; *Assam Labour Report, 1921–22* (Shillong, 1922).

21. *ITA Report, 1932* (Calcutta, 1932), p. 10. The tea industry constantly complained about restrictions and government control over its recruitment and transport of immigrant labour and lobbied for the legislation to be amended. Following the recommendations of the Royal Commission and the ITA, the Government of India passed the Tea Districts Emigrant Labour Act XXII of 1932 and repealed Act VI of 1901. Under the Act, the government appointed a Controller of Emigrant Labour whose main job was to supervise recruitment and to ensure that the manner in which labourers were transported to the Assam tea gardens complied with government regulations.

22. Guha, *Planter Raj to Swaraj*, pp. 216–236; Basudev Chatterji (ed.), *Towards Freedom, 1938* (New Delhi, 1998), chapter on the Assam Ministry.

introduced being effective against tea interests, a great step in the right direction will have been made.[23]

As part of Griffiths's action plan to deal with the political situation in Assam, it was decided to support the coalition led by Muhammad Saadulla instead of the Congress Party in return for certain considerations. Abdul Matin Chaudhury was expected to be the new Minister of Labour. As the ITA Chairman acknowledged, "we have in fact cultivated him for sometime past", and he was seen as a guarantee against any legislation hostile and detrimental to the industry. Saadulla was reported to have given his "personal assurance that he will not introduce any Legislation which directly affected the Tea Industry without full consultation with us, as his object is to be guided by those who control the tea industry".[24]

The years between 1937 and 1940 also witnessed an upsurge of labour unrest and the emergence of trade unions. The Controller of Emigrant Labour reported in 1939 that there were "an unusually large number of strikes, viz. 17 and much unrest".[25] The number of strikes reported in another official report was much larger at 37 for that year.[26] The strikes spread from the Swedish-owned Assam Match Company at Dhubri, the Assam Oil Company (a subsidiary of Burma Oil Company) in Digboi, the British-owned Assam Railways and Trading Company, to the tea gardens and government establishments.[27] The intensity of labour unrest alarmed the government. The Government of Assam expressed its anxiety over the "frequency of strikes and disturbances on the tea gardens in several parts of the province".[28] The Indian Tea Association made anxious representations to the government and the attention of the Ministry was drawn to the need for urgent action to maintain law and order.[29]

As a result the Government of Assam appointed a Tea Garden Labour Committee to investigate the causes of these recent strikes and disturbances. The members of the Committee were K.C. Ghosh, ICS [Indian Civil Services], as Chairman, F.W. Hockenhull, of the ITA, Baidyanth Mukherjee, representing the Indian plantation owners, A.K. Chanda,

23. India Office Library, London [hereafter, IOL], Indian Tea Association Papers [hereafter, ITA Papers], circular C. 159, 20 November 1939, mss Eur F 174, Bay/H.

24. IOL, ITA Papers, mss Eur F 174, bay/H circular no. 239, 17 November 1939; circular no. 159, 29 November 1939.

25. *Annual Report on the Working of the Tea Districts Emigrant Labour Act XXII of 1932* [hereafter, *RTDEL*] (Shillong, 1939), p. 386.

26. D.V. Rege, *Report on an Enquiry into Conditions of Labour in Plantations in India* (Delhi, 1946), p. 72.

27. NAI, Fortnightly Reports, Assam, Home Political Department, 1939; Guha, *Planter Raj to Swaraj*, pp. 236–263.

28. ASA, Government of Assam, General and Judicial Department, Immigration Branch B, file no. Imm 118, GIM. 49/47, 1939, p. 167.

29. *ITA Report, 1939* (Calcutta, 1939), p. 26.

MLA [Member of the Legislative Assembly] from the Surma Valley, and Debeswar Sarma, MLA from the Assam Valley, representing labour.[30] The ITA, suspicious of the Congress Party and clearly unhappy with the appointment of two Labour members, used its proximity to the colonial bureaucracy to delay and thwart the operations of this Committee from the very outset.[31] In a letter to the Chief Secretary of the Assam Government dated 26 May 1939, the ITA Chairman protested against the appointment of the two MLAs on the Committee alleging that they were "biased" against the industry and were personally associated with fomenting labour disturbances in tea gardens.[32] The ITA was willing to cooperate with the Committee only if it were carried out by persons "acceptable to the tea industry", failing which it threatened to withdraw its participation completely. It carried out the threat and withdrew from the Committee when its objections did not elicit a positive response.[33] The Committee folded even before it could start to work.

Growing labour militancy and the emergence of trade unions in the tea gardens had clearly emerged as the major concern for the ITA. Ever since the early 1920s the appearance of relatively more organized forms of labour resistance, such as strikes, in the Assam Valley tea gardens had been seen as the work of outside agitators.[34] The same refrain dominated the industry's perceptions in the late 1930s when the early signs of trade unions arrived on the scene. Under such circumstances the industry initiated discussions within tea circles to rethink strategies for control and to counter greater militancy and the emergence of collective and more organized labour protest.

In June 1939, one strategy was suggested by A.C. Turnstall, the Assistant Chief Scientific Officer of the Tocklai Tea Research Centre at Jorhat. In his proposal to the ITA, entitled "A Contribution towards the Solution of the Problem of Tea Garden Education", Turnstall attempted a

30. The Committee's terms of reference were: (1) to determine what is the root cause of recent strikes and other manifestations of discontent on tea gardens in Assam, and particularly whether there are economic grievances either generally in the district concerned or in the affected estates; (2) what measures are required in order to remove the root cause or causes or the said strikes; and (3) whether and if so what forms of organization are desirable for enabling labourers on tea gardens to communicate their grievances to the management in such effective manner as will remove any doubt that their interests are secure, and to procure settlement of such grievances, if any, by negotiation; ASA, AICC Papers, file no. P1–12, TL No. 1020, 1939, p. 3; *Amrita Bazar Patrika*, 29 May 1939; ASA, Government of Assam, General and Judicial Department, Immigration Branch B, file no. Imm. 118–GIM–49/47, 1939, p. 167.

31. IOL, ITA Circulars 92 and 115, ITA Papers, mss Eur F/174/bay/H, 1939.

32. ASA, Government of Assam, General and Judicial Department, Immigration Branch B, file no. Imm. 118–GIM 49/47, 1939, p. 137.

33. *Ibid.*; *ITA Report, 1939*, p. 28.

34. Rana P. Behal, "Forms of Labour Protest in the Assam Valley Tea Plantations 1900–1947", *The Calcutta Historical Journal*, 9 (1984), pp. 30–78.

psycho-analytical explanation of the problem of growing labour troubles and suggested a concrete plan for its solution. A summary of his proposal is revealing of the varieties of attitude and perceptions prevailing at the time among members of the European community in Assam tea circles. He argued that the "tea garden coolies require some sort of education to protect them from unscrupulous and dishonest agitation". The existing schools in the tea gardens, though increasing in number, were not "conducive to industrial peace". The educational curriculum of these schools, he felt, rendered the students of the labour community "especially susceptible to agitation of the worst type". He believed that offers of high wages and better amenities, citing the recent Digboi experience as an example, were no safeguard against strikes. He was convinced that the unrest was not due to any serious grievances but because the strikers "suffer from a feeling of inferiority which gives them an ill-defined sense of grievance". Agitators found such people easy prey.

His remedial solutions were more in the nature of long-term planning. "The only sure remedy for labour unrest of this kind is somehow or other to replace the feeling of inferiority by one of self-respect and self-reliance." That could be achieved by adopting Baden Powell's scout movement for training the younger generation of tea garden coolies on similar lines. A detailed note on the planning and its execution was submitted along with the proposal.[35] "It is important", he recommended, "to get, from the beginning, the right type of scoutmaster with the right type of training". Turnstall had already taken one such person under his wing. R.C. Mohanta, one of the younger sons of a respectable but poor *Adhikari* (chief) of a small *satra* (Vaishnavaite monastery) in a village in Jorhat, was put into the "right type of training" to become a "King's Scout". After the completion of his schooling and with the above object in mind, young Mohanta was sent for further training to the US and British Boy Scout headquarters, which entailed an adventurous international tour for him via Burma, South-East Asia, and Japan, to the USA and Europe.[36] Turnstall suggested that under his supervision, Mohanta should, on his return to Assam, be the Scoutmaster and organize training camps in the tea gardens.[37] The proposal did not elicit a favourable response from the

35. IOL, ITA circular no. 87, 12 June 1939, ITA Papers, mss Eur F 174/Bay/H, pp. 1–5.

36. A copy of the typescript entitled "Note on the General Plan of Mohanta's Education", private collection of Mohanta family papers, Jorhat, Assam. I am grateful to Jayraj Mohanta, son of the late R.C. Mohanta, for allowing access to this collection.

37. IOL, ITA circular no. 87, 12 June 1939, ITA Papers, mss Eur F 174/bay/H, pp. 1–5. The Mohanta episode lies buried as an unnoticed piece of archival material. For the Mohanta family, however, it acquired a folklorist aura, of a narratival tradition recounting the adventures of R.C. Mohanta, who joined the British Indian Army in Lord Mountbatten's commando unit, which was trained and operated in South-East Asian jungles during World War II. Mohanta later earned the reputation of being one of the toughest tea planters in Assam.

ITA hierarchy, which was busy evolving its own strategies to come to terms with the emerging trade-union movement in and around the plantations of the Assam Valley.

To begin with, the ITA was opposed to the very idea of trade unions in the tea gardens. It argued that conditions in the gardens were fundamentally different from those in industrial concerns: "In most gardens, labour is simple and primitive; and if unions are started they would most probably be run by outsiders. In such cases the prevailing opinion is that they should be discouraged."[38] However, by 1939, confronted by the new political situation of the proliferation of nationalist and, more alarmingly, communist activities in labour politics, the ITA began to review and modify its strategies.

Instead of total opposition, it was decided to follow a policy of conditional recognition of unions, so Percival Griffiths prepared and communicated detailed instructions to the superintendents and managers in conditional terms aimed at constraining the formation of labour unions in the tea gardens. For formal recognition of a union, it was laid down that only the permanent labour force residing in the gardens should be enrolled as members, and its executive should be drawn from among them, with a maximum of two persons from outside to be members. No union would be allowed to represent more than one garden. A strike could not be called without a prior ballot with a minimum of two-thirds of votes cast and approved by 50 per cent of voters. Thereafter an advance notice of fourteen days was compulsory. The union was to maintain its accounts, which were to be audited at least once a year by a government auditor. Several conditions laid emphasis on discouraging outside intervention.[39] This policy remained on paper for the time being as the Government of India imposed the Defence of India Rules in September 1939 which suppressed, for the time being, the embryonic trade-union movement in Assam.

The imposition of Defence of India Rules by the government made it harder for labour unions to carry on the momentum of the 1939 strikes. However, by 1943 labour struggle outside the plantations was leading towards the organization of labour at the provincial level. The Assam Provincial Trade Union Congress (APTUC) was formed in 1943 as a branch of the All-India Trade Union Congress (AITUC) and became fairly active over the next two years. The first conference of APTUC was held at Dibrugarh on 28 November 1943.[40] The AITUC's communist

38. *ITA Report, 1937* (Calcutta, 1937), p. 37.

39. IOL, ITA circular no. 917, 11 April 1939, ITA Papers, mss Eur F 174/bay 2 (C). The intention behind the new policy was "that Managers having done their best to prevent a Union being formed, would perforce change their attitude once such a Union had been established, and would in fact as far as possible become the guide of those running the Union in the hope that, by so doing, undesirable influences would be kept out of the Union".

40. Nehru Memorial Museum and Library, New Delhi [hereafter, NMML], All India Trade Union Congress Papers [hereafter, AITUC Papers], file no. 45, 1942–1944, p. 25.

members were also making efforts to establish contacts with tea-garden labourers. Between 1943 and 1945 the APTUC increased its strength in Assam from 4,345 members belonging to 10 affiliated and associated units to about 16,000 members with 41 affiliated and associated units. During this period the APTUC extended its activities to the oil industry too, at Digboi; to the transport industry; and to other industries such as coal, cement, match manufacture, electricity, rice mills, and banks.[41]

The most important aspect of the ITA's adaptation to new situations and its adjustment to the industry's growing strength was its shifting policies with regard to the emerging trade unions during the 1940s. From complete opposition to the very idea of trade unions in tea gardens, it shifted its stance to conditional recognition at a time when uninterrupted tea production was a priority, to meet growing demand as part of the war effort. These developments forced the ITA to implement its earlier proposals on trade unions. Trade unions were there to stay, but under the leadership of those who would be acceptable to the industry's leaders.

> It would be idle to pretend that sufficient labour leaders of the right type are likely to be forthcoming. In practice, if the Trade Union Movement develops in the Tea Industry – as indeed in other industries in this country – it is almost certain to fall under the control of people who can reasonably be described as agitators,

wrote Griffiths in July 1945 in his notes on the post-war planning of trade unions in tea gardens.[42] He went on to analyse the current situation facing the tea industry: "We know that hasty development of Trade Unions may well mean a period of difficulty and even convulsion in the Tea industry; we equally know that undue opposition to them may merely make things worse."[43] In the face of this reality, what was the industry supposed to do?

It was decided that the industry would recognize those unions which were willing to accept its conditions: no affiliation to the Communist Party; white-collar staff and labour were not to belong to the same union; and finally one-third of the garden labour force had to be paying members.[44] The ITA remained hostile to the communist-dominated unions: "with irresponsible and unrepresentative unions, organized by communist agitators, whose avowed aim is the expropriation of our estates, we have had and will have nothing whatever to do".[45] Earlier, the ITA had aligned itself with non-Congress groups when it felt the Congress

41. Report of Secretary Assam Provincial Trade Union Congress (APTUC) at its 3rd Annual Session held on 14 and 15 December 1945 in Dibrugarh, reproduced in ASA, Government of Assam, General and Judicial Department, file no. GIM 7, 1943–1947.
42. IOL, Post War Planning: Notes by the Political Advisor, Circular No. 164, 21 July 1945, ITA Papers, mss Eur F/174, bay 2 (G) 2.
43. *Ibid.*
44. Griffiths, *History of the Indian Tea Industry*, p. 391; Guha, *Planter Raj to Swaraj*, p. 293.
45. *ITA Report, 1946* (Calcutta, 1946), p. xiv.

Party was hostile towards the tea industry in matters of labour and trade unions. However, with the growth of communist-backed unions, which were seen as a bigger threat, an alliance with the Congress Party seemed prudent.

The ITA Labour Adviser, H.F. Clark, reported to its labour sub-committee in December 1946 that the Congress ministry in Assam was acutely aware of the spread of communist influence in the province and was keen to promote labour unions under the Congress umbrella.[46] A Congress labour cell was formed under the leadership of Robin Kakoti and Bijoy Bhagawati (later Head of the Indian National Trade Union Congress, INTUC) to work in the tea gardens. In May 1947 the Assam branch of the INTUC was formed, with K.P. Tripathi as its president.[47]

At the dawn of Independence the Congress-led INTUC emerged as the dominant substitute for the communist unions. The APTUC Joint Secretary complained of mounting hostilities and attacks from INTUC sponsors and the Congress Government in Assam. According to him, government machinery was freely used to build up the INTUC and to disrupt the AITUC. The Congress Government in Assam had "put behind prison bars more Trade Unionists in a month (the vast majority of them being detained without trial) than even in a year of the worst days of direct British rule".[48] Naturally, under these circumstances the Congress Party was acceptable to the ITA:

> The outstanding development in labour organization during 1947 was undoubtedly the growth of the new Indian National Trade Union Congress, formed in May by leaders of Congress Party to counteract the disruptive influence of the communist dominated All-India Trade Union Congress. In contrast to the direct action policy of the latter body, the new organization purports to encourage the settlement of labour dispute through the medium of conciliation and arbitration machinery.[49]

Following an agreement between Robin Kakoti of the INTUC, Gopinath Bordoloi, Assam's Chief Minister, and the ITA, the latter agreed to allow free access in the tea gardens only to such INTUC organizers as were accredited by Kakoti.[50] The INTUC on its part assured the ITA that its activists would conform to "legitimate" trade-union activity and would not upset existing labour–management relations.[51]

46. IOL, ITA circular no. 271, 2 December 1946, ITA Papers, mss F 174/bay 2 (G).
47. Guha, *Planter Raj to Swaraj*, p. 296.
48. NMML, AITUC Papers, TL No. 4, file no. 47, 1947–1948.
49. *ITA Report, 1947* (Calcutta, 1947), p. 41.
50. ITA circular to garden managers, no. L.D. 600, dated Dibrugarh 21 July 1947, cited in Guha, *Planter Raj to Swaraj*, p. 297.
51. *Ibid.*, p. 296.

POWER STRUCTURE AND PRODUCTION RELATIONS

While the ITA used its organizational connections and political power to influence the colonial state and its policies concerning recruitment, transport, legislation, and control of the labour force, it was the nature of the power structure and production relations which evolved within the plantation system that played a crucial role in ensuring and sustaining the employers' dominance over labour for more than a century from its inception.

From the beginning, given the nature of the process (with its intensive production methods) labour was the tea industry's major preoccupation. The Assam Valley was very sparsely populated when the Assam Company commenced its operations in the 1840s and, as a consequence, shortage of labour was a serious problem. The initial experiment of importing Chinese labour for planting turned out to be complete fiasco.[52] Serious efforts were then made to procure labour both locally and from neighbouring Bengal through *sirdars* and individual agents, mostly fortune-seeking Englishmen. These efforts constantly ran into trouble, with recruited labour running away after arrival on the plantations, or not reaching its destination even after being dispatched by boat from the recruiting areas, thereby causing a loss of advances.[53] It is interesting to note that at this stage of its enterprise the Assam Company's efforts to procure labour did not include coercion, although the wages offered were deeply inadequate. The Company's directors wrote to the Superintendent on its plantations in Upper Assam, clearly instructing him that "they positively forbid any violence on the part of the assistants to the natives of the country or to the coolies of the Association and on any such case being formally reported immediate dismissal will most assuredly be the penalty".[54]

The structure of the power hierarchy based on coercion and extra-legal authority, which had dominated production relations in tea plantations for so long, began to evolve during the 1860s with the introduction of the indenture system at the height of the speculative boom during the time of the "tea mania". The official historian of the Indian tea industry described the events of this period thus: "A madness comparable in intensity with that of the South Sea Bubble seized men's minds, and normally level headed financiers and speculators began to scramble wildly for tea shares and tea lands."[55] Greedy to make quick money, the agents on the spot

52. Guildhall Library, London [hereafter, GL], Assam Company Papers, ms 9925, vol. 1, Proceedings of Committee in Bengal, 15 February, 13 March, May and June 1840, pp. 87–144.

53. GL, Assam Company Papers, ms 9925, vol. 2, August 1841–July 1844, pp. 350–454.

54. *Ibid.*, p. 112.

55. Griffiths, *History of the Indian Tea Industry*, p. 96; J.W. Edgar attributed this to the government's wasteland policy: "There can be no doubt that the reckless speculation was very much encouraged by the way in which waste lands were dealt with by Government"; Government of Bengal, *Paper Regarding the Tea Industry in Bengal* (Calcutta, 1873), p. xv.

often misled promoters of these companies by lumping together one or two really good gardens with three or four inferior wild jungle tracts and sold the lot to the company at prices two or three times their actual value.[56] Other forms of fraud also prevailed. Often money was invested in gardens that never existed. Tea companies, with or without land, sprang up overnight and shares rose to dizzy heights. Lands were cleared without any consideration of their suitability for cultivation or the availability of labour. Highly placed civil servants resigned their posts to become planters.[57]

The immediate fall-out of this situation was a manifold increase in demand for labour supply, which in turn started the process of a very large-scale mobilization of labour from long distances in other parts of British India and its employment under indenture contract in the Assam Valley tea plantations.[58] The labour force was mobilized under appalling conditions of fraudulent recruitment and insanitary transport, leading to high mortality rates and large-scale desertions from plantations. As commissioners appointed by the Government of Bengal to enquire into the affairs of the tea industry in Assam put it in their report:

> In the mad race of speculation, when fresh clearances were made, and acre upon acre covered with tea, to meet the terms of contract entered into with the promoters of new, or to satisfy the shareholders in old companies, no one has suffered more than the unfortunate labourer, for the opening out of new Tea Cultivation has been too often synonymous with disease and death.[59]

Another contemporary official account reported that of the 85,000 labourers imported into Assam between 1863 and 1866, no fewer than 35,000 were reported to have died or deserted.[60]

56. Often a speculator started forming a company while the land was barely scratched. The company was to "start by buying the lands he had scarcely finished clearing as accomplished tea garden, and what still remained of undeniable waste, at a cost out of all proportion [...] to what it was worth"; *Friend of India*, 9 June 1874, cited in Radhe Shyam Rungta, *The Rise of Business Corporations in India, 1851–1900* (Cambridge, 1970), p. 280.

57. A contemporary, Edward Money, reported that a small garden of 30 to 40 acres was often sold to a company as 150 or 200 acres. "It was done over and over again. The price paid, moreover, was quite out of proportion even to the supposed area. Two or three lakhs (£20,000 or £30,000) have often been paid for such gardens, when not more than two years old, and forty per cent of the existing area, vacancies. The original cultivator 'retired' and the company carried on." Government of Bengal, *Papers Regarding the Tea Industry*, p. ix.

58. Behal, "Some Aspects", pp. 22–25; Rana P. Behal and Prabhu P. Mohapatra, "'Tea and Money versus Human Life': The Rise and Fall of Indenture System in Assam Valley Tea Plantations", in E. Valentine Daniel, Henry Bernstein, and Tom Brass (eds), *Plantations, Proletarians and Peasants in Colonial Asia* (London, 1992).

59. 'The excessive mortality in the Assam tea gardens was attributed to sickness, bad housing conditions, overcrowding in houses, insufficient food, impure water, and want of proper medical attention'; *Report of the Commissioners Appointed to Enquire into the State and Prospects of Tea Cultivation in Assam, Cachar and Sylhet* (Calcutta, 1868), p. 49.

60. Government of Bengal, *Papers Regarding the Tea Industry*, p. xix.

Figure 3. Clearing of the ground for establishing a new plantation. Pen and ink drawing by George M. Barker from his memoirs as a planter.
George M. Barker, A Tea Planter's Life in Assam *(Calcutta, 1884), p. 129*

Some of the contemporary colonial officials were quite appalled at the inhuman nature of such treatment, the physical coercion and economic exploitation, along with the growing racial prejudice of the European planters towards the immigrant labour. As J. Ware Edgar, another Bengal official, wrote in his *Report on Tea Cultivation*:

> The miseries of the early immigrant were in too many instances cruelly aggravated by the ill-treatment of their employers. At one time the feelings of the planters as a body towards their labourers was most deplorable. The best men looked on them as a thankless, discontented lot, for whose good it was almost useless to do anything, and who it was impossible not to dislike; while amongst the worst sort of planters this feeling of aversion deepened into a mingling of hatred and contempt that led in some instances to acts of revolting cruelty, and in far more cases than has ever been publicly known to systematic and gross treatment.[61]

To the planters it appeared quite natural that the labourers who had deserted or disobeyed should be flogged. After all, the employer had invested so much money in bringing them to the gardens. The typical planter's attitude towards the recalcitrant or deserting coolie was that displayed by W.A. Stoddard, the manager of the Maphock Tea Estate in Sibsagar district, who, in 1872, wrote to the government demanding that

61. *Ibid.*, p. xxi.

the offending labourers be whipped: "The stick has a greater terror for those innate thieves and scamps for whom flogging is useful; especially without hurting the man much, the quiet, firm systematic way the government floggings are conducted." He saw it as the best way to keep alive the goose that was laying the golden eggs.[62] Often there were cases of labourers who were really physically unfit to work being tied up and flogged. Flogging, as a form of discipline, was a universal practice in the Assam tea gardens.[63]

To the labourers, desertion appeared to be the only hope of escaping physical coercion and torture. In order to check desertions, the labourers were made to live in closely guarded areas, known as "coolie lines", within the boundaries of the garden. *Chowkidars* (security guards) maintained strict surveillance over the "coolie lines", while "savage" hill men were specially employed to track down absconders with a promise of a reward of 5 rupees per head. Dogs seem to have been specially trained for this purpose. If the absconder was caught he was tied up and flogged, and the reward paid to his captor was deducted by way of fine from his future earnings. As Edgar noted, "often runaways enfeebled by their sufferings in the jungles, died under or from the effect of the floggings they received when caught".[64]

With the amalgamation of tea gardens under the management of agent firms and the impressive growth of the tea industry from the 1870s onwards, the entire geographical landscape of the Assam Valley was transformed. Tens of thousands of acres of jungle and wasteland were converted into private estates, inhabited by labourers, Indian clerical staff, and European managers and their assistants. Through mergers of small gardens, large units averaging 1,200 acres in size had emerged as the typical plantation by the late nineteenth century. Most gardens became physically isolated both by geographical distance and deliberate exclusion by fencing off from urban settlements as well as the surrounding rural society. These huge private estates, with compulsorily resident indentured labour in the coolie lines, provided the milieu for the exercise of virtually unlimited powers by the planters over their workers. A new work regime was imposed with the rhythm of an industrial clock. In fact the clock was put ahead by an hour from standard time to produce something known as "garden time" – a practice that was discontinued only towards the end of the twentieth century.[65]

62. *Ibid.*, p. 44.
63. *Ibid.*, p. xxi.
64. *Ibid.*
65. The sun rises much earlier in eastern India compared with other parts of the Indian subcontinent. The garden-time device made it possible to utilize the extra daytime available to lengthen the working day. A uniform work regime enforced and strictly regulated short durations of water and lunch breaks in the tea gardens. Under the supervision of a hierarchical

Several factors combined with these conditions to determine the nature of the emerging organization of production and its relationships in the Assam tea plantations. First, as an agro-industrial enterprise, tea plantations used labour-intensive methods, making labour the main component of production cost. Second, producing predominantly for export made the tea industry subject to price fluctuations on the international market. It is important to note that a large part of the expansion of the tea industry during the last two decades of the nineteenth century took place at a time of steadily falling prices; between 1880 and 1900, tea prices fell by half.[66] In such a scenario the industry's profitability was sustained by keeping labour costs as low as possible. In 1901 it was reported in the Central Legislative Council that between 1883 and 1899 the wages paid to tea plantation labour were below the statutory minimum of 5 rupees for men and 4 rupees for women.[67] These remained characteristic features of the history of the tea industry until the end of colonial rule.[68] Third, the growing incidence of desertion and absconding from the Assam Valley tea plantations was now perceived by the companies as a financial loss caused by managerial failure. James Finlay & Company's instructions to its Estate Department on this issue were to

> [...] impress on Managers the absolute necessity of keeping their labour if their gardens are to be profitably worked, and they must understand that the proper handling of their labour force will be regarded as an essential point in considering a Manager for any promotion that may be going, or even his continuance in charge. An undue proportion of abscondings will be carefully noted against a Manager.[69]

For the labourers, desertion was initially the commonest way of escaping the brutalities of life in the plantations. The effort and courage involved and the risks run in this act may be seen as an indication of a growing desire to fight the plantation system. The planters referred to deserting as "absconding", and it was considered a serious offence under the existing labour laws. Prior to 1865 a deserter from the tea gardens, if caught, was punished under section 492 of the Indian Penal Code, which provided for one month's imprisonment.[70] Act VI of 1865 then further

power apparatus headed by the managers and established during the indenture period, this work regime has sustained its rigour in the tea gardens even to this day. Daylight saving time applied only to the gardens.

66. *Prices and Wages in India* (Calcutta, 1901).

67. *Proceedings of the Central Legislative Council, 1901*, vol. 40 (Calcutta, 1901), p. 94.

68. Behal, "Some Aspects", ch. 5.

69. Glasgow University Archives, Glasgow, James Finlay & Company Papers, UGD 91/139, 27 September 1900.

70. Government of Bengal, *Papers Regarding the Tea Industry*, p. xxii; S.M. Akhtar, *Emigrant Labour for Assam Tea Gardens* (Lahore, 1939), p. 42.

empowered the employers to arrest runaways without warrant. But the severity of the law could not substantially deter deserters and diminish the scale of desertion. Even the official reports bear testimony to this. The Enquiry Commission of 1868 (though it did not provide figures) reported a very large number of desertions.[71] The annual reports on immigrant labour reported 2,584 desertions in 1877, 9,855 in 1884, 6,432 in 1897, and 10,244 in 1900.[72] Actual desertions were, however, much more numerous. Many deserters were caught in the immediate vicinity of the gardens while attempting to escape. Some of the captured labourers were often not taken to police stations by their employers, although required under the law, and hence not reported as deserters. There is reference even to children deserting. In 1884 as many as 1,179 desertions were reported among children.[73]

For managers, the security of their jobs and further promotion became synonymous with ensuring uninterrupted production, and steady growth of profits for tea companies. The drive to intensify the labour process, and constant supervision to prevent coolies from running away, reinforced those elements, described by Edgar, of physical coercion, violence, and extra-legal methods of labour control by the planters during the period of "tea mania". The managers' powers acquired an omnipotent authority akin to that of white masters towards their black slave labour in the southern USA just before the Civil War. A large number of *chowkidars*, *sirdars*, and garden *mohurirs* (field staff) supervised by European managers and their assistants constituted the apparatus that controlled the labour force.[74] Penal legislation armed the planters with immense legal powers over labour, which included the power to prosecute defaulting and malingering labourers and the power of private arrest of deserters.[75]

The abuse of legal powers and recourse to extra-legal authority by planters were known to the highest colonial authorities in the province, though no action was initiated. That the planters often flogged their labourers as a form of private punishment was admitted by the Chief Commissioner of Assam, Sir Bampfylde Fuller.[76] He reported the case of a woman labourer who was stripped and flogged in a tea garden by the manager.[77] As late as the 1920s a British trade-union delegate reported that

71. *Report of the Commissioners Appointed to Enquire into the State and Prospects of Tea Cultivation in Assam, Cachar and Sylhet*, p. 54.

72. *Assam Labour Reports* for relevant years; *RALEC*, p. 81.

73. *Assam Labour Report, 1884* (Shillong, 1884), p. 26.

74. Barker, *Tea Planter's Life*, p. 134; Rege, *Report on an Enquiry into Conditions of Labour*, p. 13.

75. Behal and Mohapatra, "'Tea and Money versus Human Life'", pp. 161–163; Behal, "Some Aspects", ch. 4.

76. Sir Bampfylde Fuller, *Some Personal Experiences* (London, 1930), p. 118.

77. *Ibid.* Henry Cotton, Fuller's predecessor as Chief Commissioner of Assam, also reported the case of a woman labourer who was flogged for trying to escape from the garden. Another

"we witnessed a group of men, women and children working away together, while five yards away was a planter's young assistant proudly hugging the whip".[78] The official reasoning for condoning the exercise of such powers without explicit sanction was based on the ground that the "tea planter as a master of a large and irregular labour staff must enforce discipline by occasionally severe measures which need not be looked into too closely, because they are substantially just and for the good of the general body of coolies".[79]

Extra-legal action on the part of planters was confined neither to the workplace nor to the prevention of desertions, but permeated the whole social life of a labour force isolated in the coolie lines within the plantation complex. In his memoirs, George M. Barker, a tea planter, fondly remembered sitting in judgment every morning on cases of coolie "delinquency" reported to him by the *jamadar* (headman in the coolie lines), and meting out punishment to "evildoers".[80] Similarly, a Bengal Government official was shocked to find in 1888 a planter organizing a polyandrous marriage between five "time-expired" coolies who had completed their contract period, and a single woman. In return each man had to agree to be re-engaged to work in the same garden for five years. "The disposal in marriage of all imported female coolies", he noted, "is regarded as a matter entirely within the jurisdiction of the manager".[81]

While the operation of penal legislation and extra-legal actions by the planters helped to create this power structure, it was the introduction of several other practices that imposed and sustained the severe forms of dependency in production relations. The most significant one was the partial payment of wages in kind, by providing rations at subsidized rates; this practice was introduced in the indenture contract and remained in vogue till the end of colonial rule. The general impression of the material conditions of labour as projected by the planters and the colonial state was one of "comfort" and "well-being". That impression was reinforced by claims that labour was paid well enough not only to live in "comfort" but even to save. It was further pointed out that the cash wage did not represent the total earnings of the labourer, since it was supplemented by grants of cultivable land, either free or for nominal payments, as well as by

woman was also flogged on suspicion of helping the others to escape. He also came across a case in which labourers were confined for a number of days in a "prison-house" in the tea garden and were mercilessly beaten up. Arms of three of the labourers were broken as a result of the beating; Henry Cotton, *Indian and Home Memories* (London, 1911), p. 266.

78. A.A. Purcell and J. Hallsworth, *Report on Labour Conditions in India* (London, 1928), p. 35.

79. NAI, Government of India, Department of Revenue and Agriculture, Emigration, B Proceedings, nos 1–3, September 1893.

80. Barker, *Tea Planter's Life*, p. 171.

81. NAI, Government of India, Department of Revenue and Agriculture, Emigration, A Proceedings, nos 2–9, February 1889. The time-expired labourers were those who had completed their contract of five years under the Immigrant Labour Act.

Figure 4. "Packing the tea". This pen and ink drawing by George M. Barker subtly illustrates the power relation between British overseers and their labourers.
Barker, A Tea Planter's Life, *p. 149*

the provision of cheap subsidized rice during certain periods.[82] Elsewhere we have shown that planters were often guilty of non-compliance with the payment of minimum statutory wages and that the real wages of tea labour often declined or remained stagnant during most of the period of colonial rule. Since the statutory minimum cash payment was inadequate even for subsistence, and since even that was not fully paid, labourers and their families were forced to depend for their daily survival upon the planters' provision of subsidized rations.[83]

Another practice which enforced the dependency relationship was the grant by the planters of small plots of land to their permanent labour force for private cultivation in the plantation complex. The industry considered it to be an important "concession" that supplemented the earnings of labourers.[84] Most of the labour reports remarked that gardens with plenty of cultivable land were "popular" with labour. The 1931 Royal Commission on Labour remarked, "The garden worker is essentially an agriculturist, and his desire for the possession of a holding which he can

82. Griffiths, *History of the Indian Tea Industry*, p. 297.
83. Rana P. Behal, *Wage Structure and Labour: Assam Valley Tea Plantations, 1900–1947* (NLI Research Studies Series, no. 043/2003) (Noida, 2003).
84. Griffiths, *History of the Indian Tea Industry*, p. 302; *Report of the Royal Commission on Labour in India* (London, 1931), p. 384.

cultivate with the help of the members of his family is great."[85] However, the labourer had to pay rent on such lands and the grants were conditional on the continuation of employment.[86] The land could be taken back on "disciplinary" grounds.[87] Besides, the size of these landholdings was very small, averaging between one-quarter and one-half an acre per worker, and was hardly a source of additional earnings.[88] The Assam Labour Enquiry Committee appointed by the Government of Assam in 1921–1922 did not find that the cash value of crops so raised could be considered as a "concession".[89] But, though private cultivation did not contribute significantly to the total earnings of the labour force, in the face of constantly declining real wages, labourers' dependence on such land for survival increased. Even for those who could escape from garden employment, alternate employment was not a real option: work in other industries, such as might have existed, required different skills.

A third practice of giving "advances" or "bonuses" began when the time-expired labourers were contracted under the Workman's Breach of Contract Act XIII of 1859. It was asserted that these were popular incentives for labourers who were contracted under this Act.[90] In reality these advances, or *girmit* (agreement) money, given both in cash and kind, were to be recovered from wages. Given the extremely low level of earnings, these advances became a source of indebtedness and bondage. "It would not be unfair to hold", noted the Enquiry Committee of 1921–1922, "that the indebtedness of the labourer affects his freedom".[91] The 1931 Royal Commission found that "before the abolition of Act XIII of 1859 an outstanding advance whatever its nature, was no doubt used as an argument against the grant of a discharge certificate, and to that extent the indebtedness of the labourer may be said to have affected his freedom".[92]

The reported cases of fraudulent recruitments, high mortality both en route as well as on the plantations, and large-scale desertions triggered state intervention by the Bengal Council in the form of the labour legislation of 1863 and 1865. Act VI of 1865 introduced a penal system that sanctioned punishment for breach of contract (for three years); planters were given powers to arrest without warrant labourers who absconded,

85. *Report of the Royal Commission*, p. 384.
86. *RTDEL, 1937* (Shillong, 1937), p. 135.
87. *RALEC, 1921–22* (Shillong, 1922), p. 24.
88. Behal, "Some Aspects", pp. 186–188.
89. *RALEC, 1921–22*, p. 24.
90. Griffiths, *History of the Indian Tea Industry*, p. 281.
91. *RALEC, 1921–22*, p. 74. Similar methods used by employers to bind and control the labour force through the system of advances were also used in the Ceylon tea plantations. For details see Vijya Samaraweera, "Masters and Servants in Sri Lankan Plantations: Labour Laws and Labour Control in an Emergent Export Economy", *Indian Economic and Social History Review*, 18 (1981), pp. 123–155.
92. *Report of the Royal Commission, Written Evidence*, p. 22.

and to imprison them for refusal to work. The Act also stipulated minimum monthly wages (5 rupees for men and 4 rupees for women) and the appointment of a government inspector of labour, empowered to cancel the contract of labourers on complaints of ill treatment. Time-expired or locally recruited labourers were, however, contracted under the Workman's Breach of Contract Act XIII of 1859.[93]

Subsequently, all labourers contracted under the Labour Immigration Acts were referred to as "Act labour", while the rest of the labour force, including those contracted under Act XIII of 1859, were termed "non-Act labour" in official reports. In 1882 the Government of India, after hectic lobbying by the tea industry, passed the Labour Districts Emigration Act I, which increased the term of the indenture contract to five years. During the course of the next two decades, when the tea industry grew rapidly, the intensified labour process took its toll on labour life. Appalling working and living conditions, low wages, overwork, and undernourishment leading to high mortality and negative rates of labour reproduction were the consequences of the rigorous operation of the penal system under the 1882 Act.[94]

The working of the penal labour system drew the attention of the Calcutta-based nationalist D.N. Ganguly in 1887 and of independent missionaries such as Charles Dowding during the 1890s.[95] The labour response to the intensification of work norms and labour processes found expression in increasing cases of desertions, "rioting, mobbing, assaults and unlawful assembly" being reported in official labour reports. During 1902–1903, of fifteen serious cases of "violence" and "intimidation", in four cases managers or their assistants were seriously beaten, and in a fifth the manager saved himself only by the use of a revolver.[96] About ninety labourers were convicted and sentenced to imprisonment on charges of "intimidation", "assaults", or "rioting".[97] In 1903–1904 one of the assistant managers "who seems to have been a new man and injudicious in his treatment of the coolies, was set upon and severely beaten by a mob of coolies, who left him unconscious!"[98] During 1904–1905 one assistant manager in the Jorhat subdivision was attacked by some thirty labourers

93. *RALEC, 1906*, Appendix, p. 136.

94. Behal and Mohapatra, "'Tea and Money versus Human Life'", pp. 155–161.

95. In 1887 D.N. Ganguly, the Assistant Secretary of the Indian Association, published a series of articles in *The Bengalee* highlighting the abysmally low wages and the appalling conditions in which labour was made to work and live in Assam gardens, a situation which he compared to slavery. Dwarkanath Ganguly, *Slavery in British Dominion* (edited by S.K. Kunda, reprint of thirteen articles published in the newspaper *The Bengalee* between September 1886 and April 1887) (Calcutta, 1972); Charles Dowding, *Tea Garden Coolies in Assam* (London, 1894).

96. See the *Assam Labour Reports* for the relevant years.

97. *Assam Labour Report, 1902–03* (Shillong, 1903), p. 12.

98. *Ibid.* p. 10. In the same year sixteen other such cases of "rioting", "violence", etc., were reported.

because he had very "[...] injudiciously taken a woman by the ear to force her to return to work".[99]

Officials investigating cases of "rioting" or unrest in general repeatedly pointed out that these often occurred after "assaults" by the European staff. The Deputy Commissioner of Lakhimpur reported in 1900: "Blows given by managers, or more commonly by assistant managers, to coolies, either for bad work or refusal to work, were the immediate cause of most of the rioting cases which occurred during the year!"[100] Referring to the reaction of the labourers, it was observed that in such cases the "coolies have generally come up prepared to risk and sometimes go to the length of tempting the manager to strike them".[101] In Darrang district the labourers "assaulted" the managers of Kalakuchi and Ghoira tea estates. The reason for the "assault" in one case was that the manager had abused and "assaulted" the wife of one of the labourers.[102] The husband was sentenced to five years' rigorous imprisonment and the others received from two to six months. In the other case, one labourer was sentenced to eighteen months' rigorous imprisonment, while his friend was awarded six months' rigorous imprisonment.[103] There were cases where the labourers did not merely react to planters' acts of violence, but demanded certain social and personal rights. In Halimguri tea estate in Sibsagar district it was reported that some Santhal labourers attacked the manager, James Begg, on Kalipuja day. They had demanded a holiday on that day, but the manager not only refused it, he tried to force them to work. Though the manager was not hurt, the court sentenced one labourer to six months' rigorous imprisonment, two to five months, and seventeen to shorter terms.[104]

The news of overtly violent conflict between labourer and planter became serious enough to draw the attention of the Viceroy, Lord Curzon.[105] On his insistence, an investigation was ordered into the causes. The Chief Commissioner of Assam, J.B. Fuller, felt the penal contract system, right of private arrest, and direct managing of labour by the European planters were all factors responsible for the increasing number of outbreaks of violence.[106] On these grounds, the Government of Assam sought the withdrawal of the provision of power of private arrest from the Assam Valley. A majority of persons interviewed in the recruiting districts by the Assam Labour Enquiry Committee of 1906 named the penal clauses

99. *Assam Labour Report, 1904–05* (Shillong, 1905), p. 8; *Eastern Bengal and Assam Era*, 21 February 1906, p. 4.
100. *Assam Labour Report, 1900* (Shillong, 1900), p. 22.
101. *Ibid.*
102. *Ibid.*, p. 13.
103. *Ibid.*
104. *Ibid.*, p. 23.
105. Behal and Mohapatra, "'Tea and Money versus Human Life'", pp. 165–167.
106. NAI, Government of India, Revenue and Agriculture, Emigration A, nos 12–14, December 1904.

as a cause of the unpopularity of plantation life among the prospective emigrants.[107] Following the recommendations of this Committee, the government passed the Assam Labour and Emigration (Amendment) Act in 1908 which abolished the penal clauses of Act VI of 1901.[108] Realizing that the penal clauses were going to be abolished, planters resorted to a more stringent use of Act XIII of 1859, which ensured an even more effective control over their labour force.

The Workman's Breach of Contract Act XIII was passed in 1859 at the instance of the Calcutta Trade Association and other similar interests. They memorialized the government, setting forth losses sustained from wilful breaches of contract or desertion of service by workmen and servants, and asking for the application of summary remedies.[109] The Act was supplemented by sections 490 and 492 of the Indian Penal Code (Act XLV) of 1860, making breach of contract of service by a workman (during the journey to and at the place of work) a criminal offence in cases where the employer had paid for the journey.[110] The Act XIII of 1859 was passed for the benefit of employers in general, but tea plantations in Assam found it most useful. Initially its application was restricted to locally engaged labourers, but by the beginning of the twentieth century time-expired labourers were increasingly engaged by planters under the Act. The Enquiry Committee of 1906 observed that there was an increasing tendency on the part of tea planters to resort to Act XIII of 1859 for renewal of agreements. Apart from time-expired labourers, newly imported ones were engaged increasingly under this Act as most managers considered it "absolutely necessary that a more rigid form of contract should be retained for new arrivals".[111]

As far as labour was concerned, then, the withdrawal of the penal clauses from Act VI of 1901 did not mean any improvement in their status. The strict application by planters of Act XIII of 1859 for new contracts continued to keep labourers in bondage. In some ways they were, in fact, worse off. Even the official historian of the tea industry had to concede that

> [...] the practice of placing free labour under long term contracts under Act XIII of 1859 had to some extent deprived the labourer of such protection as was afforded by Act VI of 1901 and had largely modified the effect of the withdrawal of the provisions of that Act relating to local contract and to the power to arrest absconders.[112]

107. See the section on recruiting districts in *Proceedings of the Assam Labour Enquiry Committee in the Recruiting and Labour Districts* (Calcutta, 1906). The committee reported that out of thirty-one witnesses in the recruiting districts, twenty-eight held the view that the penal contract with its accompanying want of freedom deterred labour from going to Assam.
108. R.K. Das, *History of Indian Labour Legislation* (Calcutta, 1941), p. 23.
109. *Ibid.*; *idem*, *Plantation Labour in India* (Calcutta, 1931), p. 37.
110. Das, *History of Indian Labour Legislation*, p. 26.
111. *RALEC, 1906*, p. 75.
112. Griffiths, *History of the Indian Tea Industry*, p. 281.

Compared with the penal provisions of Act VI of 1901, the punishments awarded to the labourers under Act XIII of 1859 for "breach of contract" and absconding were even more stringent. The Enquiry Committee of 1921–1922 recorded a number of cases where labourers, both men and women, were sentenced to rigorous imprisonment and hard labour for periods ranging from three weeks to three months for refusing to work the entire period of the contract. Even minors were not spared.[113] The Committee reported that children had been arrested and sent to jail pending trial.[114] Even after Act XIII was amended in 1920, planters continued to use its oppressive provisions. In 1922 the Committee found that the practice of placing labourers, especially new immigrants, under illegal long-term agreements, illegal arrests of absconders, and the placing of minors under contract were still widespread.[115] Such irregularities were overlooked by the leading companies.[116]

During the years 1920–1922 labour resistance to the indenture system in Assam grew at an alarming rate, and suddenly the numbers involved surpassed all previous figures as the scale and scope of that resistance reached a significantly higher level. The intensity and seriousness of the revolt was sufficiently alarming for the government to appoint an Enquiry Committee to investigate the events of 1920–1922.[117] The qualitative difference between labour unrest earlier, and the phenomena witnessed from 1920 onwards, was recognized indirectly in the language of the bureaucracy. Official terminology broadened in order to classify the events of those years. Terms such as "strike", "disturbances", and "exodus" were added to the older repertoire of "unlawful assembly", "intimidation", and the rest. Between September 1920 and January 1922 cases of strikes, disturbances, and riots were reported in most tea districts in the Assam Valley.[118]

Detailed information collected by the Enquiry Committee and relating to the above incidents reveals very interesting features of plantation life. Apart from the European planters (managers and assistant managers) there were others in the hierarchy. Among their Indian staff were garden *babus* or clerks, *zamindars*, *chowkidars*, and *mohurirs*; and the *kaya* or the Marwari shopkeeper in the vicinity of the gardens. They subjected the

113. Under Act VI of 1901 it was illegal to place minors below the age of sixteen years under contract. The ITA defined as "minor" those who were below twelve years of age. See *RALEC, 1921–22*, pp. 86–87.
114. *Ibid.*
115. *Ibid.*
116. *Ibid.*, p. 92.
117. *RALEC, 1921–22*, p. 1; *The Bengalee,* 29 June 1921.
118. During the same period equally serious and more well-known cases of exodus and strikes occurred in the Surma Valley (the famous case for instance of the Chargola Exodus, May 1921). For our purposes we are concentrating only on the incidents which occurred in the Assam Valley; *Assam Labour Report, 1920–21*, p. 3; *RALEC, 1921–22*, pp. 6–7.

labour force to varying degrees of economic exploitation or physical coercion. The riots, strikes, and so on of 1920–1922 showed increasing articulation by the labourers of their grievances, and a recognition of this hierarchy of exploiters. For example, in a number of cases the labourers' targets for attack were not only the European but the Indian staff too. There were cases of the Marwari traders' shops and weekly bazaars being looted and property being attacked.[119]

The labourers' struggle during 1920–1922 certainly did succeed in dealing a death blow to that notorious labour law, the Workman's Breach of Contract Act XIII of 1859. One of the major recommendations of the Enquiry Committee was the abolition of that legislation, which was accepted in 1925 despite strong opposition from representatives of the tea industry,[120] who argued that any attempt to reform or modify such an Act was useless, as had been shown by the failure of the amendment to the Act XIII of 1920. The planters strenuously opposed the recommendation of the Committee.[121] Two members of the Committee, representing the tea industry, came out against the withdrawal of the Act on the grounds that employees had no security against absconding labourers.[122] However, pressure from the labour protests of 1921–1922 and from the Indian members of the Legislative Assembly, along with the recommendation of the Enquiry Committee, compelled the Government of India to repeal the Act in 1926.[123]

The dismantling of the last vestiges of the indenture system deprived the planters of legislative support and legitimacy in running an overtly coercive labour regime. Newer strategies were needed to deal with the changing circumstances of shifting official attitudes prompted by the growing awareness of habitual abuses, and by the display of aggressive labour militancy during 1921–1922 in the tea gardens. Planters now proceeded to work out their own internal system, which effectively curbed labour mobility within the tea districts. An elaborate set of rules was drawn up by the ITA in 1929 to discourage enticement of labour from within the tea gardens, and this became the basis of the Revised Brahmaputra and Surma Valley Labour Rules, and was agreed upon by the tea companies.[124] The Rules prohibited one manager from deliberately "enticing" or employing labourers from another garden. Rule No. 2 unambiguously laid down that:

119. *Ibid.*
120. *Ibid.*
121. ITA Report, 1921, p. 8.
122. *Ibid.*, p. 90.
123. *Central Legislative Assembly Debates*, 20 February 1923 and 2 February 1925 (Calcutta, 1923 and 1925).
124. IOL, ITA Circular no. 35, 16 October 1929, ITA Papers, mss Eur 174/bay 1/shelf 2.

> [...] no subscriber to these rules shall employ directly or indirectly or harbour or detain any coolie (whether under contract or not) who has been imported by another concern, within the period of three years after importation, it being understood, however, that no claim under this rule shall be made or entertained unless duly formulated within two calendar years after the coolie has left the importing concern.[125]

For the arbitration of disputes an internal Court was to be constituted by the ITA branch committee on receipt of written complaints. The breach of rules was punishable with fines varying from 300 to 1,000 rupees.[126] D.V. Rege, appointed to enquire into conditions of labour in the plantations in 1946, reported that, though these rules were terminated with the consent of the planters with effect from 14 September 1938, they reverted to the practice within a year. In 1939 an agreement known as the Brahmaputra and Surma Valley Local Recruitment Agreement was signed by the planters with identical provisions,[127] but to make it more effective it was stipulated that if an estate employed an "enticed" immigrant from another estate then it should be obliged to pay that original estate a "transfer fee" of 75 rupees for the first year, 50 rupees for the second, and 25 rupees for the third.[128] Thus even after the withdrawal of indentured contract and Act XIII of 1859, the planters still managed to restrain labour mobility within their plantations.

One of the most effective means of sustaining the geographical isolation of plantation labour was through control over the freedom of movement of that labour. Most of the labour working and living within the gardens was employed under the penal contract system, and, as already pointed out, kept under close surveillance. Life on the plantations under this system was perceived by most labourers as a *phatak* (literally jail). As the Deputy Commissioner of Lakhimpur ruefully noted: "Every form of punishment however mild and whether really done for the coolie's good or not is designated as phatak."[129] The successive official enquiry committees and commissions often commented disapprovingly upon the imposed immobility of labour as an irrational system, but no action to dismantle it was seriously considered.

For example, when the penal provisions were withdrawn in 1908, planters were clearly unhappy and argued that Act XIII (which was still in

125. *Ibid.*
126. *Ibid.*
127. Rege, *Report on an Enquiry into Conditions of Labour*, p. 28.
128. *Ibid.*
129. Government of India, *Special Report on the Working of Act I of 1882 (Indian Emigration Act) in the Province of Assam During the Years 1886–1889* (Calcutta, 1890), p. 240. Over a decade later the Chief Commissioner, J.B. Fuller, noted in 1903 that among the coolies the whole plantation system was commonly regarded as a *phatak*; NAI, Government of India, Department of Revenue and Agriculture, Emigration A, nos 12–14, December 1904.

force) alone could not afford the necessary control over their labour force. The Enquiry Committee of 1906 had, however, suggested that better treatment of labour by the planters and the availability of enough wasteland to settle the immigrants would be sufficient to keep the labour force under "control". The planters did not agree. The Chairman of the ITA retorted, "The majority of imported labour is not the thrifty settler, but of a type naturally indolent, who will work with a little judicious handling, but from whom some sort of security against enticement and outside influence is necessary to safeguard the employer from loss of his heavy recruiting expenses."[130]

On the question of "outsiders" and "outside influence" the planters developed a siege mentality bordering on paranoia. They considered the entire area of the plantations as their private property and therefore anyone from outside who wished to go through the gardens had to seek prior permission from the manager.[131] The Royal Commission was not impressed though, and remarked, "We do not regard as satisfactory the existing position where workers are largely isolated from outside influence and any member of the public may be effectively prevented from approaching the workers' lines except with the manager's permission." As to the planters' argument of the "danger of outsiders exploiting the 'illiterate' and 'ignorant' labour force on the tea gardens", the Commission commented that "this is a risk to which every industry in India is exposed, and we think it better to face it than to continue a policy which inevitably gives rise to suspicion and is liable to be abused". They recommended that steps should be taken to "secure public contact with workers' dwellings on all plantations".[132]

Omeo Kumar Das, the Congress MLA from the Assam Valley, was the first publicly to contest this position of the planters. In November 1937 he informed the Secretary of the Assam Legislative Assembly of his intention to move the Assam Tea Garden Labourers' Freedom of Movement Bill, and sent a communication to that effect to all concerned, including the representatives of the ITA. In the statement of objects and reasons of the intended bill he argued:

> It is generally felt that freedom of movement of tea garden labourers is limited in a manner unheard of in any other industry. They are not allowed to go out of the

130. ITA Report, 1909, p. 49.
131. *Assam Legislative Council Proceedings*, 1927, vol. 7, no. 5 (Shillong, 1927), pp. 40–103.
132. *Report of the Royal Commission*, p. 378. Planters in the Ceylon tea gardens adopted similar methods to isolate their labour force from the "mainstream of political and trade-union developments in the rest of the country. A strict surveillance was maintained on plantations and trespass laws prevented 'outside agitators' from having access to the labour force at its place of work." Samaraweera concludes from this that "these restrictive features of plantation life inhibited the rise of trade unions or any form of independent organizational activity among the workers". See Samaraweera, "Masters and Servants in Sri Lankan Plantations", p. 22.

> estate whenever they want to do so. It is a common practice to engage night chowkidars to keep watch over the lines and prevent labourers from leaving the estate. The impression has been created in the minds of labourers that they have no right to go out of the gardens of their own free will. This constant restraint on their right of free movement has reduced them to a state of slavery.

Through his bill he intended to put an end to the forced isolation of the existence of labourers in the tea gardens: "Removal of obstructions will help to establish contact with the outside world which is absolutely necessary for their moral and economic advancement."[133]

The immediate response of planters was anger and protest against these "allegations". F.W. Hockenhull, the ITA representative, threatened further action on the subject unless objectionable expressions were removed from the letter. In the conference called to discuss the bill he arrogantly dismissed the arguments: "So far as the letter is concerned in which the conditions of the tea garden labourers is so described, it is sheer nonsense. We are not here to talk about nonsense."[134] As to the complaint of preventing outsiders' entry and free movement, the ingenious explanation was that "access to outsiders was only denied for the consideration of contagious disease they might bring to the gardens"![135] At the same time, to cushion the impact of Das's bill and to prevent matters escalating into a public debate, the planters made a show of terminating the Assam and Surma Valley Labour Rule. They further assured that no restraint would be placed on labourers on attending any meeting outside the gardens. But if contact were to be attempted inside the garden, managerial permission would be required.

The bill was withdrawn, as the planters' representatives managed to convince the Congress Ministry that the grievances addressed in it would be removed.[136] That assurance was not honoured, for in 1946 Rege reported the continuation of the old practice of *chowkidars* keeping watch, and the requirement of managerial permission still in place. "Even in cases of marriages, the consent of the manager concerned is generally sought to save trouble."[137] It was only after the attainment of Independence in 1947 that rules were framed under the plantation code to guarantee freedom of movement in the tea gardens.

133. ASA, Government of Assam, General and Judicial Department, Immigration B, nos 34–63, September 1939, pp. 48–49.

134. *Ibid.*, p. 81.

135. *Ibid.*, p. 79.

136. ASA, Government of Assam, General and Judicial Department, Immigration B, nos 34–63, September 1939, p. 49; *Assam Administrative Report, 1938–39* (Shillong, 1939), p. ii; Guha, *Planter Raj to Swaraj*, p. 243; ASA, Assam Legislative Assembly Debates, 1938, vol. 2, pp. 820–821.

137. Rege, *Report on an Enquiry into Conditions of Labour*, p. 28.

"Following Custom"? Representations of Community among Indian Immigrant Labour in the West Indies, 1880–1920*

PRABHU P. MOHAPATRA

On 25 June 1887, a curious incident was reported in the *San Fernando Gazette* of Trinidad in the British West Indies. At the end of the month of Ramadan that year, on the great festival day of Eid ul-Fitr, the Indian Muslims of Victoria village and of nearby estates congregated for the mass prayer in the Little Masjid. A fracas began unexpectedly when several Muslims objected to facing east in the direction of Mecca for the prayer. They argued instead that they should face west as they were wont to do in India. Theological debates soon gave way to a free exchange of blows between the votaries of eastward and westward prayer. Peace was restored after a considerable period, but with appeals to the eminent lawyers, Messrs Wharton and Farfan, to mediate in the dispute. Was the dispute simply due to ignorance as to the true direction of Mecca? Or was it a case of "following custom", the much maligned traits that the Indian Muslims shared with their compatriots?[1]

This incident, a small footnote in the longer history of community formation, is significant for another reason – indicative as it was of the travails of travel. Migration always meant transformation of lives and styles and involved living with changes that one neither chose nor anticipated. Cultures had to be created; they could not simply be

* A version of this article was presented at the AILH International Conference on Indian Labour History, New Delhi, in March 2004 and at the SEPHIS Workshop on "Labour Migration in an Earlier Phase of Global Restructuring" in April 2004 in Xiamen, China. I would like to acknowledge the comments of the participants at those conferences. I am especially indebted to Kaushik Ghosh, University of Texas, for his thoughtful remarks. A completed version of this paper was presented at the South Asian Studies Seminar at the Centre for South Asian Studies, Cambridge University, on 17 May 2006, where I sorely missed the acute observations of Raj Chandavarkar, Director of the Centre, who passed away just over three weeks before my presentation. I dedicate this essay to the memory of this outstanding historian of labour in South Asia. I would also like to acknowledge the generous support of the Trustees of the British Indian Golden Jubilee Banquet Fund in enabling me to complete the research for this essay.

1. John Morton, the Canadian Presbyterian missionary in Trinidad, found the habit of "following custom" to be one of the most irritating obstacles to proselytization. See Sarah E. Morton (ed.), *John Morton of Trinidad [...] Journals, Letters and Papers* (Toronto, 1916), p. 196.

transplanted. The incident interests me because it provides a striking illustration of two competing and divergent theoretical formulations about the larger question of community and ethnic identity formation among Indian migrant labourers and their descendents in the British Caribbean colonies.

The first of these, the theory of cultural persistence or retention, was popularized largely though the work of anthropologists in the 1950s and 1960s. The main features of this theory may be summarized briefly. According to this theory, cultural identity is central to the process of distinctive community and ethnic formation in the diaspora, and this cultural identity is transmitted largely through deeply embedded cultural symbols and value systems. In the case of the Indian community formation, the centrality of religious, caste, and family patterns is stressed as they are institutional embodiments of these value systems. Thus, it was argued, wherever Indians emigrated in large numbers the deeply embedded institutional patterns of caste, religion, and family values (the so-called cultural baggage) were carried by the migrants to their new homeland. These cultural values transplanted to the new surroundings shaped the emergent forms of community identities. In this view "culture" is seen as deeply resistant to the changes unleashed by modernizing forces in the new society.

The classic ethnographic description of this process of cultural continuity is to be found in the work of Morton Klass and Arthur Niehoff on Trinidad, conducted in the 1950s.[2] Persistence in the diaspora of the cultural values of the homeland, it was argued, shaped the distinct ethnic identity of the diasporic community and prevented their assimilation into the prevailing cultural norms of the new societies. This explanation of ethnic distinctiveness was both reinforced and transformed by the emergence of the enormously influential theory of plural society expounded in the work of M.G. Smith in 1965 on the British West Indies. In this study Smith characterized the multi-racial societies of the West Indies as being composed of population segments marked by distinct ethnic attributes who lived in a state of "economic symbiosis and mutual avoidance".[3] Following on as it did from the work of J.S. Furnivall on colonial Burma and the Dutch East Indies, plural-society theorists emphasized the fact that each ethnic group held on to its inherited cultural

2. Morton Klass, *East Indians in Trinidad* (New York, 1961); Arthur Niehoff and Juanita Niehoff, *East Indians in the West Indies* (Milwaukee, WI, 1960). These studies followed the acculturation and cultural persistence framework of Melville Herskovits's pioneering study of African cultural survivals in Trinidad. See M. Herskovits, *Acculturation: The Study of Culture Contact* (New York, 1938), and M. Herskovits and F. Herskovits, *Trinidad Village* (New York, 1947). See also the early study by Daniel Crowley, "Plural and Differential Acculturation in Trinidad", *American Anthropologist*, 59 (1957), pp. 817–824.

3. M.G. Smith, *The Plural Society in the British West Indies* (Los Angeles, CA, 1965).

traits and interacted with each other only in the market place or if they were obliged to by the overarching political compulsions of the state. The influence of plural-society theories was largely due to the close fit they had with the emergence of the racialized politics of post-Independence West Indies.[4] As is clear, cultural-retentionist arguments focused strongly on reified cultural traits that had been inherited by the immigrant communities from their homeland – very much like the votaries of westward prayer in the example cited at the beginning of this essay.

However, the arguments of cultural retention came under scrutiny very early in historical and anthropological studies. Instead of cultural persistence, what was emphasized now was the variety of ways in which central features of a putative ethnic culture had been adapted to and changed by their context in the new world.[5] This process of adaptation and transformation was initially termed acculturation and assimilation, but it acquired theoretical prominence with the elaboration of the "creolization process" in a thesis by the cultural historian Kamau Braithwaite.[6] Initially proposed as an argument for "interculturation" traits of African and European culture during the time of slavery, the thesis has since been extended to Indian diasporic formations.

In the case of the Indian diaspora it was argued, for instance, that the institution of caste identities had been largely attenuated through the experience of migration to a new society – where caste status bore no implications for occupational or social mobility, or for resource control.[7]

4. L. Despres, *Cultural Pluralism and Nationalist Politics in British Guiana* (Chicago, IL, 1967). See also L. Despres, "Anthropological Theory, Cultural Pluralism, and the Study of Complex Societies", *Current Anthropology*, 9 (1968), pp. 3–25; C. Clarke, "Pluralism and Plural Societies: Caribbean Perspectives", in C. Clarke, D. Ley, and C. Peach (eds), *Geography and Ethnic Pluralism* (London, 1984); and C. Clarke, *East Indians in a West Indian Town* (London, 1986). The use of the plural-society perspective in historical study is best exemplified by the work of B.L. Moore on British Guiana. See B.L. Moore, *Race, Power and Social Segmentation in Colonial Society: Guyana after Slavery 1838–1891* (New York, 1987); *idem*, *Cultural Power, Resistance and Pluralism: Colonial Guyana 1838–1900* (Montreal, 1995). While being broadly framed within the pluralist paradigm, there has been a recent trend in anthropological studies of the Indian diaspora in the Caribbean towards contextualizing ethnicity. See for instance C. Clarke, C. Peach, and S. Vertovec (eds), *South Asians Overseas: Migration and Ethnicity* (Cambridge, 1990); S. Vertovec, *Hindu Trinidad: Religion, Ethnicity and Socio-Economic Change* (London, 1992); T.H. Eriksen, "The Cultural Context of Ethnic Difference", *Man* (ns), 26 (1991), pp. 127–144.

5. R.T. Smith and C. Jayawardena, "Marriage and the Family amongst East Indians in British Guiana", *Social and Economic Studies*, 8 (1959), pp. 321–376; C. Jayawardena, *Conflict and Solidarity in a Guianese Plantation* (London, 1963).

6. Kamau Braithwaite, *The Development of Creole Society in Jamaica, 1770–1820* (Oxford, 1971).

7. There are several essays along these lines in B. Schwartz (ed.), *Caste in Overseas Indian Communities* (San Francisco, CA, 1967); C. Jayawardena, "Migration and Social Change: A Survey of Indian Communities Overseas", *Geographical Review*, 58 (1968), pp. 426–449; J. Nevadomsky, "Abandoning the Retentionist Hypothesis: Family Changes Among the East

Similarly, it has been pointed out that changes in language patterns had led to extensive creolization of the migrants' original languages (Hindi, Bhojpuri) and there was evidence of distinct adaptation to the dominant creolized English. Scholars have focused on syncretic adaptations of cultural values of Creole society by Indians in the Caribbean.[8] The creolization thesis, as is clear, emphasized radical discontinuity and cultural transformation in diasporic identity formation. In recent years the creolization thesis has received much support from the postmodernist turn in the social sciences, with its celebration of hybridity, migrancy, and its emphasis on improvization in the formation of identity. One might with some qualification think of the upholders of the creolization thesis as votaries of eastward prayer in the example cited at the beginning.

While a fuller critique is not attempted here, I will briefly set out my main points of disagreement with both the creolization and cultural retentionist arguments. The first relates to the notion of community identity in the diaspora.[9] Both theories, I believe, are pitched at a general level and are applied without discriminating between the different diasporic contexts. Both these formulations assume an unproblematic notion of diaspora.[10] One implication of that is the notion of a binary relationship between two fully formed cultures – the plural-society theory emphasizing separation, and the creolization model emphasizing interaction and interculturation. The problem, of course, lies in the presumption of the wholeness of cultural identity ascribed to the immigrant and indigenous groups. What is lost sight of is the contestory process by which

Indians in Rural Trinidad", *International Journal of the Sociology of Family*, 10 (1980), pp. 181–198.

8. See for instance R.K. Jain, "The East Indian Culture in a Caribbean Context: Crisis and Creativity", *India International Centre Quarterly*, 13 (1986), pp. 153–164. For the process of creolization among Indian women in contemporary Trinidad, see P. Mohammed, "The 'Creolization' of Indian Women in Trinidad", in Selwyn Ryan (ed.), *Trinidad and Tobago: The Independence Experience, 1962–1987* (St Augustine, Trinidad, 1988). For a nuanced enunciation of the creolization process focusing on "interculturation" between the lower-class Indian and black populations in the Caribbean, see R. Reddock, "Contestations Over Culture, Class, Gender, and Identity in Trinidad and Tobago", in Verene A. Shepherd and Glen Richards (eds), *Questioning Creole: Creolisation Discourse in Caribbean Culture* (Kingston, Jamaica, 2002). Walter Rodney, *A History of the Guyanese Working People, 1881–1905* (London, 1981), argues that there was gradual creolization along class lines among Indian immigrant labourers.

9. The creolization model has been comprehensively critiqued from a Marxist dialectical standpoint by Nigel O. Bolland, "Creolization and Creole Societies: A Cultural Nationalist View of Caribbean Social History", in Alistair Hennessy (ed.), *Intellectuals in the Twentieth-Century Caribbean*, vol. 1, *Spectre of the New Class: The Commonwealth Caribbean* (London, 1992), pp. 50–79. For a pointed critique of the constructionist approach to ethnicity as applied to the diasporic Indian community see Aisha Khan's comments in "Ethnicity, Culture and Context", *Man* (ns), 27 (1992), pp. 873–879.

10. For a critique of the notion of diaspora as applied to the Indians in the West Indies see Prabhu P. Mohapatra, "Longing and Belonging: The Dilemma of Return among Indian Immigrants in the West Indies 1850–1950", *IIAS Yearbook 1995* (Leiden, 1996), pp. 134–155.

immigrant communities are formed through their insertion and emplacement in social relations engendered by specific social formations.

In the case of Indian immigrants to the West Indies, the way in which the immigrants were forced to relate to the wider society through their position in the labour regime on the plantations has been insufficiently explored in studies on community-identity formation. I intend to demonstrate in this essay the crucial role of the changing labour regime in shaping the formation of the community identity of Indian immigrants. However, by emphasizing the relationship between labourers and the labour regime, I do not at all mean to suggest that the community identity was in some sense directly derived from the structure of the labour regime. It is here that I wish to focus on the ways in which identities are formed in the crucible of practices of representation, for it is through those that the structures of the labour regime impinged on the process of identity formation. However, it is also my contention that there exists no preformed cultural identity that is then expressed through representation. In cognitive terms, there is no identity imaginable outside representation. This allows one to think also of identities as historically amenable to transformation and to imagine the coexistence of multiple identities along with different practices of representation. Instead of a single reified ethnic identity, we can imagine a repertoire of community identities being constituted by acts of representations.

Despite this preliminary excursus on the weighty question of identity, what I propose to explore here is far more modest. I shall examine four different sets of self-representations of community identity among Indian immigrants to the West Indies during the period 1880–1920, the last phase of the career of the indentured labour regime there. The first of these is about collective representations of community staged in the Muharram festival by Indian immigrants to the West Indies. Next, I shall take up three different styles of representation of community identity in the public sphere propounded by three individuals. Two of them were irrepressible and prolific letter-writers to the colonial newspapers, while the third is the author of one of the rare literary texts produced by an Indian during the period of indenture in the West Indies. What I will focus on is the different styles of representation of community identity in relation to the dominant labour regime, and I hope thereby to provide some clues as to the contradictory and often contested nature of the process by which community identity was fashioned during the period of indenture.

CHANGING LABOUR REGIME ON CARIBBEAN PLANTATIONS

Before I undertake this analysis, it will be useful to mark out the terrain of the labour regime on which these acts of representation were staged. The labour regime to which the immigrants came was marked by transformations along two axes – that of the economic cycles of growth and stagnation, benchmarked by international sugar prices; and the long-term process by which indentured labourers were transformed into permanent settlers.

Indentured labour from India was imported to the Caribbean colonies of British Guiana, Trinidad, and Jamaica following the abolition of slavery in 1838. Resistance by former slave labourers to the unreconstructed labour regime on the sugar plantations forced planters to find sources of "cheap and reliable labourers" from India. Several private experiments beginning in 1838 gave way to organized labour import under the colonial aegis. Planters and the colonial state jointly met the cost of recruiting and disciplining immigrant labour, effected now under a series of ordinances promulgated from the 1840s onward and collectively known as the Coolie Ordinances (consolidated in the late 1890s as Immigration Ordinances of British Guiana (1893) and Trinidad (1899)). Between 1838 and 1917, excepting a few years in the early decades, there was continuous annual import of labour from India – totalling 238,000 to British Guiana, 145,000 to Trinidad, 50,000 to Jamaica, and 40,000 to Surinam, which was a Dutch colony. Smaller numbers came to St Lucia, Nevis, and Grenada.

Indentured labour resuscitated the flagging sugar industry. Acreage under cane and sugar production increased greatly between the 1840s and 1880s, buoyed by favourable sugar prices and the continuous flow of indentured labour. From the mid 1880s, sugar prices dropped precipitously, to half the level of 1880. Cane acreage and sugar production stagnated until the end of World War I.[11] The Caribbean sugar industry is thus marked by two distinct phases: of growth, from the 1840s to 1880, and crisis and stagnation, from 1884–1917. Interestingly, the import of indentured labour from India remained roughly equal in both those phases, indicating the crucial role played by low-wage indentured labourers in ensuring growth in the early phase, and stabilization of the plantation system in the period of crisis.

These immigration ordinances and the apparatus of enforcement and "protection" that came into existence regulated every aspect of the working lives of the immigrants and to a large extent their non-working lives too (including marriages and festivals, sickness, housing, and their return to India). The central feature of the labour system that came into being was contractual servitude at fixed wages (25 cents or 1 shilling per day) for a period of five years on a plantation, where the labourer was also

11. Cane acreage in British Guiana and Trinidad rose from 45,000 acres in 1850 to 135,000 acres in 1884; in the same period, sugar production increased from 55,000 tonnes to 187,000 tonnes. By 1915, cane acreage in these two colonies had fallen to 121,000 acres and sugar production was 162,000 tonnes.

obliged to reside. He or she was forbidden to be outside the plantation without the explicit permission of the planter, since the essence of indenture lay in prohibiting the labourer from taking advantage of the competition for labour, which was scarce. Contracts were enforced by making any breach of the provisions of the ordinances a criminal offence, punishable by a fine or imprisonment.[12] It was into this extremely restrictive and oppressive labour regime that Indian immigrants were placed to serve out five or ten years of their working lives. After ten years of industrial residence in the colonies, the immigrant could seek repatriation to India,[13] a provision explicitly inserted in the contract in order to distinguish indentured servitude from slavery.

While immigrants came from practically every province of India, the overwhelming bulk – up to 80 per cent in fact – were drawn from United Province and Bihar in the Gangetic plains of northern India. While the social composition of immigrant labour reflected the religious and caste structures of those regions, the gender and age compositions were markedly skewed. Immigrants were predominantly single, male, and in the prime age group of twenty to thirty-five. Family migration was not the norm, with only 15 per cent of immigrants being married couples; very few migrants were children, and only 28 per cent were female, of whom 70 per cent were single. All the evidence points to the recruitment of immigrants individually rather than in groups, and not usually from their home villages, with most already having been mobile in search of employment before they were recruited in the major cities or rail and road junctions of the region.[14]

The nature of recruitment reflected the particular nature of the demand from planters for able-bodied young men fit for hard labour, which was geared more towards continuous import than local reproduction to meet its need for a servile labour force. Indeed, colonial labour policy militated against settlement of the labour force for the greater part of the period when indenture was in place. Deaths outstripped births among Indian immigrants right up to the end of the nineteenth century – not an unexpected result given this skewed gender composition of the immigrants.

Community formation on the plantations was thus beset with structural problems, but in spite of them there emerged an embryonic community

12. For the process of formation and enforcement of indenture laws in the West Indies see K.O. Laurence, *A Question of Labour* (Kingston, Jamaica, 1994), and Prabhu P. Mohapatra, "Assam and the West Indies, 1860–1920: Immobilizing Plantation Labor", in Douglas Hay and Paul Craven (eds), *Masters, Servants, and Magistrates in Britain and the Empire, 1562–1955* (Chapel Hill, NC [etc.], 2004), pp. 455–480. Between 1880 and 1915 an average of 25 per cent of indentured labourers in British Guiana and Trinidad were prosecuted for breach of contract offences every year; nearly one-third of those prosecuted were imprisoned.

13. On the changing policy of repatriation see Laurence, *Question of Labour*, and Mohapatra, "Longing and Belonging".

14. Laurence, *Question of Labour*; George A. Grierson, *Report on Colonial Emigration from the Bengal Presidency* (Calcutta, 1893).

centred on the sugar estates. The spearhead was embodied in the time-expired labourers, whose terms of indenture had ended. According to the indenture contract, they could apply for a free return passage to India after completing a further five years of residence in the colonies, so around the estates there grew small settlements or villages of former indentured labourers who worked on the estates but took up diverse other occupations too. After completing their ten years, many immigrants either did not return at all or decided to delay their return. On the whole, of the sum total of immigrants who came to the colonies, only about 20 per cent ever returned to India. This process of villagization accelerated in the late nineteenth century as the sugar economy plunged headlong into extended crisis.

A slow but steady mutation occurred in the plantation labour regime in the late nineteenth century as the policy changed to induce settlement of immigrant labour. That was done mainly by encouraging former indentured labourers to become part-time estate workers and then to bear the cost of reproduction in small parcelized holdings. Thus a cane-farming smallholder community grew in Trinidad by the turn of the century, and in British Guiana a rice-farming and paddy proletariat emerged among Indian immigrants. This process of villagization transformed the character of community formation among Indians, with the slow emergence of differentiation within their community.

This brief excursus was necessary to describe the changing nature of community formation among Indians. I have identified three phases in the process by which Indian labourers were transformed from temporary sojourners to permanent settlers in the colonies. The first phase from 1838–1880 was a phase of growth in the plantation economy, with the centre of an immigrant community being strongly anchored on the estates and nearby. Between 1880 and the end of indenture came the phase of villagization, with increasing diversification of occupation and the shifting of the centre of gravity of the community away from the estates and into villages and settlements. The third phase, in the post-indenture period, is marked by continuing decline in the social prevalence of the plantations and greater occupational mobility, differentiation among the Indian settlers themselves, and a move to urban areas by professionals and educated people. These are necessarily broad phases – and there were overlaps between them – and the tendency towards settlement was accelerated or retarded according to the pace of the economic and political processes.

MUHARRAM IN THE CARIBBEAN

A bemused "sightseer" was once witness to the celebration of Muharram (or Tadja as it was called in British Guiana) on a sugar plantation in Demerara in British Guiana in 1897 and exclaimed:

> There is something very striking in the thought that this Muslim "Miracle play" should be so firmly rooted in this single corner of the American continent. If we count Trinidad as part of the British Guiana then this must be the only spot in the whole of the Western hemisphere where the martyrdom of Hassan and Hossein is annually commemorated. It is as though Good Friday were religiously observed in a single province in the middle of China.

This singular incongruity led him onto philosophical speculation about the East in the West and he further ejaculated:

> The Coolies bring their Tadjas and Tom Toms and we give them trousers and other advantages of civilisation. They come here with their strange customs and superstitions and we give them in return free schooling and Western standard of living. What the result of this strange conjunction of the Orient in the Occident will be, what sort of a social cosmos it is going to produce I leave to others to foretell.[15]

He may not have been right about Good Friday in China nor about the advantages of trousers and civilization, but he was not very far from the truth in his observation about the strange location of Muharram performances in the heart of the West – except that he should have included Jamaica, Surinam, and the tiny island of Grenada, where Muharram was celebrated too. In fact, wherever Indian indentured labourers were sent, be it the African continent or the American, from Mauritius to Natal, Fiji to the Caribbean colonies, Muharram emerged in the nineteenth century as the most important and spectacular festival of Indian immigrants. If our "sightseer" had been more knowledgeable he would have been acquainted with the Hosay massacre in Trinidad of 1884. Undoubtedly many of the contemporary missionaries knew of it. Our man would have exclaimed in even greater surprise at the fact that Hindus and Sunni Muslim labourers had even laid down their lives in order to assert their right to celebrate a minority Shia sect festival.[16]

On 30 October 1884, 6,000 Indian labourers, residents of sugar estates around the town of San Fernando, brought out their processions of *tazias* – replica tombs of the grandsons of the Prophet – and marched towards the town to complete the ceremony of immersion of these *tabuts* to end the festival of Muharram, just as they had done for the previous thirty years. But that year the government had banned the procession from entering the town and threatened to punish severely any infringement of the ban. Yet the procession marched on to fulfil what they said was their "religious

15. *The Daily Chronicle* [hereafter, *DC*], Georgetown, 1897.
16. For a detailed account of the Hosay massacre of 1884, see Kelvin Singh, *The Bloodstained Tombs* (Basingstoke, 1988), and Prabhu P. Mohapatra, "The Hosay Massacre of 1884: Class and Community among Indian Immigrant Labourers in Trinidad", in Arvind N. Das and Marcel van der Linden (eds), *Work and Social Change in Asia: Essays in Honour of Jan Breman* (New Delhi, 2003), pp. 187–230.

obligation". A short distance from the town troops and police, mustered to stop the procession, opened fire from two of the entrances to the town. Twenty-two Indian labourers were shot dead and 100 more were injured. None of them had attacked the police nor had they even entered the town. When the dead were counted and the injuries totted up, a startling statistic emerged: 17 of those killed were Hindus and 5 Muslims, while 76 of the injured were Hindus, with 19 Muslims and 1 Christian.

The government had banned the procession, ostensibly arguing that Hindu and other non-Muslim participation indicated that it was not a religious event, so that banning it would not amount to religious suppression of the immigrants. Enquiries followed and the Governor of Jamaica, Sir Henry Norman, exonerated the government from allegations of interference with the religion of the immigrants. Yet a timid Hindu labourer, when asked by the Commissioner as to why he, a Hindu, had joined the Muslim festival, replied "I did so because it is the custom of all the coolies in Trinidad to join Hosay". Strange indeed are the effects of travelling cultures and customs, the more so because in that same year Muharram processions in Agra in the Northwest Provinces had become the site of a major riot between Hindus and Muslims. In the 1880s and 1890s there were more conflicts between Hindus and Muslims over the Muharram procession in several cities of northern India, and following them came the great round of conflicts over cow-killing during Bakr-Eid. Why indeed did Muslims and Hindus who fought and killed over Muharram in India jointly lay down their lives in far-off Trinidad while defending their right to celebrate the same festival?

I have elsewhere analysed the reasons for the unprecedented hostility of both the colonial state and planters to mass public manifestations of community among the Indians, and the obstinacy with which the workers staked a claim to public performance of that community.[17] What I wish to note here is the historical trajectory of the story of this popular community festival in the Caribbean.

If our bemused sightseer had lived to see the third decade of the twentieth century, he would have seen the passing into history of the system of indentured labour and with it the passing of Muharram as the prime celebration of the descendants of Indian immigrants. In 1932 Tadja was banned in British Guiana by the colonial state, but for some time before then it was certainly on the wane.[18] In Trinidad, Hosay, as

17. *Ibid.*.

18. B.F. Williams, *Stains on My Name, War in My Veins: Guyana and the Politics of Cultural Struggle* (Durham, 1991). B.L. Moore argues that the decline of Tadjas in British Guiana was due to increasing Creole participation and the consequent withdrawal of Indians from the celebration. However, except for citing the disapproval by missionaries and planter newspapers he provides no evidence to support his argument. Moreover, since he reproduces the missionary and newspaper accounts uncritically he continues to misread the Tadja as a Hindu festival, since

Muharram was called, had been pushed into a corner of the suburb of St James in Port of Spain and survives to date only because of its value as an exotic tourist attraction. In Surinam, as in Fiji, the 1930s saw the decline of Muharram, which was by then a minor festival in certain rural locations and was devoid equally of its past grandeur and wide participation.[19] In all these locations several other forms of religious festival had overtaken Muharram. For example, Hindus were celebrating Ramlila and Deepavali; while Muslims enjoyed Eid ul-Fitr.

What then accounts for the dazzling rise of Muharram during the nineteenth century among the Indian labour diaspora and its subsequent fall from grace? In this section I shall try to explain some puzzling aspects of this phenomenon associated with Muharram; first of all its immense popularity with the predominantly Hindu and Sunni Muslim emigrants, the cultural meanings they derived from its performance, and its unique place in community formation in the nineteenth century; and then the factors leading to its decline in the period after the demise of indenture. I shall do so with reference mainly to Muharram in British Guiana and Trinidad, which were the two most important Indian labour-importing colonies.

I will anticipate here the main thrust of my exposition, although to some extent it is already evident in the presentation of the problem itself. The coeval emergence and decline of Muharram and the indentured labour system is an important feature of the problem as I have set it out. My contention is that Muharram's unique features and its wide popularity as the premier religious and community festival bore an important relation to the labour regime in which the emigrants found themselves. It follows from another proposition that community-identity formation among Indian emigrants and their descendents was closely shaped by their relationship, both involuntary and expressive, with the labour regime. The colonial state played a constitutive role in the labour regime on the plantations and the changes it underwent over time, and it directly influenced the recruitment, organization, and discipline of labourers. So to the extent that Muharram symbolically expressed the community aspirations of emigrants, it was necessarily refracted through their own experience of the labour regime and the colonial state; the relationship was no doubt not a simple unilinear one, it was multiplex.

Yet what has marked several contemporary as well as later anthropological accounts of diasporic community formation in general and

"the Hindus would have been more anxious to put on their own show rather than simply join ranks with the Muslim compatriots and rivals". This is specious reasoning, to peddle the plural-society thesis against the historical evidence; Moore, *Cultural Power, Resistance and Pluralism*, pp. 218–223.

19. J.D. Kelly, "From Holi to Diwali in Fiji: An Essay on Ritual and History", *Man* (ns), 23 (1988), pp. 40–55.

Muharram or similar cultural performances is a deliberate erasure of the relationships they bore to the labour regime and the colonial state. They focus instead on pre-existing cultural attributes and the ethnic identity markers of the community. But ethnicity or community identity are subject to historical processes and remain part of the problem to be explained rather than being its explanation.[20]

The origins of the celebration of Muharram in the Caribbean are quite certainly to be found in the early years of indenture. In Trinidad, the earliest celebration of Muharram can be traced to 1855 in the Philippine estate in the Naparima area. In British Guiana its origin is not well recorded. Yet by the late 1850s contemporary newspapers had taken notice of the celebration of this "tumultuous festival" of the coolies in Trinidad and British Guiana. They noted with wonder the parade through the main cities of the island of "coolie castles" or "locomotive temples", as the *tabut* replica tombs of the martyred grandsons of the Prophet were termed. They remarked on the high spirits of the "noisy crowds of coolies exhibiting much earnest gesticulation, making a great noise, dancing and capering" and their vigorous fencing with sticks. There was a certain amused tolerance of this "false and foolish worship" on the part of the heathen crowd.[21] These early reports noted that the local black population participated in these parades in great numbers as onlookers in search of novelty, while they scarcely mentioned the religious denominations of the Indian immigrants. It remained for a long time a festival of coolie religion, which was broadly termed "idolatry".

What was noticed consistently was the public display of Muharram – which by the late 1850s was called "Hosay" or "Hosein" in Trinidad in imitation of the lamenting chant of "hai hassan hai hosein" and simply "Tadja" in British Guiana. (In Jamaica it was known as Hussay.) The ignorance of the religious importance of the festival was widespread and it was left to missionaries especially interested in proselytizing among Indian immigrants in the 1870s to decode it for the edification of public and officials alike. However, missionaries both in Guiana and Trinidad, disliking its idolatrous aspects, were deeply hostile to the celebration of Muharram, an unruly congregation in their eyes; and, just as much, they deplored the attractions it held for the black, lower-class Christian population. From the 1870s, Christian missionary opposition to the

20. But see C. Jayawardena, "Religious Belief and Social Change: Aspects of the Development of Hinduism in British Guiana", *Comparative Studies in Society and History*, 8 (1966), pp. 211–240, for changes in religious belief coinciding with changing status of Indian labourers after indenture. See too Kelly, "From Holi to Diwali in Fiji", for a nuanced account of the transformation of rituals and festivals and the relationship of this transformation to changes in plantation regimes in Fiji.

21. *The Trinidad Sentinel*, 6 August 1857; *Port of Spain Gazette* [hereafter, *POSG*], 13 July 1859.

festival's public aspect was an important ingredient in the making of the colonial state and in shaping reactions to Muharram among planters.[22]

In the nineteenth century Hosay, Tadja, or Hussay was celebrated in the first ten days of the first Islamic month of Muharram, or twelve new moons after the last celebration, since the Islamic calendar is lunar, with alternating months of thirty and twenty-nine days. Processions of *tazias* from various estates were sent off to be immersed in a river, or the sea, in a grand procession accompanied by women singing ritual laments or Mersiahs. For most of the nineteenth century, the grand spectacle of the Muharram procession found its culmination in the coastal cities of the colonies: Georgetown, Port of Spain, and San Fernando. It was there that the elite of the colonies witnessed the parade of *tazias* from their balconies, and as the years passed they saw with horror the growing size of the processions and the "diabolical activities accompanying it", namely stick fighting and the incessant chants of "hai hassan hai hosein". By the 1880s, for instance, San Fernando, a quaint planter town with a population of barely 5,000, was invaded annually by the Hosay procession, consisting of anything from 15,000 to 20,000 Indian labourers.

It is clear from accounts of the nineteenth century, from which the above descriptions of the festival have been gathered, that Muharram was by far the most important community festival for labourers. The question that must be answered is what cultural meanings did they seek to represent in this festival and how was the community identity of these Indian immigrant labourers expressed through it? By answering it, we can understand the reasons for the marginalization of Muharram in the late-indenture and post-indenture periods. The primary identity of Indian immigrants in the plantation setting remained that of "coolie", nominally meaning an unskilled wage labourer, but in fact a pejorative racial appellation applied to all Indians.

What is interesting is that the racial stigma and low-status ascribed to Indian labourers were rooted in laws and ordinances based on the voluntary and free labour contract. Yet nothing marked out the Indian immigrant as the member of the lowest social group in Trinidad more than the spatial and temporal immobilization which was imposed by the five-year indenture. It was the very attribute of immobilized labour implicit in the term "coolie" which was extended to the whole community of Indian immigrants and their descendants. Understandably, community aspirations of Indians were asserted in opposition to the "coolie" identity and to the physical and cultural immobilization imposed by the indentured labour regime.

It was the processional aspect of Muharram which was perhaps the most

22. Singh, *Bloodstained Tombs*. The details of Muharram celebrations in the following sections are from Mohapatra, "The Hosay Massacre"

important reason for its popularity among immigrants. The articulation of community identity in a processional form was especially important in the context of the spatial immobility of the community engendered by the indentured labour system. Through the Hosay procession, the community manipulated already existing spaces and places but gave them a new, albeit temporary, meaning. The Hosay procession performed at least three functions which were crucial to the expression of community identity: an integrative, a transgressive, and a reiterative one.

The route of the procession connected normally segregated plantation communities and physically linked the enclosed space of the plantations with the city or town centre. So it was that the community was structured by the procession and at the same time imprinted itself on the existing space. In its transgressive aspect, the procession narrated a counter discourse to the normal spatial immobility imposed on the immigrants. By occupying the highway and marching through the centres of towns, Indian immigrants laid claim to the public spaces which were ordinarily denied to them. Public spaces, highways, and towns were especially fraught places for Indians. By occupying such spaces with the procession, even though only temporarily, Indian labourers symbolically transcended both their "coolie" status and the spatio-temporal restrictions under which they lived. The Muharram procession quite literally mobilized an immobile community.

However, the counter discourse of space was not formulated in opposition to established authority even though the procession did not draw its legitimacy from any explicit legal right to occupy space. Rather, the transgressive and liminal aspects were normalized through the reiterative function of the procession. By establishing over the years fixed routes, destinations, and an order among estates for their participation in the procession, the community claimed for itself an implicit right to occupy and march through public spaces. By integrating, mobilizing, and investing customary rights to public spaces, the Muharram festival and its procession powerfully articulated community aspirations and religious belief. The sacred and the profane were not separated; neither in the practices nor in the minds of the participants.

A final feature of the processional form of Muharram needs to be noted here. While I have drawn attention to the relation between the expressive forms of community and the specific condition of labouring existence (integration, mobilization, public representation) it must not be inferred from this that the procession was in any sense a direct expression of the labouring identity of the indentured immigrant workers. In fact in Muharram and the procession if any thing was visually absent it was precisely any direct reference to the labouring condition on the plantations. I would even suggest that the Muharram procession allowed Indian immigrants to deny their overwhelming existence as coolie labour by representing themselves as a fully fledged moral and cultural community.

Muharram drew its sharpest meaning for the participants in the evident contrast with their daily condition of labour – and that was the meaning so powerfully conveyed to the wider public through the procession.

However, despite this caveat, because of the way in which the processional form of Muharram became an expression of community assertion, it emerged as a potentially powerful vehicle for representing collective grievances. In my analysis of the 1884 Hosay massacre I have demonstrated the special conditions in which community assertion and class grievances were uniquely combined in the Muharram procession in Trinidad.[23] The Muharram of 1884 in Trinidad came in the wake of an unprecedented wave of strikes that swept through the colony between 1882 and 1884 as planters tried to counter the crisis of falling sugar prices by an intensification of work. To planters and the colonial state the threat of insurrection appeared imminent as they panicked in the face of the massed display of the Muharram procession. By brutally enforcing a ban on the procession the colonial state sought to separate the class and community assertions expressed in Muharram.

Having elaborated the cultural meanings whose expression was sought in Muharram, I shall now explain its eventual gradual decline as the premier community festival of Indians in the diaspora. Muharram grew in size and importance with the spread of the plantation economy, and although its decline coincided with the plantation's severe crisis of the late nineteenth century, the most important factor in its decline remained the unabashed hostility of the colonial state to its procession. The first attempts at controlling the procession had been initiated in British Guiana in 1869 when a special ordinance required specially chosen headmen to ask permission for it and to be responsible for its good order. That was followed in Trinidad by the promulgation of ordinances banning the procession from towns and public roads and confining it to the estates. Finally, the large-scale shooting down of workers in 1884 to enforce the ordinance broke the back of this community festival. A Trinidad ordinance of 1885 made the celebration of the festival a Muslim affair, with punishment for non-Muslim celebration.

I have argued that community representation in public spaces was the most powerful source of the popularity of the festival. Denied this vital expressive quality, and confined to individual estates, the festival was starved of the chance of public support. Allied to this was the sustained hostility of missionaries and orthodox Muslims to the pagan display in the festival. But the factor that worked incessantly in the background was the gradual move away from the plantation and the process of villagization that was initiated as a response to the crisis of the late nineteenth century. As the locus of community formation shifted away from the plantation

23. *Ibid.*

and the estates, Muharram could no longer remain the preferred mode of community assertion. There was a definite shift from public display of community to more inward and exclusive forms of religious observance, such as flag worship for Hindus, and Eid among Muslims. The process of retreat from public display was soon overtaken by a new form of engagement in the emerging public sphere in the colonies.

VOICE OF THE SETTLER INDIAN: "A SON OF INDIA" IN TRINIDAD

In the aftermath of the crisis of 1884, a new mode of public activity emerged quite suddenly in the Caribbean, in the form of writing letters to the leading journals of the colonies. The first letter-writer to emerge from the ranks of the Indians wrote in the *San Fernando Gazette,* a daily paper widely circulated in Trinidad, in 1888 under the *nom de plume* "A Son of India". This was the leading Creole (black) newspaper of the colony and it championed the cause of educated Creoles who were demanding a greater share in the affairs of the colony. It was in this newspaper that "A Son of India" began writing a series of letters and essays drawing attention to the demands of the Indian community.

Three factors seem to have given rise to this public form of representation. First, the emergence of a substantial number of Indians, former indentured labourers who had diversified from the plantations and formed the nucleus of the Indian settler community. Second, from within this small but rapidly growing section there emerged a minuscule group of Indians educated in English largely through the proselytizing effort of the Canadian Presbyterian mission in Trinidad, which opened its first school for Indian children in 1871.[24] Third, the institution of the Royal Franchise Commission enquiring into the question of electoral enfranchizement in the colony in 1888 gave a fillip to public agitation for elected and representative government largely led by a progressive Creole middle class.[25]

It is significant that the first letter from "A Son of India", written in December 1888, was an address to the new Governor William Robinson, articulating the demands of the growing settler Indian community.[26] The themes set out in the letter seemed to have persisted throughout the career of this pioneer Indian letter writer. First, there was the demand that efforts should be made by the government to retain the Indian labourers in the colony rather than repatriate them. Second, the most important incentive for them so stay would be if the government should intervene actively to

24. By 1888 there were 52 schools in several estates and villages, with 3,000 children of settler Indians. Ten educated Indians were employed as interpreters and shop clerks in 1880.
25. On the Royal Franchise Commission see *POSG*, 12 September 1888.
26. Letter from "A Son of India", *San Fernando Gazette* [hereafter, *SFG*], 8 December 1888.

provide education for Indians, taking into account their special needs, considering that the bulk of them were outside the purview of any education effort at all. In it there was the demand to provide for compulsory education to all Indian children. Third, the language of imperial citizenship is deployed by the author to seek government welfare and to stake a permanent claim on the colony. ("It is not too much to ask from the Government these privileges, for we consider ourselves part and parcel of the great British Empire and not aliens".) Finally there is a conscious effort to refute the ascription of low status to the Indian community on the ground of their low-caste origins, illiteracy, and position as bound labourers on estates. This was done in several subsequent letters by drawing on the glorious past of the Indians and noting the fact that not all immigrants were of low caste; a fair proportion were of high and middling castes.[27]

In demanding special attention by the government for the education of the Indian community, "A Son of India" irked several pro-planter lobbies as well as the Creole middle class. The former thought it useless expenditure on a class whose main occupation should be and would remain labouring on the estates as "coolies". The *Port of Spain Gazette*, the colony's pro-planter newspaper, reacted to this novel form of public activity and demand for education by asserting that most Indians would "enter the school as a coolie and emerge from it the same coolie".[28] The emergent Creole middle class continued to deprecate immigration and the immigrants as causes of demoralization to the colony and a potent factor depressing the labour market.[29] They saw in the demand for education emanating from the settled Indian community another instance of state pampering and special privilege. Even John Morton, the Canadian Presbyterian missionary who played a leading role in setting up schools for Indians, was irritated by the demand for non-denominational education for Indians demanded by "A Son of India".[30] The author, who was himself a Christian and had been trained in a missionary school, was acutely aware of the reluctance of Indians to enter denominational schools for fear of losing their religion. He sought to highlight the need for advancement of the settler population through education rather than conversion as a means of "amalgamating to Western civilization".[31] Through his letters "A Son of India" also commented on the major legislation affecting the Indian community, such as the Immigration Ordinances and ordinances on Indian marriages.[32]

27. See letters from "A Son of India", *SFG*, 4 December 1889 and 25 February 1892.
28. See letter from "A Son of a Gun", *POSG*, 16 December 1892.
29. See, for example, the letter from "Fairplay", *SFG*, 16 December 1892.
30. Letters from John Morton, *SFG*, 18 February 1892 and 24 March 1892.
31. Letter from "A Son of India", *SFG*, 21 January 1892.
32. Letter from "A Son of India", *SFG*, 4 July 1896.

How was Indian community identity expressed in this new form of public activity by the letter-writers? The community that was imagined had as its nucleus those who had made Trinidad their home – this included the rapidly growing peasant proprietors involved in cultivating Crown land and others who had diversified into activities outside the plantation, such as trading, huckstering, and market gardening. The spearhead of this group was the small number of educated Indians, most of whom were Christians. There was no attempt to exclude indentured immigrants, but it was evident that they were seen as the source of recruits into this rapidly expanding nucleus. Thus, the letter writers did not oppose immigration as the Creole middle class did, but were all for its encouragement. All the same, it was imagined that they could become full members of the community only by graduating out of the estates. The emphasis on education as a means of acquiring citizenship and permanence was indicative of the character of this putative community.

While the problems of indentured labourers were sometimes raised in "A Son of India's" letters, there was no attempt at criticizing the indenture system directly, nor did he express any substantial complaint about wages, working conditions, or terms of contract. The ascription of the low status of "coolie" identity to the whole Indian community was contested, but in some sense too there was an implicit acceptance of their condition. By 1889, the term "coolie" was thought to be too degrading to be used to designate Indians in general. The Presbyterian mission led the way in this, under pressure from its exclusively Indian members to change the name of the mission from "Coolie mission" to "East Indian mission". As a new community began to be imagined around the settlers, there were attempts to begin rudimentary organization of the Indian community around 1897 with the establishment of the East Indian Congress in Trinidad.

While the settler community of Indians eventually came to chart a different path of involvement with the colonial public sphere in the late nineteenth century, what do we see happen to the indentured Indian workers, and what was their response to the crisis of the plantation economy? In the next two sections I shall look at two different styles of representation of community in the work of songwriter Lalbehari Sharma and of "coolie" publicist Bechu in British Guiana.

THE POETRY OF INDENTURE: LALBEHARI'S *DAMRA PHAG BAHAR*

It is widely assumed that Indian immigrants were illiterate and that their education happened after their entry into a plantation. This image fits neatly into the idea of the plantation and indenture as a school for the development of immigrants. However, there is enough evidence contrary to this popular image to suggest that literacy was not entirely absent among the immigrants – a fair number were literate in the native languages of India, such as Hindi, Urdu, and Hindustani. In the first place, familiarity with and reading of important religious texts was fairly common among Indians. It is possible that the upper-caste Brahmins and Muslim clerics and ritual specialists were perhaps over-represented among this group. Despite that, it is also true that the Indian diaspora has produced far too few public texts for posterity in the forms of memoirs, autobiographies, and other literary texts.[33]

It is in this context of the near absence of any public record authored by the immigrants that the rare work of Lalbehari Sharma has some significance. Lalbehari was an indentured labourer in Guiana whose work was published in 1916, just as indenture was coming to its end.[34] His work entitled *Damra Phag Bahar* (*Holi Songs of Demerara*) was written in Nagri script and in a mixture of the Bhojpuri and Awadhi languages, and was a collection of original songs meant for recitation during Holi festivals. The language of the text and the construction of the poems followed the sixteenth-century textual forms of the epic *Ramcharit Manas* [*The Story of Rama*] by Tulsidas, with a mixture of couplets [*doha*], quatrains [*choupai*], free verse [*kabita*], and rhymes [*chautal, ulara*] well-known in the main recruiting ground of the immigrant population in eastern Uttar Pradesh and western Bihar.

It is evident from the mixture of forms utilized in the text that the author expected familiarity from his readers and audience not just with the themes but also with the sequences and rhythm of the text. The text is eminently suitable for recitation, quite apart from being highly readable too. The explicitly intended audience is a collective of singers and listeners or, as he wrote in his preface, *gayanpriya rasik* [connoisseurs of songs]. Yet it is evident from the structure of the collection, and from the references to the landscape sprinkled with the names of settlements and estates where Indians resided, that the expected audience and readership is the Indian community of British Guiana.

While ostensibly meant to entertain, the text was also confessional, in that the poems were intended to cleanse the inner world (*antah karan pavitra*) and provide an outlet for the anxieties and worries of the readers. The collection of songs is in three parts. The first introduces the author to the audience and relates the story of his present condition and daily life in British Guiana; the second part is a collection of songs touching upon the Holi being played out by the epic characters Rama, Sita, Krishna, and

33. But see the recent publication of an autobiography of Munshi Rahman Khan, an ex-indentured labourer from Suriname: Kathinka Sinha-Kerkhoff, Ellen Bal, and Alok Deo Singh, *Autobiography of an Indian Indentured Labourer: Munshi Rahman Khan (1874–1972)* (Delhi, 2005).

34. Lalbehari Sharma, *Damra Phag Bahar* (Georgetown, 1916).

Radha; the third part consists of philosophical and esoteric prayers (*bhajans*).

The introductory section of the collection is of obvious interest in this analysis, although I shall refer as well to the overall theme of anxiety, lament, and alienation (*viraha*) that pervades the text. The story of the author is briefly described. He was born in the village of Mairatand in Chapra, a district in the Bhojpur region of Bihar, and is currently resident on the Goldenfleece estate in Essequibo on British Guiana. The first description of the country is of a "bad country" (*Kudesh*) bereft of *dharma* and conscience (*vivek*) where the author has enlisted himself as a coolie after abandoning the path of Vedas and so having to submit to doing lowly work (*kukarma*). From this it appears that the author had been a Brahmin who now feels disgraced by becoming a coolie.,

A brief account of daily life on the plantation follows, beginning with the work bell at 5 in the morning at the barracks and the call to work of the sardar (headman or driver). In the field following the sardar arrives the sahib (overseer/manager) dressed in hat and with whip and workbook in hand ready to deduct pay for short work. This supervision distresses the author as he contemplates his work in a country surrounded by police stations, and laments seeing the poor deceived into emigrating to such a country as this. This distressing theme is interrupted by a description of a Saturday pay day, when men and women gaily dressed receive their pay from the sardar. Then in the final section the author ponders how to carry on thus for five years of worrying about when he will become eligible for his ticket to leave the plantation.

The passage of time on the plantation and the constant anxiety leads some to become renouncers (*sadhus* and *fakir*s), while others wander in distress and anxiety wondering how to carry on. The section ends with the advice to the indentured workers to remain patient and stay on the plantation and try to live as they would in the village, "back home", under the benign guidance of the sardars. In this account we have a story of the overturning of the moral order and descent into moral anomie produced by plantation work, and the anxious desire to escape the discomfiture of coolie status. It is significant that the answer provided in this section of the text is to reinstate the order of the village, but under the sardar.

However, it is in the next two sections that the author displays his poetic prowess by weaving in themes of gay abandon represented in the play of Holi by Ram, Sita, Krishna, and Radha, with an acute sense of the longing felt by the women abandoned by their husbands. The theme of erotic play and *viraha* permeates these songs, but is often interrupted by philosophical exhortations to abandon the illusions of worldly goods. The world is after all a false dream – the world of money, power, family, and fame is mere illusion and not one's own.

While clearly the author here draws on perennial themes in the Bhakti and Nirgun poetry of Kabir and Dadu about the illusory nature of the world, what is interesting is the juxtaposition with the description of the plantation world in Guiana. To the audience and singers of this collection, the resonance with their daily life under plantation rules must have been strong. By describing the world of money, power, and fame as illusory, the author seeks to strike a parallel with the world of the plantation and its life, which is itself in a sense morally degraded. Similar parallels could be found in the intense desire of the abandoned woman for her distant husband or that of Radha for Krishna, and the desire for release from the plantation. Yet the response to both these predicaments should be patient inward contemplation about the true nature of the world to establish stability and harmony through outward compliance with the village-like order on the plantation and by chanting the name of god ("Without the name of Ram the world is like a beautiful woman without her nose") in the company of the good (*satsang*).

What the author is advocating is a sense of detachment from the surrounding world that will enable the community to pass through the period of moral degradation forced on the immigrants by their insertion into the plantation regime. Thus there is an existential critique of the indenture system through which a potentially moral community can be established, but this critique by itself is not enough. What is required is an inward transformation and detachment from the outer world. Significant in this text is first of all a complete lack of engagement with the labour regime (except in a moral sense) and with the public sphere of the colony: there is no attempt to imagine a better world, nor bettering oneself or the community through any such engagement. I suggest that the identity which this text tries to represent is one of disengaged community; and the style in which this imagined community is represented is one of inward contemplation. Yet this may not be enough of a characterization, since what destabilizes the attempted normalization is the intense, almost erotic desire to escape the conditions of existence imposed by the real world of the plantation.

We must now explore the final aspect of the representation of identity, developed under the indenture system. I shall address the question through the account of a remarkable and in some ways atypical attempt by one individual to engage with the plantation order and the colonial public sphere.

BECHU: A "COOLIE" CRITIQUE OF INDENTURE

On a presumably balmy Sunday morning on 1 November 1896, readers of Guiana's largest circulating daily newspaper, the *Daily Chronicle*, were surprised by the appearance in its columns of a letter signed by Bechu, Indentured Immigrant of Enmore estate Ex Sheila 1894. If the fact that a letter written in flawless English by an indentured coolie was itself an unprecedented phenomenon, what must have astonished the newspaper's readers even further was the letter's content and style.

> Will you kindly permit me through the medium of your widely circulated paper to say a few words with regard to the official investigation which has been made concerning the rate of wages paid to the indentured labourers in Plantation Non Pareil? Being a coolie myself, and an indentured one in the bargain I have up to now refrained from saying anything in the matter [...].

With this modest disclaimer began the career of Bechu the indentured coolie, who wrote letters to the editors of several of the colony's newspapers for the next four and a half years, championing the cause of the immigrant labourers by brilliantly dissecting and exposing the façade of legality and claims of public good made by planters and the colonial State. So powerful was his indictment of the indenture system that the West India Royal Commission which visited Guiana in 1897 invited him to present evidence and a written submission – a rare honour for a mere coolie. His exposés stung the planter class so much that he was twice prosecuted for libel (1898 and 1899). The jury being equally divided each time, neither convicted him.

He found admirers galore among leading Creole politicians, and sworn and bitter enemies among planters. His mordant wit, erudition, catchy style, and precise and irrefutable arguments brought a whiff of fresh air to the stuffy, flowery prose normal to any public discourse conducted in the colonial newspapers. He made defence of the public good an admirable cause and his success emboldened a few Indian immigrants to follow in his footsteps. But as suddenly as he had arrived, he one day bade farewell, to return to India in 1901. In his brief but incandescent career, Bechu developed a sharp and completely new perspective on Indian immigration, a view from below, nevertheless, in dialogue with the perspective from above.[35]

I shall now turn to the elaboration of this perspective of Bechu, with reference to some of his letters to the *Daily Chronicle* and the debates he entered into in the pubic domain, as well as to his submission to the Royal Commission.

It will be useful to place the career of Bechu in the context of the last decade of the nineteenth century.[36] Sugar prices had steadily declined up to that time, reaching their lowest level between 1896 and 1903. In British

35. Bechu's letter and submission to the West India Royal Commission, along with a number of annotations, was published in C. Seecharan, *Bechu: 'Bound Coolie' Radical in British Guiana 1894–1901* (Kingston, 1999).
36. On the condition of Indian indentured workers and the sugar industry in British Guiana in the last two decades of the nineteenth century see A.H. Adamson, *Sugar Without Slaves* (New Haven, CT, 1972); Rodney, *A History of the Guyanese Working People*.

Guiana, the acreage under sugar cane reached a peak of 80,000 acres in 1890 and fell by a quarter to 67,000 acres by 1900. Sugar exports fell from 130,000 tonnes in 1888 to 84,000 tonnes in 1900, their lowest level in 30 years. Buffeted by lower prices and competition from bounty-fed continental beet sugar, Guianese plantations were in deep crisis, as estate after estate was merged with others or abandoned. Of the 113 estates in 1880, only 52 remained in 1901.

Cost-cutting and wage reductions were the preferred weapons of the planters to counter plummeting profits. Intensification of work and reduced wages became endemic to the plantations and unemployment ran rampant. Yet surprisingly the average annual import to the plantations of indentured labour (4,000) remained almost the same between the 1880s and 1890s. The incessant gluttony for bound labour, even when free labour was in abundance, was the characteristic response of planters to such a crisis. It is against this background that naked exploitation of immigrants was visible beneath the carapace of an indentured system based on supposedly voluntary contract.[37] Bechu's critique was not only probing and pointed; it made its mark because of the crisis.

The immediate context for Bechu's letter of November 1896 was the riot by indentured labourers at Non Pareil in October.[38] Indentured workers protesting against low wages and a heavier workload at the plantation came out on strike en masse and went to the Protector's Office to complain. They were allowed this right under the immigration ordinances, but on their return they were confronted by police who rounded up the leaders on the pretext of conspiring to create disturbances. The workers refused to give up the men, and police fired seventy-two rounds at them, killing four and severely injuring forty others. Bechu's letter was the first public protest against this brutal repression.

Bechu began by questioning the inquiry into wages, which was carried out *post facto* and found wages to be "ample". Bechu produced his own contract which mentioned explicitly that every indentured labourer was entitled to a wage of 1 shilling for seven hours of field work, and if working on a task his wage could not be lower than this guaranteed minimum. Any work or task other than that specified was to be paid at overtime rates, by the hour. Bechu argued that the protest of punt loaders at Non Pareil was justified, since they received wages below the guaranteed minimum and worked nearly fourteen hours without being paid overtime. He followed this up by arguing that while indentured workers were frequently convicted of breach of contract for trivial matters, no planter was ever

37. Adamson has calculated that on average there were thirteen strikes per annum on British Guiana's estates between 1884 and 1903: Adamson, *Sugar without Slaves*, pp. 106–109.

38. Rodney, *A History of the Guyanese Working People*, p. 158. See also the account of the Non Pareil riot in *DC*, 18–21 October 1896.

prosecuted for the rampant violation of this contract to pay a minimum wage. While acknowledging the prevailing depression in trade he wondered, "Why should the indentured worker bear the sole burden for that?" He ended by quoting the Bible: "Unto every one that hath shall be given, and he shall have abundantly, but unto him that hath not shall be taken away even that which he hath."[39]

The letter was received in stunned silence and in the next six days only one letter appeared heartily supporting Bechu's argument.[40] But within a few days a planter named Langton published a lengthy essay in the *Argosy* entitled "A History of East Indian Immigration" which argued against Bechu.[41] Apart from the stereotyped planter's view of coolie immigration as a benefit to the indentured labourers and that indentured immigration was crucial for the survival of the colony's economy, Langton addressed the key issue of guaranteed minimum wages. He argued that the coolies had it explained to them on their arrival in the colony that their earnings were dependent on the successful completion of their tasks, and that average effort would earn them the guaranteed minimum wage. It was the laziness of the coolies which prevented them from completing their tasks and so earning the minimum wage. Bechu replied point by point to Langton and other planter correspondents, arguing that the government must ensure that the coolies received the minimum wage of 1 shilling a day.[42]

In a subsequent letter Bechu exposed the planters' attempt to use the fact of the Non Pareil riot to demand protection for West Indian sugar. Planters had started a campaign in the London press, arguing that the condition of the sugar industry under competition from bounty-fed sugar from the continent was so bad that they were compelled to reduce wages and that social unrest like the Non Pareil riots would recur ever more frequently if protection were not granted to their sugar through countervailing duties. Bechu pointed out that under no circumstances could the planters reduce the wages of indentured coolies, and if the planters claimed that then they were in blatant violation of the contracts. He also pointed to the hypocrisy of planters at the same time demanding more indentured labourers when they could not pay them minimum wages.[43] He had written in one of his letters:

> We are all alive to the fact that these are hard times, but if the planters are unable to keep to the terms of their contract let them liberate those who wish to be

39. Letter from Bechu, *DC*, 1 November 1896.
40. Letter from J. Wharton, *DC*, 5 November 1896.
41. Langton, *Argosy*, 21 November 1896.
42. Letter from Bechu, *DC*, 9 December 1896.
43. Letter from Bechu, *DC*, 7 January 1897.

> liberated – set [them] free and then there will be no occasion for dissatisfaction even if the men can not earn six pence per diem.[44]

In taking up the question of the guaranteed minimum wage, Bechu made plain the contradictions in the indenture contract and exposed the blatant violation that went on in the name of freedom of contract. Contracts should bind both parties; not provide freedom for planters and bondage for labourers. Bechu's exposé irritated the planters – several of them doubted his existence, thought he was hankering for notoriety, and wondered how, if he was so educated, he could escape the scrutiny of the recruiting agencies in India? One planter even suggested that he should be packed off back there![45] Bechu's reply to this calumny was humorous and full of wit.[46] To the question "Who is Bechu?", he replied in one of his letters

> A queer looking specimen of – it is believed – the human race (but evidently the rarest description) because when I was exhibited in the Calcutta Zoo most people, naturalists included, were ready to swear for true that I was the Missing Link, but since there was no Darwin to declare me to be the *Simian Pure*, I unfortunately lost my chance of making a fortune.

When planters wondered if he were a real live indentured emigrant he replied "It is a positive fact that I am a real live animal and what is more surprising I am allowed to go about *unchained*." To the question about his education Bechu replied

> If it is possible to educate monkeys why should not the "connecting link" between man and him be taught as well. If the Planter is death on education he should lose no time to shut up schools and do away with the Education Commission else in course of time he will find "too much educated *coolyman*" in this colony.

As Bechu's letters caused a mounting furore, the issue of coolie immigration and countervailing duties came up for discussion when the West India Royal Commission came calling in the colony in February 1897. Bechu's notoriety earned him an invitation to attend the Commission.

It was in his evidence before the West India Royal Commission that Bechu displayed his full analytical and rhetorical powers. Quoting from previous inquiry commissions, from the famous novelist Trollope, and other literary luminaries, Bechu argued that the indenture system was a veiled system of slavery, or a "despotism tempered by sugar".[47] Citing his

44. Letter from Bechu, *DC*, 22 December 1896.

45. See letters from Langton, *DC*, 12 December 1896; Planter, *DC*, 9 January 1897.

46. Letter from Bechu, *DC*, 12 January 1897.

47. See Bechu's written evidence in *Report of the West India Royal Commission*, vol. 2, Appendix C, p. 131 (London, 1897), and his evidence in vol. 3, p. 1131. See also *DC*, 2 February 1897.

own experience as an indentured worker, Bechu pointed out that the concept of equality embodied in the contract was never applied in practice, nor were the specific provisions of the contract adhered to by the planters or enforced by the colonial State. Hours of work were long and the task system allowed the planters to pay wages regularly lower than the stipulated minimum.

He pointed out that even though safeguards appeared in the contracts, the structure of plantation authority easily negated them. Workers found it difficult to complain against the drivers and overseers for fear of being prosecuted on trumped-up charges under breach of contract provisions. He pointed out that the prosecution by planters of large numbers of immigrants was a device to lower the earnings of immigrants as much as it was a way of terrorizing them into submission. He also noted the unrestrained practice of concubinage and sexual exploitation of Indian women by overseers and managers, which was a potent source of conflict. Indeed, a direct result of it was the prevalence of wife murders among Indians.

The most important critique of indenture that Bechu advanced was twofold: first it was explicitly inequitable, especially on the issue of the payment of minimum wages; second, indentured immigration was a weapon in the hand of planters used to keep the labour market permanently depressed. The irony of it was that government revenue through custom duties, which subsidized immigration expenditure, was largely derived from the consumption of goods produced by the labourers. He opposed further immigration because it was in fact directly contrary to the interests of all Indians, whether indentured or free, who were resident in the colony. Instead he suggested that time-expired Indian immigrants be offered an incentive to settle down by providing them with land instead of a return passage to India.

Although elements of Bechu's critique of indenture (such as lowering of wages, subsidy to the planters) had been articulated earlier by the rising Creole middle class, opposition to indentured immigration often meant opposition to the Indian community's very presence. Bechu's position was distinct, in that he argued from the experience of an indentured coolie, showing that it was in fact not in the interest of Indians to support further immigration, and that the interests of both Creole and Indian labourers, free and indentured immigrants alike, were harmed by the indentured immigration system.

From the evidence before the Commission the question was answered that had so bothered the planters. Who was Bechu, and how had he arrived in the colony? He submitted that he was a Bengali orphan raised by a Presbyterian missionary lady in Calcutta and that he had lived and worked with other missionaries as a copyist and domestic servant. Though never educated in a school, as a child he had been taught by the missionary lady.

His interest in literature he had cultivated himself. As to his arrival in the colony, he said he had been in much reduced circumstances when a recruiter offered him a job in the colonies. His preference had been for Trinidad, and to be a clerk, but he was forced to come to Guiana because the recruiter refused to let him leave without paying for the time he had spent waiting for the ship. He was assigned to plantation Enmore and worked in the fields for five months, when due to repeated fever he was allowed to work in the deputy manager's house. His employers were obviously kind and he had had no cause to complain against them as he was always paid his due of 1 shilling a day.

Bechu's evidence before the commission made him an instant hero among the Indian community and among the reform-minded Creoles. Planters were understandably upset and attempted to malign Bechu before the commission and even more so afterwards.[48] Planters stooped to insult not just Bechu but all Indians as born liars. One planter quoted Macaulay's infamous statement about the effeminacy and low cunning of Bengalis: "What the horns are to the buffalo, what the paws are to tiger, what the sting is to the bee [...] deceit is to the Bengali."[49] To this Bechu characteristically replied by quoting Shakespeare's "Cursed be he who moves my bones" and Longfellow's "Lives of great men".[50] Planters were often at a loss to match his barbs, while several defenders of Bechu arose from the ranks of Indians and Creoles.[51] Throughout the next three years Bechu kept up his attack on the plantation system both at the level of policy and by exposing specific instances of oppression practised by the planters.[52] He exposed individual acts of cruelty, such as the case of a sick indentured worker forced out of hospital and sent to work, after which he died.[53] Bechu's letter to the newspaper landed him in a libel suit which dragged on for a whole year. He was acquitted only when the jury twice failed to reach a verdict.

He also periodically brought up the mater of the stoppage of wages, the despatching of armed police to stop immigrants from complaining, and the plight of Indian hawkers who were rounded up by police and prevented from hawking their wares in towns.[54] He vigorously pursued the question of minimum wages for labourers by several times challenging the planters to produce evidence of such payments. It is interesting to note that never

48. See J. Thomson's evidence in *Report of the West India Royal Commission*, vol. 3.
49. Letter from "Civis Mundi", *DC*, 12 February 1897.
50. Letters from Bechu, *DC*, 14 February 1897.
51. See letters from East Indian Descendent and Ramswammy, *DC*, 9 February 1897, 15 February 1897, and 22 February 1897.
52. See letters from Bechu, *DC*, 28 July 1898 and 27 August 1898, on stopping of wages and repatriation problems.
53. Letter from Bechu, *DC*, 18 September 1898.
54. See for example letters from Bechu, *DC*, 5 March 1899, 22 August 1899, and 14 April 1900.

once were the planters able to produce such evidence, falling back on spouting inanities like the moral development of immigrants under indenture, the quasi-paternal care of the planters, and the economic benefit to Indians of emigration.[55]

Politically, one interesting debate that Bechu initiated was about reindenture of time-expired immigrants. Bechu had suggested very early on that instead of the expense of the continued immigration of ever more indentured labour, time-expired labourers could be persuaded to re-indenture themselves with the suitable incentive of a 50-dollar bonus. He kept on repeating this alternative suggestion for some time.[56] His idea might appear to go against the grain of the general critique of indenture as it would only lengthen its duration, but the suggestion was not at all contradictory because it was pitched at a different level. Central to Bechu's critique was the claim that continuous importation of labour under indenture served to depress wages to starvation level and led to unemployment among both Creole and Indian free labourers. The only long-term solution was the complete abolition of indentured immigration, although in the short term the solution to unemployment among free labourers might be found in reindenture if planters could be persuaded to forsake costly importation and instead pay statutory minimum wages.

Bechu's advocacy of reindenture must be understood in the context of his insistence that the indenture contract legally guaranteed the 1 shilling a day wage, for this was at a time when pay offered to free labour had fallen well below the minimum guaranteed wage of indentured workers. It is interesting that none of his planter opponents ever took up the suggestion of reindenture as an alternative, because they realized that it would be the thin end of a wedge which would dislodge the whole indenture system. Bechu had always argued that the main prop and life blood of so obviously oppressive a system was the annual importation. Towards the end of his stay in Guiana Bechu's letters became increasingly strident in their denunciation of the immigration system.

In his last letter to the newspaper before he left for India, Bechu pleaded that immigration be stopped for three years as an experiment,[57] but what he thought of the indenture system on the plantations is evident from one of his letters citing several of his compatriots who preferred to be in jail,

55. See letters from Planter, Norman Bascom, Creole planter, *et al.*, *DC*, 5 February 1899 and 8 February 1899, and Bechu's replies in 7 February 1899, 8 February 1899 and 11 February 1899. As evidence of the last point one planter pointed out that all the letters sent from India to the colony were without paid postage while the letters from the colony were all with paid post. Bechu replied to this by saying that that was a reflection on the postage service of the colony since anyone who wanted his letter to definitely reach its destination made sure that it was "bearing", since that at least ensured its receipt.

56. Letters from Bechu, *DC*, 2 February 1897, 18 April 1899, and 12 January 1900.

57. Letter from Bechu, *DC*, 5 February 1901.

where they were assured a meal a day, rather than to work on the plantation. He wrote "In India, Sir, we look down with contempt on a man who has been to the Jail, but here the best of us dare not do so for we can hardly tell when we shall have the misfortune to be sent ourselves."[58]

Bechu left for India some time in April 1901; he had been released from indenture in 1898 when a prosperous Indian shopkeeper, impressed by his advocacy, paid his indenture fees to the colony. Why did he stay on for three more years and why did he decide to go back? We have no idea. And about his career back in India, we do not know. He vanished as suddenly as he had arrived on the public scene with his letter of 1 November 1896. But for a period of five years Bechu represented the indentured immigrants and sought to give them a public presence and voice.

The essence of the indentured labour regime was the denial of the public existence of the workers, for in a sense the coolies were the planter's children, which was the effect of their immobilization, peculiar legal subordination, and ethnic separation from the larger body of labourers. By making the wider public aware of their presence, Bechu gave theoretical articulation to the practical criticisms indentured workers made in their various complaints against the whole indenture system. His mode of representing the indentured workers provided the basis for solidarity among the different sectors of workers throughout the colony. In other words, he made possible a labouring identity for the Indians. In many ways his critique was far superior to the nationalist critique of indenture that emerged in the first decades of the twentieth century, which explicitly denigrated the labouring identity of the indentured immigrants and focused on their moral degradation.

CONCLUSION

In this essay I have tried to argue against the emergence of a singular identity in the Indian labour diaspora in the West Indies during the period of indenture. Neither cultural persistence nor creolization theories of identity formation can capture the multiple possibilities that could and did coexist in the period under study. I have demonstrated that by examining four different styles of representation of identity which emerged in the last decades of the nineteenth century, when the plantation societies were in the throes of a deep crisis.

What was common to all of these was that they shared the same relational field that I have identified as the labour regime. Each of these forms of identity bore a relation to the labour regime without in any way being derived from or determined by it. Representational practices ranging from the collective to the individual mediated those relationships, and

58. Letter from Bechu, *DC*, 9 January 1901.

certain styles of representation of identity emerged in the last decades of the nineteenth century when plantation societies were in the throes of a deep crisis. My aim in this essay has been to try to transcend the dualities of culture and economy, class and community, which have plagued the study of diasporic formations, especially those formed through long-distance labour migration.

Masculinity, Respect, and the Tragic: Themes of Proletarian Humor in Contemporary Industrial Delhi*

SHANKAR RAMASWAMI

INTRODUCTION

This essay will explore themes of proletarian masculinity (*mardaangi*) and humor (*mazaak*) arising from research amongst male migrant workers in a metalworking export factory in contemporary Delhi. The paper seeks to describe and critique metalworkers' vocabularies and practises of joking and horseplay, with particular reference to their homoerotic and hetero-erotic imageries, as well as to their subtle auto-critiques. The paper attempts to view *mazaak*, despite its often vulgar, dualistic, and otherizing imageries, as an assertion of the *erosic* drive to affirm life, beyond the desire to merely survive, and contra the *thanotic* will to submit to the life-denying conditions of urban-proletarian existence. The paper probes the capacities and potentialities of certain styles of workers' *mazaak*, such as satirical and sarcastic humor (*vyang*), to critique exploitation, oppression, and associated dominant imageries of masculinity and work, and to suggest alternative visions and possibilities for proletarian inter-relations.

My research focuses on migrant workers working in a metal-polishing factory in the Okhla Industrial Area of south-east Delhi, exporting high-end steel artware (cutlery, serving-ware, vases, display items) for sale in department stores and boutiques in America and Europe. The employment in the factory has varied from twenty to sixty workers, all male, from the states of Uttar Pradesh, Madhya Pradesh, Bihar, Jharkhand, and Kerala. The workers range in age from seventeen to fifty years, and are comprised of backward castes, scheduled castes, *aadivaasis*, Muslims, and Christians. Although a varying segment of workers are kept as casual workers, the majority of workers have been brought onto the company muster rolls, and receive statutory minimum wages (approximately $2.50 per day), along with Employees' State Insurance and Employees' Provident Fund.

* An earlier version of this essay was presented at the conference, "Towards Global Labour History: New Comparisons", organized by the Association of Indian Labour Historians and the V.V. Giri National Labour Institute (under the aegis of the SEPHIS Programme and the International Institute of Social History), Noida, Uttar Pradesh, India, 10–12 November 2005. I am very grateful for the remarks and observations of Rana Behal, Jan Breman, Marcel van der Linden, Prabhu Mohapatra, Cláudio Costa Pinheiro, Dilip Simeon, and others present at this conference.

Figure 1. *Mazaak* in the bathing area at the end of the shift.
Photograph by the author. Used with permission.

Steel polish-work is extremely strenuous and exacting work, under very dirty and noxious conditions. The polish process generates a blackish-grey, malodorous, foggy haze consisting of metal dust and fine particles, fibres from leather, synthetic, and cloth polish buffs, and chemicals and animal fats discharged from the glue and brick-like *masaalaas* applied to the buffs. The shopfloor, a single large room in a factory shed, is an excruciating place to inhabit, with fans and coolers blowing the particulate black haze rising from the machines into one's face and nostrils. Workers' tattered clothes and bodies are blackened throughout the day by metal dust, debris, and fibres. Amidst the whirring, deafening noise of the metal-cutting belt machine and the rumbling of the pollution exhaust fan-filter system, one hears the sounds of coughing, sputtering, and hawking, as workers spit out blackish phlegm into the piles of debris that accumulate in the air-ducting in front of their machines.

Polishers' bodies, while muscular, are thin, stretched, and emaciated, revealing the strain not only of bodily exertions within an ever-intensifying production process, but also of austere diets, and the difficult, congested, and unhygienic environmental conditions of the urban villages and slums where workers reside. Colds, coughs, fevers, stomach disorders, chest pains, jaundice, and tuberculosis abound amongst these workers, and make the doctor's clinic and ESI medical dispensary the third coordinate, along with the factory and residence, of the orbits of workers' everyday lives. Bodily soreness and fatigue make a fourth coordinate of the liquor and *tambaaku-bidi-paan* shops, which dispense their own brand of medicines for the ailing body and spirit.

In this paper, I focus on one aspect of workers' factory lives, their styles of *hamsi-mazaak* (humor and horseplay), as an entry point into questions and issues of masculinity, respect, work, resistance, and proletarian interrelations. One of the first things I noticed within the factory was the style, content, and prevalence of metal workers' *mazaak.* It struck me as somewhat odd that there could be such energy, creativity, and vivacity within an environment otherwise so dark, depressing, and hostile to life. *Mazaak* begins at the very start of the workday, continues at the machines, during tea and lunch breaks, at bathing time, and while coming and going from the factory. Indeed, *mazaak* might occur whenever metalworkers gather, in meetings, in visits to each other's residences (under conditions of relative privacy), or while moving about the industrial area. I describe and analyze some of the themes of this *mazaak* below.

HOMOEROTIC *MAZAAK*: HORSEPLAY, VULGARITY, AND SUBSTITUTION

On the shopfloor, *mazaak* is most immediately visible in physical horseplay. When workers move around the shopfloor to pick up buffs and *masaalaas,* rest, take a glass of water, or go to the latrine, they engage in teasing, banter, and insults, sometimes escalating into wrestling, in which one worker may be brought to the ground as nearby others observe, cheer, and goad them on. A worker who feels he has been outwitted or out-insulted in banter might in frustration grab the other around the chest, pick him up, carry him out of the shopfloor, and drop him on the open road. During tea breaks, taken on the dusty road outside due to the lack of space inside the factory, one might be calmly sitting in conversation one moment, and then suddenly see two workers spring up and bolt down the road, throwing up dust as one chases the other, catches hold of him, brings him to the ground, then sits on him until some apology or request for mercy is exacted. In these ways, the factory becomes a kind of school playground for workers, especially for younger ones in their late teens and twenties, who perhaps never got enough of a childhood of play in the village, often leaving school due to the pressures to work in their family fields or in *mazduri* (wage-work in fields, stone-breaking, truck-loading, etc.). It may also be seen as an effort to seek a continuation, or a

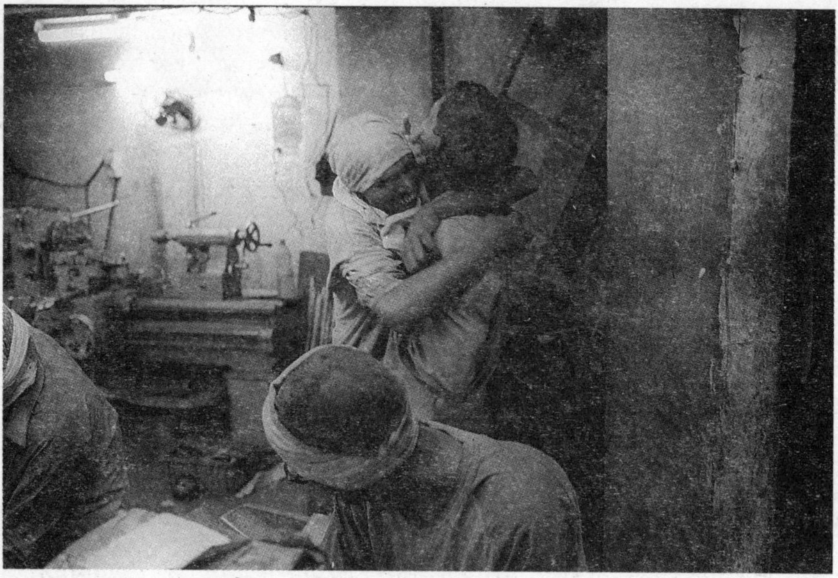

Figure 2. A worker unexpectedly greets another with a vigorous embrace.
Photograph by the author. Used with permission.

reincarnation, of the childlike joy of *physical* play, within the hellish and hostile context of an urban metal factory.

At the machines, *mazaak* goes on throughout the day, punctuating and embellishing the production process. After a *kaarigar* (skilled worker) finishes with a polish buff, he removes it from his machine, and if he feels in the mood, hurls the buff with an arc-like trajectory so that it lands with a huge thud on the metal duct hood near the face of the polish *kaarigar* directly opposite him or at his diagonal. The targeted polisher, bent over into his machine, engrossed in his work, jolts in shock at the noise and tremor to the ducting. Although the *kaarigar* jerks in reaction, as one does when caught off guard, I never witnessed any accidents from this horseplay. Polish work is otherwise quite dangerous, with *kaarigars*' wrists, hands, arms, faces, and legs bearing scars, the most common injury being induced by the treacherous jean-cloth buff, which catches hold of the worker's glove and pulls the worker's hand into the machine, scraping, flaying, and burning the skin around the wrist. During my research, one *kaarigar* had his forearm pulled into the machine while working with the jean-cloth buff, resulting in permanent disability. Thus, when engaging in *mazaak,* hurlers of buffs make sure the target *kaarigar* is not working on the jean-cloth buff at the time.

This buff-throwing becomes more unruly, with small hard fiber and cloth buffs thrown at the person's body rather than at the ducting, towards the end of the shift, while *kaarigars* are engaged in final polishing and repairing, or resting while their pieces are checked in the office above the shopfloor. This provides much diversion and relief at the end of an eleven-, twelve-, or at times seventeen-hour working day. There is a rather inclusive promiscuity of this buff-throwing, in that anyone may become a potential instigator or target, whether *kaarigar* or helper, whether from UP or Bihar or Jharkhand, whether Hindu or Muslim, whether located close by or far away on the shopfloor. While there is little attempt to hide one's agency in the deliberate, emphatic, and taunting buff-throwing that goes on during the day, in this later game, one uses various means and methods to try to hit others with buffs while keeping one's identity obscured, and if need be, implicating others as targets of retaliation. One may hide behind the cement pillars, the gas fan, or another worker's body, or keep moving purposefully across the shopfloor while underhandedly tossing the buff at its target. Surveillance and timing are everything if one is to successfully maintain anonymity. If one manages to first dab a cloth buff in white *masaalaa* powder, it creates an amusing and silly puff of white smoke on impact with the target body.

Much of the *mazaa* (enjoyment, thrill) of these buff-throwing transactions is in the observation, the targeting, the passionate reactions upon impact, and the subsequent retaliation, either with a buff or by getting up from the machine, pursuing and catching hold of the hurler, and inflicting some punishment, such as neck-locking or aggressive rubbing of the knuckles on the skull. Although buff-throwing is an anarchic affair, there are occasional coordinations between persons to attack a target in sync, but without any stable or reliable structure. A person who was collaborating with you a moment ago might unexpectedly hurl a powder-laden buff at you as well, from behind the obscuring ducting of his own machine, while maintaining a straight poker face.[1] A challenge of this game is also to execute one's throws and retaliations such that the foreman or managers, who may unexpectedly descend to the shopfloor from the office, do not catch you in the act, which would be taken as an affront to the pretence of discipline in the factory.

Mazaak may also take on more vulgar, homoerotic forms, in the flows and economies of touching, feeling, grasping, grabbing, and mock penetrating that goes on amongst polish workers. I watched with some astonishment how a young worker, arriving at the factory gate early on a foggy morning, went up to a fellow worker from behind and cheerfully greeted him with a large, circular, swooping motion of his left middle

1. On the fluidity and interchangeability of aggressors and targets within the context of horseplay amongst German factory workers at the turn of the twentieth century, see Alf Luedtke, "Cash, Coffee Breaks, Horseplay: *Eigensinn* and Politics among Factory Workers in Germany circa 1900", in Michael Hanagan and Charles Stephenson (eds), *Confrontation, Class Consciousness, and the Labor Process: Studies in Proletarian Class Formation* (Westport, CT, 1986), pp. 65–95.

finger directed straight into his rear end (*gaand*). Near the machines, workers may tweak the other's nipples, sometimes lowering their mouth to them in *mazaak*, or grasp the other's breast area generously with one's open hand, while making a longing, desirous expression on the face. I asked a worker, Arun, why he did this and what he purported to get out of it. "When I grab the chest of Mithilesh [a friend sitting nearby on the metal cutting machine], it reminds me of my wife, it's like I am holding her breasts. She's not here, she's far away. So one makes do with this". Arun's wife, along with many of the polishers' wives, live in the villages, and workers get to meet them only a few times in the year, at *Holi*, *Divaali*, *Chath*, or during the summer wedding season. *Mazaak* thrives on a kind of substitution effect, with workers' bodies evoking for each other the tactile memory of absent, inaccessible, and desired wives.

There is also, however, the sheer delight in the play of touching, grabbing, and displaying the male genitalia, as a way of embarrassing and entertaining each other. At the end of the shift, when several workers cram into a single-person latrine and adjoining small chamber to bathe, one must not only struggle to scrub oneself off of the caked dust and grime of the day with the abrasive detergent soap provided by the company, while taking care to avoid accidental fingers, elbows, or knees in the eyes within the congested space. One must also keep a check on one's underwear, which everyone wears inside the bath, lest it be pulled down to one's knees by someone or some persons working in concert (*kacchaa kholnaa*), followed by uproarious laughter as the hapless fellow pathetically tries to pull it back up.

One worker, Babloo Khan, avoids these embarrassing possibilities by waiting for the crowd to subside before entering the bath. But he is one of the most mischievous and lascivious of the group, freely pulling down the underwear of others as they emerge from the bath and rub mustard oil on their bodies, leaving themselves vulnerable to blind side attacks. Babloo also enjoys shocking people in the changing room (a small room which houses two welding machines), by proudly flashing his phallus to whomever may be there, inviting them to be introduced to his *chotaa bhaai* (little brother) or his *Khaan saahab.* The spectacle is enhanced by the fact that Babloo Khan is circumcised, a marker for many of his Muslim identity, and about which there is much *mazaak* in the factory. These *darshans* (spiritual viewings) were one of Babloo's ways of retaliating and expressing pride in his anatomy.

I too was not safe or immune from such vulgar behavior, and was treated to many unexpected *darshans* of Babloo's *chotaa bhaai* if I happened to be in the vicinity, or if I was called to the site by workers as word spread of an impending *darshan*. Narayan, an elderly, beefy, and somewhat boorish polisher from Bihar, and a wrestler in a previous life, would also routinely grab at my phallus, posterior, and chest if I happened to pass by his

Figure 3. Two workers revive an unaware and drowsy polisher on the night shift. *Photograph by the author. Used with permission.*

machine. He would do this surreptitiously, unpredictably, and with a straight face, sometimes not even looking up from his machine. When I would be jolted by these acts and turn towards him in objection and disbelief, he would raise his eyebrows and widen his eyes behind his thick plastic goggles, in mock surprise and feigned sympathy at the atrocity committed. But if I did not move away from the area, further atrocities were forthcoming.

The male genitalia were a constant referent in various spheres of shopoor talk. When a worker took too long in the latrine, while someone else was waiting, he might emerge and return to the machine to hear loud speculations, "Are time lagtaa hai, yaar, muth maar rahaa thaa" ("Oh, it takes time [in the latrine], as he was masturbating there"). The worker himself might offer this as a defense to explain his delay. If a worker is walking by the water cooler on the way to the latrine, and is casually asked, "Kahaam jaa rahe ho, bhaai?" ("Where are you going, brother?"), the pat reply might be, "Muth maarne jaa raha hum aur kyaa?" ("I'm going to jerk off, what else?"), or simply, "Khaanpur-Badarpur",a reference to the bus route up and down the Mehrauli-Badarpur road of south Delhi, traversed by many workers on their way to and from Okhla. One worker treats others to his own version of the famous Hindi lm song, "Pyaar kiyaa to darnaa kyaa" ("If you have loved, why should you fear anything")? with the alteration, "Muth maaraa to darnaa kyaa"("If you have masturbated, what is there to fear")?

Babloo Khan introduced the evocative, parting phrase, "Calo, nikal lo khambaa bacaake" ("Go on, look out for your phallus and get out of here"). This phrase caught on and took on a wider, expansive social life in workers' discourses within the residential boundaries and elsewhere, in part because its meaning was not always so clear to bystanders. In a small room in Okhla, where I conducted many of my interviews, when there were others present whom I wanted to kindly and inoffensively ask to leave so I could begin an interview with an individual worker, I needed only say, "Aap log zaraa bacaaie" ("You folks please save [your phalluses]"). People would smile, chuckle, and get up immediately, saying, "Thik hai, bacaa hi rahe haim" ("Okay, we're protecting them [and going]").

Besides the phallus, the other anatomical referent in workers' banter was the *gaand* (anus). No matter what might be the topic of conversation, Babloo Khan would unexpectedly interject, "Are teri gaand mem daal do" ("Oh stick it in your ass"). He might also act out these impulses. In winter time, when a space heater was used inside the store room to dry the leather buffs prepared for polishing, Babloo and others would gather near the heater at rest times. He asked workers to put the cord into his *gaand* for added warmth, and they obliged, creating a bizarre spectacle. "Are bas teri ek baar de do yaar" ("Come on, give me your ass just once"), one often heard in the banter at the machines. Such requests over longer distances, between machines diagonal from each other, were done by simply showing an "o" shape with the fingers and then the number "1" with the index finger, accompanied by a pouting expression of desire and hope. If I happened to be nearby while two *kaarigars* were so non-verbally bantering, one would appeal to me, "Maim uski maang rahaa hum, magar de nahim rahaa hai. Aap zaraa usse baat kar lo" ("I am asking [for his ass] but he is not giving it. You please talk to him for me").

One *kaarigar,* Rampal, short, thin, and very pleasant in nature, became a favored target of many such proposals, *kacchaa kholnaa* attacks, and buff-throwing, in part because he never took offense to *mazaak*, and indeed was quite adept at initiating and retaliating. A worker explained the collective affection for Rampal thus: "Raampaal ki gaand compani mem sabse pyaari hai" ("Rampal's ass is the most adored in the company"). I was once in the vicinity when the night shift foreman, Govind, a polisher of many years, who despite his promotion to management, still shared much of the *mazaak* culture of the shopfloor, bantered with Rambachan, a helper turned welder, who was also one of his suspected *camcaas* (yes-men). Govind was coaxing him to get onto the welding machine at the start of the shift, while the latter was sitting outside near the fire. Rambachan responded that the welding machine was under repair by the company. Govind teased him that he should then go back home, as he would not get any wages for doing no work. Rambachan replied that it was not his fault that the machine was broken, and that he should be marked "present" in the attendance register. "Koi baat nahim" ("Okay, no matter"), said Govind, giggling. "Ek baar de do. Haajri lag jaaegi" ("Give me [your ass] once. Your attendance will be marked").

One of the most favored taunts and threats on the shopfloor was "Maim teri gaand maarumgaa!" ("I'll f*** you in the ass!") This could be said calmly, quietly, or in mock rage, escalating into such colorful utterances as, "Teri itnaa maarumgaa ki tere ko Bihaar nazar aayegaa!" ("I'll ream your ass so hard that you'll see Bihar in your sights!"). In spontaneous wrestling bouts that would break out on the shopfloor, vulgar gestures and simulations of *gaand maarnaa* would be presented for the nearby onlookers. Once on the night shift, as a polisher was nodding off at his machine, two workers lined up behind him, grabbed him around the chest, and simulated vigorous sexual intercourse in a line of three, for the amusement of the rest of the otherwise weary polishers on the shopfloor. (He woke up with quite a start.)

The homoerotic sexual act (*gaand maarnaa)* could be referred to in the act of greeting itself. An elderly, grey-haired worker and master of vulgar *mazaak,* Rajender, whose every word was laden with *double entendre,* would sometimes greet me, "Kaise haim Shankarji? Atthani abhi tak piti yaa baci?" ("How are you, Shankar? Has your ass been pounded yet or is it still intact?") If I would arrive at the factory or at a meeting, the respectful act of offering a place to sit would be folded into *mazaak* in Rajender's greeting, "Aaie Shankarji, is par baitho" ("Come here, Shankar, sit on this")! As he said this, he would look me in the eye, with a slight, sharp nod of the head, without gesturing to any actual chair or stool or bench nearby. A proximate bystander, suspecting a double meaning, would ask, "Kis par baithem ("Sit on what")? "Are kursi par, yaar" ("On this chair, man"), Rajender would answer with a grin, as he pointed to a nearby vacant seat, or got up from the chair he was occupying. This expression also caught on. If a worker on cycle would see me walking in the industrial area, and his passenger carrier was empty, he might ride up alongside and greet me with the words, "Namaskaar Shankarji is par baitho" ("Hello Shankar sit on this")!

But the vocabularies and imageries of homoerotics and masculinity took on particular valences when deployed in relation to the work of metal-polishing itself. When I would greet a certain polisher at his machine, Bhagvati, who was among the more elderly workers, and also one of the most active in vulgar horseplay, his face would be thoroughly covered with the second-hand *dhoti* fragments given to workers as pollution masks. Instead of responding verbally, which would require undoing his *dhoti* around his mouth, he would simply put his left palm under his right elbow and pump his right forearm up and down, simulating an erect phallus. Later into the shift, however, if I would go by and ask him how he was doing, he would put his left palm under his right elbow, but hold his right forearm vertical, with the right hand limp and waving from side to side, as he made a weary, droopy face with what was visible of his eyes and cheeks (a limp, spent phallus). Sometimes other *kaarigars* would call over to me, smiling, and make this latter sign, pointing to Bhagvati, to tease and taunt him, implying that Bhagvati was done for the day, out of strength, and incapable of properly finishing his day's production. To which Bhagvati would fight back with his erection symbol, vigorously pumping, claiming that he still had energy and life (*jaan*) left in him, as he leaned into his polish wheel and kicked up black-grey smoke from the pressure and force of his exertions.

Here was masculinity identified as the capacity, energy, and power to do *mehnat* (hard labor), and moreover, as exclusively defined by one's hard, honest, and sincere work, and not by any of the other activities that one can engage in as a factory worker for upward mobility, such as *cugalkhori* and *camcaagiri* (informing, reporting, collaborating). Ironically, Bhagvati was a *camcaa,* and was teased (along with other suspected *camcaas)* by workers at large for staying on after the end of the shift for extra minutes at the bidding of the foreman, to finish up repairs on pieces. "Iske baad vo upar jaake gaand maraaegaa" ("After this, he'll go upstairs to the office and get screwed in the ass [by the manager]"), workers would say in *mazaak* as they passed him on the way to bathe. To be a *camcaa*, workers suggested, was to open oneself up to such possibilities of manipulation, dependence, and humiliation, in one's *svaarthi* (self-interested) quest for individual advancement. Perhaps such perceptions and insinuations (however true) of Bhagvati as a *camcaa* made it all the more important for him to deploy such masculine, defensive symbols as the erect phallus, as a defiant proclamation of the actual *mehnat* he felt he did at the machines.

But the idiom of *gaand maraanaa* ("getting oneself screwed in the ass") was not reserved only for *camcaas.* After Rajender had been working all day on the task of *saan lagaanaa,* a tiring operation in which hot, noxious glue and fine, sharp sand particles are applied by hand to the leather buffs, and the foreman, with about an hour left in the shift, told him to get onto the polish machines for some last minute final polishing work, Rajender revolted. He said that he had already spent the entire day working on one task, which was now nearing completion (and for which he would implicitly be entitled to a bit of rest), and now he was being asked to start on a new, different task. The foreman backed off. To me, Rajender vented, "Saaraa din yahaam saan lagaane mem gaand marvaayaa, aur abhi kah rahaa hai machine par baitho aur vahaam gaand marvaayegaa?!" ("The whole day the foreman got me screwed in the ass doing this buff preparation and now he wants me to sit on the machine and get me buggered there?!")

This imagery is used with respect to polishing the metal pieces as well. When Mithilesh sat down at Arun's machine to help him polish some steel bowls (*katoris*), he directed him, "Maim upar ki gaand marvaaumgaa, tum andar ki gaand marvaao" ("I'll get the outer portion of the piece screwed in the ass, you get the inside of it screwed in the ass"). I wonder, however, if a hidden meaning of these references to *gaand maarnaa* and *marvaanaa* by steel polish workers is actually the tacit awareness and feeling that day in and day out, they are, figuratively speaking, "getting their asses reamed" by the difficulty of the weighty sizes and complicated shapes of the steel artware pieces, the high production levels and finishing requirements imposed from above, and the entire complex of management strategies and tactics of maintaining and intensifying discipline, control, and exploitation-oppression (*shoshan-atyaacaar*).

Homoerotic *mazaak* also could slide into references to and discussions of *hijraas* (eunuchs), who move about in the industrial area especially at *Holi* and *Divaali* to collect customary donations from companies, and are said to engage in prostitution in the evenings inside the large storage containers stacked near the railway crossing or "siding", as it is referred to, between the Okhla Industrial Area and Mathura Road. (Heterosexual prostitution also occurs at the siding, in the forested areas along the tracks.) References to siding would arise if one asked about the whereabouts of an absent worker: "Are vo siding gayaa, uski double kamaai ho rahi hai" [showing an "o" with the fingers]! ("Oh he went to the siding, he's earning a double income [from the factory and from sex work]!"). Narayan was once planning to go to the village, and was saying to Hanif Khan, who was sitting opposite from his machine, that he expected a loan from him for this purpose. Hanif smiled, and answered, swaying his head as if in the trance of a *qavvaali*, "Abhi time hai. Siding jaao, paisaa kamaao, apnaa balance banaake ghar jaao!" ("There's still time. Go to the siding, earn some money [from sex], accumulate a [bank] balance and then go home!"). Part of the play here is on the word "balance", as a monetary accumulation, and also as the physical balance required of the person on the receiving end of homoerotic intercourse. Narayan, heated and flustered, shouted, "Paise nahim degaa, to teri gaand bahut maarumgaa, Hanifaa!" ("If you don't give me some money [to borrow], I'll f*** your ass real bad, Hanif!").

Although the words for eunuchs (*hijraa, chakke*) are often pejoratively deployed in wider society to mean effeminate, weak, and impotent, as opposed to masculine, tough, and strong, I found very few such negative usages in the metal factory. There were continual references to weakness and impotence, say when describing workers one could not count on to be firm and stable in opposing management initiatives. But here the symbolism was of the limp hand described earlier, or in expressions such as "jiskaa land pakadne kaa dhang bhi nahim hai" ("those who don't even know how to grab their own phallus"). Eunuchs were accorded more respect than the fully sexually equipped, but weak, flaccid, and impotent man, for *hijraas* at least were true to their own gender and sexuality.

Hijraas could on occasion even be invoked in solidarity, as for example when a group of eunuchs had come for a donation upon the inauguration of a new metal factory a few blocks away, where half of the polish-workers had been ignominiously transferred by the company. The senior manager resisted giving the *hijraas* a respectable contribution, in exchange for their blessings for the success of the new factory, and they stormed out in a huff, with one publicly and dramatically urinating on the factory gate. This was seen by workers as a terrible but potentially well-deserved curse on the unit and the management, given the oppressive and miserly strategies that the senior manager and the company had pursued thus far. For all the joking about the railway siding, workers did accord *hijraas* certain powers to bless and curse, drew inspiration and vindication from their irreverence, and made unwitting allies of them in their own struggles against *shoshan-atyaacaar*.

HETEROEROTICS: MACHINE AND *MAAL*

Alongside these styles of homoerotic joking and horseplay, metal workers also engaged in heteroerotic *mazaak*. Workers affixed photos of film heroines and models to their machines, cut out from the second-hand newspapers used as packing material in the factory. Sometimes these pictures were of large-busted supermodels or international actresses, wearing bikinis or lingerie, as found in say the *Delhi Times* supplement to *The Times of India*. Workers might strategically amend these photos in vulgar ways (making holes in them, etc.) and invite others to their machines to rate and comment on their selections and alterations. On the wide, square base of the fan-filter system, located close to the back wall of the shopfloor, where there was no managerial traffic, several photos would be affixed close to each other in a collage. Babloo Khan, whose machine was close to the stairs to the office, cleverly layered the scrap cardboard material above his polish wheel (used as a guard against flying debris), such that the inside layer had several affixed photos, for his own occasional viewing and displaying, but which no one could see unless he lifted the outside covering layer. Conversations otherwise referenced sightings of female prostitutes in the siding area, accounts of sexual acts observed there, as well as discussions of scenes, bodies, and activities witnessed in "blue" (pornographic) films, viewed in working-class colonies via video cable, rental VCDs, and illicit, makeshift theaters.

A dominant word which gained currency in heteroerotic *mazaak* was "machine". "Bhagvati ki machine aa gai hai!" ("Bhagvati's machine has come [from the village]!"), workers would shout across the shopfloor, if they learned that his wife had come to Delhi. Bhagvati might himself call me over to his polishing machine, and whisper into my ear, "Ganne ke ras nikaalnevaali machine mere paas aai hai" ("A sugar-cane juicing machine has arrived at my place"). Sometimes workers' wives, and women in general, might be referred to as *jhuk machines* (bending, stooping machines), conjuring the sexual *aasan* in which a woman leans forward and is entered from behind. This instrumentalized, otherizing, and life-denying terminology, where women are spoken of as sex machines, is striking and disturbing. The *mazdur*-machine relation becomes darkly transposed onto the man–woman relation.

But I have heard the word "machine" used by proletarians also for the male *gaand*, as when a worker from an Okhla factory was standing in the back of a jam-packed truck returning from a union rally in central Delhi, and was bizarrely bumping his pelvis alternately into the posteriors of two friends in front of him, while saying, "Bataao, ab kis machine mem daal dum, is mem yaa us mem?" ("Tell me, now which machine should I stick [my phallus] in, this one or that one?").[2] Also, one of Babloo Khan's favorite pieces of advice to workers, if they were showing pimples or boil-type skin eruptions (*phoraa-phunsi*), was, "Apni garmi nikaalo. Jaao, jugaar dhumdho, mobilail change kar lo" ("Get rid of your heat [semen]. Go, find someone, and change your [motor] oil"). The male body here is compared to a machine, a vehicle, whose smooth running requires periodic servicing and maintenance.[3] Within Capital, the cold logic of instrumentalization spares no one.

And perhaps there is a tacit, subtle awareness of this amongst metalworkers. When Hanif Khan was getting ready for a trip to his village in eastern Uttar Pradesh, to assist with wheat cutting on his family fields, he told me that it would be very hard work, where one has to bend down, stoop, and cut for hours at a stretch. With a chuckle of discovery, he said, "Aadmi ko bhi jhuk machine bannaa partaa hai!" ("A man also has to become a bending, stooping machine!"). Humor is perhaps at its most radical and subversive when it pulls out the rug and reveals how we ourselves, seen from a different perspective, are actually the very same as the objects, the "them", the targets of our jokes, slurs, and ridicule. Are not metal polish *kaarigars,* as they bend, lean, and incline their bodies into their polish wheels, rhythmically, back and forth, all day, with the foreman on their backs prodding them to go faster, not *jhuk machines* of a kind? Treated as barely living creatures by Capital, useable, exploitable, drainable, interchangeable, and discardable, made to endure noise, filth, and pollution, in exchange for subsistence wages only?

2. For a vivid illustration of how "machine" is deployed to describe the phallus, witness the discourse of the street purveyor of anti-impotence potions in Anand Patwardhan's documentary film, *Father, Son and Holy War* (1994).

3. For a richly insightful and evocative account of language, ideas, and experiences within truck drivers' milieus in north India, with specific reference to *mobilail change* as sexual metaphor, see Dilip Simeon, "O.K. TATA: Mobiloil Change and World Revolution", in Rukun Advani, Ivan Hutnik, Mukul Kesavan, and Dharma Kumar (eds), *Civil Lines 3: New Writing from India* (Delhi, 1997), pp. 4–30.

In struggle after struggle in the company, workers' *taalmel* activities ("togethering") would be repeatedly broken from outside and subverted from within, with workers having to ultimately accept whatever policies or practises management was seeking to institute at the time. This was also described as *jhuknaa*, to bend down and submit to power, and was perhaps the most humiliating aspect and experience of being in this factory. I wonder if the heteroerotic expression *jhuk machine*, along with the homoerotic *gaand maraanaa*, do not betray a disturbing self-awareness, cognizance, and realization of workers' own instrumentalized, machine-ized, and humiliating condition.

The other dominant term used in heteroerotic *mazaak* was the word, *maal*, meaning things, stuff, goods, materials, stock. Unlike the word *machine*, which at least carries connotations of movement, activity, electricity, energy, and power, *maal* is generally used for static and inert objects. *Things.* In the factory, *maal* is used to refer to raw metal pieces (*koraa maal*); metal pieces polished and sent upstairs by specific *kaarigars* (*Bhagvati kaa maal*); pieces which have been designated for repairs (*repair kaa maal*); pieces which have major defects and are set aside as rejects (*reject kaa maal*); pieces which are approved, packed, and loaded into the delivery vehicle; and a range of other materials and supplies used in the factory.

What was disturbing was how this language insidiously crept into the ratings system of the looks and beauty of women as seen in newspaper and magazine photos, of workers' wives whose photos on ESI cards might be viewed and scrutinized by workers, and of women working in neighboring companies or walking along the road in front of the metal factory. *Koraa*, *repair,* and *reject kaa maal* became the terms of evaluation and adjudication of these women in this *mazaak*. Sometimes one heard the rhetorical lament, "Industrial area mem koraa kahaam miltaa hai" ("In the industrial area, one can't find any virgin girls"), reflecting the general suspicions about the sexual character of women who work in factories, not to mention that of the "modern"-dressed, educated women who work as clerical and technical staff in the industrial area. "Koraa maal cahie to dehaat hi jaanaa paregaa"("If you want fresh, untouched girls, you have to go to the countryside only").

When this kind of talk was done outside the factory or on the streets of the industrial area, as women passed by, it came dangerously close to harassment, even if the women were not being directly addressed. At the beginning and end of shift timings, when two to three female staff members arrived and exited from the companies adjacent and opposite to the metal factory, one heard workers' comments to each other such as, "Dekho, maal aa gayaa" ("Look, the stuff has come"), "Maal jaa rahaa hai" ("The thing is going [by]"), "Machine calegaa bhaiyaa?" ("Will this machine work [for you], brother?"), followed by, "Are calegaa nahim,

Figure 4. Workers gaze at a neighboring employee briskly exiting the industrial area. *Photograph by the author. Used with permission.*

bhaai, dauregaa!" ("Oh it won't just work, brother, it'll run!"). While these women, who generally walk with eyes lowered, facing forward, never looking to either side, did not openly react to these comments, and also did not admit in interviews to hearing such things from the factory workers, it is true that on one morning, a male manager from the opposite company came over and scolded the workers, as one of their female employees had just walked by and heard the word *maal,*and had not taken kindly to it. Workers present at the time deployed the fall-back and rather cowardly defense that the word *maal,*if it had been overheard, could have been used by a worker in reference to any of various objects, materials, and supplies in the factory.

Although I have separated the homoerotic and heteroerotic themes above for the purpose of analysis, in practise, anatomies, genders, and sexualities owed seamlessly and irreverently together within the crucible of factory *mazaak,*as in the phrase offered as advice to a worker, "Siding jaao, gaand maraao, kuch kamaao, tabhi to apni bivi cavani de degi!" ("Go to the railway siding, get screwed in the ass, earn some money [to give to your wife], only then will she give you her vagina!").

MAZAAK, RESPECTABILITY, AND LIFE-AFFIRMATION

When I asked workers, away from the factory, how they felt about this *mazaak*, I often got an embarrassed response. Indeed, they said that the *mazaak* in the factory was as *gandaa* (dirty, filthy) as the work itself. Some suggested (in half-*mazaak*) that it was the by-product of the work, as so much *kuraa-kabaaraa* (debris, rubbish) gets stuffed and lodged in the head that it becomes difficult to express any "clean", civilized thoughts. Because of the degeneracy of the *mazaak*, workers confessed that it degraded the *izzat* (respectability) of working in this factory.

Why then did this kind of *mazaak* flourish in the factory? One reason workers gave was that unlike in their residential boundaries, where one rarely encountered such *gandaa mazaak* (vulgar humor), there were no close *rishte* (familial, kinship, or village relations) with each other in the factory that would place constraints on *mazaak*. In the absence of such checks, the *mazaak* was free to go to extremes.[4] But it is not quite the case that there were no *rishte* within the factory. A group of metal workers, distributed across the day and night shifts, comprised brothers, cousin brothers, and other relatives, from a single district of Jharkhand state. When they were together, on the way to and from the factory, or on the shopfloor, they made sure not to engage in vulgar *mazaak*. When they were spatially separated on the shopfloor, *mazaak* had more breathing room, so the Jharkhandis broke themselves up across the machines, as well as across shifts, according to relevant kin relations, such that *mazaak* could be less constrained.

The respect for elders also acted as a control on *mazaak* in the factory, and around certain senior workers, younger persons censored their speech and behavior to an extent. But when elder workers such as Rajender and Narayan engaged in such extreme and ceaseless vulgarity with the youngest of workers, with no eye for generational *izzat,* then social controls collapsed, permitting a downward spiral in conduct and civility. This became a symptom, for some, of the lack of proper *izzat* norms in the factory society (*samaaj*), and contributed to the substratum anxiety about the deeper and longer term effects of inhabiting such a context (*maahaul*) for so many hours of the day. Workers worried that there might be seepages and leakages of the vulgar vocabularies they picked up in the factory into their language use more generally, which could come out unpredictably at home or in the village if they did not remain vigilant in censoring their speech and thought.

In the factory sphere, there were some who consciously chose to stay away from horseplay and vulgar humor, out of practical concerns for safety at the machines, and also out of considerations of *izzat*. "Ham kaam karne

4. Management, on occasion, could also participate in this *mazaak* with workers. When it involved lower-level management, this *mazaak* could create a kind of levity and joviality across hierarchical divisions, but it took on a different, somewhat humiliating tone when the senior manager would prod and tease workers about their wives, as a way of rubbing his power in their faces, and would watch as they grew embarrassed and silent, unable to answer back fully, as they would amongst each other.

aae haim" ("I've come here to work"), as one worker put it. "Aatma kabul nahim kartaa hai" ("My soul doesn't sanction [this kind of *mazaak*]"). And so some workers preferred to develop and deploy different *mazaak* styles, such as *vyang* (irony, satire, sarcasm), which relied more on wit and mental alacrity than vulgarity and profanity. Some became extremely effective at turning *vyang* into a ludic critique of the moves, deceptions, and stratagem of management in their ongoing efforts to tighten discipline and intensify production, while granting little by way of wage increases or other benefits. Expressions of the manager, such as, "hamaari koshish jaari hai (my efforts [for you] are continually going on [at the head office])", in response to requests or demands, say for wage increases or restoration of *samosaas* during overtime, became a sarcastic, circulating motto in workers' discussions about the company and its policies.

One helper developed an entire, elaborate style of commentary about whatever *shoshan-atyaacaar* was going on in the company, by drawing comparisons of work tasks, posts, personalities, policies, and events in the factory to what life was once like within the Red Fort. These bizarre analogies, often very cutting and incisive, would begin and end with, "Yah Laal Qilaa se kam nahim hai (This place is no less than the Red Fort)". Hanif Khan found a way to use the term *hisaab-kitaab* (tallies, accounts) as a virtually free-floating signifier to stand in for anything he wished to refer to, which was itself a very subtle, unwitting communication, I would suggest, of the pervasiveness of economic instrumentality in human dealings in the present, decivilizing epoch (the *Kalyug*[5] in workers' cosmology). The veiled, non-direct quality of *vyang*, and its capacity to carry and convey also "serious" feelings and meanings, made it a very vital and useful mode of expression of workers' discontent, particularly given the omnipresence of informers, reporters, and collaborators in the factory *samaaj*. Indeed, *vyang* also became a means of poking fun at those suspected of being agents (*mohraas*), information gatherers (*camcaas*), and loyalists (*vafaadaar log*) of management.

Workers' non-vulgar *mazaak* could also reveal a darker underside when it articulated otherizing sentiments, competitive envy, and laden hostility towards fellow workers (*jalan*). Such *mazaak* featured terms like *Bihaari* (for those from eastern Uttar Pradesh and Bihar), *jangli* (wild, savage, for *aadivaasi* workers from Jharkhand), *katuaa* (a slur for Muslim), and in more discreet contexts, *camaar* and *harijan* (for Dalits). Another form of non-vulgar *mazaak*, also flowing perhaps from the narcissism of minor differences, was banter between those who lived in rented rooms in urban

5. The *Kalyug* is the final epoch in the four-*yug* cycle of cosmic time, which according to the *Mahabharata* and *Puranas*, begins in approximately 3102 BCE, but according to metalworkers' narratives, as recently as 10, 50, or 100 years ago. The *Kalyug* is characterized by the intensifying prevalence of exploitative oppression, covetousness, deception, and stratagem, the principles and effects of which percolate into social contexts (*maahauls*) and the soul (*aatmaa*) itself.

village colonies (considered slightly more "up-scale") and workers who lived in *jhuggi-jhompris* (slums). The former would tease the *jhuggi*-dwellers that the latter consumed extra water and time while they bathed at the factory, because they did not have adequate water facilities in their *jhuggis*. Also, if evicted, room-renters would easily adjust themselves into rented quarters elsewhere, whereas the *jhuggi*-dwellers would only leave their illegal settlements if they were kicked in the *gaand* by the government bulldozer. The *jhuggi*-dwelling workers retorted that unlike the renters who always lived under the oppressive rule of local landlords, they lived in their own houses, and even if evicted, would be entitled to a secure, legal plot somewhere else in the city.

Mazaak involving *mardaangi* and women, but of a non-vulgar kind, was also common, in the ways in which workers teased each other about their wives. Amlakant's wife was rumored to be very thrifty and miserly, and kept a tight control on their finances. Amlakant was also one of the most stingy (*kanjus*) of the workers, never willing to loan money to or spend on others, asking *tambaaku* from others rather than offering his own, and that too, despite being one of the most senior and respected members of the *samaaj*. So when Naresh Singh was moving about the shopfloor one day, asking for small loans in anticipation of a trip to the village, Varmaji, a senior worker on the other extreme from *kanjusi*, advised Naresh aloud, stabbing at Amlakant's *mardaangi*, "Amlaakaant se kuch nahim milegaa, har din ghar jaakar uski bivi ko hisaab-kitaab denaa partaa hai!" ("You won't get anything from Amlakant, every day he goes home and has to report to his wife the details of whatever he spent!"). When Bhagvati returned from his village, a few days before the end of his two-week vacation leave, while workers normally stretch it and return late by a few days or even weeks, workers teased him extensively, suggesting that his wife had had enough of him after ten days, kicked him in the *gaand*, and told him to get back to the city and start earning again.

Workers' non-vulgar, witty, and sarcastic exchanges not only indicate the plurality of forms *mazaak* may take, but also illuminate the importance of respectability within the factory, and the desires and aspirations of some workers to rise above the general styles and themes of vulgar *mazaak*. But vulgar *mazaak* flourished, and the ones who were the best at it were often the most popular. People gravitated at tea and lunch breaks, for example, to Babloo Khan, because one never knew what vulgar insinuation or insult might fly out from his raspy, deadpan voice. This had its costs for workers' *taalmel*, because Babloo was actually a *mohraa-camcaa* (agent-informer), who never actively joined with workers in their grievances, and at critical moments in struggles would attempt to break down the *taalmel* and persuade others to comply with management wishes. Though workers suspected and even joked that Babloo shared a special, secret, and sinister relationship with the senior manager (who was also Muslim and from the same home town in Uttar Pradesh), they often sat near to him whenever they had free time to rest and relax at the factory.

One of the deeper reasons for this *aakarshan* (attraction) to Babloo, as well as to Rajender, whose true affiliations in struggles were also dubious, I believe, has to do with the psychic desperation that workers felt for any kind of momentary diversion, distraction, and relief from the bodily strain and psychic tensions that they endured and suffered. In defending vulgar *mazaak*, workers invoked what one might call a *manoranjan* (entertainment) imperative, within the context of extremely dirty, lowly paid, and strenuous polish-work; myriad mental worries, anxieties, and pressures associated with the factory *maahaul;* financial requirements and demands in the city and village; chronic and serious illnesses to self and family members; and domestic quarrels and discord (*klesh*) involving wives, brothers, sisters-in-law, and parents. "Yah itni mehnat kaa kaam hai, mazaak bahut zaruri hai, yaa to phir, bas, ragaro! Aur aadmi hameshaa apni tension mem uljhegaa" ("This is such hard work, *mazaak* is very important, otherwise it's just grind away [at the polish wheel]! And a person will always remain entangled in his tensions"), workers explained. With *mazaak,* however, "Aadmi kaa man bahl jaataa hai" ("A person is entertained, diverted, distracted"). "Man parivartan ho jaataa hai" ("A person's mind/heart is transformed").

It is difficult to overlook here the references in migrant workers' discourses to the psyche (*man*) embedded in the expressions *maansik tension* (mental tension), *man bahlnaa, man parivartan,* and *manoranjan* (amusement, entertainment, recreation for the psyche). I suspect that in the physical energy, absorption, and concentration demanded in the very process of steel polish work, some heavily stressed workers found a kind of diversionary escape from mental tensions. But others admit that even while working away at the wheels, they cogitate on how to confront an immediate financial or medical crisis in the home, or how to accumulate enough savings to handle the next family *shaadi* (wedding) or the construction and repair expenses required in their village home. *Mazaak,* perhaps because of its unpredictable, surprising, disrupting quality, allows workers, even those who disapprove of it but nevertheless partake of it, to somehow break out of this tension-saturated psychic condition, and more easily "pass", "traverse", and complete some finite portion of an otherwise burdensome temporal existence (*timepass karnaa, samay kaatnaa*). I noticed that on free days, like occasional Sundays, some workers expressed serious difficulties in getting through the day, alone in their rooms or *jhuggis,* without the aid and stimulus of work and also of *mazaak.* And as an *ilaaj* (cure, treatment) for tension, *mazaak* does have certain merits over the alternatives of intense, mind-occupying *mehnat* under exploitative and noxious conditions; holding one's tensions quietly and solitarily within, making oneself vulnerable to outbursts of violent rage; passive *manoranjan* such as television which suck the conversational life out of a room; or the ubiquitous varieties of body-numbing proletarian *nashaa* (*tambaaku, bidis, paan, daaru, bhaang*). In practise, all of these *ilaajes* are resorted to in varying doses by workers. But *mazaak's* virtue is that it *requires other people*. It cannot be done in alienated isolation. Indeed, it throws people in the direction of, rather than away from, each other.

Proletarian *mazaak* has another great virtue, beyond its negative justification as diversion, distraction, and relief "from" other things. Even in its vulgar forms, *mazaak* stimulates, energizes, activates, exercises, and gives expression to metal workers' repressed, oft-ignored, and unrecognized mental faculties (of quickness, cleverness, wordplay, the ability to answer back), creative and imaginative powers (to invent, imply, insinuate), and moreover, the sheer will to *play*. *Mazaak* is how metal workers *re-create* themselves (*manoranjan* is "recreation"), through individual *mazaak* styles, all different, and ever evolving with the changing contexts, situations, and times. Through this plurality of styles, metal workers come to express unique personalities, within a setting which enforces monotonous, dreary, physical repetition, cog-like discipline, and the hard commensurability and interchangeability of persons. In the alchemy of *mazaak*, metalworkers transform from blackened *jhuk machines* into colorful, entertaining, *tension kaa ilaaj*-dispensing characters. And in so doing, they affirm that there is more to their existence than merely grinding away into the polish wheels, and more to their lives than stress, darkness, depression, and tragedy.

Mazaak affirms *life*. This is why I wish to see in the "erotic" themes of metal workers' *mazaak*, a deeper sense of *eros*, as the psychic drive energy which asserts the urge and passion to create, connect, and unify, and the *desire to live*, contra the drives of mere self-preservation (*ananke*) and the will to death (*thanatos* in Freud). The continuous, irrepressible, constraint-denying, subterranean energies and flows of *mazaak*, within the otherwise dark, decivilizing, *thanotic* context of the metal factory, are the life-asserting, life-demanding signatures of *eros*.

MAZAAK AND *MARDAANGI*: PERILS AND POSSIBILITIES

But what would it take to give fuller, more liberated expression to this *eros*? I discuss here three considerations for how workers' imageries and practises of *mardaangi* and *mazaak* might evolve, if proletarians are to more effectively resist *shoshan-atyaacaar* and regenerate their interrelations with each other.

First, as mentioned above, *mardaangi* gets dangerously identified and associated, often through the media of *mazaak*, with hard, conscientious, diligent, and speedy work, "getting the job done",[6] even when ill or injured, as opposed to the "flaccidity" of slacking, shirking, foot-dragging, *kaamcori* (stealing away from work), and *haraamkhori* (making illegitimate, undeserved earnings). While the *mardaangi* of *mehnat* was set off against the homoerotic *ghulaami* (enslavement, dependence) of the *camcaas,* who increased production and worked for extra time after the end of the shift, the imagery inadvertently worked in favor of the *shoshan-atyaacaar* regime, by giving value and legitimacy to hard, honest work, regardless of the oppressive details of the context. Hard, sincere *mehnat* is rightly valorized within a range of contexts, say in one's efforts to study and master a skill or art, or in one's own farming activities, or in the practise of struggle itself. And it is indeed from such contexts (the school, the farm, a life of deprivation and struggle) that migrants have inherited the *mehnat* ethic.

But when out of *majburi* (compulsion, difficulty), one is thrown into a modern factory, with its vertical hierarchies, alienating production process, and systematic methods of extracting, intimidating, and sucking workers dry (the metaphors are just these – *khun cusnaa* (to suck blood), *aadmi ko nicodnaa* (to squeeze, milk, bleed a person; the company is actually Bhagvati's *ras nikaalnevaali machine* writ large)), while also holding out false promises to workers that if they simply work hard, they will be rewarded with money and mobility, then it becomes vital for workers to reconsider and re-evaluate their otherwise non-context-specific teachings about the close correlations of *mehnat* (hard labor), *acche phal* (rewards), and *mardaangi* (masculinity). Indeed, in the course of metalworkers' repeated experiences of management's refusals to reward *mehnat*, the witnessing of serious illnesses which befell the most vigorous, hard-working, and masculinity-asserting workers, and the development of workers' own subtle resistance methods at and beyond the machines, the above trinity was radically disturbed.

Those who were looked up to by the *samaaj* were those who produced at quantities and speeds decided by social consensus, and who did not budge even when tempted or pressured from above. This was not considered *kaamcori* as much as working-and-resisting according to the circumstances of the situation (*hisaab se kaam karnaa*). Those who cut away from the *samaaj,* increased production or pace out of the desire for personal gain, or could not be counted upon in a struggle, became the "flaccid" or *dhilaa* (slack) members of the group. The ideal of sincerity and transparency, at the core of the valorization of *mehnat*, was preserved, but with respect to the *samaaj* one was trying to develop with one's co-resistors and co-sufferers, and not with respect to the company. I would

6. See Paul Willis, *Learning to Labour: Why Working Class Kids Get Working Class Jobs* (New York, 1982).

also argue that "character", rather than "*mardaangi*", became far more important a criterion of respectability (*izzat)* within the workers' *samaaj*.

Second, the inherited imageries and associated strategies of what one might call "militant *mardaangi*" were also disturbed by the *manthan* (internal churning) of workers' struggles. The elements of militant *mardaangi* which were questioned included the ideal and strategy of *khulaa virodh* (open defiance), in say, openly removing and casting aside extra pieces which the foreman put down at the machines to induce and encourage production increases. This practise made one into a target in the eyes of management, as opposed to working away on whatever quantity of pieces that were given, but *hisaab se,* using one's hands and *kaarigari* (skill) to decide and determine how well and how fast they actually would be made. Also, the core image of *ektaa,* as unity, solidarity, and the fist in symbolic representation, in which workers are loyal and obedient to the direction of a hierarchically constituted leadership (a parallel management?), was questioned and criticized, as the vulnerabilities of the *ektaa* model became more evident. These vulnerabilities included the dependence *ektaa* created on the actions and decrees of an allegedly enlightened few; the ease with which singular, rather than multiple, oppositional strategies could be addressed and thwarted by management; and the tacit reliance of militant *ektaa* on a palette of potentially self-destructive passions such as *krodh* (rage), *zid* (stubbornness), *ahamkaar* (hubris), and the impatient urge for immediate and extreme outcomes (*aar-paar vaali baatem).*

The practical and passionate repertoire of militant *mardaangi* rendered workers more exposed, vulnerable, and strategically constrained when confronted by management initiatives and attacks, such as bonus reductions, withdrawals of advances and of overtime *samosaas*, suspensions, a lockout, and large-scale terminations. So-called leaders and tough talkers could seamlessly transform into *mohraas,* become *taalmel*-breakers, or flee from a struggle. Multiple resistance styles (in working, speaking, writing, and meeting) which flowed from the plurality of strengths and personalities of workers could at times be more effective than the naked singularity of *ektaa* strategies. And cool-headed, well-considered, prudential modes of expressing and articulating inner rage, through varied, improvised, and situation-specific combinations of open and covert resistance, could have advantages over the dominant *josh-jazbaati* (passionate) repertoire alone of demand letters, tool-downs, and public *pradarshans* (protests, demonstrations). While management knew precisely how to break down the hard fist of *ektaa* and render it limp and flaccid, it did not know quite what to do with the more de-centred, non-hierarchical, deliberative, and unpredictable resistances of workers' autonomous *taalmel.*

Finally, there are aspects of *mardaangi* and *mazaak* which deserve to be discussed, reconsidered, and re-imagined, particularly with respect to the dualistic, otherizing imageries of gender identity which downgrade *izzat* and obstruct *taalmel.* One of the causes of the burdensome tensions of male proletarians is the persistent clinging to a vision of the male as the sole earner, provider, and accumulator in the family. This vision might have been sustainable within a world of stable, permanent, well-paying jobs, but within a scenario of extremely low-wage, ephemeral, and perpetually uncertain work situations, vulnerable to larger forces and agencies beyond the control of the individual or even a company (markets, competition, state policies), it becomes absurdly unrealistic and punishing for workers to assume total responsibility, as individuals, for their failures to advance their incomes and accumulate according to the family's escalating needs and demands (which are themselves being shaped by larger forces including the push to the cities and the rise of market-engendered new desires). It is thus difficult for anyone in the present epoch (the *Kalyug*) to live up to the *mardaangi* ideal of "possessing one's destiny in one's hand".

And it is the impotency anxieties of this loss of destiny control that I believe are being articulated in *mazaak* themes regarding the allegedly compromised character of women who work in factories, the rising materialistic demands and *svaarth* (self-interestedness) of wives, and the imperatives and exigencies of earning *paisaa* (cash) at all costs, even if it means selling one's body and *izzat* at the siding, which is only a displaced substitute for the polish factory itself, where men are pounded into *jhuk machines*. By holding to dualistic, otherizing terminologies and imageries regarding women – as *maal, machine, auratjaat* (woman as caste/genus), of wily and ever-suspect character (*triyaa caritra*), nagging and needling (*pin maarnaa*), envy-infused and relishing discord (*klesh*) – the family becomes more of a *cakravyuh* (tragic, encircling trap) than a sphere of *taalmel* and true respect (*sahi izzat*).

From workers' fragmentary confessions, however, away from the *mazaak* and *manoranjan* imperatives of the factory, one finds a different, potentially deeper set of ideas and imageries about women. These images are of woman as possessing greater strength and inner fortitude than men (*sahnshakti*), as deserving of the highest and deepest *izzat* (which they do not receive in actually existing society), and of their wives as their most intimate confidants, advisors, and ultimate refuge in this world, practically, psychically, and passionately. It is from workers themselves that I heard the most incisive (and ludic) critiques of their own *mazaak* styles regarding women, whom they say are actually *mahaan* (great), *devi* (goddess), and not fundamentally different from men, for the soul itself (*aatmaa*) lacks any specific gender. The soul is of only one kind (*aatmaa ek hi hai*), workers repeatedly asserted, and if some workers see the greatest possibilities for close, intimate, non-instrumental, truly respectful, soul–soul relations in the world (*aatmik sambandh*) with their wives only, I suspect it is because of this deeper awareness and conviction.

And perhaps it is the task of a truer *mardaangi* to bring this awareness more to the fore, directing our attention to the underlying *erosic* complementarities and unities of soul between and across genders and sexualities, from which *taalmel,* the collective struggle against *shoshan-atyaacaar,* and *aatmik sambandh* may gain life, strength, and power (*shakti*). This endeavor might also take the vital help of *mazaak*, which instead of preying merely on dualistic imageries, might also dabble in the *vyang*-style self-ridicule of dominant, otherizing, false premises and prescriptions, as workers do at times when they see themselves in their own categories for others (such as Hanif as a *jhuk machine).* Otherizing *mazaak,* although provoking us to laugh (indeed, perhaps because the humor *is* in the distortion of the deeper truth that we are also the other), and momentarily rescuing us from our tensions, also potentially deepens our alienation, distance from one another, aloneness, isolation, and ultimately, our despair. If workers' ideas and practises of *mardaangi* and *mazaak* could evolve in these ways, they could become far more formidable weapons of life-affirming struggle against the *thanatos* of Capital and the *Kalyug.*

GLOSSARY

aasan	posture, position
aatmik sambandh	soul–soul bonds
camcaa	yes-man, collaborator, informer
camcaagiri	informing and reporting to management on workers' activities, remarks, conversations; close collaborations with management directives and schemes
chotaa bhaai	younger brother
cugalkhori	reporting on workers
darshan	viewing, especially in a spiritual context
dhoti	cotton sari
ektaa	unity, solidarity; one-ness
gaand	rear-end, anus
gaand maarnaa	to bugger
gaand maraanaa, gaand marvaanaa	to get buggered
hamsi-mazaak	(see *mazaak*)
hijraa	eunuch
hisaab se kaam karnaa	to work accordingly, taking surrounding conditions and circumstances into consideration

Holi, Divaali, Chath	major festivals in north India
ilaaj	cure, treatment
izzat	respect, respectability
jalan	envy
jhuggi-jhompris	slums, shanties
jhuknaa	to bend down, lean, stoop; to submit, bow down, give in
kaamcori	slacking, shirking, stealing away from one's work
kaarigar	skilled worker, craftsman
kacchaa kholnaa	to take off underwear
kanjusi	stinginess
Khaan saahab	honorific term of address for male Muslims
koraa	raw, new, un-worked on
qavvaali	Sufi devotional song
maahaul	context, environment, atmosphere
maal	things, goods, materials, stuff
man	psyche; mind; heart
manoranjan	amusement, entertainment, recreation
mardaangi	maleness, masculinity
masaalaa	colored bricks used in metal-polishing made of quartz powder, tallow, wax, and other ingredients; also, the white dolomite powder used in the final stage of polishing
mazaak	humor, joking, horseplay
mazdur	wage worker
mazduri	wage work
mehnat	hard work, effort, labor
mohraa	worker secretly acting as a manipulative agent of management
nashaa	intoxicant, narcotic, hallucinogen
ras nikaalnevaali machine	juice extracting machine
rishte	relations
samaaj	micro-society of face-to-face relations; also society writ large
shoshan-atyaacaar	exploitation and oppression
taalmel	togethering activities
tambaaku-bidi-paan-daaru-bhaang	tobacco; leaf-wrapped small cigarettes; betel leaf and nut, often taken with tobacco; liquor; cannabis
vyang	irony, sarcasm, satire

Stretching Labour Historiography: Pointers from South Asia

WILLEM VAN SCHENDEL

PRIVILEGING FREE LABOUR

Studies of working people have long been framed by the concepts of "free" and "unfree" labour, a pair that distinguishes workers who are fully proletarianized from those who are not. Proletarians are working people without property, and therefore compelled to sell their capacities for money, but at the same time personally free to choose whom to sell their capacities to. Such (double-) free labour is contrasted with labour that is unfree, either because workers are compelled to offer their capacities to specific takers – under conditions established by those takers rather than by means of a labour market – or because these workers are not completely propertyless. Throughout the twentieth century, a dominant assumption among labour historians has been that the two concepts of free and unfree labour also reflect a basic trend in modern world history: the progressive replacement of unfree labour by free labour – or the progressive proletarianization of the world's workers.

Today, labour historians are much less sanguine about this belief. They have come to realize that the history of labour has never been a unilinear process in which unfree labour is being replaced by free labour. This realization has much to do with the fact that the study of labour is becoming de-provincialized. It used to be highly occidentalist in outlook. Based on empirical knowledge of labour in industrialized parts of Europe and North America (the "West", or now more frequently: the "North"), it sought to construct theories that were deemed to be universally applicable. But as detailed empirical studies of labour in Africa, Latin America, and Asia became available and labour historians began to take these more seriously, it became clear that the basic concepts derived from labour history do not suffice. For one, in the world beyond the West it was impossible to construct the history of labour as a march from unfree to free. Gradually, labour historians realised that it is necessary to revitalize the field by de-occidentalizing it and devising a truly comparative approach.

The extent to which comparisons will refashion the way we think about labour history is difficult to gauge. What is clear, however, is that they have begun to challenge the adequacy of basic categories and intellectual mindsets. Already, they have influenced how labour historians think about Northern trajectories. The "free wage-labourer" is now treated much more gingerly as an ideal type rather than a category of Northern historical reality, wage labour independent of the rise of industrial capitalism is taken more seriously (e.g. in debates about European proto-industrialization and worker-peasants), and it is realized that in the North unfreer forms of labour have sometimes succeeded freer forms.

One major world region that has recently produced conceptual challenges is South Asia.[1] Histories of labour in South Asia show many finely shaded degrees of labour relations that fall between the two theoretical constructs of free and unfree labour, and many shifts between these. Some are the outcome of transformations of traditional arrangements but many others have developed *de novo* in recent times. Predictions about the effects of capitalism on labour – particularly regarding its proletarianization, the making of a working class, and labour movements – have proved almost consistently off the mark in South Asia. For Dipesh Chakrabarty and Peter Robb, this signals that the universalist claims of Marxist theory are based on cultural assumptions that are far from universal.[2] In particular, the continuing salience of religion and social status "in determining identities and perceptions of self-interest [in South Asia] may be regarded not as a temporary imperfection in the march to a 'true' working class, but as a persistent feature flowing from specific conditions."[3]

If this is true, the contribution of labour-histories-beyond-the-North may lie not just in a rethinking of the *teleological* assumptions of the older occidentalist labour history, or a finer grading of categories. It may also lie in a call to reconsider the *cultural* assumptions underlying the field's main categories.[4] While the former is already being taken up seriously, the latter is by far the more difficult and radical.[5]

SOUTH ASIAN LABOUR HISTORY

In South Asia the systematic study of labour relations dates back over 200 years. Making sense of labour in various forms has been a concern for

1. The region of south Asia is usually understood to cover the territories of Pakistan, India, Nepal, Bangladesh, Bhutan, Sri Lanka, and the Maldives. It is home to about 1,500 million people, or one-fifth of mankind.
2. Dipesh Chakrabarty, *Rethinking Working Class History: Bengal 1890–1940* (Delhi, 1989); Peter Robb, "Introduction: Meanings of Labour in Indian Social Context", in Peter Robb (ed.), *Dalit Movements and the Meanings of Labour in India* (Delhi [etc.], 1993), pp. 1–67.
3. Robb, "Introduction", p. 8.
4. For example, the legal, religious and intellectual pre-histories of Europe, especially ideas of liberty, freedom, egalitarianism and modernity that are usually associated with Europe and the Enlightenment.
5. Cf. Shahid Amin and Marcel van der Linden (eds), *"Peripheral Labour"? Studies in the History of Partial Proletarianization* (Cambridge, 1997).

administrators, politicians, entrepreneurs, and academics since early colonial times but a recognizable field of labour history has developed here only very recently, and only in one country of South Asia: India. Historically, much of what we know about labour, labourers, employers, and state policies regarding labour has been subsumed under other fields of study, notably caste, law, and development studies. The links between these fields and labour history have been quite weak, with the result that labour studies have largely failed to deal with the position of labour as it mostly appeared in South Asia.

Peter Robb puts it like this: "The consequence of not connecting questions of work and status is in the end to separate out, even within the category of 'labour', all but one type of work. The norm is always the wage labourer, and often labour organised under a capitalist or proto-capitalist system."[6] This obsession with the wage-worker is also noted by Ranajit Das Gupta, who describes the approach of many labour historians to what they perceive as the emergence of a homogeneous Indian working class under capitalism as "celebratory".[7] In South Asia, however, wage-workers in the "organized sector" never formed more than one-tenth of the working population, and in many regions much less.[8]

The invisibility, within the study of South Asian labour history, of other, numerically far more prominent, forms of labour (tenancy, bondedness, sharecropping, domestic labour, family production, etc.) and the forms of social coercion that often accompany these, is increasingly being considered as a serious shortcoming. The assumption that the industrial proletariat was the advance guard of modern labour – the model that all other workers would (be forced to) emulate – has been proven wrong. Not only did the organized sector remain remarkably

6. Robb, "Introduction", p. 10.

7. "Writing on the history of labour in India from a Marxian point of view has a respectable lineage. But till a few years back most such writings tended to proceed from an assumption of a uni-directional, uni-linear process entailing the dissolution of all pre-capitalist social relations and eventually clear articulation of class relations under capitalism, that is, generalization of commodity production and polarization between capital and labour. Related to this has also been the assumption of the working of a process of homogenization of labour and the linear view of a progression of class struggle and class consciousness from lower to higher and to still higher levels, ultimately reaching a crescendo of revolutionary and socialist struggle and consciousness. In consequence, though radical labour historians have made notable contributions, particularly in the area of workers' struggles and the influence of political and ideological movements on these struggles, their writings have by and large adopted celebratory approaches, ignored the complexities of the historical formation and growth of working class in India and have not dealt with many critical areas"; Ranajit Das Gupta, *Labour and Working Class in Eastern India: Studies in Colonial History* (Calcutta [etc.], 1994), pp. xv–xvi.

8. Arjan de Haan claims 10 to 12 per cent for India; the proportion of the organized sector in other south Asian countries is lower; Arjan de Haan, "Towards a 'Total History' of Bengal Labour", in Sekhar Bandyopadhyay (ed.), *Bengal: Rethinking History: Essays in Historiography* (Delhi, 2001), pp. 119–134, 133.

small, but its workers, though wage-workers, were usually not proletarians.[9] It is fair to say, with Sabyasachi Bhattacharya, that the revolutionary role of industrial labourers has been exaggerated. We would imprison labour history in an obsolete paradigm if we were to continue privileging them analytically, on the assumption that they act as the vanguard to effect a social revolution.[10] In other words, we could be accused of indulging in wage fetishism.

These findings should be of great interest to any labour theorist because they fly in the face of received predictions. The universalist claim of these predictions shows itself in the question that is often asked next: why does the transformation of labour relations in South Asia not live up to the Northern example? Or more generally: why do labour relations in the world's south not conform to those in the "advanced" capitalist countries of the North? Such questions are misdirected because they take the organized sector and proletarian labour as natural yardsticks for modern labour relations, from which the bulk of the world's labour force happens persistently to deviate.[11] A more relevant question is what this persistence implies for the theoretical underpinnings of labour history:

> We, historians and social scientists of the South, have been battling with the possibility of histories that are not constituted in terms framed by long-standing Northern discourses. The crucial question [...] is the universalist claims of Euro-American theories. How do these claims fare when viewed through our own particular historical experiences? Most grand theories sustain themselves by pleading large exceptions around much of the globe. Yet we continue to seek to explain the exception rather than question the theory that underpins such descriptions.[12]

In this connection the field of South Asian labour history has thrown up several useful debates. There is now a near consensus that processes of industrialization in South Asia have been predicated on labour relations that differed from those in the North. From its inception, some 150 years ago, factory labour was not free but remained rooted in family labour on rural holdings, and this had far-reaching consequences for gender relations, wage levels, patterns of labour control, and worker politics.

If these findings qualify classic assumptions about relations between capital and industrial labour, an equally serious challenge is thrown up by

9. This was true for jute labourers but even more so for labourers in the tea industry because the latter were tied down by penal contracts that were intended to bind them to employers for long periods and turn them into a stable captive workforce.

10. Sabyasachi Bhattacharya, *The Labouring Poor and Their Notion of Poverty: Late 19th and Early 20th Century Bengal* (Noida, 1998), pp. 8–9.

11. Samita Sen calls these "questions of lack" in her "Beyond the 'Working Class': Women's Role in Indian Industrialisation", *South Asia*, 22 (1999), pp. 95–117.

12. Samita Sen and Shamil Jeppie, "Editorial", *SEPHIS E-Magazine*, 1 (2004), p. 1.

Gyan Prakash. On the basis of a study of *kamias* (agricultural labourers with long-terms ties to landlords in Bihar, India), he argues that the categories of free and unfree labour need thorough reconsideration. These categories are based on an "ideology rooted in the post-Enlightenment belief that freedom constituted the natural human condition" and that "the universalization of free labour [was] the *raison d'être* of history". This discourse of freedom led to the banishment of unfree labour (servitude, slavery, bondage) from the life of capital by defining it "in opposition to free labour, as the suppression of the innate condition of freedom".[13] And yet the emergence of capitalism as a global system "took shape in and profited from structures ranging from peasant production to plantation slavery, though it represented them as its opposite. In this sense, the history of unfreedom is the history of capital in disguise."[14] For this reason, Prakash concludes that:

> [...] if servitude was the form that the capital-labour relationship was compelled to assume in the process of its universalization, then colonial servitude must be included into the account of free labour. Because slavery and bondage contain the displaced history of freedom, the history of unfreedom in the colonies must be written into the history of freedom in the metropole.[15]

In other words, Prakash challenges labour historians to undo the discourse of freedom that permeates their work and to discard the oppositional categories of free and unfree labour that structure it.[16]

13. "[C]apital enacts servitude as the suppression of a prior human essence, as a system of *restrictions* on freedom to exchange labour power as a commodity. Power is banished from the realm of free labour and manifests itself in servitude alone; it becomes visible only in its juridical form, not in the realm of the economy but as 'extra-economic coercion' – as an economy of suspended rights and suppressed essence. Such a naturalization of free labour conceals capitalism's role in constituting bondage as a condition defined in relation to itself, and presents servitude as a condition outside its field of operation, as a form of social existence identifiable and analysable as alien and opposed to capitalism"; Gyan Prakash, "Colonialism, Capitalism and the Discourse of Freedom", in Amin and Van der Linden, *"Peripheral Labour"?*, pp. 9–25, 9, 10.
14. "To recognize in the history of unfreedom in India the history of free labour in disguise is to question the absolute separation maintained between the two, and to dismantle the opposition between the history of free labour in the West and unfree labour in the non-West"; Prakash, "Colonialism", p. 22.
15. *Ibid.*, p. 23.
16. Prakash takes a position in an ongoing controversy among neo-Marxist theorists that cannot be covered in this paper. For South Asian contributions that framed the battlefield in terms of modes of production in the 1970s, see Ashok Rudra *et al.*, *Studies in the Development of Capitalism in India* (Lahore, 1978). Recently the debate has been rekindled. For example, Banaji takes a position close to that of Prakash, which Brass denounces as aligning oneself with "anti-Marxist theory in general, and neoclassical economic historiography in particular"; Jairus Banaji, "The Fictions of Free Labour: Contract, Coercion, and So-Called Unfree Labour", *Historical Materialism*, 11:3 (2003), pp. 69–95; and Tom Brass, "Why Unfree Labour is Not 'So-Called': The Fictions of Jairus Banaji", *Journal of Peasant Studies*, 31 (2003), pp. 101–136. Cf. Tom Brass and Marcel van der Linden (eds), *Free and Unfree Labour: The Debate Continues* (Berne [etc.],

Clearly, then, the contributions of labour-histories-beyond-the-North go far beyond "accretions of knowledge that can be accessed when the need arises to understand the working-class history of one or several non-Western societies".[17] They go beyond providing students of the labour histories of Northern societies with an opportunity to benefit from a larger database to compare with. They have outgrown the role once assigned to them in the practices of labour history: to provide a cast of supporting characters exemplifying less successful or less complete transitions to modern forms of labour. Their real potential lies in revealing and challenging the cultural underpinnings of the entire field. In other words, labour historians need to reconsider their most precious assumptions, or, in the words of one labour historian: "we should re-examine all the schemas we were educated in on their merits".[18]

LABOUR HISTORY IN BENGAL AND NORTH-EAST INDIA

It is with this potential in mind that we need to develop the study of labour history in the world beyond the North. Rather than holding up the history of South Asian labour as if it were caught in a time warp or failed to advance according to some world-historical norm, it is essential to analyse what actually did happen to labour in South Asia. We will look at the achievements of labour historians and suggest links with findings in adjacent fields that may advance the search for new general interpretations.

South Asia as a whole is too broad a canvas for this purpose. This paper focuses on labour in the north-eastern region of South Asia. For lack of a better term, I refer to this region as "Bengal and north-east India" (see Figure 1).[19] Currently inhabited by some 300 million people, the area is economically diverse. Many inhabitants find employment in its mega-cities – Kolkata (Calcutta), Dhaka, Chittagong, Guwahati – and rural industrial complexes (tea plantations; oil, gas, and coal extraction). Far more subsist on the labour they put into agriculture, fisheries, domestic service, trade, state employment, and crafts.

The region is of interest because labour historians have done especially

1997). For a critique of Prakash, see also Neeladri Bhattacharya, *Labouring Histories: Agrarian Labour and Colonialism* (Noida, 2004), pp. 16–19.

17. Shahid Amin and Marcel van der Linden, "Introduction", in Amin and Van der Linden, *"Peripheral Labour"?*, pp. 1–7, 5.

18. Marcel van der Linden, "Refuting Labour History's Occidentalism", in Arvind N. Das and Marcel van der Linden (eds), *Work and Social Change in Asia: Essays in Honour of Jan Breman* (Delhi, 2003), pp. 249–261, 261.

19. Because of frequent name changes in this region during the twentieth century, and the intense political sensitivities connected with them, it is difficult to designate it with a single term. Today the region is divided between Bangladesh and India. The Indian part covers the states of West Bengal, Assam, Meghalaya, Tripura, Mizoram, Manipur, Nagaland, and Arunachal Pradesh.

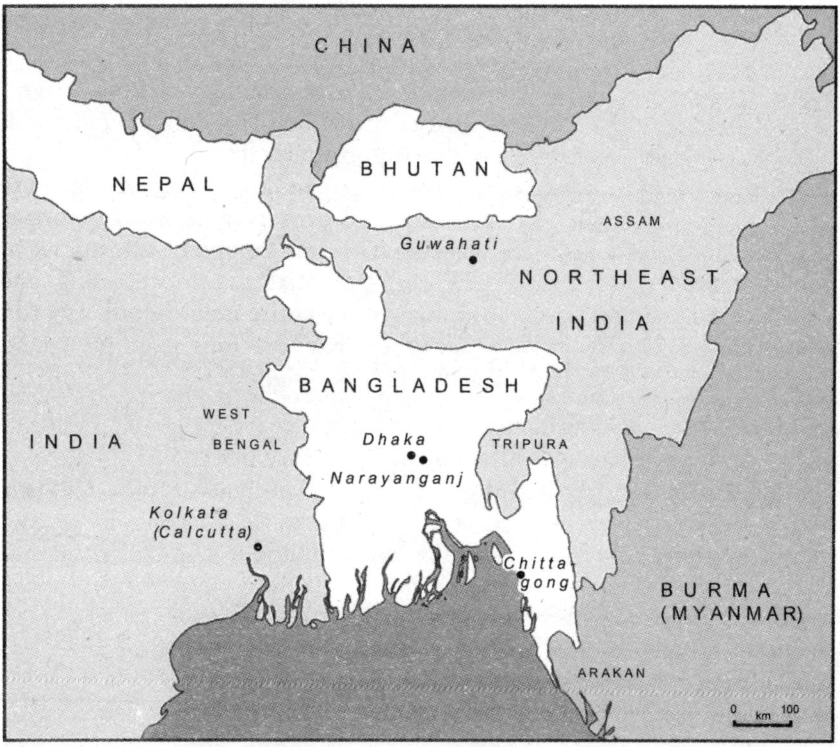

Figure 1. Bengal and north-east India

innovative work here.[20] They have concentrated their efforts in four specific and related loci: jute factories, tea plantations, coal mines, and steel factories. These large-scale capitalist enterprises developed during the colonial period largely on the basis of foreign capital and a migratory labour force consisting of hundreds of thousands. It is from these studies that insights have emerged about regional features of working-class formation. Three dimensions have been especially highlighted: the importance and heterogeneity of non-economic factors – notably gender, religious community, caste, and regional identity – the persistence of links between industrial workers and their villages of origin, and the diversity of workers' experiences. As expected, an important lesson drawn is that rather than viewing "the history of the Bengal working class as a deviation from the European model, particularly the model of the making of the

20. For a review of the historiography, see Arjan de Haan and Samita Sen, "'New Lamps for Old'? Debates in Eastern Indian Labour Historiography", in Arjan de Haan and Samita Sen (eds), *A Case for Labour History: The Jute Industry in Eastern India* (Calcutta, 1999), pp. 1–22.

English working class [...] we should look for its own specificities and dynamism".[21] Samita Sen points to a crucial specificity:

> In South Asia [...] [n]o clear separation of the household and production was effected: the household's own productive functions proved tenacious and in poor households, especially, women combined consumption, wage earning and reproduction, often simultaneously. The notion of a male wage earner as the single source of the household's sustenance – the single male breadwinner – was not a ubiquitous one and the inception of the modern factory system was not critical in this regard.[22]

In a recent overview of the labour historiography of West Bengal, Arjan de Haan suggests that the empirical focus of Bengal labour studies is too narrow and needs to be expanded to help include the diversity of workers' experiences: "their continuing link with rural areas, religious, cultural, ethnic, caste and linguistic differences[, and an understanding of class] as constituted by gender, and by other non-economic factors".[23] Such broadening, he argues, should take place in terms of economic sector, period, the nature of labour politics, geographical reach, and labourers' narratives. De Haan is not alone in his call; there is now broad support among Indian labour historians for studying the "multiplicity of worker practices and identities [and] the heterogeneity of labour forms".[24]

And yet, this understanding that the field must be renewed by broadening it still hovers at the level of exhortation rather than that of execution. Perhaps held back by a fear to step outside the familiar unified theoretical framework, labour historians have not yet set out research strategies that will deliver the goods. Starting from their suggestions, this paper examines eight partly overlapping themes that promise to be especially effective in broadening the history of labour in this region.

Industrial labour: jute and beyond

So far debates about the history of labour in Bengal and north-east India have been restricted chiefly to labour in large industrial enterprises. Within this sector, there has been a remarkable concentration on the jute factories in colonial Calcutta (or Kolkata, as it is now spelled). On the one hand, this has been a felicitous development because it allowed for productive, well-focused conversations between scholars thoroughly familiar with each

21. Sekhar Bandyopadhyay, "Introduction", in Bandyopadhyay, *Bengal: Rethinking History*, pp. 13–35, 25. Cf. De Haan, "Towards a 'Total History'", p. 127.
22. Samita Sen, "Gendered Exclusion: Domesticity and Dependence in Bengal", *International Review of Social History*, 42 (1997), pp. 65–86, 65.
23. De Haan, "Towards a 'Total History'", p. 132.
24. Prabhu Mohapatra, *Situating the Renewal: Reflections on Labour Studies in India* (Noida, 1998), p. 34. Cf. De Haan and Sen, "'New Lamps for Old'?"; Bhattacharya, *The Labouring Poor*.

other's turf, as reported in *A Case for Labour History: The Jute Industry in Eastern India*.[25] On the other hand, it remains unclear what relevance these findings might have for labour beyond the colonial jute factory in Calcutta. The operative words here are "colonial", "jute", "factory", and "Calcutta". For example, little work has been done on Calcutta's jute factories after British rule ended in 1947, and even less on labour relations in the new jute factories that were set up in Dhaka and Narayanganj (East Pakistan, later Bangladesh) after 1947.[26] Such comparative work could fruitfully examine a number of themes. For example, in the existing literature much is made of the ways in which caste identities structured the workforce. This makes comparisons with East Pakistan/Bangladesh highly relevant for here jute labourers lacked caste identities because they were overwhelmingly Muslim. Did this absence lead to any differences in recruitment, the labour process, or labour politics? Were these workers less constrained to make themselves into a working class? And if not, why?

Similarly, the existing literature strongly emphasizes the colonial nature of labour relations in the Calcutta jute industry. Anthony Cox's study of jute manufacturing in Dundee (Scotland) and Calcutta during the colonial period has begun to qualify this by arguing that the two were rather similar in their treatment of labour.[27] Studies of post-colonial labour relations in both Calcutta and Dhaka/Narayanganj could examine this argument further. To what extent can we actually attribute the behaviour of jute labourers in the colonial period to the fact that they were subjected to the "mad and violent agency of imperialism"?[28] How important was the *colonial* dimension of capital in the equation?

And what do findings on jute labour tell us about industrial labour here in general? Were labour relations similar in other large-scale urban industries (such as chemicals, paper manufacturing, tobacco, or engineering) and in small-scale enterprises (such as leather, ceramics, brick-making, rice milling, or medicinal drugs[29])? One obvious comparison is to look at cotton and silk textile production because, unlike jute, these covered the

25. See n. 20.

26. On Calcutta, see Arjan de Haan, *Unsettled Settlers: Migrant Workers and Industrial Capitalism in Calcutta* (Hilversum, 1994); Leela Fernandes, *Producing Workers: The Politics of Gender, Class and Culture in the Calcutta Jute Mills* (Philadelphia, PA, 1997). On Dhaka/Narayanganj, see V. Bhaskar and Mushtaq Khan, "Privatization and Employment: A Study of the Jute Industry in Bangladesh", *American Economic Review*, 85 (1995), pp. 267–273.

27. Anthony Cox, "Rationalisation and Resistance: The Imperial Jute Industries of Dundee and Calcutta, 1930–40" (University of Cambridge, Fellowship Dissertation, 1997), cited in De Haan, "Towards a 'Total History'", p. 128.

28. Chakrabarty, *Rethinking Working Class History*, p. 225.

29. See e.g. Amit Bhattacharyya, *Swadeshi Enterprise in Bengal, 1900–1920* (Calcutta, 1986); Smriti Kumar Saha, "The Rice Milling Industry in Bengal, 1920–1950: A Case Study of the Impact of Mechanization on the Local Peasant Economy", *Calcutta Historical Journal*, 13 (1988–89), pp. 1–111.

entire spectrum from small- to large-scale enterprises, from local to European capital, from traditional handloom to modern machinery, from local to migrant labour, and from domestic to export markets.[30] Moreover, studies of labour in silk and cotton production, both with a long and important pre-colonial history in the region, would allow us to develop a better understanding of what the transition to colonial rule actually meant for labour relations. This could be a crucial contribution to a field that bristles with assumptions about the impact of colonial capitalism on South Asian labour relations.[31]

Another potentially important line of enquiry is to explore to what extent workers' experiences differed between Indian-owned and foreign-owned industrial enterprises.[32] Such research would, significantly, also allow labour historians to push their analyses of industrial relations beyond the metropolis of Calcutta, not only to other cities and towns but also to industries – such as indigo or brick-making – that were located in rural areas because of the perishable or mineral nature of their raw materials or, possibly, because of special characteristics of their labour supply.

Agriculture: proletarianization or pauperization?

In 150 years of large-scale capitalist production, industrial labour in South Asia did not bear out the assumption that, under capitalism, labour is proletarianized. Labour historians have tried to explain this by pointing to cultural and social specificities, and to the colonial nature of capitalism up

30. For references to the literature on labour in the silk industry, see Willem van Schendel, *Reviving a Rural Industry: Silk Producers and Officials in India and Bangladesh, 1880s to 1980s* (Dhaka, 1995). For labour in the modern export-oriented garments industry of Bangladesh, see Hameeda Hossain *et al.*, *No Better Option? Industrial Women Workers in Bangladesh* (Dhaka, 1990); Pratima Paul-Majumdar and Salma Choudhuri, *The Conditions of Garments Workers in Bangladesh: An Appraisal* (Dhaka, 1991); Dina M. Siddiqi, "Gender and Labor in Bangladeshi Factories" (Ph.D. Dissertation, University of Michigan, 1996); Petra Dannecker, *Conformity or Resistance? Women Workers in the Garment Factories in Bangladesh* (Bielefeld, 1999); Dina M. Siddiqi, "Miracle Worker or Womanmachine? Tracking (Trans)national Realities in Bangladeshi Factories", *Economic and Political Weekly* (27 May 2000), L-11–L-17; Naila Kabeer, *The Power to Choose: Bangladeshi Women and Labour Market Decisions in London and Dhaka* (London [etc.], 2000); Naila Kabeer and Simeen Mahmud, "Globalization, Gender and Poverty: Bangladeshi Women Workers in Export and Local Markets", *Journal of International Development*, 16 (2004), pp. 93–109.

31. To give but one example, Amiya Kumar Bagchi asserts that colonial rule resulted in "the retardation of the forces of production by inhibiting technical change, routinising coercive and brutalising (and not just dehumanising) labour process, and sustaining a social process that requires the regular waste of a considerable amount of human and non-human resources"; Amiya Kumar Bagchi, "Colonialism and the Nature of Capitalist Enterprise in India", *Economic and Political Weekly*, 30 July 1988, PE 38.

32. See Bhattacharyya, *Swadeshi Enterprise in Bengal.*

Figure 2. Indigo factory, 1850s.
From Rural Life in Bengal Illustrative of Anglo-Indian Suburban Life; More Particularly in Connection with the Planter and Peasantry, the Varied Produce of the Soil and Seasons; With Copious Details of the Culture and Manufacture of Indigo – Letters from an Artist in India to His Sisters in England *(London, 1860).*

to 1947. Similarly, the assumption that capitalism in agriculture would produce a separation of capital and labour has failed to materialize. Although agriculture in most of Bengal and north-east India has been considerably market-oriented and monetized for centuries, agricultural production has shown no signs of falling into step with the model of capitalist entrepreneurs in possession of the means of production – land, production technology, knowledge, capital – and landless agricultural labourers freely offering their labour.

This is not to say that wage-labour has not developed in the region's agriculture. It existed before colonial rule commenced and it has expanded enormously in the colonial and post-colonial periods. But students of agricultural labour have continually warned against the tendency to read wage-labour as shorthand for proletarianization. They have made a distinction between that process, emerging from the workings of capitalism, and pauperization, the dispossession of producers through interlinked processes of impoverishment, inheritance and population growth.[33]

33. Other terms for this process in the literature on Bengal are "depeasantisation" and "non-proletarian immiserisation".

Although wage-labour has been an important element in agricultural production, labour historians of Bengal and north-east India have not concerned themselves much with the history of agricultural labour. Remarkably little historical research is available, with the exception of research on the tea plantations of Assam and north Bengal.[34] Beyond these enclaves of colonial capitalist agriculture, our picture of agricultural labour remains dim and patchy. And yet, it appears that the transformations that took place are of wider conceptual relevance. From the late eighteenth century, various state attempts were afoot to foster capitalist agriculture, by creating a class of landlords and by introducing a range of commercial crops. Despite the fact that agriculture became more market-oriented, unambiguously capitalist relations of agricultural production did not materialize. By the early nineteenth century very few wage labourers could be found in the rural parts of the region, a situation that contrasted with that in many other parts of South Asia. This scarcity of local wage labour was an important reason to use migrant wage labourers for the emerging tea and jute industries.

From the third quarter of the nineteenth century, however, observers noticed a clear shift. While the official image of Bengal as a land without rural wage-labourers lingered on, the dominant system of autonomous peasant production based on family labour began to weaken. Significantly, this shift did not take the form of either wage-labour or sharecropping, but of both at the same time. In 1888 the first survey of the "lower classes" in Bengal demonstrated that 26 per cent of the rural households now had wage-labour as their sole or principal source of income, and another 13 per cent depended on wage-labour as a subsidiary source of income.[35] A

34. Amalendu Guha, *Planter-Raj to Swaraj: Freedom Struggle and Electoral Politics in Assam, 1826–1947* (Delhi, 1977); Sharit Kumar Bhowmik, *Class Formation in the Plantation System* (New Delhi, 1981); Das Gupta, *Labour and Working Class in Eastern India*; Ranajit Das Gupta, *Economy, Society and Politics in Bengal: Jalpaiguri 1869–1947* (Delhi [etc.], 1992); Samita Sen, "Questions of Consent: Women's Recruitment for Assam Tea Gardens, 1859–1900", *Studies in History*, 18 n.s. (2002), pp. 231–260.

35. This *Report on the Condition of the Lower Classes of Population in Bengal* (Calcutta, 1888), also known as the Dufferin Report, is available in the British Library (IOR L/E/7/185). Its main conclusions on labour have been summarized as follows: "The rural labour market was fragmented and male labour fetched a higher wage than that of women and children. Wage rates for day-labour diminished as one travelled westwards. The investigators tended to relate this fact to the general level of prosperity which also declined towards the west. No correlation with differences in population density or with the proportion of labourers to the total local population was demonstrated, and no mention was made of any form of collective bargaining by rural labourers. However, there was a clear correlation of wage levels with the proportion of landlessness and thus of full-time dependence on labour. Contrary to common belief, the relation between labour dependence and landlessness was not straightforward. Not all labourers were landless; many owned some land and a few even a considerable quantity. Households generally took to wage labour for survival but some households used (seasonal) labour as a way of augmenting an already adequate income"; Willem van Schendel and Aminul Haque Faraizi,

century later, the majority (at least 55 per cent) of rural people in Bengal had become wage-dependent and, because of population increase between 1880 and 1980, their numbers had grown from 13 to 60 million.[36]

But outright expropriation of peasant producers was not the major trend. On the contrary, the dominant change that affected rural Bengal in this period was the rapid growth of sharecropping, mainly, it appears, by means of the transformation of fixed cash rents into share arrangements and by the enforcement of share contracts on newly cultivated lands. Furthermore, most wage-labouring households retained small plots of land. Thus rural proletarianization remained restricted, and surplus extraction through other means (notably credit, crop-sharing, and land mortgage) flourished.[37] Researchers have resisted the tendency to think of these arrangements as representing classes of landlords, peasants, sharecroppers, and wage labourers, or to apply designations such as "semi-feudal" to them, because such hasty labels are unhelpful in framing a system of exceptional fluidity and complexity. In Bengal agriculture, even smallholding households would typically own numerous minuscule and dispersed fragments of land, a result of ecological conditions and a partible system of inheritance. Such households often gave their distant plots to sharecroppers but they might well cultivate other plots as sharecroppers themselves. They were also likely to hire in wage labourers and at the same time hire themselves out for wages to others as well.[38]

Such dynamic and persistently finely graded labour relations in a largely market-oriented system of agricultural production form an exciting field for labour historians. Fortunately, they can benefit from a body of sophisticated studies of agricultural labour relations that deal with many of the conceptual issues to be understood in a longer time perspective. These

Rural Labourers in Bengal, 1880 to 1980 (Rotterdam, 1984), p. 21, cf. p. 9. For a summary, see Willem van Schendel, "Economy of the Working Classes", in Sirajul Islam, *History of Bangladesh, 1704–1971* (Dhaka, 1992), pp. ii, 542–599. For an introduction to the literature on agricultural labourers in other parts of South Asia, see Bhattacharya, *Labouring Histories.*

36. Van Schendel and Faraizi, *Rural Labourers*, p. 46.

37. The relative importance of appropriation by means of sharecropping as against wage labour in colonial and postcolonial Bengal remains an unexplored area. It is clear that there have been considerable local differences as well as fluctuations over time. For example, in 1939 sharecroppers outnumbered wage labourers in some districts of north and central Bengal but, on the whole, wage labourers were far more numerous than sharecroppers, who cultivated 21 per cent of the cultivable land; Government of Bengal, *Report of the Land Revenue Commission Bengal* (Alipore, 1940), vol. 2, pp. 117–119 (the "Floud Report"). Cf. Van Schendel and Faraizi, *Rural Labourers*, p. 108. For further references to the historical literature, see Willem van Schendel, *Three Deltas: Accumulation and Poverty in Rural Burma, Bengal and South India* (Delhi [etc.], 1991).

38. For example, in three villages in different parts of Bangladesh in the 1970s, about 15 per cent of the households were found to be engaged in complex combinations of sharecropping and mortgaging land in and out simultaneously; Willem van Schendel, *Peasant Mobility: The Odds of Life in Rural Bangladesh* (Assen/Delhi, 1981/1982), pp. 300, 309, 318.

Figure 3. Agricultural labourers, Bangladesh, 2003.
Photograph by the author

studies by economists, anthropologists, and development scholars are based on careful surveys, mainly in a small corner of the region (West Bengal). From the work of Ashok Rudra and his collaborators in the 1970s to that of Ben Rogaly and his collaborators in recent years, a baffling complexity of multiple and coexisting contractual forms has gradually come to light.[39]

Criticizing "abstract models" for ignoring the agency of rural workers and the ways in which labour markets are socially as well as economically

39. For example, Ashok Rudra and Madan Mohan Mukhopadhya, "Hiring of Labour by Poor Peasants", *Economic and Political Weekly*, 10 January 1976, pp. 33–36; Ben Rogaly, "Embedded Markets: Hired Labour Arrangements in West Bengal", *Oxford Development Studies*, 15 (1997), pp. 209–223; Molly Chattopadhyay, "Waged Labour Arrangements in a West Bengal Village", *Economic and Political Weekly*, 17 February 2001, pp. 569–575; Ben Rogaly and Abdur Rafique, "Struggling to Save Cash: Seasonal Migration and Vulnerability in West Bengal, India", *Development and Change*, 34 (2003), pp. 659–681; Ben Rogaly and Daniel Coppard, "'They Used to Go To Eat, Now They Go To Earn': The Changing Meanings of Seasonal Migration from Puruliya District in West Bengal, India", *Journal of Agrarian Change*, 3 (2003), pp. 395–433. On agricultural labourers and the labour *sardar* system in Bangladesh, see Geoffrey D. Wood, *Bangladesh: Whose Ideas, Whose Interests?* (Dhaka, 1994), pp. 259–289. On labour brokers in urban markets, see Aftab E.A. Opel, "The Social Content of Labour Markets in Dhaka Slums", *Journal of International Development*, 12 (2000), pp. 735–750.

embedded, recent contributions pay special attention to the decisions that rural workers make. One of the conceptual challenges thrown up is the rejection of notions of a labour market segmented into "casual" and "permanent" contracts.[40] Another raises questions about the very categories of "migrant" and "person who stays put" because decisions to migrate involve entire households and their "stretched lifeworlds": "for some, migration, and the earnings that accrue from it, form part of a struggle not to have to migrate."[41] These studies also demonstrate the possibilities for labour historians to make effective use of alternative methodologies to study labour in South Asia, especially the practices bracketed under the term oral history.[42]

Gender and stretched lifeworlds

According to labour historians, a gender shift occurred within labouring households in the region after the middle of the nineteenth century. Women and children took on more unpaid "family" labour and less wage-labour, and men moved in the opposite direction. At the same time, men dominated in the more capital-intensive forms of labour and women's activities became more labour-intensive, low-status, and poorly rewarded.[43] This gender division of labour varied markedly between social groups, between economic activities, between periods, and geographically.[44] For example, in rice cultivation in western Bengal, men ploughed and sowed and women transplanted and weeded. In eastern Bengal, however, women did not work the fields but concentrated on crop-processing. Non-Bengali groups in Bengal (such as Santals and Oraons) had another division of labour between the sexes and shifting cultivators in north-east India had yet another. In fact, among groups

40. Rogaly, "Embedded Markets".

41. Ben Rogaly, "Who Goes? Who Stays Back? Seasonal Migration and Staying Put Among Rural Manual Workers in Eastern India", *Journal of International Development*, 15 (2003), pp. 623–632, 631. Cf. *idem et al.*, "Seasonal Migration, Social Change and Migrants' Rights: Lessons from West Bengal", *Economic and Political Weekly*, 36 (2001), pp. 4547–4559; *idem et al*, "Seasonal Migration and Illfare/Welfare in Eastern India", *Journal of Development Studies*, 38:4 (2002), pp. 89–114. For a similar argument regarding the stretched lifeworlds of households engaged in both industrial labour in colonial Calcutta and agricultural production rural areas, see Sen, "Beyond the 'Working Class'".

42. This point is also made by De Haan who argues that oral history has been neglected by Bengal's labour historians: "The step that was taken in Britain after the seminal work of E.P. Thompson – projects to document local histories, for example in Dundee, including the workers' voices – has not been made in Bengal"; De Haan, "Towards a 'Total History'", pp. 133–134.

43. Banerjee, "Working Women"; Sen, "Gendered Exclusion", pp. 66–67.

44. On women in the labour force in Bangladesh, see Salma Khan, *The Fifty Percent: Women in Development and Policy in Bangladesh* (Dhaka, 1988).

practising shifting cultivation, there were numerous variations in the way they divided agricultural labour between men and women. And whereas the urban industrial workforce became increasingly male, labour in the tea industry feminized.[45]

If agriculture threw up a variety of gender roles, so did other important economic activities: fishery, animal husbandry, trade, cottage industries, and, from the mid-nineteenth century, factory labour. Labour historians have begun to explore these gender roles, the ideologies of kinship and family supporting them, their transformations over time, and how they were interconnected.[46] Clearly, however, there is still a long way to go. Progress has been made in linking the gendering of jute factory and tea plantation labour with the rural systems on which these industries depended for their labour supply. These studies indicate that the peculiarities of the industrial working class in Bengal were predicated upon the structural adaptability of rural families, factory managers' preference for a flexible labour force, the emergence of a male-provider ideology and a secular impoverishment of rural producers. It is here that connections with the literature on the "stretched lifeworlds" of migrant labourers, mentioned above, could be especially helpful: those lifeworlds, described for contemporary migrants, clearly have a long history. Speaking of the colonial period, Sen points out that:

> [...] the typical working-class family was spatially fragmented and was as crucially dependent on the unpaid (or poorly paid) labour of women and children in the rural economy as on men's industrial wages [...] women operated at a remove from the emerging "modern" sectors and the urban labour market which helped entrench the notion of the male provider.[47]

These findings may shift the practice of labour history away from a fascination with the sheer power of capital to transform societies and recreate them in its own image, as well as with state interventions such as taxation and legislation to facilitate this. The power of kinship and family ideologies in deploying the labour of household members, parcelling out entitlements and shaping household strategies needs to be taken more seriously. This requires us to focus on the agency of workers and the transformative role of their living strategies, cumulating over generations.[48] If stretched lifeworlds were the outcome, then these lifeworlds

45. Sen, "Questions of Consent".
46. *Idem*, "Gendered Exclusion".
47. *Ibid.*, pp. 73, 86. Cf. *idem*, "Beyond the "Working Class"."
48. These strategies include long-term ones, such as fertility strategies, heirship, and the manipulation of household composition. See Jack Goody, *Production and Reproduction: A Comparative Study of the Domestic Domain* (Cambridge, 1976); Van Schendel, *Peasant Mobility*.

were stretched by workers themselves as much as by the contexts in which they had to operate. This point can be driven home only if we learn more about workers' decision making and about struggles within households regarding the gendered deployment of family labour.[49]

Labour and rice: a special case?

The region's agriculture holds other attractions for labour historians as well. Among them is the possibility of a crop-specific explanation of the historical trajectories of labour relations in Asian societies. Not really pursued by any scholar of the region so far, this eco-technological explanation links social structure to the botanical properties of the rice plant. Writing about Asian agriculture, Clifford Geertz and Francesca Bray have, in different ways, pointed to these features of rice as a crop: much higher yield-to-seed ratios than wheat, barley, maize, or rye, and a short cropping season that does not exhaust the soil and thus allows two or three crops a year from the same field. These features imply that wet-rice cultivation can always be intensified by applying more labour.[50]

In such systems, technological changes that absorb labour and reduce agricultural unemployment are preferable to those that increase output at the cost of reducing the labour force.[51] Geertz and Bray argue that, historically, wet-rice cultivation has not been subject to economies of scale, nor has it responded positively to the centralization of management or the introduction of machinery. On the contrary, rice producers selected innovations that favoured both land productivity and labour demands. Unlike the European pattern, "skill-oriented technologies" proved more effective than "mechanical technologies", and the historical trend was not towards larger and more efficient, but towards smaller and more efficient units of production. In this way, "where the plantation sector becomes addicted to capital, the peasant sector becomes addicted to labor – the more they use, the more they need".[52]

Of course, we may question the extent to which the ecological and technological specificities of wet-rice cultivation actually did put

49. Greenough's study of the collapse of employment and the abandonment of family "dependents" during the great Bengal Famine of 1943 provides perspectives on household living strategies in extremis. Although it is true that acute starvation forces extraordinary decisions, the crisis exposed intra-household power relations that operate to deploy labour in less desperate times; Paul R. Greenough, *Prosperity and Misery in Modern Bengal: The Famine of 1943–44* (New York [etc.], 1982), pp. 183–236.

50. Clifford Geertz, *Agricultural Involution: The Processes of Ecological Change in Indonesia* (Berkeley, CA, 1963); Francesca Bray, *The Rice Economies: Technology and Development in Asian Societies* (Oxford, 1986).

51. *Ibid.*, p. 4.

52. Geertz, *Agricultural Involution*, p. 101.

Figure 4. Cigarette (*biri*) maker, West Bengal, India, 2005.
Photograph by the author

constraints upon agrarian capitalism in rice economies.[53] Still, it is clear that the enormous tenacity of the family farm in rice production under both capitalism and state socialism in Asia provides labour historians with an important problematic that concerns not only agricultural labour but

53. For a critique of Bray, see Willem van Schendel, "Rural Transformation in Asia: Models and the Interpretation of Local Change", in Jan Breman and Sudipto Mundle (eds), *Rural Transformation in Asia* (Delhi [etc.], 1991), pp. 281–309.

also its links with industrial labour, as discussed above.[54] Are we to analyse this persistence in Prakashian terms, as a history of capital in disguise? Was it a form that the capital-labour relationship was compelled to assume in the process of its universalisation in rice-growing societies? If so, we must include the history of peasant production into the account of free labour and we must discard the oppositional categories of peasant and labourer.

The evolving labour systems of shifting cultivation

The cultivation of rice may be of exceptional importance in the regional economy but there are several other forms of agrarian production that deserve more attention from labour historians as well. In about half of the region, particularly the north and east, wet rice cannot be cultivated. Here steep hills, mediocre soil quality, and extremes in rainfall do not allow even for the rice terraces of Java. Instead, agriculture takes the form of shifting cultivation, locally known as *jhum*.[55] Nothing could perhaps be further from the classic concerns of labour historians than this system of

54. This tenacity was demonstrated by the emergence of a prawn export industry in coastal Bangladesh from the 1970s. Here, according to Ito, "institutional forms traditionally associated with the rice economy have been carried over into the new process of prawn farming". Despite predictions that "prawn-lords" would appropriate large areas of land, this did not happen. After an initial spurt in land sales, entrepreneurs/absentee landowners were gradually pushed out, either giving up completely or deciding to lease out their properties. Small landholders, combining family labour with hired wage labour, became important beneficiaries of the new production regime, and even landless households leased in plots in order to breed prawns. Sanae Ito, "From Rice to Prawns: Economic Transformation and Agrarian Structure in Rural Bangladesh", *Journal of Peasant Studies*, 29 (2002), pp. 47–70.

55. Shifting cultivation is a term that refers to a diversity of agricultural systems. Another term for the *jhum* systems is *taungya* (Burmese: hill agriculture). Recent studies of these systems in north-east India and Bangladesh have been inspired almost exclusively by socio-ecological concerns, especially social forestry, resource management technology, and carrying capacity. These studies usually provide very little information about labour relations, often treating it as having no exchange value. Even basics such as labour inputs are either vaguely referred to as ruled by traditional arrangements or are pronounced difficult to measure. For introductions to *jhum*, see. P.S. Ramakrishnan, *Shifting Agriculture and Sustainable Development: An Interdisciplinary Study from North-Eastern India* (Paris [etc.], 1993); Raymond L. Bryant, "Shifting the Cultivator: The Politics of Teak Regeneration in Colonial Burma", *Modern Asian Studies*, 28 (1994), pp. 225–250; Daman Singh, *The Last Frontier: People and Forests in Mizoram* (New Delhi, 1996); Golam Rasul *et al.*, "Determinants of Land-Use Changes in the Chittagong Hill Tracts of Bangladesh", *Applied Geography*, 24 (2004), pp. 217–240. One study that does concern itself with labour, and shows shifting cultivation (in the Orissa hills) to be more labour-intensive than wetland cultivation, while giving comparable returns to labour, is Smita Mishra Panda, "Towards Sustainable Natural Resource Management of Tribal Communities: Findings from a Study of Swidden and Wetland Cultivation in Remote Hill Regions of Eastern India", *Environmental Management*, 23 (1999), pp. 205–216. See also *Chittagong Hill Tracts Region Development Plan, Final Report No. 10: Life Histories and Livelihoods in CHT* (Rangamati, 2001).

Figure 5. Shifting cultivation, Bangladesh, 1957.
Photograph by Lorenz G. Löffler

agriculture in which wage-labour does not normally play a role and cooperative labour systems based on rules of mutual assistance dominate.[56]

From the earliest colonial writings, *jhum* cultivation has been represented as "primitive" and on its way to the dunghill of history.[57] State policies in colonial and post-colonial times generally misrepresented it as static and unchanging, and they have striven to replace it by more "advanced" plough cultivation, usually with little effect. Such evolutionist biases have placed *jhum* cultivation in opposition to capitalist production, suggesting that its interest is largely antiquarian or anthropological. It is no surprise, then, that labour history, a field that itself is suffused with

56. For a description of such cooperative labour systems in shifting cultivation in another part of the humid tropics, see Tereza Ximenez, "Division of Labor and Resource Management in Eastern Pará, Brazil", *Agriculture and Human Values*, 18 (2001), pp. 49–56.

57. Kaushik Ghosh shows how "primitivism" was a term used not just to classify shifting cultivation but also to classify shifting cultivators, and how it became an important element in structuring the market for plantation labour. What remains to be explained, however, is why "hunting the primitive for the plantations of colonial civilization" was well developed in the Chhota Nagpur hills on the western borders of our region but not in the much larger eastern areas of Assam, Tripura, and the Chittagong Hill Tracts. Kaushik Ghosh, "A Market for Aboriginality: Primitivism and Race Classification in the Indentured Labour Market of Colonial India", in Gautam Bhadra *et al.* (eds), *Subaltern Studies X: Writings on South Asian History and Society* (New Delhi, [etc.], 1999), pp. 8–48.

evolutionist assumptions, has given it no attention. And yet, if we are to follow Prakash's suggestion that the history of labour unfreedom is the history of capital in disguise, the field broadens and the study of the labour process in *jhum* cultivation takes on more urgency.[58]

How did this system survive, develop, transform and become market-oriented, without a separation of capital and labour? Which links did develop between kin-determined labour relations in *jhum* production and capitalist forms of production? How and why, for example, did *jhuming* communities free labour to work in far-away plantations, factories, and road construction?[59] And why did generations of experience with capitalist labour relations have so little effect on labour arrangements in shifting cultivation? In other words, it is the very persistence and adaptation of these presumably "primitive" forms of production today that make them so interesting for historians of labour. To some extent, such studies can benefit from earlier theoretical work, especially in African history, that attempted to capture similar questions in terms of the "articulation" of modes of production.

New coercions: labour trafficking

Perhaps the most pressing task for historians of labour in Bengal and north-east India is to analyse the historical processes that have given rise to the massive labour migrations that are currently taking place in the region. Predicated upon the movement of cultivators from the Bengal delta to surrounding areas (notably Assam, Tripura, and Arakan) in the nineteenth century, the streams of Bengalis in search of work and land beyond Bengal itself have never stopped growing. More than anything else, it is this migration that makes it essential to study the region of Bengal and north-east India as a unit.

The administrative separation into two states in 1947 has complicated the processes of migration because, first, it led to two additional streams of people fleeing from one part of the region to the other and, second, it turned labour migration into an international affair. Today, most migrants are Bangladeshis who end up in West Bengal (India) and north-east India, although the Bangladeshi diaspora has now become worldwide. The

58. *Jhum*ing communities also knew forms of labour bondage that historians have largely ignored. In colonial reports these forms, usually equated with slavery, were said to emerge from three mechanisms: capture in war, sanctuary seeking, and debt bondage. Whereas slavery was abolished by law in the lowlands in 1843, hill slavery was not outlawed till the 1920s. On hill slavery, see e.g. T.H. Lewin, *Wild Races of the Eastern Frontier of India* (Delhi, 1984 [1870]; N.E. Parry, *The Lakhers* (Calcutta, 1976 [1932]), pp. 223–228.

59. For an example of shifting cultivators from the Orissa hills migrating long-distance to build roads in Arunachal Pradesh, see Mishra Panda, "Towards Sustainable Natural Resource Management".

Indian government claims that some 20 million undocumented Bangladeshis are living in India today. The arrival of so many migrants has led to a host of political repercussions in India: anti-Bangladeshi pogroms, forcible deportations to Bangladesh, the building up of vote banks, and so on. Many economic repercussions have also been noted: low real wages in areas with many immigrants, the existence of enterprises in India that can be run only on the basis of undocumented Bangladeshi labour, and particular labour market niches (brick-making, construction, weaving, cigarette-factory work, domestic service, sex work, rag-picking, rickshaw-pulling) being taken over by immigrants.

Very little is actually known about the identities of the migrants and their motives for leaving Bangladesh, their migration strategies, the mechanisms that allow them to cross the border and find work, their further careers, and their return migration. As far as organizations are concerned, we get hints of Indian-run agencies recruiting labourers in Bangladesh to work in brickfields, in factories, and on public works in India; of Bangladeshi brokers helping migrants across the border; of cross-border kin networks facilitating migration and finding employment; and of Bangladeshi migrants striking out on their own and "self-smuggling" themselves across the border.[60]

One of the core conceptual issues here is the agency of labour migrants. In a general discussion of human smuggling, Kyle and Dale distinguish two ideal-types.[61] A *migrant-exporting industry* is driven by migrant demand. It provides a package migration service out of a sending region, most of the organizational activity is at the sending side, and the contract is terminated once the migrant has arrived at the destination. A *slave-importing operation*, on the other hand, is set up to import weak labour for ongoing enterprises. It is usually carried out by relatively stable (criminal or semi-legitimate) organizations in the destination country and nearly always depends on corruption of state officials in all countries involved. In most cases, victims of such operations – who tend to come from weaker social backgrounds than the customers of migrant-exporting schemes – are duped into believing that they are embarking in a migrant exporting scheme.

In order to create this false image, seemingly well-to-do women often act as initial contact persons in slave-importing schemes.[62] The victims'

60. For details, see Willem van Schendel, *The Bengal Borderland: Beyond State and Nation in South Asia* (London, 2005).

61. David Kyle and John Dale, "Smuggling the State Back In: Agents of Human Smuggling Reconsidered", in *idem* (eds), *Global Human Smuggling Comparative Perspectives* (Baltimore, MD [etc.], 2001), pp. 29–57.

62. *Ibid.*, p. 34. See Van Schendel, *The Bengal Borderland*, for some examples of the role of women in procuring Bangladeshi workers for the Indian sex industry. In a similar way, women had been used to lure female labour to the tea plantations in colonial times. On this, and a

Figure 6. Brickfield, West Bengal, India, 2004.
Photograph by the author

own complicity is then used to facilitate making them pay off a rolling debt through coerced labour.

> Contrary to the conventions of enforcement agencies and news reporting, which tend to identify "the bad guys" and their victims, much migrant smuggling or trafficking operates in an ambiguous area that is neither purely voluntary nor involuntary from the perspective of the migrant. Many contemporary slaves know that they will be smuggled illegally across borders to work, and they sometimes know the nature of the work – what they often do not know is the terms of the "contract".[63]

Both men and women, children and adults, are smuggled across the Bangladesh-India border but the trafficking of women has attracted most attention. In many cases it is only after the women reach their final destination that they realise they have been tricked: often they are sold to sweatshops or brothels. Middle-men play the same trick on boys and men

discussion of "kidnapping" of tea labourers, See Sen, "Questions of Consent".

63. David Kyle and Rey Koslowski, "Introduction", in *idem* (eds) *Global Human Smuggling*, p. 9.

when they offer them jobs in faraway factories, only to sell them as bonded labourers to rural landlords or sweatshop owners.[64]

The prospect of employment or marriage is commonly used to entice women to cross the border.[65] In the case of many women and children, however, it is not consent or enticement but force or sale that makes them cross the border. Kidnapping is common, especially of young children, even babies, but some parents sell their children. In this way, about 15,000 children are said to cross the border from Bangladesh to India every year, a practice that has been going on for a long time. Boys aged between 2 and 12 are in high demand in the Gulf states as jockeys in camel races.[66] Young girls and boys are sought after as domestics,[67] and as sex workers.[68] Very young girls are said to "command a high price as they are likely to be free from HIV/AIDS", and,

> [...] in West Bengal, children used as jockeys in camel races are the most expensive, followed by those used for prostitution, while those pushed into begging or used as labourers cost the least. In Bangladesh, the prices are said to be very low, with the average ranging between Rs 1,000 and Rs 5,000.[69]

Exploring the history of coerced migration in Bengal and northeast India is a pressing task for labour historians for three reasons: it is a

64. Ranabir Samaddar, *The Marginal Nation: Transborder Migration from Bangladesh to West Bengal* (New Delhi [etc.], 1999); Van Schendel, *Bengal Borderland.*

65. John Frederick and Thomas L. Kelly (eds), *Fallen Angels: The Sex Workers of South Asia* (New Delhi, 2000), pp. 67–68, 74.

66. For a documentary about the working conditions of these boys, see *United Arab Emirates: Camel Jockeys,* by Geoff Thompson (in the series Foreign Correspondent, Australian Broadcasting Corporation, 2003).

67. Historical studies of domestic service in colonial Bengal and north-east India are still rare. See Indrani Chatterjee, *Gender, Slavery and Law in Colonial India* (Delhi [etc.], 1999); Tanika Sarkar, "Bondage in the Colonial Context", in Utsa Patnaik and Manjari Dingwaney (eds), *Chains of Servitude: Bondage and Slavery in India* (Madras, 1985), pp. 97–126; Raka Ray, "Masculinity, Femininity, and Servitude: Domestic Workers in Calcutta in the Twentieth Century", *Feminist Studies*, 26 (2000), pp. 691–718; Swapna M. Banerjee, "Down Memory Lane: Representations of Domestic Workers in Middle Class Personal Narratives of Colonial Bengal", *Journal of Social History*, 37 (2004), pp. 681–708. Cf. *Employment of Domestic Servants in Dacca City* (Dacca, 1963); Thérèse Blanchet, *Lost Innocence, Stolen Childhoods* (Dhaka, 1996), pp. 97–121. For an impressive evocation of the labour conditions of child domestic servants in middle-class Calcutta, see Mrinal Sen's film, *Kharij (The Case Is Closed)*, 1982.

68. According to a United Nations report, around 300,000 Bangladeshi women and children were sold to Indian brothels in the mid-1990s; *The Daily Star*, 15 December 1998. The market for sex workers is a highly complex one: Bangladeshi women ended up in the sex industry in India and Pakistan, but at the same time Indian sex workers were active in Bangladeshi border towns. Boys from the borderland were also known to end up in the sex industry in India. "Rajshahi Most Vulnerable to AIDS Onslaught", *The Independent*, 19 June 2002; "Rescue Blows Lid Off Boy Trafficking", *The Telegraph*, 22 August 2003.

69. i.e. between about US$25 and US$125. "27,000 Bangladeshis Trapped in Indian Brothels", *Dawn*, 8 April 1998; Sanghamitra Chakraborty, "Repatriated Bangla Children May Never See Their Real Families Again", *Times of India*, 19 April 1998.

neglected aspect of this region's social transformation that has huge contemporary political significance; it concerns important categories of labour that have been disregarded in the region's labour historiography (women, children, domestic service, sex work, "illegal" labour[70]); and it provides a link with the debate on forms of migrant labour control in capitalist enterprise (e.g. the *sardar* system) that have been analysed for colonial jute factories and tea plantations. Are there historical continuities between these forms of migration?

Cultures and meanings of labour

As labour historians are re-examining the universalist claims of theoretical constructs that have long underpinned their efforts, the study of cultures of labour has proved to be particularly helpful. In Bengal and north-east India, this has meant taking labour beyond the gate of the jute factory and into the communities that provided factory labour; it meant interpreting

70. The importance of highlighting the gendered nature of labour has been stressed continually in recent times. See e.g. Nirmala Banerjee, "Working Women in Colonial Bengal: Modernization and Marginalization", in Kumkum Sangari and Sudesh Vaid (eds), *Recasting Women: Essays in Colonial History* (New Delhi, 1989), pp. 269–301; Samita Sen, *Women and Labour in Late Colonial India: The Case of the Jute Industry, 1890–1940* (Cambridge, 1999); *idem*, "Beyond the 'Working Class'"; *idem*, "Gendered Exclusion"; *idem*, "Questions of Consent"; Chatterjee, *Gender, Slavery*; Banerjee, "Down Memory Lane". Cf. Mead Cain, S.R. Khanam, and S. Nahar, "Class, Patriarchy and Women's Work in Bangladesh", *Population and Development Review*, 5 (1979), pp. 405–438.

The history of child labour has not been taken up, although there are studies by anthropologists and others to build on, e.g. Mead T. Cain, "The Economic Activities of Children in a Village in Bangladesh", *Population and Development Review*, 3 (1977), pp. 201–277; Mead Cain and A.B.M. Khorshed Alam Mozumder, "Labor Market Structure, Child Employment, and Reproductive Behavior in Rural South Asia", in Gerry Rogers and Guy Standing (eds), *Child Work, Poverty and Underdevelopment* (Geneva, 1981), pp. 245–287; Alia Ahmed and M.A. Quasem, *Child Labour in Bangladesh* (Dhaka/Lund, 1991); Blanchet, *Lost Innocence*, pp. 97–143; Arup Maharatna, "Children's Work Activities, Surplus Labour and Fertility: Case Study of Six Villages in Birbhum", *Economic and Political Weekly*, 15 February 1997, pp. 363–369; Emily Delap, "Child Housework in Urban Bangladesh: An Exploration of Intra-Household Labour Deployment", *Journal of International Development*, 12 (2000), pp. 723–734; Sarah C. White, "From the Politics of Poverty to the Politics of Identity? Child Rights and Working Children in Bangladesh", *Journal of International Development*, 14 (2002), pp. 725–735.

The history of prostitution is still in its initial stages: Zarina Rahman Khan and Helaluddin Khan Arefeen, *Potita Nari: A Study of Prostitution in Bangladesh* (Dhaka, 1989); Zarina Rahman Khan and H.K. Arefeen, *The Situation of Child Prostitutes in Bangladesh* (Dhaka, 1990); Kamal Siddiqui *et al.*, *Social Formation in Dhaka City* (Dhaka, 1990), pp. 277–345; Blanchet, *Lost Innocence*, pp. 123–143; Carolyn Sleightholme and Indrani Sinha, *Guilty Without Trial: Women in the Sex Trade in Calcutta* (Calcutta [etc.], 1996–1997); Sumanta Banerjee, *Dangerous Outcast: The Prostitute in Nineteenth Century Bengal* (Calcutta, 1998).

For the history of "illegal" (undocumented, unauthorized) labour, see references in Van Schendel, *Bengal Borderland*.

labour practices as embedded in a broader urban culture in Calcutta. Although some have posited that jute labourers were driven by "vertical" pre-capitalist community consciousness rather than by "horizontal" capitalist class-consciousness, others have criticized this juxtaposition.[71] Research on workers' culture continues to explore to what extent a "working-class" experience was a "relatively insignificant dimension in the world experienced by the migrant workers in Bengal's industries".[72]

In this endeavour it is essential to avoid a dichotomous approach in which urban and rural are used as categories of opposition. If we take the idea of stretched lifeworlds seriously, we have to steer clear of ideas that equate urban with the more modern and class-conscious, and rural with the more traditional/pre-capitalist and community conscious. Studies of workers' culture should themselves be stretched to embrace the rural–urban continuum rather than focusing on urban neighbourhoods alone. There was a continual two-way exchange of ideas, identities, and individuals between villages and towns. In shaping workers' identities, rural forms of class-consciousness may have been just as important as urban forms of community consciousness.[73]

Another way of probing more deeply into the culture of labour is to consider what labour means to those who engage in it. Such meanings are not self-evident but a matter of empirical inquiry. For starters, it would seem highly relevant to study terms relating to labour. What terms do workers use, and what are the connotations of those terms? How do these change over time? To take but one example from the largest of dozens of languages spoken in the region: the Bengali language is rich in terms for what the English language would describe as labour, work, or toil. Some of these terms are: *srom*, *kaj*, *kormo*, *karjo*, *kam*, *chakori*, *khatuni*, *porisrom*, and *mehonot*. There are many more, and much regional and historical variation. It is easy to suggest similar multiple terms for wages, day-labourer, employer, unemployment, labour-broker, factory, and so on.

When do Bengalis employ which terms for labour, and why? Are there

71. See e.g. Subho Basu's study of strikes in Calcutta and his critique of the historiography of labour politics: "Historians have been wrongfooted by a set of assumptions based upon the notions of class consciousness. This has resulted in the search for set behavioural models among workers, and the absence of such archetypes has led them to construct alternative monolithic models like 'community consciousness' in explaining labour politics that deny Calcutta workers even agency to make their own history"; Subho Basu, "Strikes and 'Communal' Riots in Calcutta in the 1890s: Industrial Workers, Bhadralok Nationalist Leadership and the Colonial State", *Modern Asian Studies*, 32 (1998), pp. 949–983, 983.

72. De Haan and Sen, "'New Lamps for Old'?", p. 7.

73. In studying culture, we should be mindful of De Haan and Sen's call for balance: "Doubtless, questions of 'labour' and, more specifically, of the industrial working classes, have to be enriched by a better understanding of culture, as well as of gender and agency. But these new concerns should include rather than displace examination of the material conditions of the working classes"; De Haan and Sen, "'New Lamps for Old'?", p. 2.

class, gender and generational variations in use? Which terms for labour are privileged in political or academic discourse in Bengali? If we are to develop an understanding of the cultural assumptions underlying labour relations, a socio-linguistic approach could be extremely elucidating. So far, the field of labour history has largely neglected this angle. Of course, labour history is strewn with problems regarding the translation of key concepts of labour between European languages. Did German *Arbeit*, Italian *lavoro*, Russian *trud*, English *labour*, and French *travail* really refer to the same phenomenon?

South Asian labour historians, who have access to this historiography almost exclusively through English, are well placed to examine the problem of translatability in a much wider context. First there is the level of academic and political discourse. Which vernacular terms did South Asian labour historians select to indicate "labour" or "wages" when discussing labour history in their own languages? What repercussions did these choices have for their understanding of the historical realities they were studying? Second, how did this politico-academic vocabulary relate to the vocabularies of working people? What has been the effect of these choices on the permutation of their identities? And last but not least, what were the vocabularies of working people? How can we use these to come to better interpretations of what labour meant to them and how these meanings changed over time?

It is clear that we know most about these matters regarding Calcutta's jute labourers; however, this is only a sub-field if we think about the labour history of the entire region. Now that there is an increasing emphasis in labour history on the agency of labourers, their living strategies and their lifeworlds, we need to know how they conceptualized work. We need to know how a household head in rural Chittagong talked about labour when she decided to send her teenage son to the Karnaphuli paper factory in Chandraghona. Or how tea labourers in Assam discussed their jobs. What words did Sylheti dockworkers in Calcutta use? Or Rakhain cigar-makers in Cox's Bazar? Did Garo maids in Shillong use the same terms as Garo maids in Mymensingh? There is a range of sources that labour historians could use to explore these questions. In addition to records and oral testimony, songs may be an important source, as suggested by Sabyasachi Bhattacharya.[74]

The comparative potential of labour histories in Bengal and north-east India

To the labour historian, the region of Bengal and north-east India provides an important research site for comparative research because of the fluid

74. Bhattacharya, *The Labouring Poor.*

complexities of its labour relations, the quality and volume of its historical sources, the sophistication of studies already done, and the sheer fact that the number of its labouring poor runs into the hundreds of millions. In addition, the region is also a unique research site for comparative research because it was divided between two independent states after 1947. This partition has created a veritable laboratory in which to test theoretical notions about how state policies affect labour and how labour impinges on state formation. During the second half of the twentieth century, India and East Pakistan/Bangladesh devised divergent policies regarding wages, labour conditions, sharecropping, etc. Labour historians, unlike agricultural economists and development scholars,[75] have not yet plotted, compared, and explained the resulting trajectories.

The creation of an international border right through the region also affected the strategies of the labouring poor in many ways. Circuits of labour migration had to be adapted or fell apart – seasonal migrants from north India to East Bengal and Burma, tea labourers from central India to plantations in East Bengal, East Bengal labourers to industries, ports and mines in West Bengal, and so on.[76] Seasonal migrants either created new patterns of migration that steered clear of the international border, or, if they did cross the border, adapted to the now unauthorized character of their migration. The borderland itself became a new site of employment for boatmen, porters, sex workers, petty traders, factory workers, smugglers, and various state employees: policemen, clerks, border guards, *peons* (orderlies), and watchmen.[77]

There was also much settler migration across the border and among these migrants were many small land holders, tenants, and labourers. One strategy for those with some land was to exchange it for land across the border, a strategy that allowed many poor and middling families to start their new life with some assets. Many others lost their land in the process of migrating across the border and so joined the ranks of the labouring poor.[78] In other words, the partition of Bengal and north-east India provides labour historians with an unique opportunity for studying comparatively both institutional transformations affecting labour and the agency of the labouring poor themselves.

75. James K. Boyce, *Agrarian Impasse in Bengal: Institutional Constraints to Technological Change* (Oxford, 1987); Abhijit Dasgupta, *Growth with Equity: The New Technology and Agrarian Change in Bengal* (Delhi, 1998).

76. See Van Schendel and Faraizi, *Rural Labourers*, pp. 46–57; Willem van Schendel, "Working Through Partition: Making a Living in the Bengal Borderlands", *International Review of Social History*, 46 (2001), pp. 393–421.

77. Van Schendel, "Working Through Partition"; *idem*, *Bengal Borderland*. Cf. *idem*, "Stateless in South Asia: The Making of the India-Bangladesh Enclaves", *The Journal of Asian Studies*, 61 (2002), pp. 115–147.

78. Md. Mahbubar Rahman and Willem van Schendel, "'I Am *Not* A Refugee': Rethinking Partition Migration", *Modern Asian Studies*, 37 (2003), pp. 551–584.

THE LABOURING POOR

Labour historians of Bengal and north-east India have given short shrift to most labour relations discussed above. One explanation could be that they considered these forms of labour to be less modern and dynamic, and therefore less important for explaining the transformation of society than "the making of working classes".[79] In this perspective, these other forms of labour could be interpreted as survivals from an earlier age that some contemporary societies had not yet shed completely.

If this is indeed the reasoning behind the research choices of so many labour historians, then their reasoning shows some parallels with that of classical evolutionist anthropologists such as E.D. Tylor, who developed the concept of "survivals" to indicate customs or institutions that had lost their function but had been carried on into a later stage of society by force of habit. Survivals were of interest because they proved the existence of earlier, more primitive stages of society. Evolutionist anthropologists were later criticized by functionalist colleagues such as Bronislaw Malinowski, who insisted that there could not be non-functioning aspects of society. In this view, the customs and institutions labelled as "survivals" need to be explained, not as past forms, but as aspects of contemporary culture.

In similar vein, labour historians who believe in a historical movement, under capitalism, from unfree labour to progressively freer labour, must present unfree labour as a marginal and increasingly peripheral survival. The historical support for this position is now highly contested. Many authors maintain that there is no necessary correlation between capitalist expansion and a decline of unfree labour; indeed, unfree labour has emerged repeatedly within capitalist industrial societies.

Rather than treating unfree labour as essentially a survival – as somehow outside of capitalism or persisting peripherally despite a capitalist context – labour historians need to study forms of non-proletarian and non-wage labour as functioning aspects of a worldwide political economy dominated by the dynamics of capitalist production. After all, it could be argued that partial rather than full proletarianization has been the hallmark of most labour in the modern world.

Gyan Prakash challenges us to accept that the current conceptual apparatus of labour history is unable to cope with these insights. As Juan

79. E.P. Thompson's study, *The Making of the English Working Class* (Harmondsworth, 1970) has had an extraordinary impact on late twentieth-century labour history, not least in south Asia. As Dipesh Chakrabarty reminisced in 1998: "I remember the day Barun De gave me E.P. Thompson's book *The Making of the English Working Class* and said: 'We have nothing like this, try and do this'"; Dipesh Chakrabarty, *Culture in Working Class History: A Discussion* (Noida, 1998), p. 6. The iconic role of Thompson's book is also reflected in the title of Vinay Bahl's study of steel workers in Jamshedpur (eastern India), *The Making of the Indian Working Class: The Case of the Tata Iron and Steel Co., 1880–1946* (New Delhi [etc.], 1995).

Giusti-Cordero suggests in an analysis of the historiography of labour in the Caribbean, attempts to recombine the concepts of "peasant" and "rural proletarian" can go "no further than their own deeply dichotomous structure [...] [they] first enrich, then constrain our vision".[80] It seems that for the moment we have only negative terms to analyse the major embodiment of labour in the modern world – terms that tell us more about what it is not than what it is: partly free, disguised wage-worker, peripheral labour, intermediate forms, semi-proletarian, and so on. As Shahid Amin and Marcel van der Linden demonstrate, whenever we construct schematic representations of free and unfree labour in the tradition of labour history, we end up by placing the historically most common form (partly-proletarianized labour) outside our scheme, relegated to grey zones of our own making.[81]

Prakash's suggestion to understand these as the hidden history of capital and include them all within the category of free labour is one way of resolving the conundrum. It points the way to a reconstitution of the concepts and practices of labour history based on a far more informed understanding of these "grey zones" than is currently available.

Sabyasachi Bhattacharya takes another route. He does not insist on subsuming unfree labour under free labour but proposes to use the term "the labouring poor" because the historical description of the plural, fluid, and transforming forms of labour that simultaneously existed in Bengal "cannot be achieved by the categories currently in use".[82] He argues that if we take the perspective of the poor themselves, there is no point in privileging the industrial proletariat.

> There is a commonality in cultural terms among the labouring poor cutting across the wage/non-wage labour boundary [...]. The reference point in this culture is not "wage slavery" under capital, but poverty and the life of labour in everyday experience. In the language of this culture the significance attached to poverty, indigence, destitution and hunger is far greater than to wage work and non-wage work, to proletarianness or its absence.[83]

This approach may help push the study of labour in Bengal and north-east India in new directions. Not only does it enable labour historians to explore labour beyond the confines of the waged proletariat but it also

80. Juan A. Giusti-Cordero, "Labour, Ecology and History in a Puerto Rican Plantation Region: 'Classic' Rural Proletarians Revisited", in Amin and Van der Linden (eds), *"Peripheral Labour"?*, pp. 53–82, 54.
81. Amin and Van der Linden, "Introduction", in *idem*, *"Peripheral Labour"?*, p. 3.
82. "The labouring poor is a fuzzy concept without sharp edges at the boundaries and hence suits the fuzziness of the reality of 'transitional' economies where gradations shade into each other, class boundaries are porous, and individuals and families are simultaneously located in more than one of the conventional class categories (i.e. categories contraposing wage labour and non-wage labour)"; Bhattacharya, *The Labouring Poor*, p. 5. The quotation is from p. 3.
83. *Ibid.*, p. 6.

brings to the fore the ways in which working poor people in this region themselves have conceptualized both labour and poverty. This allows a new engagement with themes brought up in the historiography on urban jute labourers (e.g. the "precapitalist, communal forms of organization and consciousness" that Dipesh Chakrabarty explored[84]) by juxtaposing them to other conditions of labour as well as with insights gained from other disciplines, especially anthropology and development studies. Understanding the lifeworlds and worldviews of the labouring poor requires utilizing, but also going beyond, the archives of the colonial and post-colonial states. It is here that alternative sources of history become crucially important: poetry, stories and songs; life stories; mental maps; and the memory sites (*lieux de mémoire*) of the labouring poor.

GLOBALIZING HISTORIES OF LABOUR

In the past few years labour historians of Bengal and north-east India have reached near-consensus about the need to broaden their scope and to see the region's labour history beyond the looking-glass of the North. The next step is to put this consensus into practice by implementing research projects that provincialize the labour historiography of Europe.

This effort is certainly not unique to Bengal and northeast India. It is being replicated by historians and social scientists all over the South who are "battling with the possibility of histories that are not constituted in terms framed by long-standing Northern discourses [or] seek to explain the exception rather than question the theory that underpins such descriptions".[85] Such battles are part of a general stock-taking that is currently taking place in the social sciences. Prominent among the reasons for this stock-taking is the challenge thrown up by post-colonial studies. This challenge is directed against dominant social-science practices that, from their inception in early nineteenth-century Europe up to the present, have constructed and perpetuated dichotomies between the superiority of a modern, rational North and the inferiority and "otherness" of Southern peoples and cultures.[86] Post-colonial thinkers argue that any serious attempt at globalizing social science practices requires a thorough overhaul of these inherited categories.

There are lessons for labour historians here, and these are not restricted to rethinking categories such as free and unfree labour. Do labour historians study the histories of labour, or are they actually interested in studying the progress of capitalism by means of the study of free wage

84. Chakrabarty, *Rethinking Working Class History*, p. 226.
85. Sen and Jeppie, "Editorial", p. 1.
86. For example, Fernando Coronil, "Beyond Occidentalism: Towards Nonimperial Geohistorical Categories", *Cultural Anthropology*, 11 (1996), pp. 51–87.

labour? There can be no doubt that the development of capitalism has been a major determinant of human life worldwide during the past few centuries. In that sense the study of labour during that period always addresses capitalism head-on, and it is essential to understand proletarianization as a most significant expression of it. But the focus on free wage labour as the embodiment of "modern" labour is clearly problematic. If this focus persists, those who argue that the history of labour is too important to be left to labour historians do have a point. In a period in which ideas about what is modern and what is not are being rethought, labour history must do so too.

In this context Marcel van der Linden refers to a choice between a "universal history of work" and a "history of globalized work". Suggesting that the former consists of "recounting the development of contractual relationships and labor movements all over the globe as comprehensively as possible", he chooses the latter view, which he defines as follows: "a global labor history is first and foremost the history of an important aspect of the present capitalist global economy, namely its labor aspect". In his opinion, global labour history is a modified form of classical Marxist analysis whose research spectrum should include not only wage labour but also slavery, sharecropping, and debt peonage.[87]

This manner of broadening the scope of labour history to include forms of labour that are not "free" raises a number of important questions of theory. We have seen that labour history in the classical Marxist mould assumes a basic trend in modern world history: the progressive replacement of unfree labour by free labour, or the progressive proletarianization of the world's workers. Marxists have studied slavery, sharecropping, and debt peonage as forms of "unfree" labour, and they have understood unfree labour as either a precursor of free labour or its contemporary other. Van der Linden's plea is to treat slavery, sharecropping, and debt peonage on a par with free labour in a new practice of global labour history. This is certainly possible, but it is much less clear how this relates to Marxist analysis, classical or modified, or how it meets the post-colonial critique. As we have seen, Prakash, Bhattacharya, and Giusti-Cordero point out that there are fundamental problems with Marxist categorizations of labour and that the required theoretical modifications are very considerable.

A moot point is why a globalized labour history should posit its Marxist credentials *a priori*. In this light, the choice that Van der Linden puts in front of us is perhaps not such a stark choice after all. A "universal history of work" need not be merely a pedestrian, theory-challenged "recounting

87. Marcel van der Linden, "The 'Globalization' of Labour and Working-Class History and its Consequences", *International Labor and Working-Class History*, 65 (2004), pp. 136–156, 141, 142, 144.

[of] the development of contractual relationships and labor movements all over the globe as comprehensively as possible". It could just as well be a dynamic and crucial field of inquiry in which the histories and identities of working people are compared and analysed from different theoretical vantage points that attempt to see beyond the looking-glass of the North. The "history of globalized work" (histories of labour seen as studies of capitalism through its labour aspect) could then be understood as a special interest within this larger field and it, too, could be approached from various theoretical angles.

It would be a mistake to think of labour-histories-beyond-the-North as new arenas in which to fight old Northern theoretical debates. The contribution of Southern labour histories lies first and foremost in their capacity to allow, indeed compel, globally thinking labour historians to reinvent the field. The endeavour to create a globalized labour history will not be successful unless we discard the teleological biases of the older occidentalist historiography, sensitize ourselves to the cultural limitations of its main categories, undo its construction of inferior "otherness" and superior "selfhood," and challenge its universalist presumptions.

Since it is various strands of Marxism that have dominated Northern labour history, it is this theoretical tradition in particular that needs to be reconsidered in the process of constructing a globalized labour history. The urgency is evident, in view of the fact that Marxist labour historians of the South have found it so very hard to break out of their conceptual shells and to study labour beyond a narrow terrain. Many have come to realize that the core dichotomies that they start from, e.g. free/unfree labour, "first enrich, then constrain our vision". We may find that a successful globalization of labour history demands a more agnostic, open-minded approach.

DOCUMENT

EDITORIAL INTRODUCTION

Below we print the draft of Rajnarayan (Raj) Chandavarkar's chapter for this collection of essays. Due to his untimely death, Raj could not finalize his text. Yet, it is reproduced here as a document because it deals with a crucial, but neglected, problem of modern Indian labour history, the decline of the so-called jobbers (labour contractors). Almost thirty years ago, Dick Kooiman characterized the jobbers in this journal as follows:

> In the mid-nineteenth century Indian entrepreneurs started a textile industry, which proved to be a new way to invest capital and to make profit. The management functions in their Bombay mills were filled by Europeans and Indians with an educated, middle-class background. The social and linguistic position of these people prevented their easy communication with the local labour-force of Marathi-speaking peasant origin. Therefore, from the creation of the industry, mill-owners and management cadres delegated the task of labour recruitment to a special class of men, called jobbers.
>
> These jobbers were both a pragmatic bridging of the social gap between mill management and labour, and the result of considerations of convenience as mill-owners were unwilling to invest into a regular system of personnel management. Coming from the rank and file, the jobbers were empowered to engage, to discipline and to dismiss workers and to give what elementary training was required. [...]
>
> The jobber's position as foreman and supervisor enabled him to build up a position of considerable influence. Since he was entrusted with the distribution of eagerly sought employment opportunities labour looked up to him for jobs. The employment relationship may be said to have been set up between the jobbers and the labour-force rather than between the factory-management and labour. In that way every jobber had his own following, numbering about thirty or forty men. [...]
>
> The jobber functioned as a broker between management and labour. He acted as the spokesman for labour and as the protector of their interests, which were partly his own. For the mill managements the jobber formed the only communication channel with the workers, and for information about their labour-force they were almost completely dependent on him.[1]

It was the spring of 2005 when Raj, on Sabbatical, was in India working in the Mumbai and Delhi archives, that I spoke to him about contributing a paper to this Supplement on Indian labour history. He regaled me with the stories of his personal experiences of working at the police record room in

1. Dick Kooiman, "Jobbers and the Emergence of Trade Unions in Bombay City", *International Review of Social History*, 22 (1977), pp. 313–328, 313–315.

Mumbai. On a more serious note he talked about his keenness to write a substantial paper dealing exclusively with the institution of jobbers within the larger world of Indian labour history. He believed that while jobbers occupy a very crucial place in the Indian labour historiography, the loss of their position and influence, both with the employers and workers, during the last decade of colonial rule and early years of Independence had eluded any serious discussion. Thus, the idea of writing a paper on this subject for the Supplement crystallized during the course of our discussion.

He kept his promise, despite his huge commitments to research, teaching, and managing the affairs of the Centre of South Asian Studies in Cambridge University, as its Director and, despite missing several deadlines of schedule, he informed us on 10 April that we would be soon receiving his paper for the Supplement. He didn't get time to put in the final touches he would have very much liked to add, given his reputation as a stickler for the minute details of his final products.

Rana P. Behal

The War on the Shopfloor

RAJNARAYAN CHANDAVARKAR

The outbreak of World War II accentuated, and its conduct and immediate aftermath sustained, the mounting pressures on the jobber system and exposed its weaknesses more fully. These pressures upon the jobber emanated from three sources. First, the imperatives of the war economy facilitated the more intensive exploitation of labour. The jobber's traditional task, to reconcile workers to the demands of the mill-owners, became almost impossible to sustain. Indeed, it drew the full wrath of the workers upon the jobber.

Second, the 1940s witnessed deepening tensions and bitter conflicts at the workplace. Attempts to enforce labour discipline under these conditions met with fierce, sometimes violent, resistance. The general strikes of 1940 and 1950, co-ordinated across the industry, revealed the perennial weakness of jobbers, when called upon to operate at a supra-mill level. Conversely, strikes occurred with greater frequency in individual mills in the mid 1940s. These were fractious disputes, often accompanied by violence directed at jobbers as well as supervisors and managers. To some extent, these disputes were fuelled by rivalries within the managerial hierarchy, as various ranks of managers intervened in the jobber's domain and as power balances shifted within the supervisory apparatus of the mills.

Third, the decade was marked by political volatility. Apart from the increasing number of strikes between 1943 and 1947, the Quit India movement, launched from Bombay, proved the most powerful of the Gandhian agitations and the most ruthlessly suppressed. In 1941 and 1944, the city was wracked by communal riots. When they recurred in 1946–1947, they raged with an unprecedented ferocity. The Royal Indian Naval Mutiny unfolded dramatically in the city in 1946 and attracted widespread support from the working classes. In anticipation of the 1946 elections, and even more extensively with the advent of universal suffrage, political parties strove to form trade unions and to compete for working-class votes. The passage of the Bombay Industrial Relations Act in 1946 stimulated frenetic competition for members between various parties, but most acutely between the new Congress union, the Rashtriya Mill Mazdoor Sangh, and the communist Girni Kamgar Union. Jobbers, no less than *dadas* or neighbourhood power-brokers of diverse sorts, necessarily became pivotal figures in the conduct of these rivalries, and especially in the competitive drive of various unions to expand their membership. Each of these sources of conflict and competition focused upon the jobber and made his intermediary position almost impossible to sustain.

The war rescued the Bombay mills from the slump into which they had entered since the early 1920s and to which they returned at the end of the 1930s, after a brief period of recovery in 1937–1938. The military demand was estimated to amount to about one-quarter of the industry's output in 1940.[1] In addition, by disrupting international trade, the war created new opportunities in both the domestic market and in some third markets, deprived of Japanese and Lancashire imports. The Bombay mills quickly found that the attempt to supply military needs and to make the most of these new potential markets placed their productive capacity under severe strain. The Bombay mill-owners who had, for the most part, been reluctant to invest in machinery during the slump of the 1920s and 1930s, now found it difficult to increase output, let alone improve productivity.

Mill-owners and managers responded to the severe structural constraints that they faced in increasing production by driving their workers hard. In this objective, the jobber was their blunt instrument. Irrespective of the widely acknowledged weaknesses of the jobber system to prevent or break strikes when they were coordinated across the industry as a whole, mill-owners had continued to place their faith in their instrument of labour control at the level of the individual mill. Yet it was precisely at the workplace that the pressure on the jobbers now mounted.

As the mills now sought to take advantage of the new market opportunities during World War II, they tried to set and meet high production targets on the basis of deteriorating machinery, scarce supplies, and inferior and expensive raw materials. Machinery supplies could no longer be imported on a substantial scale. Old machinery had to be pressed into service more intensively and deployed with a mixture of improvization, strategic running repairs, and optimism. In other words, mill-owners and managers were forced to rely upon the skills and ingenuity of the jobbers and supervisors, at a time when their position was scarcely secure and their relationship with each other highly conflictual. Managers exerted considerable pressure on jobbers to repair and maintain machinery under increasingly adverse conditions. Shortages of equipment and deteriorating plant continued to plague the industry for most of the decade. Some mills reported in 1946 that they had to run their spindles at lower speeds in the hope of ensuring that they would last longer. The lack of bobbins, and sometimes a shortage of cards, forced mills to spin finer counts of yarn, or else leave their frames idle while consequent interruptions in the supply of yarn to the looms reduced the output of cloth and created excess capacity.[2]

1. V.B. Kulkarni.

2. *Interim Report by the Industrial Conditions Enquiry Committee on the Cotton Textile Industry in Bombay City and Bombay Suburban District* (Bombay, 1948), p. 31.

In 1940, the price of raw cotton quickly soared. Necessarily, the quality of cotton mixings declined and from 1943, they deteriorated steadily.[3] Dyestuffs and bleaching powder quickly became scarce. As the quality of materials declined, they required more skilful treatment, even manipulation, in the preparatory processes. Problems at these early stages of production were magnified, often in the form of broken threads on the ring frames or damaged cloth on the looms. Rising prices, like the poor quality of materials, provided a further incentive for the mill-owners to manipulate cotton mixings, the quality of yarn and the varieties of cloth.

Conflicts over damaged cloth, resulting in fines and lost earnings, or the slowing down of production because of supply failures, had been a recurrent theme in the history of the mills. Attempts to expand output or speed it up ordinarily intensified these conflicts. The manipulation of machine settings and speeds, deteriorating and poorly maintained machinery, sudden changes in the quality and character of cotton mixings or the quality of yarn, or the composition of output sometimes resulted in damaged cloth and a loss of earnings for line jobbers and weavers and thus necessarily provoked bitter disputes between them.[4] In particular, it was reported in 1946, workers objected vociferously to "the constant infliction of fines" by jobbers, supervisory staff and managers.[5]

At the same time, new varieties of cloth called for adjustments in their methods, materials, and machine settings. Workers had to adapt to new production schedules and new types of cloth. The government of Bombay suspended the provisions of the Trade Disputes Act that required mill-owners to give adequate notice before changes were effected in the conditions of production and composition of output. Changes in the composition of output usually meant that the labour needs of a mill would vary from day to day, perhaps even in the course of a day. Workers might have to be laid off or hired in larger numbers at short notice. The jobber was now called upon to fulfil his original task of ensuring a regular supply of skilled and experienced labour in the face of fluctuating demand. Yet his own influence in the neighbourhood and, as a consequence, also in the workplace had been pared down.

These daily conflicts of the workplace, which had always characterized

3. *Interim Report by the Industrial Conditions Enquiry Committee*

4. Opportunities to manipulate materials and output increased under the Standard Cloth Scheme, which imposed on mills quotas of output for military demand. Its purpose was to ensure that a supply of cheap cloth for domestic consumption was maintained. Mills could boost their profits within the Standard Cloth Scheme by using cheaper mixings of cotton and making imperceptible reductions in the counts of yarn and density of cloth. Increased output under the Standard Cloth Scheme enabled them to place a larger volume of cloth on the unregulated market.

5. K. B. Wassodew, "Report of the Court of Inquiry in the Trade Dispute between the Textile Mills and its employees regarding the dismissal of certain workers", *Labour Gazette*, 26:2 (October 1946), p. 111.

the industry, were now engaged with increasing acrimony and they were played out in the context of declining real wages for the workers and rising profits for the mills.[6] Moreover, while the power and authority of the jobber had been diminishing, the mill-workers had been increasingly assertive and had built up a considerable momentum of industrial action in the preceding two decades. Thus in 1946, adjudicating on a dispute in Textile Mills, Justice Wassodew noted: "It seems that the workers with a growing consciousness of their rights [...] resented abusive language, personal violence and the like from their superior officers, including jobbers."[7]

Significantly, the general strike, that was launched in March 1940, by millworkers seeking a "dearness allowance to match the rising cost of living",[8] had been characterized by a higher degree of violence against jobbers, head jobbers, and mill supervisors than any of the previous eight general strikes since 1919. Of course, some jobbers, recognizing the need to secure their own future within the supervisory structure of the mills, played an active part in taking blacklegs across the picket lines, often in closed vans and with police escorts, and in some cases, especially in Bhoiwada and in the Kohinoor Mills, they were reported to have held workers in the mills overnight, so that they could keep the mill running on the following day. Similarly, the final stages of the strikes was marked by "stray assaults practised by the bullies", sometimes used by the police as a euphemism for *dadas*, against strike-breakers, jobbers, and mill supervisory or technical staff.[9]

Rivalries and divisions between workers also developed ferocious antagonisms and could culminate in violence between jobbers and against them. But they also reflected the weakening of the jobbers' position and the intensifying conflicts on the shopfloor, both within the managerial hierarchy and between jobbers and workers. That violence against jobbers and supervisors were given greater prominence in police and press reports in 1940 suggests a growing anxiety among mill-owners and officials about the jobbers' failing grip, the breakdown of discipline in the mills and indeed, more widely, the threat to the social order in the neighbourhoods of Girangaon.

Strikes and *hartals* in the mills continued in the early 1940s. The Quit India movement led to the closure of numerous mills until the agitation was suppressed. The Gandhian *satyagraha* did not transcend the divisions

6. According to the Government of Bombay's Labour Office, the "working class cost of living index", based on 1933–1934, had risen from 105 in 1939 to 279 in 1947 for all items, while for food alone, the price index rose steadily from 252 in 1943, a year of famine, to 344 in 1947; *Labour Gazette*, 27:11 (July 1948), pp. 1397, 1400–1401.
7. *Ibid.*, p. 111.
8. GOB, Home (Special) File 550 (23) C (2) of 1940, pp. 76–77, MSA.
9. GOB, Home (Special) File 550 (23) C (1) of 1940, MSA.

between the mill-workers that had been so clearly expressed during the general strike of 1940. Indeed, it opened up differences between the mill-owners, who were divided in their response to the nationalist agitation. Although the communist leaders of the Girni Kamgar Union stood aloof from the Quit India campaign, workers participated in the *satyagraha* on a sufficient scale to pose an awkward challenge to the Left. Once the Quit India movement was quickly repressed, with the communist leadership encouraged by the People's War to adopt a conciliatory stance, the frequency of strikes in the mills declined. Managers, supervisors, and jobbers found it easier once more to thwart industrial action at the level of the workplace. On the other hand, workers found it more difficult to coordinate action across the industry. In addition to the quotidian sanctions of the workplace, any decision to strike would now first have to fulfil the conditions and comply with the procedures stipulated in the trade disputes legislation and it would inevitably encounter the repressive reactions of not only the mill-owners but also the state, now fortified by the Defence of India Rules.

From 1945, however, strikes became more frequent and then in 1946 and 1947, their number rose steeply.[10] These strikes occurred at the level of the individual mills and departments. Some were driven by inflation; others were provoked by disputes over discipline and dismissals. The reorganization of work, sometimes real, and sometimes anticipated, also provoked industrial conflict. At the end of the war, the mill-owners anticipated the introduction of standardization and rationalization schemes. In the late 1920s and 1930s, the introduction of rationalization and standardization schemes had been pressed upon them by the colonial state as an alternative to the introduction of tariffs. Faced with severe foreign and domestic competition in a period of declining demand, the mill-owners had been unwilling to carry the risk of investment in the reorganization of their industry. They had proceeded cautiously, implementing changes in uneven and piecemeal fashion. In the 1920s and 1930s, rationalization had amounted to little more than the reduction of wages, the retrenchment of labour, and increased workloads.[11] Nonetheless, the introduction of rationalization schemes inevitably had an effect on wage differentials and increased the variations in production conditions between mills. As a result, mills competed for labour and wage differentials provoked strikes.

It had been apparent from the earliest days of the industry that the standardization of wages would remove a significant and avoidable cause of labour unrest.[12] However, the Mill-owners' Association had found it impossible to impose a standard wage list on their members in the 1930s.

10. *Labour Gazette*, 27:11 (July 1948), p. 1491.
11. Chandavarkar, *Origins of Industrial Capitalism*, ch. 8.
12. *Report of the Industrial Disputes Committee* (Bombay, 1922). Also CK 1890s.

Not only did individual mills resist any meddling in their mechanisms of labour discipline and control, but they were also fully aware that a standard list might force them to raise their wages in particular occupations. In the slump of the 1930s, they remained averse to this outcome. In seeking to postpone the implementation of a standardization scheme in the late 1930s, the Mill-owners' Association had observed that it would be easier to secure the acceptance of its members in a period of buoyant demand, swelling profits, and rising wages.[13] In the mid 1940s, the Mill-owners' Association recognized that the drift towards a minimum wage for workers paid according to time, the effects of changes in piece-rates as a result of conciliation proceedings and the adoption of a uniform scale for the payment of a dearness allowance had tended in the preceding few years to iron out some variations in earnings between mills had been.[14] It might now be easier to devise a standard list acceptable to their members.

At the same time, with the disruption of international trade and the destruction of Japan, the Bombay mills, in the aftermath of World War II, encountered less fierce foreign competition and experienced more favourable conditions both in their domestic and their export markets. In a period in which they anticipated rising profits, the mill-owners regarded the task of a more comprehensive programme of "rationalization" with more enthusiasm. In the late 1920s and 1930s, the mill-owners had already recognized that rationalization could enable them to reduce the status of the weavers and break the resistance of their most recalcitrant workers. During World War II, their productive capacity had severely limited their ability to make the most of expanding opportunities. "The first duty of the prudent mill-owner", their Chairman intoned at their annual general meeting in 1941, "is to ensure that provision is made for the renewal and renovation of productive equipment".[15] On the eve of Independence and in its aftermath, the mill-owners welcomed the Congress doctrine that industrial production was vital to the task of nation building and that strikes were a blow aimed at the Indian people as a whole. Simultaneously, in 1946, the Millowners' Association decided to introduce a standardization scheme, rather similar in structure to the one they had presented to the Textile Labour Inquiry Committee in 1939.[16] The Industrial Court's arbitration award, following the Girni Kamgar

13. Chandavarkar, *Origins of Industrial Capitalism*, ch. 8.

14. S.R. Deshpande, *Report on an Enquiry into the Conditions of Labour in the Cotton Mill Industry in India, The Labour Investigation Committee, Government of India* (Simla, 1946), p. 13; *Annual Report of the BMOA*, 1945.

15. *Annual Report of the BMOA*, 1940, p. iii.

16. "Proceedings of the Industrial Court", *Labour Gazette*, 26:10 (June 1947), p. 781. The scheme did, however, incorporate some minor revisions.

Union's rejection of the scheme, ensured that the standardized wage list was put into effect from 1 January 1947.[17]

In anticipation of a standard wage list and changes in working conditions associated with "rationalization", mill-owners and managers reported that workers had begun in 1946 to slow down production. In addition, rates of absenteeism rose steadily, reaching by 1946–1947 twice the level of 1937–1938.[18] By slowing down production, workers calculated that piece rates would have to be fixed at a low level of output. Once the standardized rates came into effect, the weaver, for instance, could expect to increase his earnings by working normally. Similarly, workers hoped that going slow would provide some defence against rationalization schemes being pegged at levels that enabled the retrenchment of labour and demanded considerably increased workloads.[19]

The attempt by workers to slow down production coincided with the efforts of the mill-owners to increase production to take full advantage of their buoyant markets. Managers, supervisors and jobbers now sought to extract higher levels of production. Workers were driven harder under the threat of disciplinary sanctions.[20] Inevitably, the tensions and conflicts that marked labour relations were not only focused upon, but also heightened at, the point of production. They were concentrated upon the increasingly fractious relationship between jobbers and workers. By 1946–1947, mill-owners made demands on the jobbers that the latter could now barely deliver. Jobbers could no longer, under these conditions, reconcile workers to the demands of the mill management without alienating them and they had less space in which to represent, let alone, remedy the workers' grievances. The Industrial Conditions Enquiry Committee observed that "the driving force of discipline and supervision" could no longer contain the widespread "insubordination and indiscipline" of the workers.[21] In other words, the jobber system was no longer able to maintain discipline at the point of production.

As the jobber's position weakened at the level of the individual mill by the mid 1940s, it was further compromised by the political volatility and in particular, the deepening rivalries and antagonisms manifested in workers' politics. Of course, there was nothing new or surprising about rivalries and factionalism that marked the politics of labour in Bombay. However, these rivalries quickened and expanded after the collapse of the general strike of 1934 and they intensified during the Congress ministry between 1937 and 1939. In the late 1930s, the city's Congress revived its efforts to establish a political base within the mill districts, largely under the direction of the

17. *Ibid.*, pp. 770–787.
18. *Interim Report of the Industrial Conditions Committee*, p. 31.
19. *Ibid.*, pp. 25, 19; *Labour Gazette*, 26:2 (August 1947), pp. 977–978.
20. *Interim Report of the Industrial Conditions Enquiry Committee*, p. 19.
21. *Ibid.*, p. 25.

S.K. Patil, and his "right-hand man", Keshav dada Borkar, and formed the Rashtriya Girni Kamgar Sangh. At the same time, Ambedkar's Independent Labour Party and, with far more modest success, the Royists and the Congress Socialists and sundry other aspirants to lead labour formed trade unions, attempted to recruit members and tried to draw workers away from their rivals. The recriminations that followed the 1940 general strike developed the differences between trade unions and their leaders into bitter conflicts and antagonisms.

In the 1940s, the apparent decline of the communists in the mill districts of Bombay provided an impetus to the conduct of these rivalries. In the 1920s and 1930s, the communist leadership of the Girni Kamgar Union had appealed to the working classes by its stance of unremitting opposition to the mill-owners and the state. In the 1940s, now waging the People's War, they adopted a resolutely conciliatory posture. By contrast, the Congress in Bombay, which had shown little sympathy for or interest in the concerns of the working classes, now appeared far more consistently hostile to the state than the communists did.[22] In the early 1940s, as the communists found their support among the working classes waning, the Congress sensed an opportunity to establish a firm presence in Girangaon.

In 1945, they had every reason to do so. Building a significant following in the mill districts might pay dividends both in the elections that were imminent and, in the longer run, as independence and universal suffrage beckoned. Seeking to capitalize on its gains during the 1940s, the Congress founded its own union textile workers' union, the Rashtriya Mill Mazdoor Sangh (RMMS), in 1945. Immediately, the RMMS began to compete with the Girni Kamgar Union for members and subscriptions. In this task, the RMMS was sometimes blessed with the active support or, at least, with the benevolence and encouragement of some mill-owners and mill managers. To compete for working-class support with other better established rivals in the mill districts, the RMMS and its protagonists had to enter into the political networks of the working-class neighbourhoods, based upon jobbers and mill supervisors, landlords and grain dealers, dadas and moneylenders. In competing for alliances within the political networks of Girangaon, the Congress had a major, and increasingly significant, advantage in their proximity to power and their access to patronage. The city's Congress could almost immediately measure the efficacy of their strategies with some satisfaction. In the 1946 elections, M.Y. Nurie, the Congress candidate for the Bombay City and Suburban Districts Textile Unions very nearly defeated Dange, the doyen of the Girni Kamgar Union and once the dominant political leader in Girangaon.[23]

Soon after accepting office in 1946, the Congress Government swiftly

22. GOB, Home (Special), File 1110 (6) – A (1) of 1942, MSA.
23. *Labour Gazette*, 25:7 (March 1946), p. 489; P.D. Kulkarni.

introduced and passed the Bombay Industrial Relations Act. Its immediate effect was to bring the ferocious and often violent rivalries between trade unions into the workplace. When the previous Congress Ministry had introduced the Bombay Trades Disputes Bill in 1938, it had hoped to undermine the communist Mill Mazdoor Union and to blunt its threat to the Textile Labour Association in Ahmedabad. In 1946, they were seeking to entrench the position of the RMMS in Bombay. Indeed, the new legislation in 1946 sought to establish a single union within the industry. The government explained that its aim, in introducing the Act, was "to supply a very real impetus for the growth of sound organizations of industrial and other workers" and "to ensure that [...] efficient production is not hampered by thoughtless and needless stoppages of work".[24]

By the provisions of the Trade Disputes Act of 1938, to be deemed "representative", a trade union had to claim one-quarter of the industry's workforce for its membership. With the exception of the Girni Kamgar Union in 1928–1929, no union had ever achieved this strength. The Bombay Industrial Relations Act of 1946 introduced a new category of "approved" unions. These unions could secure "representative" status by enrolling as their members only 15 per cent of the workforce. To qualify, trade unions had to renounce the option to strike until all other means of resolution had been exhausted and they had to undertake not to initiate action, unless it was sanctioned by a majority vote by secret ballot. The implementation of this procedure would ensure that when workers began to organize a strike, their employers would have sufficient time to dismiss them or, alternatively, to break their organization. In effect, this provision meant that trade unions would have to renounce strikes in return for "approved" status. Conversely, the Registrar of Trade Unions could deny "approval" if he was "satisfied that it is not being conducted bona fide in the interests of its members, but to their prejudice".[25] Since the communists had long been characterized by the mill-owners, officials, and propertied elites as acting against the workers' "real" interests, it was not unrealistic to expect that this discretionary power would be deployed against the red-flag unions.

An "approved" union was allowed access to the workplace. It could collect dues from workers on wage payment day. It could deploy

24. *Labour Gazette*, 25:9 (1946), pp. 670–671. The mill-owners had long shared this objective, but they did not welcome the measure. They suspected that it was simply an attempt to fabricate a place for the RMMS in the industry. In their interpretation, the Congress was simply attempting to usurp the position that communists had occupied in the industry. In 1947, on the eve of Independence, the mill-owners were extremely reluctant to surrender their freedom to "manage" their labour force to the Congress Raj; Chairman's Speech, Annual General Meeting, 15 May 1947, *Annual Report of the BMOA*, 1946, pp. iii–iv.

25. These sweeping powers were contained in clause 23(vi) of the Bombay Industrial Relations Act, 1946. The text of the Act was published in the *Labour Gazette*, 26:9, (May 1947), pp. 681–713.

conciliation procedures on behalf of the workers. It also acquired the exclusive right to negotiate on behalf of the workforce and to represent it in conciliation and arbitration proceedings.[26] While the 1938 legislation had established a Court of Industrial Arbitration, it had made the agreement of both parties to the dispute a precondition for the institution of arbitration proceedings. During the war, in 1941, however, the Act had been amended to make arbitration compulsory. In effect, the 1946 Act defined yet more closely the limits within trade unions could act by stipulating that only "approved" unions would be allowed to represent the workers in arbitration proceedings. By requiring the single "approved" and "registered" industry to invoke the conciliation and arbitration procedures before embarking on a strike, extending the sanctions that the employers and state could command against strikers and tightening measures to exclude the Girni Kamgar Union from the industry, the new act considerably raised the impediments to the organization of general strikes. No legislation could have been more specifically designed to undermine and destroy the Girni Kamgar Union, or indeed any seemingly recalcitrant union.

As soon as the Bombay Industrial Relations Act was passed, trades unions scrambled to recruit members, establish agents in various mill departments, and claim "representative" status. Fierce competition to enrol members led to considerable turmoil and violence in the mills in the late 1940s.[27] Strikes occurred often as a consequence of the attempt by rival groups of workers, dadas, trade unions, and political parties tried to claim, or manoeuvred to develop, a following in the workplace.[28] The advent of independence, and, with it, the prospect of universal adult franchise, provided an incentive for political parties to create their own unions as means of gathering workers' votes and mobilizing support during elections. As unions proliferated, the competition for members and for a foothold in the industry and in Girangaon only intensified.

In 1949, the RMMS was officially granted representative status on the basis of the membership list it claimed. No ballot was held to establish the preferences of the workers. The fact that the RMMS could collect its dues at the pay desk was a convenience for the union. That it was allowed access to the workplace and to seek redress for the daily problems of the workers proved a major advantage. As Bhai Bhonsle, later the General Secretary of the RMMS recalled,[29] workers "felt that all they have to do is give twelve rupees a year to these people and we have our problems solved; so what is

26. See M.D. Morris, *The Emergence of an Industrial Labour Force in India: A Study of the Bombay Cotton Mills, 1854–1947* (Berkeley, CA [etc.], 1965), pp. 185–194.
27. *Interim Report of the Industrial Conditions Enquiry Committee*, p. 18.
28. M.P. Gandhi (ed.), *The Cotton Textile Industry Annual, 1946–47* (Calcutta, 1947/8), p. 32.
29. N. Adarkar and M. Menon, *100 Years, 100 Voices: The Millworkers of Mumbai: A Vanishing History* (Calcutta, forthcoming), pp. [ch. 2, p. 45].

the loss in doing this? Textile workers always know where their interests lie." The representative status of the RMMS was challenged almost immediately and was repeatedly called into question over the following decades. Certainly, the general strike of 1950, called by the Girni Kamgar Union and the socialist Mill Mazdoor Sabha and sustained for over two months, cast grave doubt on the "representative" character of the RMMS.

The daily social relations of the workplace in the late 1940s were marked by an apparently high incidence of violence. In addition, strikes that related directly to the jobber occurred more regularly. In some cases, workers demanded the dismissal of the jobber, head jobber, or supervisory staff; in others, they demanded their reinstatement. In several cases, they merely protested against the treatment meted out by mill officials and jobbers. Underlying the proliferation of strikes was the mill-owners' concern that their reforms had sufficiently weakened the jobber's position that he could no longer maintain discipline at the level of the individual mill.

Measures taken in the 1930s to check the jobber's power had limited his control over casual labour and weakened his position within the social organization of the neighbourhood. It had also tended to create opportunities for managers, supervisors, and departmental heads to intervene in the recruitment, supervision and control of the workers. Managers, spinning and weaving masters, and timekeepers had sometimes attempted to enter into the social and commercial networks of the neighbourhood. They sought, acquired and profited from a stake in its patronage networks. As they were drawn into a wider and more competitive social nexus, so they impinged more substantially upon the jobber's domain.

While the tensions and conflicts of the workplace intensified, they were played out along a very wide front in the neighbourhoods. During the war, managerial demands upon the jobber increased both to drive workers harder and to reconcile them to falling real wages. By the mid 1940s, therefore, the jobbers found themselves beleaguered on every front. Their authority at the workplace as mill officials intervened more freely in their domain. Their influence with the workers declined as the patronage they once commanded was circumscribed, while tensions and conflict in the workplace deepened. Their place in the neighbourhood was subjected to severe competition both by political parties and trade union organizations, on the one hand, and, as their influence within the workplace was undermined, by commercial and social rivals in the neighbourhood.

Squeezed between managerial imperatives and workers' resistance, jobbers were left with a narrowing freedom of manoeuvre. Like many others in a similarly intermediary position, their options were either to align themselves with the managers or to lead the resistance of the workers. By moving in the latter direction, they might hope to retain some influence with the workers in their connection, but it incurred an increased risk of dismissal. In addition, if they attempted to act as the workers' champions, they would find themselves in competition with a wider array of political parties and trade-union leaders, power-brokers and neighbourhood bosses, even as their base within the workplace continued to weaken. On the other hand, if they aligned themselves with the mill management, they would quickly sacrifice their influence with the workers and lose such leverage as they commanded with the managers. Consequently, they were often either sucked into a lowly position within the managerial hierarchy or driven out of the mill.

During the ferocious conflicts of the workplace that occurred in the late 1940s, jobbers became either the objects of attack by workers who sensed an opportunity to get even, or, alternatively, they became engaged in a bitter contest for precedence and influence with the serried ranks of supervisors, "masters", and managers. Ten years earlier, while the mill-owners recognized that the jobber system was no longer an reliable instrument for preventing or breaking strikes coordinated across several mills, they valued its efficacy in maintaining discipline within the individual mill. By 1946, the jobber's position within the mill was beginning to appear untenable.

As the jobber's power declined, mill-owners saw less reason to defend their now apparently obsolete instrument of labour discipline. Indeed, during the volatile and panic-stricken years of the mid 1940s, it was far from clear that the jobber was capable of maintaining discipline at work. In fact, the jobber's presence in the workplace may have contributed to its collapse. On the other hand, as the mill-owners reclaimed their "right to manage" from the jobbers, it seemed as if the serried ranks of mill officials could not adequately handle its complex demands either. Increasingly, however, policy and legislation protected the mill-owners' position. The Bombay Industrial Relations Act now placed severe restrictions on the expression of workers' militancy. Following the Industrial Court's ruling, the standardized wage list had been put into effect. Individual mill-owners were now less averse to rationalization than they had been in the 1930s. As a result, the Millowners' Association could hope that some limits would be placed on the range of differences in the production conditions of their member mills. The Congress government could be relied upon to protect Indian industry in the domestic market, from foreign competition, if not from the increasingly subsidized hand-loom sector. The mill-owners found themselves by the end of the decade in a favourable political and economic climate for revamping their methods of labour recruitment and control.

In 1949, the Bombay government introduced a "de-casualization scheme" to regulate more closely the hiring of casual labour. Ostensibly, the state's objectives in intervening the industry's labour relations was "to eliminate bribery, corruption and favouritism in the recruitment of textile workers", to improve efficiency by "reducing labour turnover", to minimize the "waiting period" of unemployed textile workers between jobs and to establish a system of training for *badlis* to ensure "a steady supply of efficient workers"..

[Handwritten page missing. Top of next page to be added.]

The "de-casualization scheme" replaced the jobber's role in supplying *badlis* with an employment exchange and established rules by which it would operate. The scheme attempted to create a pool of casual labour that was attached to the industry and to ensure transparency in their hiring. In effect, it signalled the end of direct recruitment to the Bombay mills. In the 1930s, the mill-owners had argued that a central employment exchange would be impractical, largely because jobbers preferred to know the workers they hired. Now that a concerted attempt was being made to take recruitment out of the jobber's hands, the old arguments became redundant. In the textile industry's centenary volume, an anonymous writer declared triumphantly in 1951 that "crude and corrupt methods have now thoroughly been discredited".[30]

However, the celebrations were premature. By the mid-1950s, it was reported, nearly three-quarters of the casual workers in the mills had been hired through the employment exchange.[31] The employment exchanges could not offer the flexibility that the business methods of the industry had always demanded. The jobber's skill lay in expanding and contracting the supply of casual labour according to short-term fluctuations in demand. The employment exchanges simply could not cope with periodic labour shortages, created for instance, when workers returned to their villages to help with the harvest or for the marriage season in April and May. Nor could they cope with the expansion of labour needs created, for instance, by the re-opening of a mill or the adoption of an extra shift by one or more mills. In these circumstances, mills resorted to direct recruitment, inevitably subverting the order of seniority or even the occupational categories so crucial to the procedures of the employment exchange. In matters of recruitment, if not of discipline, the jobber's functions had to be periodically revived, even if they were no longer performed by him alone or by the methods he had traditionally adopted.

30. Anon., [M.P. Gandhi?], "Labour in the Cotton Textile Industry", in M.P. Gandhi (ed.), *Indian Cotton Textile Industry, 1851–1950: 1st Centenary Volume* (Bombay, 1951).

31. R.C. James, "Labour Mobility, Unemployment and Economic Change: An Indian Case", *Journal of Political Economy*, 67:6 (1959), p. 549.

Select Bibliography[1]

AHUJA, Ravi, "The Origins of Colonial Labour Policy in Late Eighteenth-Century Madras", *International Review of Social History*, 44 (1999), pp. 159–195.
——, "Labour Relations in an Early Colonial Context: Madras, c.1750–1800", *Modern Asian Studies*, 36 (2002), pp. 793–826.

AMIN, Shahid, *Sugarcane and Sugar in Gorakhpur: An Inquiry into Peasant Production for Capitalist Enterprise in Colonial India* (Delhi, 1984).

ANDERSON, Michael, "India 1858–1930: The Illusion of Free Labor", in: Douglas Hay and Paul Craven (eds), *Masters, Servants, and Magistrates in Britain and the Empire, 1562–1955* (Chapel Hill, NC [etc.], 2004), pp. 422–454.

BAAK, Paul E., *Plantation Production and Political Power: Plantation Development in South West India 1743–1963* (Delhi, 1997).

BAHL, Vinay, *The Making of the Indian Working Class: The Case of the Tata Iron and Steel Co., 1880–1946* (Delhi, 1995).

BALACHANDRAN, Gopalan, "Searching for the *Sardar*: The State, Pre-Capitalist Institutions and Human Agency in the Maritime Labour Market, Calcutta, 1880–1935", in Burton Stein and Sanjay Subrahmanyam (eds), *Institutions and Economic Change in South Asia* (Delhi, 1996), pp. 206–236.
——, "Conflicts in the International Maritime Labour Market: British and Indian Seamen, Employers, and the State, 1890–1939", *IESHR*, 39, (2002), pp. 71–100.

BANERJEE, Nirmala, *Women Workers in the Unorganized Sector: The Calcutta Experience* (Hyderabad, 1985).

BASTIAMPILLAI, Bertram, "The South Indian Immigrant's Trek to Ceylon (Sri Lanka) in the Mid-Nineteenth Century", *Sri Lanka Journal of Social Science*, 7 (1984), pp. 41–66.

BASU, Amrita, *Two Faces of Protest: Contrasting Modes of Women's Activism* (Berkeley, CA, 1992).

1. Compiled by Marcel van der Linden. Only publications in the English language after 1970 have been included. Abbreviations: *EPW* = *Economic and Political Weekly* (Bombay/Mumbai); *IESHR* = *Indian Economic and Social History Review*.

BASU, Subho, *Does Class Matter? Colonial Capital and Workers' Resistance in Bengal (1890–1937)* (Delhi, 2004).

BEHAL, Rana P., "Forms of Labour Protest in the Assam Valley Tea Plantations, 1900–1930", *EPW*, 20 (1985), 4, pp. PE19–PE26.
——, "Forms of Labour Protest in the Assam Valley Plantations 1900–1947", *Calcutta Historical Journal*, 9 (July–December 1984), pp. 30–78.
——, "Wage Structure and Labour: Assam Valley Tea Plantations, 1900–1947", *V.V. Giri National Labour Institute Studies Series*, No. 043/2003.
—— and Prabhu P. MOHAPATRA, "'Tea and Money versus Human Life': The Rise and Fall of the Indenture System in the Assam Tea Plantations 1840–1908", *Journal of Peasant Studies*, 19 (1992), pp. 142–172.

BHATTACHARYA, Sabyasachi, "Capital and Labour in Bombay City, 1928–29", *EPW*, 16 (1981), 41, pp. PE36–PE44.
——, "The Outsiders: A Historical Note", in Ashok Mitra (ed.), *The Truth Unites: Essays in Tribute to Samar Sen* (Calcutta,1985), pp. 90–100.
——, "The Labouring Poor and their Notion of Poverty: Late 19th and early 20th Century Bengal", *Labour and History Series, Working Paper no. 1, V.V. Giri, National Labour Institute* (Noida, 1998), pp. 1–33. [Reprinted in *Labour and Development*, vol. 3, no. 1–2, July 1997, pp. 1–23.]

BHATTACHERJEE, Debashish, "Unions, State and Capital in Western India: Structural Determinants of the 1982 Bombay Textile Strike", in Roger Southall (ed.), *Labour and Unions in Asia and Africa: Contemporary Issues* (Basingstoke, 1988), pp. 211–237.

BHOWMIK, Sharit, *Class Formation in the Plantation System* (New Delhi, 1981).

BOSE, Sanat, "'Industrial Unrest' and Growth of Labour Unions in Bengal, 1920–1924", *EPW*, 16 (1981), pp.1849–1860.

BREMAN, Jan C., *Patronage and Exploitation: Changing Agrarian Relations in South Gujarat, India* (Berkeley, CA, 1974).
——, *Of Peasants, Migrants and Paupers: Rural Labour Circulation and Capitalist Production in West Bengal* (Delhi, 1985).
——, *Beyond Patronage and Exploitation: Changing Agrarian Relations in South Gujarat* (Delhi, 1993).
——, *Wage Hunters and Gatherers: Search for Work in the Urban and Rural Economy of South Gujarat* (Delhi, 1994).
——, *Footloose Labour: Working in India's Informal Economy* (Cambridge, 1996).
——, "Industrial Labour in Post-Colonial India", *International Review of Social History*, 44 (1999), pp. 249–300 and 451–483.

——, *The Making and Unmaking of an Industrial Working Class: Sliding Down the Labour Hierarchy in Ahmedabad, India* (Delhi, 2004).

BRENNAN, Lance and Brij LAL (eds), *Across the Kala Pani: Indian Overseas Migration and Settlement*, Special Issue of *South Asia: Journal of South Asian Studies*, 21 (1998), pp. 1–237.

BRENNAN, Lance and Ralph SHLOMOWITZ, "Mortality and Indian Labour in Malaya, 1877–1913", *IESHR*, 29 (1992), pp. 57–75.

BROEZE, F.J.A., "The Muscles of Empire: Indian Seamen and the Raj, 1919–1929", *IESHR*, 18 (1981), pp. 43–67.

CARTER, Marina, *Servants, Sirdars, and Settlers: Indians in Mauritius 1834–1874* (Delhi, 1992).

CHAKRABARTY, Dipesh, *Rethinking Working-Class History, Bengal 1890–1940* (Princeton, NJ, 1989).

CHAKRAVARTY, Lalitha, "Emergence of an Industrial Labour Force in a Dual Economy – British India, 1880–1920", *IESHR*, 15 (1978), pp. 249–327.

CHANDAVARKAR, Rajnarayan, *The Origins of Industrial Capitalism in India: Business Strategies and the Working Classes in Bombay, 1900–1940* (Cambridge, 1994).

——, *Imperial Power and Popular Politics: Class, Resistance and the State in India, c.1850–1950* (Cambridge, 1998).

CHATTERJEE, Piya, *A Time for Tea: Women, Labour, and Post/Colonial Politics on an Indian Plantation* (Durham, NC, 2001.).

CHATTERJEE, Suranjan and Ratan DAS GUPTA, "Tea-Labour in Assam: Recruitment and Government Policy, 1840–80", *EPW*, 16 (1981), pp. 1861–1868.

CHOUDHURI, Deep Kanta Lahiri, "India's First Virtual Community and the Telegraph Strike of 1908", *International Review of Social History*, 48 (2003), Supplement 11, pp. 45–71.

CHOWDHURY, Sukhbir, *Peasants' and Workers Movement in India, 1905–29* (Delhi, 1971).

DAS, Amal, *Urban Politics in an Industrial Area: Aspects of Municipal and Labour Politics in Howrah, West Bengal, 1850–1928* (Calcutta, 1998).

DAS GUPTA, Ranajit, *Labour and Working Class in Eastern India: Studies in Colonial History* (Calcutta [etc.], 1994).

DATTA, Partho, "Strikes in the Greater Calcutta Region, 1918–1924", *IESHR*, 30 (1993), pp. 57–84.

DATTA, Satya Brata, *Capital Accumulation and Workers' Struggle in Indian*

Industrialisation: The Case of Tata Iron and Steel Company, 1910–1970 (Stockholm, 1986).

DIXON, Conrad, "Lascars: The Forgotten Seamen", in: Rosemary Ommer and Gerald Panting (eds), *Working Men Who Got Wet* (Newfoundland, 1980), pp. 263–281.

DUTTA, Amita, "An Econometric Study of Indo-Ceylon Labour Migration, 1920–1938: A Critique", *Economic Development and Cultural Change*, 21 (1972), pp. 142–156.

FERNANDES, Leela, *Producing Workers: The Politics of Gender, Class and Culture in the Calcutta Jute Mills* (Philadelphia, PA, 1997).

GBAH BEAR, Laura, "Miscegenations of Modernity: Constructing European Respectability and Race in the Indian Railway Colony, 1857–1931", *Women's History Review*, 3 (1994), pp. 531–548.

GHOSH, Parimal, "Communalism and Colonial Labour. Experience of Calcutta Jute Mill Workers, 1880–1930", *EPW*, 25 (1990), 30, pp. PE61–PE72.

——, "Colonialism, Communalism and Labour: A Belaboured Matter of Consciousness and Experience of the Calcutta Mill workers, 1880–1930", in Sekhar Bandopadhyay and Suranjan Das (eds), *Caste and Communal Politics in South Asia* (Calcutta, 1993), pp. 47–97.

GOOPTU, Nandini, *The Politics of the Urban Poor in Early Twentieth-Century India* (Cambridge, 2000).

GOSWAMI, Omkar, *Industry, Trade and Peasant Society. The Jute Economy of Eastern India, 1900–47* (Delhi, 1991).

GUPTA, P.S., "Notes on the Origin and Structuring of the Industrial Labour Force in India, 1880–1920", in R.S. Sharma (ed.), *Indian Society: Historical Probings: In Memory of D.D. Kosambi* (Delhi, 1974), pp. 414–434.

DE HAAN, Arjan, *Unsettled Settlers: Migrant Workers and Industrial Capitalism in Calcutta* (Hilversum, 1994).

—— and Samita SEN (eds), *A Case for Labour History: The Jute Industry in Eastern India* (Calcutta, 1999).

HEUZÉ, Gérard (ed.), *The Context of Work in India/Travailler en Inde* (Paris, 1992).

HOLMSTROM, Mark, *South Indian Factory Workers: Their Life and their World* (Cambridge, 1976).

——, *Industry and Inequality: The Social Anthropology of Indian Labour* (Cambridge, 1984).

—— (ed.), *Work for Wages in South Asia* (Delhi, 1990).

JAGGA, Lajpat, "Colonial Railwaymen and British Rule: A Probe into Railway Labour Agitation in India, 1919–22", *Studies in History*, 3 (1981), pp. 103–145.

JOSHI, Chitra, *Lost Worlds: Indian Labour and its Forgotten Histories* (Delhi, 2003).

KABIR, Ekhlasul, "Wages and Cost of Livings of the Working Classes of Bengal in the Second Half of the Nineteenth Century", *Journal of Pakistani Historical Society*, 11 (January 1992), pp. 21–31.

KALE, Madhavi, *Fragments of Empire: Capital, Slavery, and Indentured Labor Migration in the British Caribbean* (Philadelphia, PA, 1998).

KAMAT, Manjiri N., "The War Years and the Sholapur Cotton Textile Industry", *Social Scientist*, 26, 11–12 (1998), pp. 67–82.

KARNIK, V.B., *Strikes in India* (Bombay, 1967).

KERR, Ian J., *Building the Railways of the Raj, 1850–1900* (Delhi, 1995).
——, "Labour Control and Labour Legislation in Colonial India: A Tale of Two Mid-Nineteenth Century Acts", *South Asia*, 27 (2004), pp. 7–25.

KHAN, Munshi Rahman, *Autobiography of an Indian Indentured Labourer*, Kathinka Sinha-Kerkhoff, Ellen Bal, and Alok Deo Singh (eds & tr.) (Delhi, 2005).

KIDAMBI, Prashant, "Housing the Poor in Colonial Bombay: The City Improvement Trust, 1898–1918", *Studies in History*, 17 (2001), pp. 57–79.

KOOIMAN, Dick, *Bombay Textile Labour: Managers, Trade Unionists and Officials 1918–1939* (Delhi, 1989).

KRISHNAMURTY, J., "The Distribution of the Indian Working Force, 1901–1951", in K.N. Chaudhuri and Clive J. Dewey (eds), *Economy and Society. Essays in Indian Economic and Social History* (Delhi, 1979), pp. 258–276.

KRISHNAMURTY, Sunanda, "Real Wages of Agricultural Labourers in the Bombay Deccan, 1874–1922", *IESHR*, 24 (1987), pp. 81–98.

KUMAR, Nita, *The Artisans of Benares: Popular Culture and Identity, 1880–1986* (Princeton, NJ, 1988).

KUMAR, Radha, "Family and Factory: Women in the Bombay Textile Industry, 1919–1939", *IESHR*, 20 (1983), pp. 81–110.
——, "City Lives: Workers' Housing and Rent in Bombay, 1911–1947", *EPW*, 22 (1987), 30, pp. PE47–PE56.

LAKSHMANAN, M., "Industrial Conflict in Madras, 1918–1920", *Indian Historical Review*, 22, 1–2 (1995–1996), pp. 126–156.

LAL, Brij V., *Girmitiyas: The Origins of the Fiji Indians* (Canberra, 1983).
——, "Kunty's Cry: Indentured Women on Fiji Plantations", *IESHR*, 22 (1985), pp. 55–72.
——, "Murmurs of Dissent: Non-Resistance on Fiji Plantations", *Hawaiian Journal of History*, 20 (1986), pp. 188–214. [Revised version published as: "'Nonresistance' on Fiji Plantations: The Fiji Indian Experience, 1879–1920", in: Brij V. Lal, Doug Munro, and Edward D. Beechert (eds), *Plantation Workers: Resistance and Accomodation* (Honolulu, HI, 1993), pp. 187–216.]

LAURENCE, K.O., *A Question of Labour: Indentured Immigration into Trinidad and British Guiana, 1875–1917* (New York, 1994).

LIETEN, G.K., *Colonialism, Class and Nation: The Confrontation in Bombay around 1930* (Calcutta, 1984).
——, Ravi SRIVASTAVA and Sukhadeo THORAT (eds), *Small Hands in South Asia: Child Labour in Perspective* (Delhi, 2004).

LINDBERG, Anna, *Experience and Identity: A Historical Account of Class, Caste, and Gender among the Cashew Workers of Kerala, 1930–2000* (Lund, 2001).

MASKIELL, Michelle, "Gender, Kinship and Rural Work in Colonial Punjab", *Journal of Women's History*, 2 (1990), pp. 35–72.

MAZUMDAR, D., "Labour Supply in Early Industrialization: The Case of the Bombay Textile Industry", *Economic History Review*, 2nd series, 26 (1973), pp. 477–496.

MISRA, Baniprasanna, "Factory Labour during the Early Years of Industrialization: An Appraisal in the Light of the Indian Factory Commission, 1890", *IESHR*, 12 (1975), pp. 203–228.

MITRA, Ira, "Growth of Trade Union Consciousness among Jute Mill Workers, 1920–40", *EPW*, 16 (1981), pp. 1839–1848.

MOHAPATRA, Prabhu P., "Coolies and Colliers: A Study of the Agrarian Context of Labour Migration from Chota Nagpur, 1880–1920", *Studies in History*, New Series, 1, 2 (1985), pp. 13–42.
——, "The Hosay Massacre of 1884: Class and Community among Indian Immigrant Labourers in Trinidad", in Arvind N. Das and Marcel van der Linden (eds), *Work and Social Change in Asia: Essays in Honour of Jan Breman* (Delhi, 2003), pp. 187–230.
——, "Assam and the West Indies, 1860–1920: Immobilizing Plantation Labor", in Douglas Hay and Paul Craven (eds), *Masters, Servants, and Magistrates in Britain and the Empire, 1562–1955* (Chapel Hill, NC [etc.], 2004), pp. 455–480.

MURPHY, Eamon, *Unions in Conflict: A Comparative Study of Four South Indian Textile Centres, 1918–39* (Delhi, 1981).

NAIR, Janaki, *Miners and Millhands: Work, Culture and Politics in Princely Mysore* (Delhi, 1998).

NEWMAN, Richard, *Workers and Unions in Bombay, 1918–1929: A Study of Organisation in the Cotton Mills* (Canberra, 1981).

NORTH-COOMBES, M.D., "From Slavery to Indenture: Forced Labour in the Political Economy of Mauritius 1834–1867", in Kay Saunders (ed.), *Indentured Labour in the British Empire 1834–1920* (London [etc.], 1984), pp. 78–125.

PARTHASARATHI, Prasannan, *The Transition to a Colonial Economy: Weavers, Merchants and Kings in South India 1720–1800* (Cambridge, 2001).

PARRY, Jonathan P., Jan BREMAN, and Karin KAPADIA (eds), *The World of Indian Industrial Labour* (Delhi, 1999).

PATEL, Sujata, *The Making of Industrial Relations: The Ahmedabad Textile Industry 1918–1939* (Delhi, 1987).

PEEBLES, Patrick, *The Plantation Tamils of Ceylon* (London [etc.], 2001).

PRAKASH, Gyan, *Bonded Histories: Genealogies of Labour Servitude in Colonial India* (Cambridge, 1990).
—— (ed.), *The World of the Rural Labourer in Colonial India* (Delhi, 1993).

PRASHAD, Vijay, *Untouchable Freedom: A Social History of a Dalit Community* (Delhi, 2000).

RAO, G.N., "Transition from Subsistence to Commercialised Agriculture. A Study of Krishna District of Andhra, c.1850–1900", *EPW*, 20 (1985), 25–26, pp. A60–A69.

RAO, P.D.P. Prasado, *Strikes in India (1860–1970)* (Hyderabad, 1972).

REDDOCK, Rhoda, "Freedom Denied. Indian Women and Indentureship in Trinidad and Tobago, 1845–1917", *EPW*, 20 (1985), pp. WS79–WS87.

REVRI, Chamanlal, *The Indian Trade Union Movement: An Outline History 1880–1947* (Delhi, 1972).

ROBB, Peter (ed.), *Dalit Movements and the Meanings of Labour in India* (Delhi, 1993).

SATYANARAYANA, Adapa, "'Birds of Passage': Migration of South Indian Labourers to Southeast Asia", *Critical Asian Studies*, 34, (2002), pp. 89–115.

Van SCHENDEL, Willem, *Three Deltas: Accumulation and Poverty in Rural Burma, Bengal and South India* (Delhi, 1991).
——, "Working Through Partition: Making a Living in the Bengal Borderlands", *International Review of Social History*, 46 (2001), pp. 393–421. [Also in: Arvind N. Das and Marcel van der Linden (eds), *Work and Social Change in Asia. Essays in Honour of Jan Breman* (Delhi, 2003), pp. 55–89.]
—— and Aminul Haque FARAIZI, *Rural Labourers in Bengal, 1880 to 1981* (Rotterdam, 1984).

SEN, Samita, *Women and Labour in Late Colonial India: The Bengal Jute Industry* (Cambridge, 1999).

SEN, Sukomal, *Working Class of India: History of Emergence and Movement, 1830–1990, with an Overview up to 1995* (Calcutta, 1997).

SEN, Sunil K., *Working Class Movements in India, 1885–1975* (Delhi, 1994).

SHERLOCK, Stephen, *The Indian Railways Strike of 1974: A Study of Power and Organised Labour* (Delhi, 2001).

SHLOMOWITZ, Ralph, "Infant Mortality and Fiji's Indian Migrants, 1879–1919", *IESHR*, 23 (1986), pp. 289–302.
——, "Fertility and Fiji's Indian Migrants, 1879–1919", *IESHR*, 24 (1987), pp. 205–213.

SIMEON, Dilip, *The Politics of Labour Under Late Colonialism: Workers, Unions and the State in Chota Nagpur, 1928–1939* (Delhi, 1995).

SIMMONS, Colin P., "Recruiting and Organising an Industrial Labour Force in Colonial India: The Case of the Coal Mining Industry, c. 1880–1939", *IESHR*, 13 (1976), pp. 455–485.

SPECTOR, Ronald, "The Royal Indian Navy Strike of 1946: A Study of Cohesion and Disintegration in Colonial Armed Forces", *Armed Forces and Society*, 7 (1981), pp. 271–284.

SWARNALATHA, Potukuchi, "Revolt, Testimony, Petition: Artisanal Protests in Colonial Andhra", *International Review of Social History*, 46 (2001), Supplement 9, pp. 107–129.

UPADHYAYA, Shashi Bhushan, "Communalism and Working Class: Riot of 1893 in Bombay City", *EPW*, 24 (1989), pp. PE69–PE75.
——, "Cotton Mill Workers in Bombay, 1875–1918: Conditions of Work and Life", *EPW*, 25 (1990), 30, pp. PE87–PE99.

VEERARAGHAVAN, D. and T. THANKAPPAN, "Class Conflict and the Colonial State in Madras Presidency up to 1918", *South Asia Bulletin*, 10–11 (1990), pp. 1–11.

WERSCH, Huub van, *The Bombay Textile Strike, 1982–83* (Bombay, 1992).